Youth sport in Australia

edited by Steve Georgakis and Kate Russell

SYDNEY UNIVERSITY PRESS

Published 2011 by Sydney University Press

SYDNEY UNIVERSITY PRESS
University of Sydney Library
sydney.edu.au/sup

© Steve Georgakis and Kate Russell 2011
© Individual contributors 2011
© Sydney University Press 2011

Reproduction and Communication for other purposes
Except as permitted under the Act, no part of this edition may be reproduced, stored in a retrieval system, or communicated in any form or by any means without prior written permission. All requests for reproduction or communication should be made to Sydney University Press at the address below:

Sydney University Press
Fisher Library F03
University of Sydney NSW 2006 AUSTRALIA
Email: sup.info@sydney.edu.au

Readers are advised that protocols can exist in Indigenous Australian communities against speaking names and displaying images of the deceased. Please check with local Indigenous Elders before using this publication in their communities.

National Library of Australia Cataloguing-in-Publication entry

Title: Youth sport in Australia / edited by Steve Georgakis and Kate Russell.
ISBN: 9781920899646 (pbk.).
Notes: Includes bibliographical references and index.
Subjects: Sports--Australia.
           Youth--Australia--Recreation.
           Sports for children--Australia.
Other Authors/Contributors:
           Georgakis, Steve.
           Russell, Katrina Marie.
Dewey Number:
           796.0994

Cover design by Miguel Yamin, the University Publishing Service

Contents

Introduction v
Steve Georgakis and Kate Russell

About the contributors xi

1. Making sense of Australian sport history 1
   Daryl Adair

2. The role of educational institutions in Australian sport 27
   Steve Georgakis

3. Sport policy in Australia 43
   Matthew Nicholson and Russell Hoye

4. Accessing youth sport in Australia: schools and clubs 59
   Richard Light

5. Compulsory heterosexuality and the construction of femininity and masculinity:
   issues of performance versus presentation 71
   Kate Russell

6. Sport, the body and boys' constructions of masculinity 85
   Murray Drummond

7. Can any*body* play? An introduction to the sociology of sport and disability 97
   Nikki Wedgwood

8. A critical history of the Gay Games movement 115
   Kellie Burns

9. Black and White in Australian sport 133
   Colin Tatz

10. Beach sports 149
    Douglas Booth

11. The role of physical education in promoting sport participation in school and beyond ...165
    Murray Drummond and Shane Pill

12. Are schools responsible for engaging youth in sport and physical activity?....................179
   Louisa Peralta

13. Factors influencing talent identification and athlete development in youth sport............193
   Donna O'Connor

14. Coaching and adherence issues in youth sport..211
   Andrew Bennie

15. Seen but not heard: child protection in sport..229
   Kate Russell

16. The media, body image and youth sport..241
   Kate Russell

17. Celebrity, popular culture and sport..255
   Bob Petersen

18. Research methodology for youth sport..265
   Rachel Wilson

Index 287

Introduction

Steve Georgakis and Kate Russell

Late in November 2010, while waiting for the train at Goulburn train station to travel to Sydney, we came across a plaque, hidden in bushes, which commemorated the first train journey from Sydney to Goulburn in 1869. The plaque read, 'The first railway steamed into Goulburn on 26 March 1869, bringing up the Warwick Cricket Team from Sydney to play in a match against Goulburn.' On the same day the 'Cobb & Co Coach' was held up by bushrangers at Run-O-Waters Creek (three kilometres from Goulburn). While bushrangers have disappeared it is important to note that a cricket game was used to celebrate the newly built train line not a dramatic production, not fireworks and certainly not an opera. Sport has been a privileged social phenomenon in Australia since British colonisation and continues to be so in the second decade of the 21st century.

For more than a century scholars of Australian history and sociology have documented the important role that sport plays in the cultural and social identity of Australians. In 1912 English historian Inglis noted that as far as he could see Australians seemed to be interested in sport and nothing else, while Cashman (1995) more than 80 years later proclaimed Australia a 'paradise of sport'. The place of sport is so privileged in Australian society that a number of athletes, both male and female, have received the highest annual award 'Australian of the Year'. It is the only country in the world where four football codes (Football, Rugby Union, Rugby League and Australian Rules) battle for dominance. There are also a number of scholarly works, both historical and sociological which have highlighted the strong link between Australian identity and sport; the most authoritative and interpretative of these include Stoddart's (1986) *Saturday afternoon fever,* Cashman's (1995) *Paradise of sport,* Adair and Vamplew's (1997) *Sport in Australian history,* and Booth and Tatz's (2001) *One-eyed: a view of Australian sport.* There are also an innumerable number of popular texts which have looked at sport using a 'who won, what and where' mentality. Almost all of these texts deal with sport at the elite level, and include titles such as '100 greatest moments', 'cricket diaries' or 'biographies'.

While there are a plethora of books, very few studies have looked at issues related to youth sport specifically. This neglect has been unusual because study in youth sport can provide important insights to the understanding of Australian sport history and culture through the eyes of those that access it from a young age. This book is therefore an effort to produce a synthesis of contemporary issues related to Australian youth sport.

This edited book of scholarly chapters is primarily a response to the publication of the Crawford Report (2009) when youth sport issues took centre stage. In particular, the report highlighted two important but neglected themes in the academic literature. Firstly, the assumed privileging of elite sport over grassroots participation; and secondly, the diminished status of physical education and school sport. Upon its publication, debates in the media and elsewhere raged for months and centred on issues related to motivation, participation, role models, funding models, national curriculum, low status of physical education and school sport, marginalised experiences, and competitive sport versus inclusive sport. Some of the views were polarised; for example, the editor of the *Sunday Telegraph* (2009) noted that:

> One thing is for certain: *The Sunday Telegraph* wants the Government to continue to spend heavily to fund Olympic sports. Olympic and other sporting heroes inspire generations of kids to get up and get active. Olympic and other sporting heroes cut obesity rates. End of story (22 November 2009, p. 37).

Relevant academic arguments did not find their way into these debates at the time, partly because there was little available research. At the very least the Crawford Report (2009) highlighted that government funding in sport should benefit *all* Australians. Philosophical perspectives were espoused and many argued that youth sport should be an end in itself, not a beginning for fame and fortune for the few. Many sports which historically boasted large entry-level programs very rarely discussed retention rates or how many dropped out due to not being identified by talent identification programs.

As the title suggests this book looks at youth sport. Since the relationship between youth and sport could cause debate it is worthwhile clarifying the use of the term. Sport is a collective noun and will refer to a range of organised activities including physical education, school sport, and organised community sport. For many youth, physical education and school sport is the main societal institution for the development of sport. This is because the latest participation rate figures demonstrate that for almost 40% of youth, school provides the main opportunity for regular organised and structured sport (ABS 2010). While school-based sport offers opportunities for teachers to introduce students to the benefits of sport within a safe and supportive network, the introduction of the national curriculum has raised significant questions about its future. Similarly, organised community club sport which has dominated the scene is in decline for a number of reasons, including economic pressures, competitive nature and parental concerns for safety.

Youth is a fluid term and is a transitional stage of physical and mental human development between childhood and adulthood. Youth as a social category, with its special concerns and theoretical issues, became visible at the time of the industrial revolution and is a Western construct that emerged in the 19th century. For the purposes of the book youth is defined very loosely as starting when childhood finishes and ending when someone 'settles down'. Because of the 'Peter Pan Syndrome', youth marrying much later in life, and also childhood finishing earlier, the period of youth is ever expanding. We have not included a definitive age range for that reason but suggest investigating the years between five and 25. The end of youth is when 'one gets one's act together for life' and the key theme is 'independency' and the so-called transition into adulthood. The Australian Sports Commission, which amongst other roles promotes the national sports system, uses the term 'junior sport' for participants aged between five to 17 years. This of course coincides with the school years.

The link between youth and sport is a strong one and historically youth have been encouraged to play sport for a myriad of benefits. Bailey (2006) summarised the benefits under the following developmental categories: physical, lifestyle, affective, social and cognitive. Regarding lifestyle development, physical inactivity has been identified as a risk factor for a number of lifestyle diseases and participating in sport promotes general health. In the affective domain, sport can have a positive effect on the psychological wellbeing of youth and can build self-esteem, and decrease stress and anxiety. It is well documented that sport affects how youths develop socially. Through sport, individuals can experience equality, freedom and empowerment. Youth sport can teach essential values and life skills including self-confidence, teamwork, communication, inclusion, discipline, respect and fair play. Regarding cognitive development, there has long been a tradition 'that a healthy body leads to a healthy mind' and that sport can support intellectual development in youth. School sport can improve a child's ability to learn, increases concentration, attendance and overall achievement. Therefore in each of the developmental categories noted above, there is overwhelming evidence to suggest that sport can have an undeniably positive effect. Although as Bailey (2006) highlighted 'further research and evaluation will help us better understand the nature of these contributions'(p. 399). This edited collection will shed light on these contributions.

This book explore several themes related to youth sport in the Australian context. In the first chapter, Daryl Adair provides an overview of sport in Australian history and culture identifying the many influences that have helped shape Australian sporting traditions. In the second chapter, Steve Georgakis asserts that while Australian schools and community clubs have been nurseries for major sports, there is a tendency for scholars of Australian sport to ignore the important role played by educational institutions in this process. There is one exception to this: elite independent schools and associations. The chapter argues that governmental educational institutions were central to this growth and consolidation of Australian sport, although their contribution has yet to be fully documented.

Since the release of the Crawford Report (2009) there has been much debate regarding the current funding privileging of elite sport over grassroots level sport. Matthew Nicholson and Russell Hoye provide an historical account of the development of a professional sporting system in Australia; in particular, the authors focus on the 1970s when Australia still had in place an amateur sports system in contrast to many other countries that had government funded sporting organisations. Such developments left Australia behind in terms of the development of elite athletes and this led to a complete rethink in the funding model and elite sport policy was prioritised. Richard Light's chapter on youth sport policy provides an account of the Australian youth sport model using the example of swimming. A well-established youth sport system is available, with 1.6 million of 2.6 million youth, involved in organised sport outside school. Within this system swimming is the most popular sport for youth (aged 5–14) in Australia with almost 500,000 participating (17% of all children). According to Light, competitive swimming is organised in Australia through two structures: the community-based club system and the school system. Swimming is part of the physical education syllabus but the focus is on 'learning to swim' and developing competency in the water. Both the primary and secondary school systems offer access to competitive swimming structures for students who excel in the sport. This is achieved through levels – school, region, state and national titles. While an organised program exists for elite swimmers it is the club system that provides extensive training and preparation and most competitive swimmers compete outside school.

As sport plays a major role in the construction of feminine and masculine identities, a section of the book looks at issues related to sport and the construction of gender. Kate Russell explores the heterosexism of sport and its impact on girls and girls' participation in sport. Russell argues that the central component in the defining practices of appropriate and inappropriate activities for women and men is in the perception of the gendered identity that participation in an activity produces. Notions of acceptable body shapes and sizes often influence the ways in which a person or an observer may either accept or reject an individual's gender. These arguments fail to address the notion of 'functionality', which suggests that body shapes that enhance successful athletic performance are both valuable and valued. This practice also facilitates the validation of compulsory heterosexuality – the practice whereby heterosexuality is presented as the only valid, and therefore valued, form of sexuality. Murray Drummond adds to this work by identifying the sporting issues and discourses faced by male youth. He achieves this by examining the complex relationship between sport, masculinity and the body. He argues that being competent in sport serves as a rite of passage for males and youths who are not well versed in sport and have a weaker sense of masculine identity than others.

The next section of the book looks at marginalised sporting experiences. With over 2.5 million youths aged between five and 14 taking part in organised community sport, it is imperative to understand the motives for and against involvement. The Australian Bureau of Statistics (2010) notes that almost two in five school-aged youth do not participate in sport after school hours. Research would suggest that this group is overrepresented by immigrant youth from low socioeconomic areas of Australian and disabled youth. This section will look at issues related to marginalisation by focusing on disabled, LGBT (lesbian, gay, bisexual, transgendered) and Indigenous Australians, and aspects of their associated sporting experiences. Nikki Wedgwood's chapter looks at issues related to disability and argues that understanding sociology is beneficial to sports providers. The chapter highlights the fact that sporting practice in Australian society is heavily influenced by social structures like gender and ableism but also the fact that people who play sport or provide physical education are not completely constrained by these structures. Kellie Burns provides an overview of the Gay Games and raises some important issues related to their promotion and consolidation. The chapter analyses the event as a site of production, where normative meanings around sex, gender, citizenship and global living are constructed and contested. Colin Tatz's chapter notes that Indigenous athletes are overrepresented in professional sports such as boxing, Australian Rules football and Rugby League while there are still economic and social barriers to sports such as Rugby Union and swimming. Racial vilification and abuse is still common while paradoxically sport is one of the few areas in which Indigenous Australians compete on equal terms. Sport is important in maintaining a sense of community and Colin Tatz claims that sport is the 'cement' that binds so many communities together.

The following section of the book highlights the link between learning and sport by looking at how the Australian beach and various aspects of physical education and school sport are linked to learning. Doug Booth's chapter looks at the intersection between sport and youth on the Australian beach. The Australian beach is one of the great symbols of Australian culture. Perhaps Australia's most defining moment on Sunday 25 April 1915 occurred on a beach, not in Australia but in Turkey, when thousands of ANZAC troops landed on Z Beach (later called ANZAC Cove) and were slaughtered. In recent times the Australian beach gained world-wide publicity after riots broke out on the Sydney's Cronulla Beach. Most of the literature on the Australian beach has concentrated on aspects such as surfing and criminal youth subcultures, but failed to mention the learning and other sport that takes place on the beach; for example the 50,000 youths who migrate to the beach every Saturday morning to compete in sport. The following two chapters look at issues related to physical education and school sport, and highlight the complexities surrounding the promotion of lifelong physical activity. Murray Drummond and Shane Pill explore the meaning associated with contemporary physical education and highlight sociological themes related to promoting participation. In particular their chapter focuses on the model of sport education as a way to enhance the physical learning experiences of children at school suggesting a broader approach to viewing curriculum development. Louisa Peralta's philosophical chapter brings into question the school's responsibility to address health issues such as obesity and physical inactivity. In particular, the author focuses on three intervention programs and illuminates the complexity of designing appropriate interventions to combat physical inactivity and obesity.

It is only recently that scholarship has looked at community club sport and the role of the coach in a sustained manner. The two chapters by Donna O'Connor and Andrew Bennie raise important questions related to the philosophy of community sport participation by looking at the role of the coach and various sports coaching philosophies. O'Connor's chapter examines the role of talent identification strategies and the consequences for both rural and city youth in moving towards participation in elite level sport, whereas Bennie's chapter seeks to expand our understandings of the ways in which a coach's preferred leadership style and direction can both positively and negatively affect the learning experiences of youth in sport.

The final chapters of the book deals with emerging contemporary issues in youth sport, such as child protection, the media, the sporting celebrity and research methodology issues. One of Kate Russell's chapters in this section looks at the intersection between sport and child protection. Russell identifies the ways in which legislation has helped shape child welfare policy in sport. Her chapter highlights the many factors that may increase the potential for harm among young sport participants as well as identifying ways to counteract this. Russell's final chapter explores body image in youth with regards to sport participation and the media. In particular this chapter focuses on the factors that influence the development of body image in youth and how this is influenced by the sports they take part in, or observe through their exposure to a variety of media. Russell suggests that regardless of gender or age, females experience poorer body satisfaction than males and body image is influenced by a number of sociocultural factors including gender, age, race, economic status and cultural background. Bob Petersen's chapter notes the link between popular culture and the rise of the sporting celebrity. This chapter explores the role of consumerism within the sporting field, suggesting that youth can be susceptible to the 'bright lights' of money, sex appeal and talent presented to them. In so doing they can become unduly influenced by such practices and ultimately succumb to measures such as changing body shape in order to become like their idols. Consumers aren't just buying a product – they are buying into a lifestyle represented by a celebrity. The final chapter of the book, by Rachel Wilson, presents a critical review of recent and current research methods in this field. She analyses and critiques the methodological issues within youth sport; including the development of an unproductive dichotomy of quantitative versus qualitative research. This provides a very apt conclusion to our book, as she reflects on the wide range of research strategies required to make progress in a field which is driven by both physical and social understandings. She advocates the use of mixed methods which provide us with effective, evidence-based and engaging ways to promote the diverse benefits of youth sport across all sections of society.

Whilst we acknowledge that this book cannot possibly cover all areas relating to youth sport, we feel that it provides a valuable resource for both undergraduate and graduate students in the fields of sport sociology, sport studies, youth studies, coach education and leisure studies. Furthermore, researchers with a focus on the role of sport in the development of youth both within and outside the Australian context will find this an important addition to their collection.

References

Adair, D. & Vamplew, W. (1997). *Sport in Australian history.* Cambridge: Cambridge University Press.

Australian Bureau of Statistics (2010). *Children's participation in cultural and leisure activities, Australia.* Canberra: Australian Bureau of Statistics.

Bailey, R. (2006). Physical education and sport in schools: a review of benefits and outcomes. *Journal of School Health,* 76(8): 397–401.

Booth, D. & Tatz, C. (2001). *One-eyed: a view of Australian sport.* Sydney: Allen & Unwin.

Cashman, R. (1995). *Paradise of sport.* Melbourne: Oxford University Press.

Crawford Report (2009). *The future of sport in Australia.* Canberra: Commonwealth of Australia.

Inglis, G. (1912). *Sport and pastime in Australia.* London: Methuen.

Stoddart, B. (1986). *Saturday afternoon fever.* Sydney: Angus and Robertson.

About the contributors

Daryl Adair is Associate Professor of Sport Management in the UTS Business School, Sydney, Australia. His research is wide-ranging, embracing the history, sociology, politics and management of sport. Daryl's major books include *Sport in Australian history* (1997), *Sport tourism* (2004), and *Sport, race and ethnicity* (2011). He has recently edited six special issues of academic journals focused on issues of anti-racism, diversity and cross-cultural engagement in sport: *Australian Aboriginal Studies* (2009), *Sporting Traditions* (2009), *International Review for the Sociology of Sport* (2010), *Sport Management Review* (2010), *Cosmopolitan Civil Societies* (2010), and *Sport in Society* (2011).

Andrew Bennie is Lecturer in the School of Biomedical and Health Sciences at the University of Western Sydney. He was awarded his PhD in 2009 from the University of Sydney. His research focused on perceptions of effective coaching amongst a unique Australian professional sport sample. Andrew's research interests focus on coach development, coach education and sport participation and he has authored several papers in coaching and physical education journals.

Douglas Booth is Professor of Sport and Leisure Studies and Dean of the School of Physical Education at the University of Otago (New Zealand). He is interested in the broad area of sport as a form of popular culture (with a particular emphasis on political relationships and processes) and historiography. He is the author of *The race game* (1998), *Australian beach cultures* (2001), *The field* (2005) and, with Colin Tatz, *One-eyed* (2000). He serves on the editorial boards of the *Journal of Sport History* and *Sport History Review* and is an executive member of the Australian Society for Sport History.

Kellie Burns is a member of the Faculty of Education and Social Work at the University of Sydney. She was awarded her PhD from the University of Otago in 2008. Her doctoral research used the Sydney 2002 Gay Games as a case study of how sexual citizenship is produced against the increasingly neoliberal mandates governing large global gay and lesbian sport and tourism events. Kellie's more recent work uses questions of sexual citizenship to explore notions of 'girl citizenship' as produced against emergent models of 'healthy citizenship'.

Murray Drummond is an Associate Professor of Sport, Health and Physical Education at Flinders University, Adelaide, Australia. He has been the Chief Investigator on a number of qualitative health research projects and author of numerous papers relating to children's sport, health and physical activity as well as boys, sport and masculinities. He is an editorial board member of *Men and Masculinities, International Journal of Men's Health, THYMOS: Journal of Boyhood Studies, Gay and Lesbian Issues in Psychology Review, Canadian Journal of Behavioural Science* and *The Journal of Men's Health*.

Steve Georgakis is Senior Lecturer at the Faculty of Education and Social Work at the University of Sydney, Australia. He has published on various aspects of physical education and sports studies including archaeology, history, sociology, pedagogy and comparative assessment. The author of more than 40 peer-reviewed publications including books, journal articles and conference proceedings, he is currently completing a book on the delivery of Australian youth sport.

Russell Hoye is Professor in Sport Management in the School of Management and Director of the Centre for Sport and Social Impact at La Trobe University, Melbourne, Australia. His research interests focus on the governance of sport organisations, the impact of public policy on sport and the engagement of volunteers in sport. He is a co-author of *Sport and policy: issues and analysis* (2010), *Sport management: principles and applications* (2 editions) (2009) and *Sport and social capital* (2008) as well as the author of *Sport governance* (2007), all published with Elsevier, UK. He also wrote *Participation in sport: international policy perspectives* (2011) and *Working with volunteers in sport: theory and practice* (2006).

Richard Light holds the Chair in Sport Pedagogy in the Carnegie Faculty of Sport and Education, Leeds Metropolitan University in the United Kingdom. He conducts research on sport and physical education pedagogy, and in the sociocultural dimensions of sport with a focus on youth sport. He has published on sport in a range of settings and has produced over 100 peer-reviewed publications including the book *Sport in the lives of young Australians* (2008).

Matthew Nicholson is Associate Professor in Sport Management in the Centre for Sport and Social Impact and the School of Management at La Trobe University, Melbourne, Australia. Matthew's research interests focus on policy development and practice, the relationship between sport and the media and the contribution of sport and volunteering to social capital. He is a co-author of *Sport and policy: issues and analysis* (2010), *Sport management: principles and applications* (2nd edition) (2009) and *Sport and social capital* (2008) as well as the author of *Sport and the media: managing the nexus* (2007). He also wrote *A national game* (2008), *Participation in sport: international policy perspectives* (2011) and *Australian sport: better by design? The evolution of Australian sport policy* (2004).

Donna O'Connor is an Associate Professor and the course coordinator of the postgraduate program in Coach Education at the University of Sydney. Her research has focused on youth sport and high performance athlete and coach development, science and football, and injury prevention. Donna has received a Vice Chancellor's Award for Outstanding Teaching and a Carrick Citation for Outstanding Contributions to Student Learning. Donna has worked with a number of teams and coaches in Rugby Union, Rugby League, Touch, Track and Field, Basketball and Netball. She is currently a member of the NRL research board and the World Congress Science and Football Steering Committee. She is a co-author of the textbooks *Peak Performance 1* (2010) and *Peak Performance 2* (2009).

Louisa Peralta is a Lecturer in the Faculty of Education and Social Work at the University of Sydney. Louisa was awarded her PhD in 2009 at the University of Wollongong, with her research focusing on the feasibility, acceptability and potential efficacy of a school-based physical activity and healthy lifestyle intervention on targeted adolescent boys' health outcomes. Louisa is currently one of the chief investigators of a NSW DET funded Girls in Sport project, that aims to increase adolescent girls' physical activity levels during the school day (both curriculum and non-curriculum periods). Louisa's future projects aim to further evaluate the efficacy of healthy lifestyle and physical activity school-based programs among children and adolescents on both health and education outcomes.

Bob Petersen was on the staff of the Faculty of Education at the University of Sydney for many years. He has been president of the Australian and New Zealand History of Education Society and editor of its journal *History of Education*. He is a member of the Australian Society for Sports History. His biography of the boxer Peter Jackson will be published in the US by MacFarland in 2011.

Shane Pill is a former Head of the Health and Physical Education Department, now lecturing in Physical Education Studies at Flinders University, Adelaide, Australia. He is President of the Australian Council for Health, Physical Education and Recreation (SA Branch). His research focus is the enactment and blending of TGfU/Game Sense and Sport Education for pedagogically progressive sport teaching/coaching in natural settings. Shane is author of the popular game-centred teaching resource, *Play with purpose*, co-authored *S'Cool cricket*, and was co-editor of *Pick up & run V3*, and *Active children*.

Kate Russell is a Senior Lecturer at the Faculty of Education and Social Work at the University of Sydney, Australia. Her research interests and publications span the fields of child protection in sport, gendered identities in the sporting and educational context and the development of body image among sportswomen. Her most recent publications include the co-edited book *Child welfare in football: an exploration of children's welfare in the modern game* (2007), and a co-authored series *Science through sport: body image I middle secondary* and *Science through sport: body image II senior secondary* (2009).

Colin Tatz is Honorary Visiting Fellow at the Australian Institute of Aboriginal and Torres Strait Islander Studies and Visiting Fellow, Politics and International Relations, Australian National University. In his 20 books and numerous articles, he has addressed Aboriginal affairs, comparative race politics, migration issues, Holocaust and genocide studies, youth suicide and sports history.

Nikki Wedgwood is a Research Fellow of the Australian Family & Disability Studies Research Collaboration in the Faculty of Health Sciences at the University of Sydney. Her past research includes the gendered embodiment of schoolgirls, schoolboys and adult women who play Australian Rules football. Her current research focuses on how young people with physical impairments meet the developmental challenges of adolescence and emerging adulthood, including consolidation of identity, peer acceptance and increasing autonomy from family. She is also involved in a long-term project on the oral history of women who have played Australian Rules football from the 1890s to the 1970s.

Rachel Wilson has degrees in psychology, audiology, research methods and education and holds a PhD in educational development from Oxford University. She is currently Senior Lecturer in Research Methodology and Educational Assessment at the University of Sydney. Her research interests range from early childhood to higher education and she has a particular interest in research for evidence-based education policy and practice.

1
Making sense of Australian sport history

Daryl Adair

Despite the high profile of sport in Australian culture, the historical analysis of sport in this country has not attracted much coverage, whether in terms of academic research, media interest, or the reading public. Australian sport fans are eager to recount glorious performances by the nation's teams and athletes, and they certainly indulge in eulogistic books and magazines about sport. But these enthusiasts have comparatively little knowledge about, or interest in, Australian history and the role of sport in shaping its evolution. This is, in large part, a reflection of inadequate education: in many schools history has been supplanted as a key area of study, with the Australian story conveyed as part of broad brush subjects like 'social studies' or 'civics and citizenship'. Moreover, at university level Australian history is typically taught with scant regard for the explanatory potential of sport and physical culture. Too often, sport has been relegated by Australian academics to the 'toy department' rather than the history department where, incidentally, there are few scholars for whom sport is a serious focus of research (Booth 1997; Adair 2002). This is illogical, because sport can provide important insights into themes and issues that have been pivotal to the evolution of Australian culture. Indeed, as this chapter indicates, sport historians have carved out areas of research that contribute ably to the study of Australia's past. The following discussion is a thematic overview of Australian sport history with a focus on three pivotal areas: national self-image through sport, norms of sport participation, and the involvement (or otherwise) in sport of so-called minority groups. Together they provide metaphorical windows through which to try to make sense of Australian society and culture, and the role of sport in their historical evolution.

Australian self-image through sport

According to historian Geoffrey Blainey (1966), Australia has been cursed by the 'tyranny of distance'. As a British colonial outpost it was literally on the other side of the world, and, particularly before air travel and electronic communication, this meant separation from the so-called motherland. Sport was one way in which Britain and its colonies, whether in Australia or elsewhere, could be connected. It was, as both Daly (1982) and Cashman (1995) have averred, part of the cultural baggage of migrants – particularly those who arrived as free settlers in the second half of the 19th century. Efforts to establish race tracks, cricket fields and rugby pitches were part of the colonial drive to recreate – even if in the imagination – some of the cultural trappings of a distant 'homeland'. There was fanfare and excitement when sports teams and competitors from Britain toured the colonies. The locals were initially in awe of visiting athletes, such as in cricket, where English sides toyed with their colonial counterparts. But, as historians have shown, from the 1860s onwards the tide slowly turned – most notably in cricket, rowing, and Rugby Union – with Antipodean teams and crews performing creditably in Anglo-Australian contests (Adair 1994; Adair et al. 1997). The importance of this sporting relationship was firmly established in 1882, when the legend of the 'Ashes' was born in the wake of a surprise Australian win over England at The Oval in London. That victory, together with other triumphs in sport, impacted positively on colonial self-confidence; athletes and teams were eagerly representing 'Australia' abroad before the nation existed (Cashman 1992). They were still fiercely pro-Empire, but anxious to overcome negative attitudes about a convict past and rumblings about Antipodean inferiority (Hirst 1983; Hughes 1987). Sport, with its immutable scoreboard, was thus an important way of establishing a sense of Anglo-Australian parity – and ultimately rivalry.

Mandle (1973) sees in sport, though most notably in cricket, seeds of colonial nationalism that went beyond culture into politics. Australians were for many years lukewarm about the idea of Federation, and it took two referenda for that proposal to be passed – and eventually by only a small majority (Norris 1975). Mandle (1973) contends that intercolonial and Anglo-Australian sport provided examples of effective administrative cooperation at the national level, which many had thought unlikely in an era when parochial colonies protected their local economies with tariffs and, by producing differently sized railway gauges, effectively stymied regional trade and travel. This rather 'reluctant' Commonwealth of 1901 provided a very hybrid sense of nationhood (Meaney 2001; McGregor 2006). Australia remained a dominion of the British Empire and would continue to prove its loyalty to Britain by military service in the Boer War and two world wars. Through 'Empire' sports like cricket, Rugby Union and Rugby League, together with active support for British troops in Europe, Australians developed a formidable reputation on both playing fields and battlefields. This combination of sport and wartime service has received attention by scholars interested in questions of identity, loyalty and gender norms (McKernan 1979; Blair 1995; Phillips 1996, 1997; Jaggard 1996; Rodwell & Ramsland 2000; Crotty 2001; Ramsland 2004; Cohen 2006). But the subject has not been treated exhaustively – surprisingly so given the depth of interest in military history in Australia and the elevation of the ANZACs to the status of a legend (Seal 2004).

The use of space and response to climate are lynchpins of Australian history. With European annexation of land, many colonists looked to establish agricultural properties and mining operations in rural or remote areas. They were the exceptions. Most whites resided in urban centres along the outer rim of a vast, largely dry, island continent. There they had ready access to the ocean and regular supplies of water from coastal river systems – both of which also provided opportunities for aquatic sports (Drew 1994). The city of Sydney with its sunny weather, panoramic harbour and lengthy Parramatta River, provided regular opportunities for sailing and rowing regattas, which proved to be some of the most popular sporting spectacles of the 19th century (Cashman & Hickie 1987; Adair 1992). Today, of course, some of the most iconic recreational spaces in Australia are beaches, with both surfers and surf lifesavers quintessential symbols of local aquatic culture (Saunders 1998). Yet, as historians have shown, during the colonial era there was conflict between picnickers and surf bathers, and efforts to proscribe swimming in public. For many moral conservatives, bathing at the beach in daylight hours was frowned upon as improper, exposing too much flesh at a time when modesty was acute (Brawley 1995; Booth 2001b; White 2004; Jaggard 2006). Indeed, when public bathing eventually became more widely accepted, whether at the beach or in swimming pools, men and women were initially segregated (Phillips 1998; McDermott 2005). Surf lifesaving – an Australian invention – dates from 1907, but until recent decades this was a male-dominated institution. The timing and extent of gender reform is, however, still hotly debated by sport historians (Booth 2000, 2002; Jaggard 2001, 2002; Phillips 2002).

As a public space, the beach provides historians with a fascinating resource for tracking changing perceptions about the human body and norms of public behaviour. Surfing, for example, became part of a 1960s beachside 'counterculture' in which self-expression and aesthetic movement in the surf were highly prized. New swimwear was intended to accentuate body display, and was soon commercialised as a fashion item (Booth 2001b Daley 2005). Booth's research has revealed structural tensions at the modern beach. 'Surfies' preferred to stay aloof from formality and civic engagement, while surf lifesavers volunteered their time to clubs and the wider beach-going community. To the lifesavers the surfies appeared self-indulgently radical; to surfies the lifeguards seemed subservient and conformist to authority. These were convenient stereotypes; both of these male-dominated groups could, in their own way, be a law unto themselves. Lifesaving clubs were ideal places to drink heavily, and many were sponsored by alcohol companies or pubs. Surfers, meanwhile, were more likely to experiment with illicit drugs. None of these substances was conducive to optimum motor skills or water safety (Booth 1991, 1994a, 1994b, 2001a, 2001c). Today many of the best Australian surfers are part of a global professional circuit, with performance and style being rewarded in cash (Booth 1995). Concurrently, surf lifesaving clubs have sought to curb excess drinking, make membership more gender inclusive, and actively recruit volunteers from culturally and linguistically diverse backgrounds. Indeed, a positive response to the infamous Cronulla Beach riots of 2005, which involved conflict between ultranationalist 'whites' and beachgoers of Middle Eastern background, has been Surf Lifesaving's 'On the Same Wave' program, which has actively recruited volunteers from diverse ethnic and cultural backgrounds.

While space, place and geography are pivotal to our understanding of Australian history, these subjects have yet to be developed extensively by sport historians. Indeed, although regional differences have been noted about sport around Australia (Cashman & Hickie 1982; Forster 1986; Bennet 1988; O'Hara 1991, 2002; Magdalinski 2002; Topp & Nauright 2004; Atherley 2006; Horton 2006), there is no systematic geographically informed or comparative research – certainly nothing to rival the comprehensive work of John Bale in Britain (Bale 1994, 2003). Our notions about athleticism, identity and self-image are therefore lacking a demonstrated awareness of similarities *and* differences about sport and history across what is, after all, a vast continent with varying terrains, climates, populations and cultures. And, as is now discussed, there were key norms and power relationships in society that established boundaries of inclusion and exclusion within sport.

Norms of participation in Australian sport

The Australian colonies did not reproduce a class system based on nobility. There were self-styled migrant aristocrats from Britain, but in the Antipodes elevated status was shaped overwhelmingly by holding public office or 'making good' economically. Australians were not equal in wealth or power, though there was a commitment to opportunity; an achievement culture. Those who 'made it' were, however, frowned upon if they adopted 'airs' and 'graces'. Hirst (2006) has described this as 'a democracy of manners' and contends that 'it is the feel of Australian society that is markedly egalitarian, not its social structure' (p. 301). This hypothesis can also be usefully applied to Australian sport. Sociologists have done much to dispel widespread assumptions that sport is structurally egalitarian in contemporary society. Yet they also note the persistence of discourses that present sport as inherently 'open to all' (Lawrence & Rowe 1986; Stoddart 1986; Rowe & Lawrence 1990; McKay 1991). Historians, meanwhile, have tried to put inequalities in context: class and status divisions in sport were typically more pronounced in the 19th and 20th centuries than today, and some sports were more elitist than others.

In late Victorian England there was a serious divide between professional and amateur versions of sport. This schism soon impacted on Australia, particularly as rules for the amateur code tended to be drawn up in Britain (Holt 1989; Cashman 1995). In the colonies there evolved amateur and professional versions of sports like rugby football (Cunneen 1979; Horton 1994; Collins 2000, 2005; Little 2007), athletics (Ross 1984; Mason 1985; Daly 1994); cycling (Hess 1998; Weaver & Weaver 1999; Simpson 2006) and rowing (Adair 1992, 1994). A further sporting innovation from abroad was the Olympic Games, where amateur status was needed for eligibility to take part. Hence there was considerable surveillance of sports to which prize money and wagering were attached (Jobling 1988). By and large, though, the amateur code was read and applied more stringently in Britain than in Australia. With rowing, for example, English clubs not only banned participants who had competed for a wager or prize money, they eventually imposed a test of status and privilege – anyone deemed working class was proscribed from membership of an amateur club (Halladay 1990). In Australia, however, non-pecuniary amateur status was more important than class background; hence the introduction of a manual labour amateur classification at many rowing clubs (Adair 1992, 1994; Crotty 1998; Ripley 2005). In Australian sport the amateur code was open to very different interpretations, and the penalties associated with transgressions varied; officials could be very harsh while some conveniently turned a blind eye. This was very much sport and politics (Moore & Phillips 1990; Cashman 1995, pp. 54–71; Adair & Vamplew 1997, pp. 37–40; Phillips 2001a; Senyard 2002). It used to be thought that amateur and professional sport in Australia were entirely separate domains. Recent research, however, has thrown that easy assumption into disarray. In mid-19th-century rowing, for example, it was quite common to offer prizes to amateur victors and this did not compromise their amateur status. What was more, they often competed on the same program (though generally in different events) as professional competitors (Adair

1992, 1994; Senyard 2002). Most startling of all, though, Stuart Ripley (2003) revealed that some of Australia's leading sport officials presided over both amateur and professional competitions during the late 19th and early 20th centuries.

In terms of the evolution of amateur and professional modes of elite sport in Australia, much has changed since the advent of live television broadcasts in the 1970s. Significantly, neither tennis nor cricket offered long-term professional careers within Australia until players sought, in effect, a slice of the TV revenue being earned by not-for-profit sporting bodies. However, while there has been much debate about the World Series Cricket 'revolution' that spawned the rise of full-time professional cricketers in Australia (Harriss 1990; Stewart 1995; Haig & Dundas 2001), remarkably little has been written about the schism in Australian tennis, wherein some of the great players of the 1950s and 1960s turned professional at a time when the Majors were for amateurs only (Fewster 1985; Kinross-Smith 1994). Golf provides another complex scenario: professionals in private clubs of the early 20th century were modestly paid coaches or lowly paid caddies appointed to serve the interests of members, with many of the latter coming from wealthy backgrounds. This 'master and servant' relationship has now evolved to the point where a club professional holds a position of considerable status, and the burgeoning prize money offered on Australian and overseas circuits has raised the income of the elite golfer and caddy into the upper echelons of athlete income (Stoddart 1994).

Tennis and golf are also interesting historically because they have long been sites of public access or private privilege. The fees associated with membership of a private club have always acted as an economic filter, but so too has social vetting of members by club boards. Curiously, though, too little is presently known about questions of inclusion and exclusion in two of Australia's best-known participant sports (Phillips 1988, 1990; Tatz & Stoddart 1993; Kinross-Smith 1994, 1997; Blashak 2004). Indeed, there is a general lack of systematic historical analysis into questions of class, status and privilege in a range of emergent elite sports like sailing, motor racing and horse racing, where wealth and social position impact on membership of private clubs and the capacity to own yachts, grand prix cars, and thoroughbred horses (O'Hara 1994, 2007; Griffen-Foley 2000; Thompson 2004). The eminently popular Melbourne Cup is perhaps the quintessential example of Hirst's dictum about structural inequality and a 'democracy of manners' in Australia. This horse race literally stops much of the nation for two minutes on the first Tuesday in November; to that extent it is a shared celebration. However, Flemington racecourse separates spectators according to their status as club members, horse owners and 'ordinary' punters. They might be at the same event, but the idea that all classes 'rub shoulders together' on Melbourne Cup Day – whether at the race course or over a champagne lunch – is one of the nation's most alluring myths (Beresford 1982; Ahearne 1987; White 2003).

Australian schools have long been nurseries for major sports like Rugby Union, Rugby League, Australian Rules football, cricket and netball. Back in the 19th century there was a particular effort by denominational schools to instil in pupils the British-inspired athletic ideal of 'muscular Christianity', within which amateurism was a core value. This not only applied to Anglican and Protestant schools; amateurism was a hallmark of Irish sport too, hence its significance within Catholic education (Cronin 1996; McDevitt 1997; Brice 2001; Watson 2005). A major examination of sport, religion and ideology in Australian history nonetheless awaits (key publications include Crawford 1986; Brown 1987; Connellan 1988; Stewart 1992; Crotty 2000). Perhaps the biggest gap, though, is in our historical understanding of varying physical education and sport opportunities for children across the two educational systems: state-funded, secular schools and state-subsidised, private schools (Collins et al. 1990; Kirk & Twigg 1993, 1995; Kirk 1996; Wilkinson 1998). For example, in Sydney, a small elite clique known from 1892 as the Amateur Athletic Association of the Great Public Schools (AAAGPS) of New South Wales (or Great Public Schools) has provided sport facilities and resources, such as rowing sheds, swimming pools and tennis courts, that are typically absent from the grounds of non-selective state schools and second-tier independent schools. One of the major events on the GPS sporting calendar is the exclusive 'Head of the River' rowing regatta, which dates back to 1893 and is modelled on boat races among the elite public schools of England (Sherington 1983). Sydney's GPS schools have been a traditional nursery for recruitment into New South Wales Rugby Union clubs; and, since the majority of these schools catered for boys rather than girls, the social construction of masculinity through body contact sport (Light & Kirk 2000, 2001). This is not to suggest that girls have had no place in school sport, either in the state or private systems. But it has been very much a secondary place. For example, not until 1996 did female students in New South Wales have their own Head of the River regatta (Crawford 1984; Stewart 1992; Kirk 2000).

Gender identities and associated norms of physicality are indeed keys with which to investigate sport in Australian history. It has been largely a male domain, as elsewhere. Scholars have shown that for many young boys sport has been a significant rite of passage into manhood. This reflects longstanding cultural assumptions that boys are 'inherently' combative and aggressive, and that sport provides a focus for such overtly 'masculine' behaviours (Nauright & Chandler 1996; Light & Kirk 2000; Hickey 2008). For young females the reverse has been true; until the late 20th century girls had fewer opportunities to participate in sport, and they were often encouraged to undertake 'female appropriate' activities, such as netball, that did not compromise traditional notions of femininity (Treagus 2005; Taylor 2005). Even today, with important efforts to improve female access to a range of sports, the institution of sport itself remains a key to the gendering process. Not only are men and women typically separated in competitive physical activity, but at the elite level, females are celebrated as athletes of calibre on too few occasions – such as Olympic and Commonwealth Games, where they receive equal media coverage alongside men (Phillips 1997; Adair & Vamplew 1997, pp. 48–62; Payne 2004).

The history of women in Australian sport has been characterised, on the one hand, through radical feminist criticism of marginalisation and oppression by males (Randall 1988); and on the other hand, through liberal feminist arguments that women have indeed been more active in sport than many (male) historians have bothered to notice (Stell 1991). There is, however, little debate about one point: as the work of Dennis Phillips has shown, Australian women have repeatedly outperformed their male counterparts in terms of procuring medals at the Olympic Games. His research offers an alternative way of recognising and valuing female sport achievement (Phillips 1990, 1996). Similarly, Rob Hess has examined the historical importance of women as sports fans; their contribution as supporters of Australian Rules football, in particular, is unsurpassed by any other code (Hess 1996, 2000, 2005). Today, though, the analysis of women in Australian sport history seems to have reached a hiatus; the 21st century has yet to produce a wave of new research despite the welcome efforts of a small number of enthusiasts (Burroughs & Nauright 2000; Haig-Muir 2000, 2004; Brabazon 2000; Burroughs 2001; Little 2001; Hess 2000, 2005; Taylor 2005).

The historical analysis of group identity, inclusion and exclusion in Australian sport must also engage with societal issues for Indigenous peoples, other non-whites and ethnic minorities generally. As the following discussion indicates, this means taking seriously endemic problems of racism and the stereotyping of 'others' on the basis of their skin colour or ancestry.

Aborigines, non-whites and ethnic minorities in Australian sport

Well before the arrival of Europeans and the subsequent British annexation of *Terra Australis*, a vast array of Aboriginal peoples were custodians of the land and sea. They were regionally disparate and spoke different languages, but had much in common. This included an ingenious capacity to observe, understand and respect the natural environment, a constructive mutualism that enabled co-existence for at least 40,000 years. Aborigines were spatially aware and physically dexterous; they needed these attributes when fishing and hunting for food. It was here that play, games and sports provided input. Within Aboriginal communities there were games of strategy and play activities requiring athleticism and dexterity. Footraces promoted speed, ball games fostered agility, while spear and boomerang throwing contests demanded eye-to-hand coordination important for hunting (Howell & Howell 1992; Edwards 1999, 2009). However, Aboriginal societies were fragmented by European annexation of land, with many Aborigines confined subsequently to colonial reserves and missions. This dislocation meant that traditional Aboriginal sports and games began to lose their functional relevance, with the meaning and significance of such activities not passed onto later generations. A decline in these customs was part of a wider diminution of Aboriginal culture and identity under European colonisation (Smith 2008).

Recently, there have been efforts to trace, record and revive traditional Indigenous games. Using the medium of oral history, Queensland academic Ken Edwards has spent many years talking with Aboriginal and Torres Strait Islander elders. Through this dialogue, as well as by reading early anthropological accounts, he has established a formidable record of customary Aboriginal recreation (Edwards 1999). That knowledge now has applied significance because Edwards, with the assistance of the Australian Sports Commission, has produced a user-friendly booklet for schools and community groups which explains the traditional purpose of particular Indigenous games and how they may be played today (Australian Sports Commission 2009, Edwards 2009). This is a significant development: through sport and recreation non-Aboriginal Australians can be introduced to aspects of a living culture. Too often Indigenous history and customs are neglected as 'irrelevant' in discourses of modernity in Australia.

Histories of Aboriginal responses to colonialism, and the regime of controls exerted on Indigenous peoples by representatives of the British Crown, have developed significantly over the past 20 years (e.g. Reynolds 1996, 2006). So too, stories of the various missions that institutionalised Aborigines and separated them from European settlers (Stevens 1994; Mitchell 2005). This confinement introduced Indigenous people to the language, religion and customs from Britain. That process of colonial acculturation included sport – most notably the game of cricket – as a means of instilling in Aboriginal boys and men agreement on rules, respect for the decisions of those in authority, and a common goal of teamwork in a competitive setting. It seems remarkable, at first glance, that in 1868 the first 'Australian' cricket team to tour England consisted almost entirely of Aborigines. However, as historians have shown, this was an entrepreneurial initiative on the part of non-Indigenous sponsors and management, who saw an opportunity to draw big crowds and significant revenue for themselves from a series of exhibitions abroad – involving both cricket and displays of Aboriginal physical culture (Mulvaney & Harcourt 1988; Sampson 2000, 2009). The Aboriginal cricketers performed ably, winning as many games as they lost. But this did not establish Indigenous players in Australian cricket back home. Indeed, although there were some fine young Aboriginal cricketers in the late 19th and early 20th centuries, they faced significant obstacles to play at the elite level (Whimpress 1992, 1999). There were logistical problems owing to laws that constrained the movement to cities of Aborigines impounded on rural missions and reserves. What was more, as sport historians have shown, the few Indigenous players who did make it to first-class cricket had chequered experiences, such as outstanding bowlers Jack Marsh and Eddie Gilbert, both of whom had problems with cricket officials that negated their opportunity to play for Australia (Whimpress 1994; Colman & Edwards 2002; Bonnell 2003).

Despite negative Aboriginal experiences in cricket, Newlin and Moran make the salient point that 'there have always been Aboriginal achievers in sport, but few people know this' (Newlin & Moran 1999, p. 35). Sport historians, led by Colin Tatz, have tried to rectify this lack of awareness, while also detailing ways in which Aborigines have been discriminated against in sport and society (Tatz 1987, 1995). Indigenous athletes were most likely to appear in activities that offered the prospect of financial reward; amateurism was a white, middle-class philosophy of privilege that was not relevant to their circumstances. No surprise then that Aborigines featured in prize-money events, particularly pedestrianism (sprinting), boxing, and as jockeys in horse racing (Broome 1980, 1996; Blades 1985; Mooney & Ramsland 2008). But they were generally not to be seen in sports that required expensive equipment, such as sailing and rowing. For the most part, they were also absent from the membership of private clubs like golf and tennis.

When Australia was proclaimed a Commonwealth in 1901, the restrictive White Australia Policy (WAP) was enshrined in law. The focus of this federal legislation was non-English speaking immigrants and (de facto) people of 'colour' seeking to be residents of Australia. However, short-term visitors could, with the support of a local sponsor and the consent of immigration authorities, be provided with an 'exemption certificate' that temporarily overlooked their 'alien' or 'coloured' status (Honey 2001). Intriguingly, this loophole allowed occasional visits by non-white, 'foreign' athletes who performed publicly at

Australian sport venues. Notwithstanding the racial separation implicit in the WAP, local sport fans typically appreciated the athletic skills and 'exotic' appearance of these 'coloured' competitors. However, there were also differences of opinion and reaction. African-American boxer Jack Johnson was admired for his boxing prowess, but hated by many for defeating a white title holder in Sydney in 1908 (Broome 1979; Wells 1998; Headon 2009). Yet only two years earlier African-American cyclist Marshall 'Major' Taylor had beaten all comers in Sydney and was widely coveted by local sport fans (Ritchie 1996, 2010). In 1915, the man widely accredited with giving surfing a high profile, Hawaiian Duke Paoa Kahanamoku, was revered when he took to the waves in Australia (Osmond et al. 2006). Similarly, Alick Wickham, a Solomon Islander in Australia, became the most famous exponent of the 'crawl' stroke (Osmond & Phillips 2004; Phillips 2006). Visiting athletes of Asian origin were less renowned in Australia but do not seem to have been excluded from local sporting culture (Osmond & McDermott 2008). Indeed, despite local fears of eventual invasion by the so-called yellow peril from East Asia, swimmers from Japan and footballers from China were received very hospitably during the 1920s (Guoth 2007; Brawley 2009). There is plenty of irony about athletes of non-white appearance being accorded such status; not only because of the WAP, but because in the first half of the 20th century Indigenous Australians had such a low profile in the nation's sporting culture (Whimpress 2001).

There were signs of change in the 1960s and 1970s. When Aboriginal boxer Lionel Rose claimed the world bantamweight title in Japan in 1968, he was mobbed by well-wishers upon return to Australia. Not only was Rose the first Aborigine to win a world boxing title, he also became the first Indigenous person to be awarded the prestigious title of 'Australian of the Year'. A year later he reached the top of the music charts with a country and western song 'I Thank You' (Rose & Humphries 1969). Along with tennis player Evonne Goolagong, who twice won the Wimbledon singles crown, Rose presented the image of an Aborigine who had 'made it' in white society. Like Cathy Freeman, who lit the cauldron at the opening of the 2000 Olympic Games, both Rose and Goolagong appealed to many white observers who, ordinarily, had little contact with or sympathy for Aboriginal dissidents, such as those who fashioned the Aboriginal Tent Embassy in Canberra in 1972 (Goolagong-Cawley 1993; Bruce & Hallinan 2001; Lothian 2007); or, for that matter, Aborigines who took their protests about land rights to the streets during the Commonwealth Games of 1982. In the latter case the Queensland government was so 'spooked' by this Aboriginal assertiveness that it declared a state of emergency in order to constrain such public demonstrations (Tatz 1981, 1984; Shannon 2004). Rose and Goolagong presented to white Australians 'non-threatening' examples of Aboriginal advancement.

During the 1980s and 1990s increased numbers of Indigenous males participated at the elite level in the country's two largest football codes – Australian Rules and Rugby League. By the early 21st century players from Aboriginal or Torres Strait Islander heritage constituted around 10% of all professional players in both the AFL and the NRL – a staggering proportion, given that the Indigenous population of Australia is about 2% of the national total (Korf 2009). As scholars have shown, however, these footballers battled long and hard against racism on and off the field. Not until the late 1990s did football administrators have anti-vilification policies fully in place, and they were in effect pushed into doing so by outspoken and articulate players like Essendon's Michael Long (Gardiner 1997; Warren 1997, 2000; McNamara 2000). The profile, status and remuneration of professional Indigenous athletes has never been better (Tatz & Tatz 1996, 2000), but there remains more to be achieved – particularly in terms of career transition planning and retirement experiences of Aboriginal sportspeople (Stocks & East 2000; Gorman 2005; Stronach & Adair 2010).

Issues of discrimination and stereotyping in sport have also been apparent among ethnic minority groups in Australia. While soccer, for example, was an important sport for the great flood of European migrants after World War II, the game was typecast as 'foreign' by comparison to the existing staples of the rugby codes and Australian Rules (Hay 2006). Soccer was commonly ridiculed as 'wogball' and a game for 'poofters'; this derision not only impacted upon so-called New Australians playing soccer, but residents of Anglo-Celtic heritage with a passion for the sport (Warren et al. 2002). Ethnicity has, of course, been part of Australian sport since the 19th century. Scots were particularly noticeable in golf and lawn bowls, Irish Catholics were prominent as bookmakers in the racing industry, while the English were especially zealous about cricket and fox hunting. These practices were basically extensions of migrant cultural baggage in the Antipodes (Adair 1998). But it would be misleading to speak of ethnic enclaves among the Australian population or within the sporting culture of the late 19th and early 20th centuries. Indeed, despite protracted Anglo-Irish tensions, most notably after the Easter Rising of 1916, which had local impacts upon Australian society, sport appears to have been less affected by sectarianism than education, party politics and the public service (Hogan 1987; Kildea 2002). There have been suggestions that Irish-Catholic Test cricketers suffered discrimination at the hands of team mates and selectors, though there is debate among historians as to whether this was systematic persecution or merely a series of personality conflicts (Bairner 2007).

In Australia, historical research into sport and ethnicity has focused principally on the second half of the 20th century (Mosely 1997). It was given impetus as a subject for inquiry by the emergence of a federal government policy of multiculturalism, first adopted by Labor in 1973. Previously, New Australians were expected to assimilate into a dominant English-speaking, Anglo-Celtic culture. Now there was an emphasis on respect for group differences within a society that, as a consequence of mass migration – not only from Europe but increasingly Asia – had become more culturally diverse and ethnically cosmopolitan (Jupp 1991). In terms of sport, however, little seemed to change. For example, although a promising 19-year-old fast bowler, Len Durtanovich, played junior representative cricket for New South Wales, it was the pragmatically renamed Len Pascoe who played for Australia between 1977 and 1982. His parents' Yugoslavian origins were, however, still a source of derision for some cricket opponents (Lawson 1993; Haig 2004). Soccer, meanwhile, was still subject to discourses propounding it as a game for ethnic 'others' (minorities) and thus not 'true-blue' Australian (Hughson 1992; Danforth 2001). Sport therefore remained a culturally conservative institution within which traditional forms and norms of physical activity dominated.

In the past two decades, however, there has been a greater emphasis on social inclusion and the engagement of various communities into sport – with a particular focus on attracting people from culturally and linguistically diverse backgrounds (CALD) (Taylor & Toohey 1998). Yet this has coincided, ironically, with a move away from sports clubs dedicated to particular ethnic groups and towards the 'cosmopolitanising' of Australian sport culture – within which people of all ancestries and skin colours are assumed to have a place. On the one hand this has opened new opportunities, on the other hand it has represented loss. For example, sports clubs organised by and for Jews have a long lineage in Australia (Hughes 1996, 1999). This includes the Monash Golf Club in Sydney, named after Australia's renowned Jewish military commander of World War I. However, demographic and socioeconomic changes have in effect transformed Monash into a 'cosmopolitan' golf club, albeit with a Jewish past (Tatz 2002).

This theme of loss has also been noticeable among soccer clubs that were originally formed to cater for the fraternal needs of ethnic groups from non-English speaking backgrounds – Italians, Greeks, Serbs, Croats, and so on (Mosely 1995; Hay 1998). The profile and status of such clubs has been denuded since the mid-1990s by a National Soccer League (NSL) decision to in effect 'de-ethnicise' elite-level club competition in Australia (Hughson 1997). A key expectation was that club names be revamped in an attempt to garner fan support from beyond an 'ethnic' base. Greek club West Adelaide Hellas, for example, changed its name to the West Adelaide Sharks. This was part of an explicit effort to reinvent soccer as a game intended to appeal to 'mainstream' Australia, not just particular ethnic communities that many of the clubs appeared to represent (Westerbeek 2005). At the elite level, club soccer faced protracted financial and administrative difficulties, as well as a perception (sometimes created by the media) that matches between Serbs and Croats, for example, were little more than occasions for historic, European-based inter-group hostilities to be played out in an Antipodean setting (Hughson 2000, 2001; Hay 2001). Intriguingly, NSL efforts to 'mainstream' soccer were a contrast to strategies by the AFL and the NRL, both of which actively courted players and supporters from CALD backgrounds and, though they did not put it this way, a more conspicuously 'cosmopolitan' following (Stewart 2007).

No Australian sport has gone through more reform than soccer in recent decades; while this has involved loss it has also presented opportunity. The NSL has been supplanted by the A-League, which involves team franchises and single clubs representing cities or regions. It has received financial backing from Jewish-Australian property magnate Frank Lowy, while the long overdue involvement of the Socceroos in the World Cup (2006) gave the sport – renamed football in Australia – unprecedented profile and public following. Although it is early days, the 'mainstreaming' of football via the A-League and the expectation of the Socceroos participating regularly in the World Cup, appears to have the potential to put the game in a more stable financial position (Dabscheck 2007; Skinner 2008). What is more, preliminary research indicates that CALD fans of the NSL have, for the most part, not been isolated by the A-League, and that a new generation of football fans – from all sorts of backgrounds – are attending matches (Lock et al. 2008; Lock 2009). As with the Monash Golf Club there is both loss and opportunity; erosion of ethnic traditions, but a commitment to engage with a wider range of followers. It is an example of the growing diversity of Australian sport cultures. Of course sport and Australian nationalism persists, but for many people it is a hybrid sense of fan allegiance – Australian *and* Vietnamese, Australian *and* Serbian, Australian *and* Greek, and so on. Rather than a site of monolithic parochialism and patriotism, Australian sport – both in local and global contexts – appears to be moving towards a postmodern, cosmopolitan phase (Georgakis 2000; Bowden 2003).

'Re-visioning' and revisiting Australian sport history

As explained at the outset, there are very few career opportunities in Australia for academics aspiring to work as sport historians, and the vast majority of current practitioners are located in Human Movement, Sports Studies or Business environments within which historical analysis tends to have a low priority. That said, there have been some important contributions by Australians to the practice of sport history. Murray Phillips and Douglas Booth have been at the forefront of global initiatives to make the subdiscipline more receptive to innovations within social and cultural history generally. They have encouraged researchers to explicitly situate themselves within a theoretical paradigm; they have urged scholars to be more conscious of archives as sources of power, not simply evidence; they have prompted writers to reflect upon their research methods and their positions, as investigators, within that process; and they have emphasised the constructed and contingent nature of 'findings' (Phillips 1998, 2001; Booth 2004, 2005a, 2005b, 2006; Phillips 2006). Their counsel has so far received mixed responses: sport historians familiar with the 'cultural' or 'linguistic' turn in the discipline of History are well placed to benefit from both the Phillips and Booth recommendations, but those limited to conventional social history face something of a challenge from deconstructionism and postmodernism (Hay 2006b; Stoddart 2006; Johnes 2007; Guttmann 2008). Concepts like reflexivity and tropes, as well as methods of discourse analysis or semiotics are not grasped easily, in part because many who deploy them insist on highly specialised, even obtuse language. Thus the challenge for Phillips and Booth, world leaders in their own right, is to convey their arguments in a way that inspires others to follow.

While there has recently been important debate about a 're-visioning' of the craft of sport history, there are further priorities that need revisiting. First, remarkably little systematic research has been conducted into the economic history of Australian sport (Stewart 1985, 2003, 2007; Dabscheck 1991, 1998; Booth 1997, 2004). In Britain, by contrast, there is a wealth of knowledge about club ownership, profit and utility maximising behaviours, player salaries and unions, and so on. Classic examples include Vamplew (1976), Vamplew (1988) and Tranter (1998). Second, while there has been sustained research into the impact of the media on Australian sport since the late 1970s – the era when television became crucial to professionalisation and commercialisation (Lawrence & Rowe 1986; Hutchins & Phillips 1997; Rowe 1999; Phillips & Hutchines 2003) – too little is presently known about the role and significance of the print media and radio in the formative years of Australian sport (Cunneen 1981; Grow 1986; Wenn 1993; Brown 1995; Stewart 2002). Such conventional forms of mass mediated sport are less significant in the age of digital television and the internet, but they are surely of major historical import. Third, there are distinctive aspects of Australian sport history that are well known but poorly understood.

Why is it that professional clubs in the football codes and cricket have typically been member based rather than, as with soccer and baseball in Britain and the US respectively, either owned by individuals or shareholders? (Nauright & Phillips 1996, 1997; Phillips & Nauright 1999). What values and aspirations have been associated with club membership in Australian sport history? (Stemski 1986; Moore 1996; Phillips 1996; Lock et al. 2008). Why, in addition, is there no tradition (other than in soccer) of Australian sport spectators being formally segregated in stadia on the basis of team allegiance? What is more, given the passion typically associated with 'barracking' at Australian sport, why has the hard core 'hooligan' phenomenon been largely absent from the football codes Down Under? (Warren 2003). In sum, a key problem with Australian sports history is not simply a lack of theoretical or methodological vision, but a need to systematically revisit historical archives – documentary, visual and oral. Revisionism can emerge from reforms to the academic craft of sport history; equally they can arise from painstaking reading and interpretation of primary sources – many of which are as yet untouched by scholars of sport. May a new generation of scholars lead the way.

References

Adair, D. (2002). Location, location! Sports history and academic real estate. *Australian Society for Sports History Bulletin, 36*: 11–14.

Adair, D. (1998). Conformity, diversity, and difference in antipodean physical culture: the indelible influence of immigration, ethnicity, and race during the formative years of organised sport in Australia, c.1788–1918. In M. Cronin and D. Mayall (Eds). *Sporting nationalisms: identity, ethnicity, immigration, and assimilation* (pp. 14–48). London: Frank Cass.

Adair, D. (1994). Rowing and sculling. In W. Vamplew & B. Stoddart (Eds). *Sport in Australia: a social history* (pp. 172–92). Melbourne: Cambridge University Press.

Adair, D. (1992). Two dots in the distance: professional sculling as a mass spectacle in New South Wales, 1876–1907. *Sporting Traditions, 9*(1): 52–83.

Adair, D., Phillips, M. & Nauright, J. (1997). Sporting manhood in Australia: test cricket, rugby football, and the Imperial connection, 1878–1918. *Sport History Review, 28*: 46–60.

Adair, D. & Vamplew, W. (1997). *Sport in Australian history*. Oxford: Oxford University Press.

Ahearne, K. (1987). The myth lives on: cultural significance of the Melbourne Cup. *Australian Society, 6*(12): 52, 57–58.

Atherley, K. (2006). Sport, localism and social capital in rural Western Australia. *Geographical Research, 44*(4): 348–60.

Australian Sports Commission (2009). *Yulunga: traditional Aboriginal games*. [Online]. Available: www.ausport.gov.au/participating/indigenous/resources/games_and_activities/full_resource [accessed 21 February 2010].

Bairner, A. (2007). Wearing the baggie green: the Irish and Australian cricket. *Sport in Society, 10*(3): 457–75.

Bale, J. (2003). *Sports geography*. London: Routledge.

Bale, J. (1994). *Landscapes of modern sport*. Leicester: Leicester University Press.

Bennett, S. (1998). Regional sentiment and Australian sport. *Sporting Traditions*, 5(1): 98–111.

Beresford, Q. (1982). The Melbourne Cup: Australia's first national day. *Hemisphere*, 27: 180–84.

Blades, G. C. (1985). Australian Aborigines, Cricket and Pedestrianism: Culture and Conflict, 1880–1910, Honours thesis, Bachelor of Human Movement Studies, University of Queensland.

Blainey, G. (1966). *The tyranny of distance: how distance shaped Australia's history*. Melbourne: Sun Books.

Blair, D. J. (1995). The greater game: Australian football and the army at home and on the front during World War I. *Sporting Traditions*, 11(2): 91–102.

Blashak, B. (2004). 'The ignorant labelled it a ladies' game': masculinity in Australian tennis in the late nineteenth and early twentieth centuries. In I. Warren (Ed.). *Sport, gender and theory: the formative years of tennis and snowboarding* (pp. 1–59). ASSH Studies 16, Melbourne: Australian Society for Sports History.

Bonnell, M. (2003). *How many more are coming? The short life of Jack Marsh*. Petersham, NSW: Walla Walla Press.

Booth, D. (2006). Sites of truth or metaphors of power? Refiguring the archive. *Sport in History*, 26(1): 91–109.

Booth, D. (2005a). *The field: truth and fiction in sport history*. London: Taylor & Francis.

Booth, D. (2005b). Evidence revisited: interpreting historical materials in sport history. *Rethinking History*, 9(4): 459–83.

Booth, D. (2004). Escaping the past? The cultural turn and language in sport history. *Rethinking History*, 8(1): 103–25.

Booth, D. (2002). A tragic plot? A reply to Jaggard and Phillips. *Journal of Sport History*, 29(1): 41–48.

Booth, D. (2001a). The dark side of surf lifesaving. *Journal of Sport History*, 29(1): 7–14.

Booth, D. (2001b). *Australian beach cultures: the history of sun, sand, and surf*. London: Frank Cass.

Booth, D. (2001c). From bikinis to boardshorts: wahines and the paradoxes of surfing culture. *Journal of Sport History*, 28(1): 3–22.

Booth, D. (2000). Surf lifesaving: the development of an Australasian sport. *International Journal of the History of Sport*, 17(2): 166–87.

Booth, D. (1997). Sports history: what can be done? *Sport, Education and Society*, 2(2): 191–204.

Booth, D. (1995). Ambiguities in pleasure and discipline: the development of competitive surfing. *Journal of Sport History*, 22: 189–206.

Booth, D. (1994a). Swimming, surfing and surf-lifesaving. In W. Vamplew & B. Stoddart (Eds). *Sport in Australia: a social history* (pp. 231–54). Melbourne: Cambridge University Press.

Booth, D. (1994b). Surfing '60s: a case study in the history of pleasure and discipline. *Australian Historical Studies*, 26(103): 262–79.

Booth, D. (1991). War off the water: the Australian Surf Lifesaving Association and the beach. *Sporting Traditions*, 7(2): 134–62.

Bowden, B. (2003). Nationalism and cosmopolitanism: irreconcilable differences or possible bedfellows? *National Identities*, 5(3): 235–49.

Brabazon, T. (2000). Time for a change or more of the same? Les Mills and the masculinisation of aerobics. *Sporting Traditions, 17*(1): 97–112.

Brawley, S. (2009). 'They came, they saw, they conquered': the Takaishi/Saito tour of 1926–27 and Australian perceptions of Japan. *Sporting Traditions, 26*(2): 49–66.

Brawley, S. (1995). *Vigilant and victorious: a community history of the Collaroy Surf Life Saving Club, 1911–1995*. Collaroy, NSW: Collaroy Surf Life Saving Club.

Brice, I. D. (2001). Ethnic masculinities in Australian boys' schools: Scots and Irish secondary schools in late nineteenth-century Australia. *Paedagogica Historica*, 37(1): 139–52.

Broome, R. (1996). Theatres of power: tent boxing circa 1910–1970. *Aboriginal History*, 20: 1–23.

Broome, R. (1980). Professional Aboriginal boxers in eastern Australia 1930–1979. *Aboriginal History*, 4(1–2): 49–71.

Broome, R. (1979). The Australian reaction to Jack Johnson, black pugilist, 1907–09. In R. Cashman & M. McKernan (Eds). *Sport in History* (pp. 343–63). St Lucia: University of Queensland Press.

Brown, D. W. (1987). Muscular Christianity in the Antipodes: some observations on the diffusion and emergence of a Victorian ideal in Australian social theory. *Sporting Traditions*, 3(2): 173–87.

Brown, P. (1995). Gender, the press and history: coverage of women's sport in the Newcastle Herald, 1890–1990. *Media Information Australia*, 75: 24–34.

Bruce, T. & Hallinan, C. (2001). Cathy Freeman: the quest for Australian identity. In D. Andrews and S. Jackson (Eds). *Sports stars: the cultural politics of sporting celebrity* (pp. 257–70). New York: Routledge.

Burroughs, A. (2001). Women, femininity and sport: the contribution of the 'new woman' to nationhood. In R. Cashman, J. O'Hara & A. Honey (Eds). *Sport, federation, nation* (pp. 165–80). Sydney: Walla Walla Press.

Burroughs, A. & Nauright, J. (2000). Women's sports and embodiment in Australia and New Zealand. In J.A. Mangan & J. Nauright (Eds). *Sport in Australasian society: past and present* (pp. 188–205). London: Frank Cass.

Cashman, R. (1995). *Paradise of sport: the rise of organised sport in Australia*. Melbourne: Oxford University Press.

Cashman, R. (1992). Symbols of Imperial unity: Anglo-Australian cricketers, 1877–1900. In J. A. Mangan (Ed.). *The cultural bond: sport, empire, society* (pp. 129–41). Frank Cass: London.

Cashman, R. & Hickie, T. (1987). The divergent sporting cultures of Sydney and Melbourne. *Sporting Traditions*, 7(1): 24–46.

Cohen, P. (2006). Behind barbed wire: sport and Australian prisoners of war. *Sporting Traditions*, 23(1): 63–86.

Collins, T. (2005). Australian nationalism and working-class Britishness: the case of Rugby League football. *History Compass*, 3(1): 1–19.

Collins, T. (2000). From Bondi to Batley: Australian players in British rugby league, 1907–1995. *Sporting Traditions*, 16(2): 71–86.

Collins, B, Aitken, M. & Cork, B. (1990). *One hundred years of public school sport in New South Wales 1889–1989*. Sydney: New South Wales Department of School Education.

Colman, M. & Edwards, K. (2002). *Eddie Gilbert: the true story of an Aboriginal cricketing legend*. Sydney: ABC Books, Sydney.

Connellan, M. (1988). *The ideology of athleticism, its Antipodean impact, and its manifestation in two elite Catholic schools*. Bedford Park SA: ASSH Studies in Sports History, 5.

Crawford, R. (1986). Athleticism, gentlemen and Empire in Australian public schools: L. A. Adamson and Wesley College, Melbourne. In W. Vamplew (Ed.). *Sport and colonialism in 19th century Australasia* (pp. 42–64). Bedford Park SA: ASSH Studies in Sports History, 1.

Crawford, R. (1984). Sport for young ladies: the Victorian Independent Schools 1875–1925. *Sporting Traditions*, *1*(1): 61–82.

Cronin, M. (1996). Defenders of the nation? The Gaelic Athletic Association and Irish nationalist identity. *Irish Political Studies*, *11*(1): 1–19.

Crotty, M. (2001). *Making the Australian male: middle-class masculinity 1870–1920*. Melbourne: Melbourne University Publishing.

Crotty, M. (2000). Manly and moral: the making of middle-class men in the Australian public school. *International Journal of the History of Sport*, *17*(2): 10–30.

Crotty, M. (1998). Separate and distinct? The manual labour question in nineteenth-century Victorian rowing. *International Journal of the History of Sport*, *15*(2): 152–63.

Cunneen, C. (1981). Elevating and recording the people's pastimes: Sydney sporting journalism 1886–1939. In R. Cashman & M. McKernan (Eds). *Sport: money, morality, and the media* (pp. 162–76). Sydney: UNSW Press.

Cunneen, C. (1979). The rugby war: the early history of Rugby League in New South Wales. In R. Cashman & M. McKernan (Eds). *Sport in history: the making of modern sport history* (pp. 293–306). St Lucia Qld: University of Queensland Press.

Dabscheck, B. (2007). Moving beyond ethnicity: soccer's evolutionary progress. In B. Stewart (Ed.). *The games are not the same: the political economy of football in Australia* (pp. 198–235). Carlton Victoria: Melbourne University Press.

Dabscheck, B. (1998). Australian baseball's second unsuccessful attempt to establish a players' association. *Sporting Traditions*, *14*(2): 87–90.

Dabscheck, B. (1991). The Professional Cricketers Association of Australia. *Sporting Traditions*, *8*(1): 2–27.

Daley, C. (2005). From bush to beach: nudism in Australasia. *Journal of Historical Geography*, *31*(1): 149–67.

Daly, J. A. (1994). Track and field. In W. Vamplew and B. Stoddart (Eds). *Sport in Australia: a social history* (pp. 255–68). Melbourne: Cambridge University Press.

Daly, J. A. (1982). *Elysian fields: sport, class and community in colonial South Australia, 1836–1890*. Adelaide: J.A. Daly.

Danforth, L. M. (2001). Is the 'world game' an 'ethnic game' or an 'Aussie game'? Narrating the nation in Australian soccer. *American Ethnologist*, *28*(2): 363–87.

Drew, P. (1994). *The coast dwellers: Australians living on the edge*. Ringwood: Penguin.

Edwards, K. (2009). Traditional games of a timeless land: play cultures in Aboriginal and Torres Strait Islander communities. *Australian Aboriginal Studies* (2): 32–43.

Edwards, K. (1999). *Choopadoo: games from a Dreamtime*. Brisbane: Queensland University of Technology Press.

Fewster, K. (1985). Advantage Australia: Davis Cup tennis 1950–1959. *Sporting Traditions*, 2(1): 47–68.

Forster, C. (1986). Sport, society and space: the changing geography of country cricket in South Australia 1836–1914. *Sporting Traditions*, 2(2): 23–47.

Gardiner, G. (1997). Racial abuse and football: the Australian Football League's racial vilification rule in review. *Sporting Traditions*, 14(1): 3–26.

Georgakis, S. (2000). *Sport and the Australian Greek*. Sydney: Standard Publishing.

Goolagong Cawley, E. & Jarratt, P. (1993). *Home! The Evonne Goolagong story*. East Roseville, NSW: Simon & Schuster.

Gorman, S. (2005). *Brotherboys: the story of Jim and Phillip Krakouer*. Crows Nest, NSW: Allen & Unwin.

Griffen-Foley, B. (2000). Playing with princes and presidents: Sir Frank Packer and the 1962 challenge for the America's Cup. *Australian Journal of Politics & History*, 46(1): 51–66.

Grow, R. (1986). Nineteenth century football and the Melbourne press. *Sporting Traditions*, 3(1): 23–37.

Guoth, N. (2007). Kangaroos and dragons: the 1923 Chinese football tour of Australia, Paper Presented to Sporting Traditions XVI, the Biennial Conference of the Australian Society for Sports History, Canberra, 27–30 June 2007.

Guttmann, A. (2008). Review essay: the ludic and the ludicrous. *International Journal of the History of Sport*, 25(1): 100–12.

Haig-Muir, M. (2004). Handicapped from birth? Why women golfers are traditionally a fairway behind. *Sport History Review*, 35(1): 64–82.

Haig-Muir, M. (2000). Many a slip twixt cup and the lip: equal opportunity and Victorian golf clubs. *Sporting Traditions*, 17(1): 19–38.

Haigh, G. (2004). Pascoe was like a bull at a batsman. *The Age*, 21 February.

Haigh, G. & Dundas, R. (2001). *The cricket war: the inside story of Kerry Packer's World Series Cricket*, Melbourne: Text Publishing Company.

Halladay, E. (1990). *Rowing in England. A social history: the amateur debate*, Manchester: Manchester University Press.

Harriss, I. (1990). Packer, cricket and postmodernism. In D. Rowe & G. Lawrence (Eds). *Sport and leisure: trends in Australian popular culture* (pp. 109–21). Sydney: Harcourt Brace Jovanovich.

Hay, R. (2006a). 'Our wicked foreign game': why has association football (soccer) not become the main code of football in Australia? *Soccer and Society*, 7(2): 165–86.

Hay, R. (2006b). Approaches to sports history: theory and practice. *Sporting Traditions*, 22(2): 70–81.

Hay, R. (2001). 'Those bloody Croatians': Croatian soccer teams, ethnicity and violence in Australia, 1950-99. In G. Armstrong & R. Giulianotti (Eds). *Fear and loathing in world football* (pp. 77-90). Oxford: Berg.

Hay, R. (1998). Croatia: community, conflict and culture: the role of soccer clubs in migrant identity. *Immigrants And Minorities*, 17: 49-66.

Headon, D. (2009). 'World's Fistanic History', Sydney 1908: 'Flash Jack Johnson' vs 'Sinking Tommy Burns'. *Sporting Traditions*, 26(2): 1-14.

Hess, R. (2005). 'For the love of sensation': case studies in the early development of women's football in Victoria, 1921-1981. *Football Studies*, 8(2): 20-30.

Hess, R. (2000). 'Ladies are specially invited': women in the culture of Australian Rules Football. *International Journal of the History of Sport*, 17(2): 111-41.

Hess, R. (1998). A mania for bicycles: the impact of cycling on Australian Rules Football. *Sporting Traditions*, 14(2): 3-24.

Hess, R. (1996). Women and Australian Rules Football in colonial Melbourne. *International Journal of the History of Sport*, 13(3): 356-72.

Hickey, C. (2008). Physical education, sport and hyper-masculinity in schools. *Sport, Education and Society*, 13(2): 147-61.

Hirst, J. B. (2006). *Sense and nonsense in Australian history*. Melbourne: Black Inc.

Hirst, J. B. (1983). *Convict society and its enemies: a history of early New South Wales*. Sydney: Allen & Unwin.

Hogan, M. C. (1987). *The sectarian strand: religion in Australian history*. Ringwood, Vic.: Penguin Books.

Holt, R. (1989). *Sport and the British: a modern history*. Oxford: Oxford University Press.

Honey, A. (2001). Sport, immigration restriction and race: the operation of the White Australia Policy. In R. Cashman, J. O'Hara & A. Honey (Eds). *Sport, federation, nation* (pp. 26-46). Sydney: Walla Walla Press.

Horton, P. A. (2006). Football, identity, place: the emergence of rugby football in Brisbane. *International Journal of the History of Sport*, 23(8): 1341-68.

Horton, P. A. (1994). Dominant ideologies and their role in the establishment of rugby union football in Victorian Queensland. *International Journal of the History of Sport*, 11(1): 115-28.

Howell, R. A. & Howell, M. L. (1992). *The genesis of sport in Queensland*. St Lucia: University of Queensland Press, 1992.

Hughes, A. (1999). Sport in the Australian Jewish community. *Journal of Sport History*, 26(2): 376-91.

Hughes, A. (1996). Muscular Judaism and the Jewish rugby league competition in Sydney, 1924 to 1927. *Sporting Traditions*, 13(1): 61-80.

Hughes, R. (1987). *The fatal shore: a history of the transportation of convicts to Australia, 1787-1868*. New York: Random House.

Hughson, J. (2001). 'The wogs are at it again': the media reportage of Australian soccer 'riots'. *Football Studies*, (1): 40-55.

Hughson, J. (2000). The boys are back in town: soccer support and the social reproduction of masculinity. *Journal of Sport and Social Issues*, 24(1): 8-23.

Hughson, J. (1997). Football, folk dancing and fascism: diversity and difference in multicultural Australia. *Journal of Sociology*, *33*(2): 167–86.

Hughson, J. (1992). Australian soccer: 'ethnic' or 'Aussie'. The search for an image. *Current Affairs Bulletin*, *68*(10): 12–16.

Hutchins, B. & Phillips, M.G. (1997). Selling permissible violence: the commodification of Australian Rugby League 1970–1995. *International Review for the Sociology of Sport*, *32*(2): 161–76.

Jaggard, E. (Ed.) (2006). *Between the flags: one hundred summers of Australian surf lifesaving*, Kensington: UNSW Press.

Jaggard, E. (2002). Writing Australian surf lifesaving's history. *Journal of Sport History,* *29*(1): 15–24.

Jaggard, E. (2001). Tempering the testosterone: masculinity, women and Australian surf lifesaving. *The International Journal of the History of Sport*, *18*(4): 16–36.

Jaggard, E. (1996). Forgotten heroes: the 1945 Australian Services cricket team. *Sporting Traditions*, *12*(2): 61–79.

Jobling, I. (1988). The making of a nation through sport: Australia and the Olympic Games from Athens to Berlin, 1898–1916. *Australian Journal of Politics & History*, *34*(2): 160–72.

Johnes, M. (2007). Archives, truths and the historian at work: a reply to Douglas Booth's 'refiguring the archive'. *Sport in History*, *27*(1): 127–35.

Jupp, J. (1991). One among many: the relative success of Australian multiculturalism. In D. Goodman, C. Wallace-Crabbe & D. O'Hearn (Eds). *Multicultural Australia* (pp. 119–33). Newham, Vic.: Scribe.

Kildea, J. (2002). *Tearing the fabric: sectarianism in Australia 1910 to 1925*. Sydney: Citadel Books.

Kinross-Smith, G. (1997). Privilege in tennis and lawn tennis: the Geelong and Royal South Yarra examples: but not forgetting the story of the farmer's wrist. *Sporting Traditions*, *3*(2): 189–216.

Kinross-Smith, G. (1994). Lawn tennis. In W. Vamplew & B. Stoddart (Eds). *Sport in Australia: a social history* (pp. 133–52). Melbourne: Cambridge University Press.

Kirk, D. (2000). Gender associations: sport, state schools and Australian culture. *International Journal of the History of Sport*, *17*(2): 49–64.

Kirk, D. (1996). Foucault and the limits of corporeal regulation: the emergence, consolidation and decline of school medical inspection and physical training in Australia, 1909–30. *International Journal of the History of Sport*, *13*(2): 114–31.

Kirk, D. & Twigg, K. (1995). Civilising Australian bodies: the games ethic and sport in Victorian government schools, 1904–1945. *Sporting Traditions, 11*(2): 3–34.

Kirk, D. & Twigg, K. (1993). The militarization of school physical training in Australia: the rise and demise of the junior cadet training scheme, 1911–31. *History of Education*, *22*(4): 391–414.

Korff, J-U. (2009). *Aboriginal Indigenous Sport*. [Online]. Available: www.creativespirits.info/aboriginalculture /sport/ [accessed 7 January 2009].

Lawrence, G. A. & Rowe, D. (Eds) (1986). *Power play: essays in the sociology of Australian sport*, Sydney: Hale & Iremonger.

Lawson, G. (1993). *Henry: the Geoff Lawson story*. Randwick, NSW: Ironbark Press.

Light, R. & Kirk, D. (2001). Australian cultural capital – rugby's social meaning: physical assets, social advantage and Independent schools. *Culture, Sport, Society*, 4(3): 81–98.

Light, R. & Kirk, D. (2000). High school rugby, the body and the reproduction of hegemonic masculinity. *Sport, Education and Society*, 5(2): 163–76.

Little, C. (2007). The 'hidden' history of the birth of Rugby League in Australia: the significance of local factors in Sydney's rugby split. *Sport in History*, 27(3): 364–79.

Little, C. (2001). 'What a freak-show they made!' Women's rugby league in 1920s Sydney. *Football Studies*, 4(2): 25–40.

Lock, D. (2009). Fan perspectives of change in the A-League. *Soccer and Society*, 10(1): 109–23.

Lock, D., Taylor, T. & Darcy, S. (2008). Soccer and social capital in Australia: social networks in transition. In M. Nicholson and R. Hoye (Eds). *Sport and social capital* (pp. 317–38). Oxford: Butterworth-Heinemann.

Lothian, K. (2007). Moving blackwards: black power and the Aboriginal embassy. In I. MacFarlane and M. Hannah (Eds). *Transgressions: critical Australian Indigenous histories* (pp. 19–34). Aboriginal History Monograph 16, Canberra: ANU e-Press.

Magdalinksi, T. (2002). Cricket and regional development on the sunshine coast. *Sporting Traditions*, 18(2): 15–29.

Mandle, W. F. (1973). Cricket and Australian nationalism in the nineteenth century. *Journal of the Royal Australian Historical Society*, 59(4): 225–46.

Mason, P. (1985). *Professional athletics in Australia*. Adelaide: Rigby.

McGregor, R. (2006). The necessity of Britishness: ethno-cultural roots of Australian nationalism. *Nations and Nationalism*, 12(3): 493–511.

McKay, J. (1991). *No pain, no gain? Sport and Australian culture*. Sydney: Prentice Hall.

McDermott, M-L. (2005). Changing visions of baths and bathers: desegregating ocean baths in Wollongong, Kiama and Gerringong. *Sporting Traditions*, 22(1): 1–19.

McDevitt, P. F. (1997). Muscular Catholicism: nationalism, masculinity and Gaelic team sports, 1884–1916. *Gender and History*, 9(2): 262–84.

McKernan, M. (1979). Sport, war and society: Australia, 1914–1918. In R. Cashman & M. McKernan (Eds). *Sport in history: the making of modern sporting history* (pp. 1–20). St Lucia: University of Queensland Press.

McNamara, L. (2000). Tackling racial hatred: conciliation, reconciliation and football. *Australian Journal of Human Rights*, 6(2): 5–31.

Meaney, N. (2001). Britishness and Australian identity: the problem of nationalism in Australian history and historiography. *Australian Historical Studies*, 32(116): 76–90.

Mooney, C. & Ramsland, J. (2008). Dave Sands as local hero and international champion: race, family and identity in an industrial working-class suburb. *Sport in History*, 28(2): 299–312.

Moore, A. (1996). *The mighty Bears!: a social history of North Sydney Rugby League*. Sydney: Macmillan.

Moore. K. & Phillips, M. G. (1990). The sporting career of Harold Hardwick: one example of the irony of the amateur-professional dichotomy. *Sporting Traditions*, 7(1): 61–76.

Mosely, P. (1997). *Sporting immigrants: sport and ethnicity in Australia*. Sydney: Walla Walla Press.

Mosely, P. (1995). *Ethnic involvement in Australian soccer: a history 1950–1990*. Canberra: National Sports Research Centre.

Mulvaney, J & Harcourt, R. (1988). *Cricket walkabout: the Australian Aborigines in England*. South Melbourne: Macmillan.

Nauright, J. & Chandler, T. J. L. (Eds) (1996). *Making men: rugby and masculine identity*. London: Frank Cass Publishers.

Nauright, J. &. Phillips, M. (1997). Us and them: Australian professional sport and resistance to North American ownership and marketing models. *Sport Marketing Quarterly*, 6(1): 33–39.

Nauright, J. & Phillips, M. (1996). A fair go for the fans?: super leagues, sports ownership and fans in Australia. *Social Alternatives*, 15(4): 43–45.

Newlin, N. & Moran, C. (1999). Living cultures. In R. Craven, *Teaching Aboriginal studies* (p. 35). Sydney: Allen & Unwin.

Norris, R. (1975). *The emergent Commonwealth: Australian federation, expectations and fulfilment 1889–1910*. Melbourne: Melbourne University Press.

O'Hara, J. (2007). Globalisation, historical consciousness and the Melbourne Cup. *Sporting Traditions*, 23(2): 33–46.

O'Hara, J. (2002). *Big river racing: a history of the Clarence River Jockey Club 1861–2001*. Kensington: UNSW Press.

O'Hara, J. (1994). Horse racing and trotting. In W. Vamplew & B. Stoddart (Eds). *Sport in Australia: a social history* (pp. 93–111). Melbourne: Cambridge University Press.

O'Hara, J. (1991). The Jockey Club and the town in colonial Australia. *Journal of Gambling Studies*, 7(3): 207–15.

Osmond, G. & McDermott, M-L. (2008). Mixing race: the Kong Sing brothers and Australian sport. *Australian Historical Studies*, 39(3): 338–55.

Osmond, G. & Phillips, M. G. (2006). 'Look at that kid crawling': race, myth and the 'crawl' stroke. *Australian Historical Studies*, 37(127): 43–62.

Osmond, G. & Phillips, M. G. (2004). The bloke with a stroke. *Journal of Pacific History*, 39(3): 309–24.

Payne, R. (2004). Rethinking the status of female Olympians in the Australian press. *Media International Australia incorporating Culture and Policy*, 110: 120–31.

Phillips. M. G. (Ed.) (2006). *Deconstructing sport history: a postmodern analysis*. New York: State University of New York Press.

Phillips, M. G. (2002). A critical appraisal of narrative in sport history: reading the surf lifesaving debate. *Journal of Sport History*, 29(1): 25–40.

Phillips, M. G. (2001a). Diminishing contrasts and increasing varieties: globalisation theory and 'reading' amateurism in Australian sport. *Sporting Traditions*, *18*(1): 19–32.

Phillips, M. G. (1998). Public sports history, history and social memory: (re)presenting swimming in Australia. *Sporting Traditions*, *15*(1): 93–102.

Phillips, M. G. (1997). Sport, war and gender images: the Australian sportsmen's battalions and the First World War. *International Journal of the History of Sport*, *14*(1): 78–96.

Phillips, M. G. (1996). Football, class and war: the rugby codes in New South Wales, 1907–15. In J. Nauright & T. J. L. Chandler (Eds). *Making men: rugby and masculine identity* (pp. 158–80). London: Frank Cass.

Phillips, M. G. (1990). Golf and Victorian sporting values. *Sporting Traditions*, *6*(2): 120–34.

Phillips, M. G. (1988). Ethnicity and class at the Brisbane Golf Club. *Sporting Traditions*, *4*(2): 201–13.

Phillips, M. G. & Hutchins, B. (2003). Losing control of the ball: the political economy of football and the media in Australia. *Journal of Sport and Social Issues*, *27*(3): 215–32.

Phillips, M. G. & Nauright, J. (1999). Sports fan movements to save suburban-based football teams threatened with amalgamation in different football codes in Australia. *International Sports Studies*, *21*(1): 16–38.

Ramsland, J. (2004). A remarkable life: Roden Cutler as sporting, military and local hero. *Sporting Traditions*, *20*(2): 39–54.

Randall, L. M. (1988). A fair go?: women in sport in South Australia, 1945–1965, *ASSH Studies 6*, Bedford Park SA: Australian Society for Sports History.

Reynolds, H. (2006). *The other side of the frontier: Aboriginal resistance to the European invasion of Australia*. Kensington: UNSW Press.

Reynolds, H. (1996). *Dispossession: black Australians and white invaders*. Sydney: Allen & Unwin.

Ripley, S. (2005). The golden age of Australian professional sculling or skullduggery? *International Journal of the History of Sport*, *22*(5): 867–82.

Ripley, S. (2003). A social history of New South Wales professional sculling, 1876–1927, unpublished PhD thesis, School of Arts and Humanities, University of Western Sydney.

Ritchie, A. (2011). Major Taylor: understanding the complex story of a champion African-American cyclist in white Australia, 1903–04. In D. Adair (Ed.). Sport, race and ethnicity: narratives of difference and diversity. Morgantown WV: FIT Publishing, (in press).

Ritchie, A. (1996). *Major Taylor: the extraordinary career of a champion bicycle racer*. Baltimore MA: Johns Hopkins University Press.

Rodwell, G. & Ramsland, J. (2000). Cecil Healy: a soldier of the surf. *Sporting Traditions*, *16*(2): 3–16.

Rose, L & Humphries, R. (1969). *Lionel Rose Australian: the life story of a champion* [As told to Humphries by Rose]. Sydney: Angus and Robertson.

Ross, J. (1984). Pedestrianism and athletics in England and Australia in the nineteenth century: a case study in the development of sport, Bachelor of Human Movement Studies (Hons) thesis, University of Queensland, St Lucia.

Rowe, D. (1999). *Sport, culture and the media*. Buckingham: Open University Press.

Rowe, D. & Lawrence, G. (Eds) (1990). *Sport and leisure: trends in Australian popular culture*. Sydney: Harcourt Brace Jovanovich.

Sampson, D. (2009). Culture, 'race' and discrimination in the 1868 Aboriginal cricket tour of England. *Australian Aboriginal Studies*, (2): 44–60.

Sampson, D. (2000). Strangers in a strange land: the 1868 Aborigines and other Indigenous performers in mid-Victorian Britain, PhD thesis, Faculty of Humanities and Social Sciences, University of Technology Sydney, Australian Digital Thesis Repository, hdl.handle.net/2100/314.

Saunders, K. (1998). Specimens of superb manhood: the lifesaver as national icon. *Journal of Australian Studies*, 56: 96–105.

Seal, G. (2004). *Inventing ANZAC: the digger and national mythology*. St Lucia: University of Queensland Press.

Senyard, J. (2002). From gentleman to the manly: a large step for the amateur. *Sporting Traditions*, 18(2): 1–14.

Shannon, N. (2004). The friendly games? Politics, protest and Aboriginal rights at the XII Commonwealth Games, Brisbane 1982. In I. Warren (Ed.). *Buoyant nationalism: Australian identity, sport and the world stage, 1982–1983* (pp. 1–59). ASSH Studies, 14. Melbourne: Australian Society for Sports History.

Sherington, G. (1983). Athleticism in the Antipodes: the Athletic Association of the Great Public Schools of New South Wales. *History of Education Review*, 12(2): 16–28.

Simpson, C. S. (Ed.) (2006). *Scorchers, ramblers and rovers: Australasian cycling histories*, ASSH Studies 21, Melbourne: Australian Society for Sports History.

Skinner, J. (2008). Coming in from the margins: ethnicity, community support and the rebranding of Australian soccer. *Soccer and Society*, 9(3): 394–404.

Smith, L., McCalman, J., Anderson, I., Smith, S., Evans, J., McCarthy, G. & Beer, J. (2008). Fractional identities: the political arithmetic of Aboriginal Victorians. *Journal of Interdisciplinary History*, 38(4): 533–51.

Stell, M. K. (1991). *Half the race: a history of Australian women in sport*. North Ryde, NSW: Angus & Robertson.

Stremski, R. (1986). *Kill for Collingwood*. Sydney: Allen & Unwin.

Stewart, B. (Ed.) (2007). *The games are not the same: the political economy of football in Australia*. Carlton, Vic.: Melbourne University Press.

Stewart, B. (2003). The crisis of confidence in Australian first-class cricket in the 1950s. *Sporting Traditions*, 20(1): 43–62.

Stewart, B. (2002). Radio's changing relationship with Australian cricket: 1932–1950. *Sporting Traditions*, 19(1): 49–64.

Stewart, B. (1995). 'I heard it on the radio, I saw it on the television': the commercial and cultural development of Australian first class cricket: 1946–1985, Unpublished PhD thesis, School of History, La Trobe University, Melbourne.

Stewart, B. (1992). Athleticism revisited: sport, character building and Protestant school education in nineteenth century Melbourne. *Sporting Traditions*, *9*(1): 35–50.

Stewart, B. (1985). The Economic Development of the Victorian Football League 1960–1984. *Sporting Traditions*, *1*(2): 2–26.

Stocks, G. & East, A. (2000). *Lewie, Lewie. Chris Lewis: an Aboriginal champion*. Perth: Specialist Sports Management.

Stoddart, B. (2006). In search of meaning: historians and their work. *Sporting Traditions*, *22*(2): 82–87.

Stoddart, B. (1994). Golf. In W. Vamplew & B. Stoddart (Eds). *Sport in Australia: a social history* (pp. 77–92). Melbourne: Cambridge University Press.

Stoddart, B. (1986). *Saturday afternoon fever: sport in the Australian culture*. Sydney: Angus and Robertson.

Stronach, M. M. & Adair, D. (2010). Lords of the square ring: future capital and career transition issues for elite Indigenous Australian boxers. *Cosmopolitan Civil Societies: An Interdisciplinary Journal*, *2*(2): 46–70.

Tatz, C. (2002). *A course of history: Monash Country Club 1931–2001*. Sydney: Allen & Unwin.

Tatz, C. (1995). *Obstacle race: Aborigines in sport*. Kensington: UNSW Press.

Tatz, C. (1987). *Aborigines in Sport*. ASSH Studies 3: Bedford Park SA.

Tatz, C. (1984). Race, politics and sport. *Sporting Traditions*, *1*(1): 2–36.

Tatz, C. (1981). Aborigines and the Commonwealth Games. *Social Alternatives*, *3*(1): 48–51.

Tatz, C. & Stoddart, B. (1993). *The Royal Sydney Golf Club: the first hundred years*. Sydney: Allen & Unwin.

Tatz, C. & Tatz, P. (2000). *Black gold: the Aboriginal and Islander sports hall of fame*. Canberra: Aboriginal Studies Press.

Tatz, C. & Tatz, P. (1996). *Black diamonds: the Aboriginal and Islander sports hall of fame*. St. Leonards, NSW: Allen & Unwin.

Taylor, T. (2005). Gendering sport: the development of netball in Australia. *Sporting Traditions*, *22*(1): 57–74.

Taylor, T. & Toohey, K. (1998). Negotiating cultural diversity for women in sport: from assimilation to multiculturalism. *Race, Ethnicity and Education*, *1*(1): 75–90.

Thompson, C. (2004). Boats, Bondy and the boxing kangaroo: the 1983 America's Cup. In I. Warren (Ed.). *Buoyant nationalism: Australian identity, sport, and the world stage 1982–1983* (pp. 60–117). ASSH Studies 14, Balaclava, Vic.: Australian Society for Sports History.

Topp, D. & Nauright, J. (2004). Rugby league, community and identity in the Lockyer Valley, Queensland. *Sporting Traditions*, *21*(1): 53–65.

Tranter, N. (1998). *Sport, economy, and society in Britain, 1750–1914*. Cambridge: Cambridge University Press.

Treagus, M. (2005). Playing like ladies: basketball, netball and feminine restraint. *International Journal of the History of Sport*, *22*(1): 88–105.

Vamplew, W. (1988). *Pay up and play the game: professional sport in Britain, 1875–1914*. Cambridge: Cambridge University Press.

Vamplew, W. (1976). *The turf: a social and economic history of horseracing*. London: Allen Lane.

Warren, I. (2003). *Football, crowds and cultures. Comparing English and Australian law and enforcement trends*, ASSH Studies in Sport History, 13, Canberra: Australian Society for Sports History.

Warren, I. (2000). Combating vilification: the AFL and NRL anti-vilification rules. *ANZSLA Commentator*, *9*(4): 13–15.

Warren, I. (1997). Racism and the law in Australian Rules Football: a critical analysis. *Sporting Traditions*, *14*(1): 27–53.

Warren, J., Harper, A. & Whittington, J. (2002). *Sheilas, wogs and poofters: an incomplete biography of Johnny Warren and soccer in Australia*. Sydney: Random House Australia.

Watson N. J., Weir, S. & Friend, S. (2005). The development of muscular Christianity in Victorian Britain and beyond. *Journal of Religion and Society*, *7*: 1–21.

Weaver, J. & Weaver, J. T. (1999). We've had no punctures whatsoever: Dunlop, commerce and cycling in fin de siècle Australia. *International Journal of the History of Sport*, *16*(3): 94–112.

Wells, J. (1998). *Boxing Day: the fight that changed the world*. Sydney: Harper.

Wenn, S. R. (1993). Lights, camera, little action: television, Avery Brundage and the 1956 Melbourne Olympics. *Sporting Traditions*, *10*(1): 38–53.

Westerbeek, H., Deane, J. & Smith, A. (2005). De-ethnicization and Australian soccer: the strategic management dilemma. *International Journal of Sport Management*, *6*(3): pp. 270–88.

Whimpress, B. (2001). Absent Aborigines: the impact of Federation on Indigenous sport'. In R. Cashman, J. O'Hara & A. Honey (Eds). *Sport, federation, nation* (pp. 47–54). Sydney: Walla Walla Press.

Whimpress, B. (1999). *Passport to nowhere: Aborigines in Australian Cricket, 1850–1939*. Sydney: Walla Walla Press.

Whimpress, B. (1994). The Marsh-Maclaren dispute at Bathurst, 1902, and the politics of selection. *Sporting Traditions*, *10*(2): 45–58.

Whimpress, B. (1992). Few and far between: prejudice and discrimination among Aborigines in Australian first class cricket 1869–1988. *Journal of the Anthropological Society of South Australia*, *30*(1–2): 57–70.

White, C. (2004). Picnicking, surf-bathing and middle-class morality on the beach in the eastern suburbs of Sydney, 1811–1912. *Journal of Australian Studies*, *80*: 101–10.

White, R. (2003). National days and the national past in Australia. *Australian Cultural History*, *22*: 55–72.

Wilkinson, I. R. (1998). School sport and the amateur ideal: the formation of the Schools' Amateur Athletic Association of Victoria. *Sporting Traditions*, *15*(1): 51–70.

2

The role of educational institutions in Australian sport

Steve Georgakis

Australia's development as a country coincided with the rise of modern sport in the Western world. The British were central to the growth and consolidation of modern sport (Holt 1990) and when the British colonised Australia sport immediately assumed prominence as a cultural practice and became an essential element in projecting Australia internationally (Cashman 1995; Adair & Vamplew 1997). Sport also played a major role in developing Australian identity and it is therefore not surprising that there was an endorsement for sport in educational institutions (Sherington & Georgakis 2008, pp. 1–21). For example the first official game of Rugby Union in Australia was conducted at the University of Sydney in 1865; the first recorded match of football (soccer) by The King's School in 1880; while the first game of Australian Rules football was played between Melbourne Grammar and Scotch College in 1858. In the second decade of the 21st century, sport still looms large in the lives of students and it is compulsory for all students in both primary and secondary schooling. It remains a central feature of the Australian identity.

Individual school histories often document sporting achievement, but there are aspects of educational institutional sporting history which have been neglected. For example, the place of sport in the government school systems and Catholic school systems is poorly documented. In New South Wales (NSW) the literature on government school sport is limited to one text published more than two decades ago by Collins et al. (1989) while the Catholic education sporting system has not been documented, nor has the Associated School Sport Association which was established in 1929.

While the history of Australian government school sport has largely been ignored, sport in the elite independent schools has been well documented and analysed. In particular the growth of 'athleticism' in the English public schools (Mangan 1981, 1985) and its transplantation to the British colonies, such as Australia, has been the subject of rigorous analysis (Sherington 1983; Stewart 1992). This over representation of research in one sector is surprising as these elite independent schools especially after World War I represented only a small percentage of the total Australian school population.

The purpose of this chapter is threefold. First, this chapter endeavours to trace the origins and consolidation of Australian government school sport. Second, it contends that Australian government schools played a decisive and pioneering role in the development of Australian sport. Third, it argues that in order to understand the history of Australian sport a complete history and synthesis of all major educational institutions needs to be undertaken, taking into account all school types and systems.

Elite independent schools

More than two decades ago Naul (1990) predicted that the rise of the history of sport as an academic discipline would mean the decline of the historical study of physical education and school sport. The German author pointed out that the only exception to this were studies of 'athleticism' in elite independent schools. Almost a decade after Naul's prediction, this lack of scholarship was further reinforced by Kirk who reviewed the literature concerned with school sport and physical education (1998, p. 44). He researched a 12-year period in 13 well-established academic journals including the Australian *Sporting Traditions, Journal of Education, History of Education Review, The Australian Journal of Educational Studies* and found a paltry number of relevant references. Kirk (1998) only noted a line of research into 'athleticism', which he claimed, 'continues to fascinate researchers' and further that 'there is little indication of a resurgence of interest in historical study of other forms of physical education' (1998, p. 52). Kirk concluded that:

> one possible future direction for this work that as yet remains underdeveloped is the extent to which the concepts of athleticism and the games ethic might be applied to investigations of sport and physical education in schools for the masses (1998, p. 49).

Kirk (1998) was specifically referring to government schools but no-one took Kirk up on this 'future direction', although the elite independent schools continued their relentless documentation highlighting their sporting prowess. As late as 2007, the heads of the Victorian Associated Public Schools commissioned a centenary history of their sporting association (Hibbons 2008). In fact most of the Victorian independent schools of this body have their own sporting histories which clearly document the strength of school sport, with Wilkinson's (1997) history of Caulfield Grammar School being perhaps the most complete and interpretative volume, while Bate (1990) claimed that sport was the unofficial religion of Melbourne Grammar.

In Sydney, the situation is much the same and there is no shortage of publications. A typical example of this is St Ignatius' College Riverview where the promotion of sport dates back to the founding of the school in 1880 and has been documented widely. Apart from a number of Riverview histories which devote large sections to sport (Sheldon 1980; Lea-Scarlet 1989), there are individual histories of the cricket, rugby and rowing teams. A cricket team emerged in that first year, while in 1882, with a student and staff population of 71, the rowing team was established (Sheldon 1980, pp. 8–9, 63). In fact in the first decade of rowing competition, the school remained unbeaten. In 1893 the school instituted the famous Gold Cup and rowing took pride of place among all sports (Gorman 1983).

These elite independent schools were part of educational systems which organised umbrella organisations to oversee their sporting exchanges. For example in NSW the Amateur Athletic Association of Great Public School (AAAGPS) was established on 31 March 1892. The main aim of the AAAGPS was to regulate the conduct of school competitions in cricket, rugby, athletics and rowing; while in 1905 shooting was added (Sherington 1983). The AAAGPS comprised the following independent schools: The King's School, Sydney Grammar School, Newington College, Saint Ignatius' College, St Joseph's College, Sydney Church of England Grammar (Shore) and The Scots College. To this day sport remains an important part of these schools and the rivalry in the AAAGPS is still very intense. For example, in June 2009 Shore, King's and St Joseph's schools, advertised for a rowing master; former Olympians have acted as rowing masters at schools and state-of-the-art boatsheds litter Sydney harbour. Generally students train twice a week, while games are played on Saturdays and are compulsory for all students. Students can represent the NSW Combined Independent Schools teams at the NSW All-Schools Championship against NSW Combined High Schools and NSW Combined Catholic Colleges. There are also a number of sporting scholarships available. A typical example is St Ignatius' Riverview where students are able to select a winter and summer sport from a selection of over 20 sports. In 2010 the most popular sports were Rugby Union; basketball; football; cricket and rowing. Riverview has more than 110 acres of land, including a sports centre (pool, two basketball courts and gymnasium), seven basketball courts, nine tennis courts, nine football fields, cricket nets and a boatshed.

Government school sport

While elite independent schools have an unbroken line of superior sporting involvement which has been well documented in the literature, the situation in the much larger government school system is less well known. This section will document landmarks in the history of government school sport using NSW as an example. While Collins and colleagues' (1989) history of NSW public school sport is very detailed, noting the growth of public school sport, the authors focused primarily on the umbrella organisation which coordinated NSW public school sport and failed to link this material to other social and historical influences. For example, there is no analysis of the impact of the two world wars, the 1956 Melbourne Olympic Games or various educational reforms on public school sport. The material in this chapter will shed new light on the important and pioneering work played by government schools in Australian sporting history.

The first known reference to sport in government schools appears in suggestions regarding the importance of playgrounds. The *NSW National Board of Education Annual Report* noted:

> The time spent by the children in the Playground is devoted to refreshment and recreation. Advantage should be taken of the opportunity to study the characters of children, and so discover how to rule them by moral influence. At play children appear as they really are; and stripped of the artificial manner induced by the restraint of the classroom, their characters and dispositions are exhibited in their true light. Intelligent teachers will not

> fail to conclude, therefore, that the Playground, or uncovered Schoolroom, is a field in which the exercise of all their faculties is required. (1858, p. 413)

In 1862 the *NSW National Board of Education Annual Report* noted, 'The importance of supplying every school with a playground and its adjuncts can hardly be overestimated, whether considered in relation to the present discipline of the pupils or their future conduct' (1862, p. 6). Throughout the 1860s and 1870s the importance of playgrounds was highlighted and school inspectors commented on the terrible state of playgrounds that hindered opportunities for sport. The syllabus did not provide for any organised sport, this was left to the initiative of the teacher and even as late as the turn of the 20th century the 'curriculum was principally concerned with reading, writing and arithmetic. Resources were poor by today's standards. Classes were large and facilities were basic' (Hughes 2008, p. xi).

The main problem in the promotion of sport was a lack of space and fields. Independent schools had funding and land to build sports fields and by 1890 Riverview for example had one of the best cricket grounds in Australia, while the NSW Minister of Public Instruction in the same year noted the poor state of government grounds:

> The Council could as a rule, do no more than provide sufficient land to meet the then existent demands for accommodation. These areas in the course of time were encroached upon by the erection of additional buildings, rendered necessary by increase in the number of scholars and consequently as the schools grew larger, the space available for pupil's recreation often became smaller. The effect of confined playgrounds is injurious in as much as the ordinary pastimes and outdoor exercises so requisite for the health and well-being of the young cannot be indulged in, and children are compelled to seek their amusement in the streets and thoroughfares. (NSW Department of Education 1890, p. 6)

By the time compulsory public primary schooling was established in 1881, sports-minded teachers were not deterred by the lack of school sporting grounds and taught youth to play cricket and football in nearby playing fields. For many students the emancipation from school was anticipated and after school youths converged to the fields. In school hours military drill was required and for most teachers and students this drilling was dreary and repetitive compared to team sports. Drill was the only physical activity recognised by the Education Department, and this was the reason why sport took place outside of official hours. So rapidly and robustly did inter-school sport grew that in 1885 the Public Schools Amateur Athletic Association of New South Wales (PSAAA) was established to coordinate the sporting exchanges (Collins et al. 1989). The first secretaries elected were sports aficionados WJ Rooney and WF McManamey and while this PSAAA did not see out its second year, it preceded the AAAGPS by seven years.

The PSAAA was re-established in 1889, when a group of teachers met and re-formed the association with the objective of 'encouraging physical education in connection with our public schools' (*NSW Educational Gazette*, August 1891, p. 8). School sport and inter-school competitions flourished in that inaugural year and the first mass sports meeting held by the PSAAA attracted more than 12,000 spectators and took place at the Sydney

Cricket Ground. The PSAAA advocated 'on the advisability of each school having sports of their own, and the association having a championship meeting annually, and for the various schools to enter into football, cricket and tennis contests and endeavour to get grounds for themselves' (*Sydney Morning Herald,* 21 March 1890). Still the sports needed to be 'out of school activities' as the Education Department sanctioned military drill. Nevertheless, support for the PSAAA's activities came in 1892 when the *Educational Gazette* criticised the state of sport in public schools:

> One of the greatest wants in our system of public education has been the total absence of any systematic effort towards physical culture. While possessing, without a doubt, one of the finest systems of education in the world, this anomaly stands out as a feature requiring careful consideration ... Many teachers, however, still regard this very important part of their work as something which should be left to chance and beyond a few hours' drill to prepare for the 'annual concert' nothing is done. (December 1892, p. 127)

The criticism on the limits of drill, and the lack of sport in schools, helped to strengthen the PSAAA's influence with the department in the last decade of the century. By 1897, the PSAAA was securely entrenched in Sydney through its organisation of inter-school sport and the success of the annual sports meeting. The school sporting exchanges were now officially called 'after-school sport' (Crawford 1981, p. 154). The *Educational Gazette* claimed that 'teachers were now more acutely aware of their responsibilities to the adage a healthy body begets a healthy mind' (October 1897, p. 111).

In 1897 the Minister of Public Instruction noted that sport was taking place in most schools and was referred to as 'the out of school educational work'. The *Annual Report* noted:

> They have not only made the physical training more interesting and therefore more effective, but they have been the means of bringing much brightness and pleasure into students lives. It has been aptly remarked the love of games among boys is a healthy instinct and there can be no question that cricket, football, running, swimming, etc, are not only among the greatest pleasures, but are the medicine for boys. The teachers, and there are many who cheerfully give their time, their energy and their money to carrying out the objects of these associations, prove their deep interest in the welfare of their pupils and their loyalty to the Department. (1897, p. 117)

The PSAAA grew rapidly and by the mid-1890s comprised a number of sub-branches. Each branch organised local sports meetings in their respective districts and each year there was a combined sports meeting where all the districts came together. The growth of the PSAAA was clearly related to the rapid growth of government schools in the 1890s. Table 1 highlights this growth in NSW student numbers:

Further educational reform occurred after George Knibbs and John Turner provided a commissioned report on primary education in 1903 and on secondary education in 1904. The first report criticised primary education for delivering a curriculum that was narrow and bookish, and neglected students' character building (Barcan 1988, p. 177). The Knibbs-Turner reports (1903, 1904) brought with it a reconsideration of the role that sport might have in the social, as well as the physical development of students (Wooldridge 1904). Knibbs-Turner noted: 'Every effort should be made to present exercise to children in such a way that they would be both attractive to the children and of educational value' (1904, p. 174). The Knibbs-Turner report resulted in the appointment of Peter Board, PSAAA president from 1906 to 1922 (Crane & Walker 1957), as the Director of Education in 1905. With this appointment the department began to publicly support the work done by the PSAAA. It was difficult to dismiss the PSAAA as it was receiving considerable press coverage and for example, the 1904 PSAAA's annual sports meeting at the Sydney Cricket Ground was attended by more than 50,000 spectators (Collins et al. 1989).

Table 1 Growth in NSW student numbers (1881–1894).

Schools	1881	1894	Increase 1881–1894
High schools		5	5
Superior schools	58	241	183
Primary	1042	1643	601
Provisional	246	302	56
Half-time	93	449	356
House to house		71	71
Evening	57	14	43
Total schools	1496	2725	1229
Total students	98,721	231,370	132,649

The table notes the number of schools in operation in 1881, the first full year during which the department was under Ministerial control, as compared with the number of schools open in 1894 (*Report of the Minister of Public Instruction* 1894, p. 3).

The case for the inclusion of sport in normal school hours was advocated strongly by teachers, such as Lee-Pulling, graduate of Cambridge University, who endorsed games because it allowed teachers and boys 'to find a common interest'. He criticised drill for its dullness while 'games' had a 'moral tone' which could develop character in the students (Lee-Pulling 1909).

Government school sporting associations sprung up Australia-wide. The Victorian State Schools' Amateur Athletic Association (VSSAAA) was established in 1904. Games were initially extra-curricular and the Victorian Football League was most supportive of the VSSAAA as Australian Rules became the dominant football code in Victoria. The establishment of swimming clubs in Victorian schools was one of the forces behind the formation in the VSSAAA. In 1912 the South Australian Primary Schools Amateur Sports Association was established by teachers and principals to coordinate the sporting programs between schools.

In pre-World War I Australia, the influence of 'athleticism' arrived in the government schools primarily through the voluntary organisation of games as an extra-curricular pursuit. Much of it was initially teacher led, although leading up to World War I, professional sporting associations increasingly viewed schools as a nursery for their codes. In NSW, the newly established code of Rugby League in 1908 understood the importance of gaining a foothold in the government and Catholic schools and many of these schools which played Rugby Union football changed their allegiances and promoted Rugby League instead (Sherington and Georgakis 2008, pp. 178–79).

Two main developments marked the post-World War I period. Firstly the Education Department started officially promoting the educative role of physical education and school sport. The physical education syllabus was also widened to include activities such as dancing, hygiene, gymnastics and naturally games and sports. Secondly it was also recognised that involvement in sport should be for the masses and not just the minority of government students. Huck Hamilton (1941), a physical educationalist commented:

> It must not be thought that the object of games practice is to produce champions in sport ... There is a tendency in many large schools to concentrate on the instruction of the few already competent and gifted children allowing this limited number to reap the benefits of inter school competitive games ... One of the chief aims [should be] to ensure that each and every child is given the opportunity to learn games and to become to some degree skilled in them. In this way he is assured of a healthy physical exercise with a definite motivating interest. (Huck Hamilton, cited in Kirk et al. 1996, p. 238)

In order to do so, government schools began to set aside an afternoon each week for the specific purpose of inter-school competition. The organisation provided for grades and divisions making provisions for large playing numbers, different ages and levels of skills. The emphasis also shifted towards participation rates and practices for games started to take place in school time during physical education classes which previously were used for drill instruction.

Once again it was the lack of school fields which handicapped the promotion of sport and although school grounds were increased in size, very little was done in the matter of providing adequate facilities until the 1950s. The turning point occurred in 1956, when Australia hosted the Olympic Games. In that year it became general policy to make provisions for the development of sports grounds in conjunction with the construction of each new 'comprehensive' school.

With growing numbers of specialist physical education teachers in the primary and secondary schools, during the 1940s and 1950s, it was now possible to provide instruction for all children in the skills and tactics considered to be the prerequisite of games playing during physical education classes. The institutionalisation of sport was also achieved through the appearance of the NSW Physical Education Primary School Syllabus (1952), which covered amongst other aspects 'games' and 'skill practices for games'. Material learnt in physical education classes would then be translated in inter-school sport. The more talented athletes were also involved in knockout school competitions as well as representative teams at the district, region and state level. With the influx of post-World War II immigrants public sport widened in choice and sport played a significant role in the assimilation of immigrant students in the school setting. Collins et al. (1989) document the growth of sport and sporting activity in the post-World War II period.

Swimming

Swimming in the school curriculum was first advocated in the Victorian parliament in 1877 and in the following year a proposal was made to the Victorian Education Department, to introduce a scheme to teach every youth in the city over the age of nine to swim. Although the proposal was never adopted (Victorian Education Department Archives, May 1878), some Melbourne teachers took students to baths for afterschool 'learn to swim' instruction throughout the 1880s, and in 1890 the Victorian Teachers' Association attempted to formalise these activities by passing a resolution which called on the Education Department to allow swimming classes for government school students (ibid. September 1890).

Similarly in NSW, as early as the beginning of 1881, a number of teachers were making efforts to include swimming in the curriculum. Swimming instruction was held as an extra-curricular activity and the formation of classes was not discouraged by the department. In some instances schools sought permission to finish early in order to administer swimming carnivals (Crawford et al. 1981, p. 159). In 1895 the PSAAA argued that they were the proper organisation to administer 'learn to swim' programs. By 1897, the department was prepared to give the PSAAA the authority to organise and establish 'swimming clubs in schools' (*NSW Educational Gazette* April 1898, p. 253). This action was an important prelude to the compulsory 'learn to swim' programs in Australian history and the right to have time made available to it during the school day. In their first year, 1898, more than 100 school clubs were founded and 12,000 youths, including 1500 girls had been enrolled into them (Crawford et al. 1981, p. 157, 160).

The department took more than just a simple interest and resources were allocated to swim programs and instructors were appointed (NSW Department of Education 1904, p. 197). In 1907 school teacher Miss Kilminster was seconded to be the department's specialist swimming instructor. The Municipal Councils also became a hurdle for the promotion of school swimming because they resisted building swimming pools to cater for the growing number of students who wanted instruction. To avoid this bottleneck in the few existing pools students were staggered throughout the week to attend their nearest local pool (ibid. 1907, p. 42). The department also mandated that students needed to be accompanied into the water by teachers who were suitably trained (ibid. 1908, p. 19). As too few teachers were able to swim, special swimming classes were organised for teachers. Also, all pre-service teachers at the Sydney Teachers College received compulsory swimming instruction including lifesaving and rescue work (ibid. 1908, p. 39).

Prior to World War I, Friday afternoon started to be commonly used for swimming and so 'it was expected that every child attending a public school where facilities for bathing existed would become proficient in swimming' (ibid. 1912, p. 23). Interestingly, 'learn to swim' classes were obviously advocated for safety reasons although educationalists argued that more than just safety was at stake. As, later in his life, the pioneering Jack MacLean explained in his memoirs:

> the acquisition of swimming, opened the door to a whole way of life – the coast line, beaches, bays, waterways, in later years the home pool; a lifestyle involving surfing, swimming, boating, skiing, sailing, recreation/competitive swimming and diving ... not to overlook the social interactions emanating from a water lifestyle. (MacLean 1983, p. 68)

Wherever facilities were available it was expected that public school students 'would become proficient swimmers' (NSW Department of Education Annual Report 1912, p. 23). In 1916 the first vacation swimming programs were established in the Christmas vacation period and in that first year 500 of the 800 students who attended this program were successfully taught to swim (ibid. 1916, p. 42). Ella Gormley became central to the promotion of swimming and in 1921 was sent to the United States by the department to investigate the US 'learn to swim' programs. Upon her return she conducted training courses for the department to train teachers in the swimming instruction. By the end of the 1920s swimming instruction was widespread and the Department of Education *Annual Report* noted:

> Swimming instruction is divided into two sections – the weekly swimming classes conducted by those schools where baths or similar facilities are readily available, and the Christmas Vacation swimming school which comprises an intensive course of instruction covering a period of ten days. The average attendance at the weekly classes was 29,733 and the total number who learnt to swim 12,982. The vacation swimming schools had an effective enrolment (i.e. those who attended at least three lessons) of 5,477 all of whom were non-swimmers at the time of enrolment, and, when the course was completed 4,943 or 90.2% had learnt to swim. (1920, p. 10)

The program received further credibility when certification for primary school students was introduced in 1933. The certificates were issued in two grades, 'Learners Certificates' for youth who had learnt to swim during the season and had completed a 20 yards test and the 'Advanced Certificate' for youth who completed tests for 50, 100, 220, and 440 yards. Min Matheson and Olympian Harold Hardwick guided this program for almost 30 years until they both retired in 1952 and Jack MacLean took over these duties.

In the early 1950s reforms were initiated. Because of the lack of facilities specialist swim teachers travelled to various districts and taught 'learn to swim' to primary school students. The system involved each student undertaking one hour of swimming instruction for ten days per year. The staff rotated around the various districts and instructed at pools such as North Sydney, Cabarita and Enfield. Buses would collect students and they would stagger their swim classes. Up until the mid-1950s the department was the leading authority of swim instruction. At Easter 1954 the department organised a camp at the Broken Bay National Fitness Camp to discuss swimming instruction and the camp was attended by the Royal Life Saving Society. In 1958 Frank Whitebrook, from the Sydney Teachers College, went to the US to complete his PhD on the most effective method to teach youth swimming.

The hosting of the 1956 Melbourne Olympic Games not only triggered the building of sports fields in schools but also stimulated the building of school pools. In 1954 the Hurlstone Agricultural High School pool was built. High school pools were also built at Yanko Agricultural, Farrer Agricultural, Macarthur Girls, and Sydney Technical schools. The first swimming pool was built at a primary school in Lindfield in 1957, followed by Wahroonga, Pymble, Peakhurst West, Wollongong West and Denistone East primary schools. The building of pools coincided with reforms initiated by the Wyndham Report (1957), which resulted in unprecedented growth in the school population and of secondary schooling.

Discussion

Scholars such as Mangan (1981, 1985) documented the important role that sport played in English public schools. This stimulated in turn Antipodean interest in the manifestations of 'athleticism' in Australia and academics focused on the elite independent schools. Scholars found it difficult to theorise the relationship between independent and government experiences and a number of generalisations occurred.

The common perception in the literature is that all government schools used drilling, while all elite independent schools adopted the ethos of 'athleticism' and 'games playing'. That is, the children of the middle class were sophisticated enough to adopt 'games' such as cricket and football, while the working class needed to be controlled and disciplined which could only be achieved by 'drilling'. 'Athleticism' in the independent schools was advocated because it built character, teamwork, self-discipline, loyalty and commitment, and the promotion of sport in schools not only assisted the students but also the school in shaping school culture. Perhaps the most obvious inconsistency in this simplistic thesis is the fact that elite independent schools such as King's and Shore had cadet units, well before the 'athleticism' ethos had taken hold. At King's, for example, the Cadet Corps was established in 1866 and to this day has a significant presence. The great passion of Albert Weigall, headmaster of Sydney Grammar from 1867 to 1912, was the Cadet Corps, which he founded in 1872 (Turney 1969, p. 120). Clearly drilling must have accompanied 'athleticism' in elite independent schools especially leading up to World War I where eugenic concerns became paramount. Kirk (1996) noted:

> By the turn of the century, a range of institutions had emerged in Australia with specific functions relating to the propagation of populations over time and the regulation of bodies in space. Schools were just one of a series of such institutions, established under government control towards the end of the nineteenth century, in which the body was monitored, regulated and disciplined in an effort to produce good racial stock, compliant citizens and productive workers. Medical inspection and physical training were two key interrelated technologies of power within schools that were part of the process of corporal regulation and normalization. (p. 119)

Kirk and others make reference to 'schools' and 'students' but only in the context of government schools and military drill. There is no understanding of the impact of drilling in the elite independent school system. That is, the innumerable books dedicated to elite independent school sport have not been matched by histories which have looked at Cadet Corps.

The other notable inconsistency relates to the establishment of umbrella sporting organisations. As this chapter has demonstrated the PSAAA, established in 1885, preceded the establishment of the AAAGPS by seven years. Government school teachers promoted sports and introduced swimming to students in the 1880s even though they were handicapped by lack of finances and fields. Surprisingly, the AAAGPS included a government school, Sydney Boys High School into their competition in 1906. Sport was, however, taking place at government schools. Sydney Boys High School established both cricket and football in the first year of the founding of the school in 1883. The football team was coached by James MacManamey who 'was able to get the best out of the scholars and the footballers under his control'. MacManamey was instrumental in establishing the PSAAA, while the first headmaster of the school Joseph Coates, who had previously captained the inter-colonial cricket team, coached the cricket team. Coates had previously been headmaster at government-sponsored Fort Street High School where sport also flourished under him (Waugh 2008).

Government schools promoted the introduction of a range of sports and competitions. Collins et al. (1989) highlight this dynamic sporting presence in not only established sports such as cricket and Rugby Union but also sports such as baseball. For example, in 1908 the Proud Shield baseball school knockout competition was established and Fort Street High School was the inaugural winner. Many of Australia's elite baseball players were introduced to the sport at government schools. For example, Australian-born United States Major League Baseball players such as Travis Blackley, Cameron Cairncross, Peter Moylan, David Nilsson, Brad Harman and Damian Moss competed in interstate school baseball; while in the early 1970s Alan Border, future Test cricket captain, represented NSW in baseball.

This brings us to ask why elite independent school sport has been privileged in sports scholarship. Perhaps a touch of academic snobbery can be blamed as to why historians of sport seem disinterested in sport in government schools even though many great sportspeople emerged from these institutions.

Another reason may be that the independent schools are wealthy enough to undertake research into their own history, whereas struggling government schools such as Birchgrove Primary School or Strathfield South High School (both with long and distinguished sporting histories) do not have the funds to document this. Lennox concluded that independent schools used sport as a means to market their school in a competitive environment and the winning of inter-school competitions links to the 'assumption by heads and governing bodies that sporting success will attract enrolments' (2005, p. 10). There may be some merit to this, because as early as 1896 the AAAGPS had already established a publicity system which illuminated their sporting prowess. At the 1896 PSAAA annual sport meeting, Jacob Garrard, the Education Minister, drew attention to the similarly organised annual AAAGPS annual athletic meeting and noted that:

> The Public School sports had not been treated quite fairly by some who called themselves the 'great' Public schools of the colony. Their own association had been in existence for a number of years before these 'great' Public schools thought of having annual demonstration of their own, and not satisfied with having one of their own he was afraid that sometimes the 'great' Public Schools Association chipped in just before the Public School Association – using the term 'great' and robbed them of some of the kudos and some of the attendance they would otherwise have had. (*Sydney Morning Herald*, 12 October 1896)

Garrard concluded that government schools were not as skilled as promoting their sport and perhaps to this present day it continues to be the case. As Lennox states, 'public schools do not have the income to fund Saturday sport like non-government schools' (2005, p. 9). Non-government schools have the finances to hire professional coaches, to maintain and expand sporting facilities and to contribute to the overall sports development of the school. Tied in with economic differences is Kotzur's notion of the growing 'professionalism of school sport' in independent schools. This is a consequence of the increasing 'amounts of money being poured into school sport, the ever increasing status of school sport' and the 'increase [in] pressure to win' (2004, p. 56).

Another reason why scholars became preoccupied with issues concerning 'control' and 'discipline', and the belief that government schools were only firmly embedded in militarism may be related to the introduction of the Junior Cadet Scheme between 1911 and 1931 by the Commonwealth Department of Defence. This compulsory national scheme of physical training for male students between the ages of 12 and 14 reinforced the perception that government relegated physical education and school sport to the ideals of simply 'drilling' and 'controlling bodies' (Kirk 1998). This is surprising because this was almost 150 years after Gustav Techow published the first book on physical education and school sport. The book *Manual of gymnastic exercises* was published in Melbourne and supported the adoption of gymnastics. Techow ran the National Gymnasium in Melbourne and advocated the Northern European approach to sport noting that, 'discipline is almost as indispensable for a gymnasium as for an army' (1866, p. 153). Scholars of physical education and school sport history used this book as one of the justifications for lumping Australian government schools into the militarism stream and relegated student experiences to drilling. Typical of this was:

> From the 1880s on, the military were keen to have the voluntary cadet system made compulsory, a goal they eventually achieved in 1911. The military made no bones about the interest in the use of schools as a training ground for Australia's citizen army ... The legacy of these practices was to be influential for at least another 50 years after the turn of the century (Kirk et al. 1996, pp. 233–34).

> For most Australian children attending government schools from the 1870s until the early 1930s, drilling and exercising was the main form of physical education available to them. In the 1940s, games came to play an important role in physical education for working class children, as it had for privileged boys and girls for some 50 years previously. (ibid., p. 242)

There is no doubt that with no standing army there was a concerted push for military drill in schools and in the 1880s a voluntary school cadet scheme was established Australia wide. A more compulsory scheme was introduced in 1911, although by that stage umbrella government school sport associations existed throughout Australia. The 'Junior Cadet Scheme' of physical training was organised into eight categories: introduction and breathing exercises; trunk bending back and forward; arm bending and stretching; balance exercises; shoulder blade exercises; trunk turning and bending sideways; marching, running, jumping, games; and breathing exercises. Even in this scheme there were provisions for sport in the 'games' category.

The drilling literature, nevertheless, fails to note how well the Junior Cadet Scheme was established or even how successful it became. Stockings noted that the Junior Cadet Scheme was 'classes of schoolboys undergoing compulsory pseudo-military instruction during school hours on school premises' (2007, p. 17), but he fails to deal with the practical functioning of the scheme. No literature has shed light on the day-to-day working of the scheme even though it lasted for two decades (1911–1931); most of the discussion is related to the 'how and why' it was instituted (Barrett 1979; Tanner 1980; Kirk & Twigg 1993; Kirk 1998). Advocates of the scheme, including Lord Kitchener and Colonel Bjelke-Petersen, admitted that standards had been compromised. Indeed, the implementation of this form of physical training was uneven across the country and can hardly have been effective. Surprisingly there is no mention of drilling or the Cadet Corps in the elite independent schools; though as highlighted earlier it must have formed a very visible part of this school system.

Conclusion

This chapter provides an historical account of the important and yet neglected role played by government schools in the consolidation and growth of Australian sport. While elite independent schools became synonymous with 'athleticism' and 'games playing', it seems that government schools equally supported the 'games playing ethic' although their involvement has been neglected in the literature. In NSW government schools, teachers were to become responsible for drilling, which took place in the schools though it was not to the taste of all teachers and students, many of whom objected to the department's directives that part of a teacher's duty was to serve in the cadet force. Prior to the inauguration of the PSAAA some teachers had decided to demonstrate their obligations to students by using alternative activities and methods that they considered superior to military drill. Their drive and energies led to the formation of the PSAAA, which made a valuable contribution to school life, and extended the narrow and formal curriculum of physical exercises produced by drilling. The department gave qualified support to the PSAAA in their early development, and later accorded it official status in the educational system. The PSAAA was organised through the voluntary efforts of school teachers. At little cost to itself, the department could be seen to be involved in the total education of children and to happily record the interest in the promotion of a broad range of physical activities in the schools. In the 1880s and early 1890s, the department avoided any comment on the activities of the association in their annual reports, though good coverage of their displays and sports meetings appeared in the Sydney papers. The PSAAA produced athletes who went on to achieve international and national success, encouraged a love of sport and promoted grassroots level sport participation.

Scholars of curriculum history, such as Goodson (1985, 1987) advocated that the study of the past is an essential part of planning for the future; although this belief has made little impact on scholarship of Australian physical education and school sport history. Goodson concluded: 'The reluctance of historians to look behind the schoolhouse door, and of curriculum specialists to use historical methods, serves as a drag on any attempt to comprehend schools and education' (1994, p. 51).

Public school sport has made an important contribution not only to education but also to Australian sport. This contribution existed on a number of different levels. For example, public school sport has been responsible for producing many of Australia's greatest athletes such as Ian Thorpe, Mark Waugh and Shane Gould; helped in the assimilation process of post-World War II immigrant youth and helped educate students in moral education.

The latest Australian Bureau of Statistics (2010) data reveal that approximately two in five school-aged youth did not participate in any sport *outside* the school setting. While to some these figures seem impressive, almost all children viewed television or accessed the internet. The introduction of the proposed national curriculum and the threat of the expulsion of sport could result in one of the most dominant traditions of Australian education being jeopardised.

References

Adair, D. & Vamplew, W. (1997). *Sport in Australian history.* Cambridge: Cambridge University Press.

Australian Bureau of Statistics (ABS) (2010). *Children's participation in cultural and leisure activities.* Canberra: Australian Bureau of Statistics.

Barcan, A. (1988). *Two centuries of education in New South Wales.* Sydney: UNSW Press.

Barrett, J. (1979). *Falling in: Australians and 'boy conscription', 1911–1915.* Sydney: Hale and Iremonger.

Bate, W. (1990). *Light blue Down Under: the history of Geelong Grammar School.* Melbourne: Oxford University Press.

Cashman, R. (1995). *Paradise of sport.* Melbourne: Oxford University Press.

Collins, B., Aitken, M. & Cork, B. (1989). *One hundred years of public school sport in New South Wales 1889–1989.* Sydney: NSW Department of School Education.

Crane, A. & Walker, W. (1957). *Peter Board: his contribution to the development of education in New South Wales.* Melbourne: ACER.

Crawford, R. (1981). A history of physical education in Victoria and New South Wales 1872–1939: with particular reference to the English precedent. PhD. thesis, La Trobe University.

Goodson, I. (1994). *Studying curriculum: cases and methods.* Buckingham: Open University Press.

Goodson, I. (1987). *School subjects and curriculum change.* London: The Falmer Press.

Goodson, I. (1985). Towards curriculum history. In I. F. Goodson (Ed.). *Social histories of the secondary curriculum: subjects for study.* London: The Farmer Press.

Gorman, F. J. (1983). *Rowing at Riverview: the first hundred years 1882-1982.* Sydney: St Ignatius' College.

Grant, B. (2000). Games in independent schools: issues and challenges. *Independence, 25*(3): 31-33.

Hamilton, L. G. (1941). Games practice: its place and value in the school. *Education Gazette and Teachers' Aid.* Melbourne: Government Printer.

Hibbins, G. (2008). *Associated Public Schools of Victoria: celebrating 100 years 1908-2008.* Melbourne: Associated Public Schools of Victoria.

Holt, R. (1990). *Sport and the British: a modern history.* Oxford: Oxford University Press.

Hughes, J. (2008). *Reform and resistance in NSW public education: six attempts at major reform, 1905-1995.* Sydney: NSW Department of Education and Training.

Kirk, D. (1998). School sport and physical education in history. *International Journal of Physical Education, 35*(2): 44-56.

Kirk, D. (1996). Foucault and the limits of corporeal regulation: the emergence, consolidation and decline of school medical inspection and physical training in Australia, 1909-1930. *The International Journal of the History of Sport, 13*(2): 114-31.

Kirk, D., Nauright, J., Hanrahan, S., Macdonald, D. & Jobling, I. (1996). *The sociological foundations of human movement.* South Melbourne: Macmillan.

Kirk, D. & Twigg, K. (1993). The militarization of school physical training in Australia: the rise and demise of the Junior Cadet Training Scheme, 1911-1931. *History of Education, 22*(4): 391-414.

Knibbs, G. & Turner, J. (1903-05). *Report of the Royal Commission on primary schooling and other branches of education.* Sydney: Government Printer.

Kotzur, T. (2004). School sport: towards what future? *Independence, 29*(1): 52-56.

Lea-Scarlet, E. (1989). *Riverview: aspects of the story of Saint Ignatius' College and its peninsula, 1836-1988.* Sydney: Hale & Iremonger.

Lee-Pulling, J. (1909). Sport in relation to school life. *Australian Journal of Education, 7*(5): 12.

Lennox, P. (2005). School sport: marketing or education? *Independence, 30*(1): 9-14

Mangan, J. (1985). *The games ethic and imperialism: aspects of the diffusion of an ideal.* Harmondsworth: Viking.

Mangan, J. (1981). *Athleticism in the Victorian and Edwardian school: the emergence and consolidation of an ideology.* Cambridge: Cambridge University Press.

MacLean, J. (1983). Jack MacLean memoirs, 30 April, spiral bound.

National Board of Education (1858, 1862). *Annual report,* Sydney: Government Printer.

Naul, R. (1990). The renaissance of the history of school sports: back to the future? *Journal of Sport History, 17*(2): 199-213.

NSW Department of Education (1881–1966). *Annual Report,* Sydney: Australian Government Printer.

NSW Department of Education (1952). *Curriculum for primary schools.* Sydney: Government Printer.

Sheldon, L. (1980). *St Ignatius' College, Riverview jubilee book 1880–1930.* Sydney: St Ignatius' College.

Sherington, G. (1983). Athleticism in the antipodes: the AAGPS of New South Wales. *History of Education, 12*(2): 16–28.

Sherington, G. & Georgakis, S. (2008). *Sydney University sport 1852–2007: more than a club.* Sydney: Sydney University Press.

Stewart, B. (1992). Athleticism revisited: sport, character building and Protestant school education in 19th century Melbourne. *Sporting Traditions, 1*(1): 35–50.

Stockings, C. (2007). *The torch and the sword: a history of the army cadet movement in Australia.* Sydney: UNSW Press.

Tanner, T. (1980). *Compulsory citizen soldiers.* Sydney: Maxwell Printing.

Techow, G. (1866). *Manual of gymnastic exercises.* Melbourne: The author.

Turney, C. (1969). *Pioneers of Australian education.* Sydney: Sydney University Press.

Waugh, J. (2008). *Sydney Boy's High School: the foundation years 1883–1891.* Sydney: Sydney Boy's High School.

Wilkinson, I. (1997). *The fields at play: 115 years of sport at Caulfield Grammar School 1881–1996.* Sydney: Playright.

Wooldridge, G. (1904). Athletics in schools. *Australian Journal of Education, 1*(2): 6–7.

3

Sport policy in Australia

Matthew Nicholson and Russell Hoye

This chapter[1] aims to examine the development of Australian sport policy and is divided into the following sections: a brief synopsis of the development of national sport policy in Australia; an outline of the national government's administrative system for implementing sport policy; a description of the nature of the intersection of sport policy with the commercial and non-profit sectors of sport in Australia; a discussion of the prominence of sport within wider government policies; and an identification of a number of emerging and future sport policy issues germane to the Australian sport system.

The development of an Australian sport policy

For much of Australia's history, local government was the major supporter of sport, while the federal government had relatively little influence. Prior to World War II, Australian government involvement in sport at the national level was limited to sporadic funding initiatives, such as funding of Australian teams travelling to the Olympic and Empire Games (Stewart et al. 2004). By contrast, Australian local governments provided sporting infrastructure in the form of sporting grounds and facilities at public parks (Cashman 1995), while state governments provided assistance to water-safety and lifesaving bodies (Booth 2001). It was not until 1939 that the national government began its formal involvement in the development of Australia's physical fitness through the establishment of the National Coordinating Council for Physical Fitness, and the passing of the *National Fitness Act (1941)*. From World War II until the beginning of the 1970s national government continued to fund travelling Australian teams, lifesaving grants and support the physical fitness initiatives of the Commonwealth National Fitness Council. In comparison with the more traditional government policy areas of defence, trade, commerce, work and education, sport was a low priority during this period (Jaques & Pavia 1976). Furthermore, sport's relatively poor status throughout the 1950s and 1960s was largely unaffected by the shifting political ideologies of successive national governments.

Prior to the 1972 federal election, future prime minister Gough Whitlam gave an important policy speech, in which he declared that 'there is no greater social problem facing Australia

---

1 Major parts of this chapter have been reproduced from Hoye & Nicholson 2009. This material has been used with permission of Taylor and Francis.

than the good use of expanding leisure' and that the construction of community centres for cultural, artistic, educational and sporting activities would be a priority of a Labor government (Whitlam 1972). The election of Whitlam's Labor party in late 1972 resulted in a quantum leap in Australian sport policy. Three important initiatives defined the approach of what was to be a short-lived government. First, a specialist 'tourism and recreation' portfolio was established, which gave recreation, and by association sport, a legitimacy within government that it had not previously enjoyed. Second, a 'capital assistance program' was established to provide grants for the construction of community sport facilities, thereby fulfilling an election promise and the belief that governments were responsible for improving the recreational opportunities of its people (Shelton 1999). Finally, the Whitlam government commissioned two reports that became instrumental in establishing a direction for Australian sport and Australian sport policy.

The first report on 'The role, scope and development of recreation in Australia', was released in 1973 and became known as the 'Bloomfield report'. It recommended a recreational program focused on creating community recreation centres, raising community consciousness about the importance of general fitness and building Australia's elite performance. The second report, known as the 'Coles report' was released in 1975. It examined the proposition that an elite sport institute would be necessary if Australia was to improve its international sporting success, which had been waning since the highpoint of the Melbourne Olympic Games in 1956. The Whitlam government had only enough time to engage the community development aspect of the Bloomfield recommendations, before it was defeated by the more conservative Liberal Party in late 1975. As such, the Coles report and its recommendations lay dormant until pressure started to build after Australia failed to win any gold medals at the Montreal Olympic Games in 1976. In hindsight, this failure can be viewed as one of the most significant landmarks in the development of Australian sport policy.

Australia's poor performance in Montreal, growing public unrest and an increasing awareness of the political expediency of supporting the elite arm of the Australian sport system led to the Fraser government creating an Australian Institute of Sport (AIS) in 1981. Although the Rudd Labor government of 2008 described the AIS as a global pioneer, which has 'developed a reputation as the Harvard of world sport academies' (Commonwealth of Australia 2008, p. 3), the original AIS was modelled on East German and Chinese institutes of sport. It is somewhat ironic that many nations have sought to ape Australian sport structures, yet the impetus for early Australian development was successful international models. The establishment of the AIS soon paid dividends, particularly at the Olympic Games, where Australia's performance improved markedly in the 1980s and 1990s.

The national and international adulation that resulted from Australian performances, which could be linked (directly and indirectly) to the AIS, meant that the formation of an elite training institute has rightly been regarded as one of the most significant sport policy decisions in Australia's history. As previously noted, a 'tourism and recreation' portfolio was created by the Whitlam government, but this was dismantled by the Fraser government soon after it was elected in 1975. When the Hawke government was elected in 1983, it set about restoring elements of the agendas set by the Whitlam government in the early 1970s, and, in part, by the Confederation of Australian Sport in the late 1970s. Importantly, a separate Department of Sport, Recreation and Tourism was established, which was soon complemented by the Australian Sports Commission (ASC) in 1985. While it did not enjoy the same public profile as the AIS, the formation of the Australian Sports Commission in 1985 represented an important administrative and structural change to the Australian sport system. The ASC's functions were to: advise the minister on matters of sport development; raise money; administer and expend money appropriated by Parliament; coordinate activities for the development of sport; consult and cooperate with relevant federal and state authorities; initiate and facilitate research and development; and collect and distribute information (Commonwealth of Australia 1985). A 1989 Parliamentary inquiry into sports funding and administration concluded that a new structure was required to ensure that government funding was coordinated, focused and efficient. As a result, the AIS and the ASC were merged, with the ASC responsible for implementing policy and coordinating the AIS programs and activities.

The Hawke government made a significant investment in the Australian sport system throughout the 1980s in the areas of elite performance, community participation, facility development and major events. It was not surprising, therefore, that in order to protect its investment and respond to a series of national and international drug crises in the mid to late 1980s, it created the Australian Sports Drug Agency (ASDA) in 1990. The ASDA was given the authority to conduct testing and research, as well as provide education and policy advice.

Two further pieces of sport related legislation enacted in the early to mid 1990s demonstrated that the Hawke and Keating Labor governments were prepared to provide regulatory intervention in order to protect its citizens. Through the *Tobacco Advertising Prohibition Act* of 1992, the Australian government not only made it illegal for Australian media organisations to broadcast or publish a tobacco advertisement, but also made it illegal for tobacco companies to sponsor sport. As a result of this legislation Australia became one of the first democracies in the world to ban tobacco advertising and sponsorship (Chapman et al. 2003). In the mid 1990s pay television was introduced to Australia and the federal government responded by amending the *Broadcasting Services Act* to include 'anti-siphoning' provisions. These provisions, which were considered the most extensive in the world, essentially ensured that all of Australia's most culturally significant sporting events would be available on free-to-air television (Nicholson 2007).

In 1993 Sydney was granted the rights to host the 2000 Olympic Games. The Australian government complemented the 'Maintain the momentum' policy, which was scheduled to provide the sport system with $290 million between 1992 and 1996, with the Olympic Athlete Program, which injected an additional $135 million into elite athlete development in the lead-up to the Olympic Games. An additional $80 million from the Australian Olympic Committee's Gold Medal Plan supplemented this funding. Elite athlete development had not been so well funded in Australia's history, and as a result Australia recorded its best ever performance at the 2000 Games, finishing fourth on the medal tally behind three political and economic superpowers: the United States, Russia and China.

In the wake of the Sydney Olympics, the Australian federal government launched a new sport policy, *Backing Australia's sporting ability* (BASA) (Commonwealth of Australia 2001a). BASA was indicative of both the hard work that had taken place in the preceding 30 years, as well as the maturity of the Australian sport system and the government's sport policy agenda. In essence, BASA articulated a relatively simple yet effective four-pronged sport policy which focused on maintaining elite performance, increasing participation in organised sport, ensuring a drug-free sport environment, and improving the governance and management of Australian sport organisations. In many respects the emphasis on participation, drugs and management improvement appeared designed to protect the Australian government's substantial investment in elite sport, by respectively increasing the talent pool from which elite athletes are drawn, protecting Australia's sporting image and credibility, and ensuring that national sport organisations were in a position to appropriately and efficiently use the funds they had been granted.

The Australian sport policy remained relatively unchanged until the election of the Rudd Labor government in late 2007. In May 2008 the Rudd government released a discussion paper titled 'Australian sport: emerging challenges, new directions', in which it noted that new directions were needed in the way government supports elite sport and the way in which sport is used to boost participation and physical activity to help build a healthier nation. The discussion paper claimed that 'in recent times, junior and community sport has been approached with a focus, almost exclusively, on increasing the pool from which our elite athletes can be drawn' and that 'whereas early federal sports policy had a clear focus on community physical activity and "Life. Be in it" style programs, this has declined over time to become virtually non-existent' (Commonwealth of Australia 2008, p. 5). As part of a broader argument for the need for new approaches, statistics were quoted that highlighted significant health problems within Australian society, including that between 1989–90 and 2004–05 the proportion of the Australian population considered obese doubled from 9% to 18%. In its conclusion of the new direction to be taken by the Rudd government, the discussion paper revealed that moving the Sport Portfolio to the Department of Health and Ageing underscored an approach in which sport would be of benefit to the entire nation, as part of a broader health agenda.

Despite the promise of change that was inherent in the 'Australian sport: emerging challenges, new directions' discussion paper, the Australian sport policy status quo was maintained, in large part because the government soon commissioned an investigation of the Australian sport system and Australian sport policy. Formed in late August 2008, the 'Independent Sport Panel', chaired by David Crawford, was charged with making recommendations on the specific structures, programs and reform required to ensure the continuing robustness of the Australian sport system. Specifically, the panel's terms of reference focused on five key areas:

- Ensure Australia's continued elite sporting success
- Better place sport and physical activity as a key component of the government's preventative health agenda

- Strengthen pathways from junior sport to grassroots community sport right through to elite and professional sport
- Maintain Australia's cutting edge approach to sports science, research and technology
- Identify opportunities to increase and diversify the funding base for sport through corporate sponsorship, media and any recommended reforms, such as enhancing the effectiveness of the Australian Sports Foundation.

After an extensive consultation period, the panel's report, entitled 'The future of sport in Australia' was presented to the government in October 2009 and contained several recommendations with significant implications for the Australian sport system. First, the panel recommended that the government should develop a national sports policy framework, to include measurable objectives and priorities for public funding within the key areas of high performance sport and sport participation, strategies to deliver the objectives, and a clear articulation of the roles and responsibilities of the various levels of government in delivering the strategies. Second, the panel recommended that the Australian Sports Commission should provide leadership, but should not be involved in service delivery. As such, it recommended that the Australian Institute of Sport be separated from the commission. Third, the panel recommended that the various state and territory institutes of sport be merged with the Australian Institute of Sport to form a single entity funded by the federal government. Finally, the panel recommended that a national curriculum for sport and physical education be considered. The report generated considerable debate, particularly around the issue of the funding balance between high performance and participation sport. Advocates for high performance sport were critical of any suggestion that funding to high performance sport be decreased as part of broader reforms to the Australian sport system.

In May 2010 the government released 'Australian sport: the pathway to success', which it claimed was its new sport policy, as well as a response to the report of the Independent Sport Panel. The government agreed to establish a National Sport and Active Recreation Policy Framework, but did not agree that the Australian Sports Commission should be separated from the Australian Institute of Sport. Furthermore, the government did not support merging the institutes of sport into a single entity, although conceded that a national approach to high performance training was essential to an effective high performance strategy. Similarly, the panel's recommendations in the area of sport and physical education in the school curriculum were only supported in part, with the government agreeing that the hours committed to physical activity in the school curriculum should be maximised. It remains to be seen whether the Independent Sport Panel's recommendations will have a significant impact on the sport policy priorities cemented by the BASA policy in 2001.

Administering sport

As noted in the previous section, the Hawke government created a Department of Sport, Recreation and Tourism when it was elected in 1983. In late 1987 the departmental responsibility was widened to Arts, Sport, the Environment, Tourism and Territories, which remained relatively unchanged throughout the late 1980s and early 1990s, apart from the Arts and Tourism portfolios being relocated to other departments towards the end of the Keating era. When the Howard Liberal government was elected in 1996 sport lost its departmental profile – a Ministry of Sport, Territories and Local Government was created, which was located within the Department of the Environment. Subsequently, a newly named Ministry of Sport and Tourism was relocated to the Department of Industry, Science and Resources, before being renamed the Ministry of Arts and Sport and located within the Department of Communications, Information Technology and the Arts (DITA). The Sport Portfolio remained within DITA throughout the last half of the Howard government, from late 2001 till late 2007. When the Rudd government took office in late 2007 a newly named Ministry of Youth and Sport was created, which was located within the Department of Health and Ageing, which in turn became a Ministry of Sport. The allocation of departments and ministries responsible for sport since 1983 is illustrated in Table 1.

Table 1 Departments and ministries responsible for Australian sport policy 1983–2009.

Date	Department	Ministry
1983–1987	Sport, Recreation and Tourism	Sport, Recreation and Tourism
1987–1993	Arts, Sport, the Environment, Tourism and Territories	Arts, Sport, the Environment, Tourism and Territories
1993–1996	Environment, Sport and Territories	Sport and Territories
1996–1998	Environment	Sport, Territories and Local Government
1998–2001	Industry, Science and Resources	Sport and Tourism
2001–2007	Communications, Information Technology and the Arts	Arts and Sport
2007–2009	Health and Ageing	Youth and Sport
2009–	Health and Ageing	Sport

Source: Parliament of the Commonwealth of Australia (2008b, 2009b).

The somewhat chequered history of the Sport Portfolio within Australian government over the last 25 years illustrates not only that different governments have had different priorities for sport, but that is has often been difficult to find sport an appropriate home within government. At various times throughout Australian history the Sport Portfolio has been linked to recreation (Whitlam and Hawke), tourism (Whitlam, Hawke and Keating) or arts (Hawke, Keating and Howard) and has been located within government departments that appeared to have little or no affinity for sport. The election of the Rudd government in 2007 has resulted in sport being aligned with an overt health agenda for the first time in Australia's history, notwithstanding the early attempts to increase Australia's physical fitness in the 1930s, the fleeting work of the Whitlam government and the interdepartmental cooperation that marked the development and implementation of the Active Australia program. This departmental change has the potential to significantly alter the direction of Australian sport policy, a discussion of which is incorporated in the concluding section.

Since 1985 the minister for sport has been responsible for the Australian Sports Commission and, since 1990, for the Australian Sports Anti-Doping Authority (ASADA, known as the Australian Sports Drug Agency until 2006). In 2006–07 the Australian Sports Commission received $193 million in government funding, which was exclusively raised through taxation, as well as another $20 million raised by the ASC through commercial activities such as sponsorship and facility hire (Australian Sports Commission 2007). In the same year the ASADA received $12.9 million in government funding and an additional $1.7 million from the provision of drug testing services (Australian Sports Anti-Doping Agency 2007). Government funding of sport has become more important since the establishment of the AIS and the ASC, and the vast majority of government or agency funding has been appropriated from general taxation revenues. Although the possibility of an injection of funding into Australian sport through a UK style lottery has been raised in reviews and inquiries (e.g. Commonwealth of Australia 1999), state jurisdiction over gambling precludes this occurring without substantial legal and constitutional restructuring (Productivity Commission 1999).

Each Australian state and territory also has a government department that is focused on sport and recreation. For example, Sport and Recreation Victoria (SRV) is located within the Department of Planning and Community Development (DPCD) and in 2006–07 its expenditure was $94.7 million (Department for Victorian Communities 2007). The vast majority of SRV's budget is allocated to community development programs, particularly facility renewal and construction, although a significant proportion is also allocated to high performance sport through the Victorian Institute of Sport. Comparable per capita levels of funding are provided by the other states. For example, in 2006 the New South Wales state government provided $106 million to the sport and recreation component of their Department of Arts, Sport and Recreation (State of New South Wales 2006). Similarly, the Western Australian state government allocated $94 million to sport in the 2006–07 fiscal year (State of Western Australia 2006).

Local government also allocates a significant proportion of its expenditure to sport services, facilities and programs. The Commonwealth Grants Commission's analysis of local government expenditure over the period 1961–1998 revealed that there had been a relative increase in the importance of recreation and culture (Commonwealth of Australia 2001b). Australian Bureau of Statistics data for the period 2004–05 shows that local government expenditure on 'recreation and culture' was $2879 million, which represented 14.8% of total local government expenditure (Australian Bureau of Statistics 2006).

In summary, Australian federal government sport policy is largely implemented through the ASC and is focused on elite sport development. State government policies in sport are typically delivered through dedicated departments of sport and recreation and are focused on infrastructure development, supporting their respective satellite elite sport institutes and supporting the delivery of community-based sport. Local governments across Australia also invest heavily in local community sport facilities and work directly with clubs and associations to enhance participation opportunities within their regions.

Nonprofit and commercial sectors of sport

The Australian sport system is based on a complex federated model, in which the government relies on not-for-profit organisations to help deliver its public policy objectives. While government policy is set by the federal minister for sport, the responsibility for executing policy lies with the ASC. The ASC in turn relies on a range of national sport organisations (NSOs) to ensure that the vast majority of its policy goals and outcomes are achieved. In this respect, the ASC acts as an intermediary between government and Australian NSOs (Stewart et al. 2004). The ASC ensures that NSO planning is aligned with the ASC's strategic objectives through funding and service agreements with each NSO and through annual reviews that monitor performance and allocate funding on the basis of achievement. In order to receive funding through the ASC, the NSOs must also adhere to minimum mandatory requirements.

The ASC recognises approximately 80 NSOs; of these 55 were funded in 2006–07, with 21 receiving more than $1 million in government funding. For many NSOs, the funding received from government via the ASC is an important source of revenue. For example, in 2006–07 Rowing Australia received $4,059,909 in grants from the ASC and the AIS, which represented 80% of its annual income (Rowing Australia 2007). By contrast, state sporting associations rely far less on government funding. For example, in 2007–08 Rowing Victoria, one of Rowing Australia's state associations, received $84,280 in government grants, equivalent to 9% of its annual revenue of $899,188 (Rowing Victoria 2007). In 2008 the federal government acknowledged that 'the National Sporting Organisations, not governments, run sport in Australia' (Commonwealth of Australia 2008, p. 4), yet the funding agreements the ASC strike with NSOs typically attempt to influence the overall strategy of sports across the country rather than specific elements of their activities (e.g. high performance programs or coach development).

Arguably, Australia also has the most competitive professional sport marketplace in the world, with four major football codes, a national basketball league, a crowded international and domestic cricket calendar, a highly successful Grand Slam tennis tournament, a thriving horse racing industry and a host of other major sports events each year. As noted by Hoye 'the scale of commercial activity associated with professional sport in Australia and New Zealand is significant' (2005, p. 90). The major leagues attract significant broadcast rights income, including the Australian Football League valued at $140 million per year (Hess et al. 2008), Super 14 valued at $431 million for its most recent five-year deal (Sainsbury 2005), and the National Rugby League valued at $40 million per year (Walter 2005). The major professional sports attract approximately $1.3 billion in sponsorship in Australia each year (Commercial Economic Advisory Service of Australia 2001). These major professional leagues have limited interaction with federal government sport policy but there is significant interaction between respective state governments and clubs in respect to major stadia developments.

Sport's place in the public policy arena

Sport is a relatively low priority within the Australian federal government compared to traditional public policy areas, despite appearances to the contrary. Although the ASC's funding allocation increased by almost $80 million during the period from 2005–06 to 2010–11, as Table 2 demonstrates, government spending on sport as a proportion of total budget expenditure has remained static, particularly during the period between the Athens and Beijing Olympic Games. The absolute increase in sport funding has been more a result of economic conditions than a shift in policy priorities. Although it is clear that the Australian federal government's funding of sport has been politically expedient, particularly since the early 1980s, the increases in government funding for sport throughout the first decade of the 21st century have in large part been the result of Australia's growing economy and a resources boom, driven by increasing demand for Australian exports within countries such as China and India.

Table 2 Australian federal government budget and Australian Sports Commission allocation as a proportion of the total.

	2005–06	2006–07	2007–08	2008–09	2009–10	2010–11
Budget ($000)	47,371,218	53,334,597	58,986,078	60,874,689	71,283,073	71,949,922
ASC ($000)	168,631	192,428	204,409	219,785	222,044	248,032
ASC%	0.36	0.36	0.35	0.36	0.31	0.34

Source: Parliament of the Commonwealth of Australia (2005, 2006, 2007, 2008a, 2009b, 2010).

Table 3 shows that in terms of funding, the largest Australian government departments are 'defence', 'education, employment and workplace relations', 'health and ageing' and 'foreign affairs and trade'. As noted previously, the minister for sport is located within the Department of Health and Ageing and the Australian Sports Commission is the peak sport agency located within the department. In 2010–11 the Department of Health and Ageing appropriations budget was $7165 million of which $248 million, or 3.5%, was allocated to the Australian Sports Commission. In order to contextualise the place of sport within the public policy hierarchy, it is worth briefly examining three other peak agencies that are similarly funded (Parliament of the Commonwealth of Australia 2010). The Bureau of Meteorology, which sits within the Environment, Water, Heritage and Arts Portfolio, and is responsible for ensuring that 'Australia benefits from meteorological and related science and service', had an annual budget in 2010–11 of $278 million. The Australia Council, which also sits within the Environment, Water, Heritage and Arts Portfolio, is responsible for meeting two outcomes: 'Australian artists create and present a body of distinctive cultural works characterised by the pursuit of excellence' and 'Australian citizens and civic institutions appreciate, understand, participate in, enjoy and celebrate the arts'. In the 2010–11 the Australia Council's budget was $172 million. Finally, the Special

Broadcasting Service, located within the Department of Broadband, Communications and the Digital Economy, and responsible for providing 'multilingual and multicultural services that inform, educate and entertain all Australians and in doing so reflect Australia's multicultural society', had an annual budget of $211 million in 2010–11. These examples also illustrate that the Australian government, like all national governments, has a vast array of services it provides. In this context it is perhaps significant that the proportion of government spending allocated to sport has remained constant.

Table 3 Selected Australian government portfolio budgets, 2010/11 ($million).

Portfolio	Budget
Defence	23,519,162
Health and Ageing	7,164,888
Education, Employment and Workplace Relations	7,112,296
Foreign Affairs and Trade	5,509,751
Human Services	3,827,233
Environment, Water, Heritage and the Arts	3,061,446
Innovation, Industry, Science and Research	2,248,036
Immigration and Citizenship	1,996,327
Broadband, Communications and the Digital Economy	1,569,504
Agriculture, Fisheries and Forestry	655,547

Source: Parliament of the Commonwealth of Australia (2010).

The Australian Sports Commission is charged with achieving two outcomes: an effective national sports system that offers improved participation in quality sports activities by Australians and excellence in sports performances by Australians. As Table 4 shows, during the period 2005–06 to 2010–11, excellence in sports performances by Australians was regarded as the more important of the two and has been funded at significantly higher levels, a trend which has been evident since the Australian federal government engaged with sport policy (Stewart et al. 2004). Furthermore, the disparity in funding between the two objectives can be considered even greater, given the outcome that refers to 'an effective national sports system' is extremely diverse and encompasses a range of sub-outcomes that include: increasing community sport participation; increasing after school-based participation; complying with the World Anti-Doping Agency Code; executing agreements with national sport organisations; surveying sport and reaction participation; improving the governance and management of national sport organisations; providing sport-related information to sport organisations; planning and implementing sport development in the Pacific; and encouraging and increasing Indigenous and disabled participation in sport.

Table 4 Australian Sports Commission annual allocations, 2005–06 to 2010–11 ($million)

	2005–06	2006–07	2007–08	2008–09	2009–10	2010–11
Total	168,631	192,428	204,409	219,785	222,044	248,032
O1*	57,666	66,971	72,895	78,236	78,171	72,217
O2*	110,965	125,457	131,514	141,549	143,873	175,815

*Outcome 1: An effective national sports system that offers improved participation in quality sports activities by Australians; Outcome 2: Excellence in sports performances by Australians. The figures within the table only relate to government allocations and do not include Australian Sports Commission revenue from other sources, such as the sale of services and products, nor do they include cash reserves. Source: Parliament of the Commonwealth of Australia (2005, 2006, 2007, 2008a, 2009b, 2010).

Table 5 Selected* national sport organisation funding, 2005–09 ($million).

	2005–06		2006–07		2007–08		2008–09	
	Total	Elite#	Total	Elite	Total	Elite	Total	Elite
Swimming	5.46	5.14	6.35	6.04	5.98	5.66	7.99	7.64
Soccer	5.91	2.56	3.31	2.82	7.16	6.72	6.99	6.70
Athletics	4.77	4.56	6.13	5.61	5.87	5.28	6.37	5.67
Rowing	5.19	5.11	5.63	5.49	5.60	5.47	6.24	6.12
Cycling	5.06	4.89	5.28	5.12	5.78	5.59	5.97	5.80
Hockey	4.79	4.46	5.50	5.05	5.39	5.04	5.89	5.52
Basketball	4.01	3.66	4.76	4.31	4.37	4.07	4.76	4.40
Sailing	3.16	3.02	4.36	4.21	3.82	3.66	4.26	4.10
Canoeing	2.28	2.17	3.05	2.92	1.36	1.24	3.09	2.96
Volleyball	1.96	1.85	2.91	2.73	2.62	2.43	2.91	2.55

*The top ten national sport organisations based on total funding in the 2008–09 year. #The 'Elite' figure has been calculated by adding the sport's Australian Institute of Sport and high performance allocations. Source: Australian Sports Commission (2006, 2007, 2008, 2009).

The Australian Sports Commission's grants to national sport organisations focus on the outcome of 'excellence in sports performances by Australians'. Table 5 shows how much funding the top ten Australian national sport organisations received in the four-year period from 2005–06 to 2008–09 from the ASC. It demonstrates that the vast majority of funding is directed to Australian Institute of Sport and high performance programs within each of the sports. Table 5 also highlights that Olympic sports are the most popular funding targets and sports in which Australia has been particularly successful are at the top of the table (e.g. swimming, rowing, hockey and cycling). The focus of Australian government sport funding on high performance has been well established, particularly since the formation of the Australian Institute of Sport, yet the reasons for this focus are not necessarily clear. Arguments for funding elite sport and the funding bias towards elite sport have included providing Australia with a sense of national pride, social cohesion, international recognition and exposure, increased tourism and trade, as well as the creation of role models that will engender greater levels of participation among the general population. It appears clear that the Australian government, and possibly the Australian people, are attached to the notion that Australia is a successful Olympic nation and are prepared to make a financial investment in order to ensure it becomes a reality.

Future policy issues

There are arguably four major emerging or continuing policy issues that will dominate Australian sport policy in the short to medium term: (1) the continued push to support elite sport on the international stage at the expense of funding community level sport; (2) the ongoing search for effective and efficient policies to control both performance enhancing and illicit drugs in sport; (3) the ongoing relationship between the ASC and NSOs for the achievement of policy goals and the concomitant need to enhance the governance and management capacity of NSOs; and (4) the increasing desire of the government to look to sport for assistance in solving 'health-related' problems of declining physical activity levels and the increasing obesity of Australians.

Australia's performance at the 2008 Beijing Olympic Games has the potential to influence, if not change public policy within Australia. Australia won seven gold medals at the Barcelona Olympic Games, nine in Atlanta, 16 in Sydney, 17 in Athens and 14 in Beijing. At the Beijing Games Australia slipped out of the top four countries (to sixth on the basis of gold medals and fifth on the basis of total medals), replaced by Britain, which excelled in sports usually dominated by Australians, such as track cycling. Although it is difficult to conclude that a single performance at an Olympic Games is indicative of broader trends, it does appear that the sports in which Australia has been most successful at the Olympic Games are becoming more competitive and that rival nations with larger economies are investing more heavily in high performance sport. Throughout the Beijing Games, Youth and Sport Minister Kate Ellis repeatedly fielded questions in the media about the level of sport funding, and whether the government would respond to calls by Australian Olympic Committee President John Coates to increase funding. Ellis was non-committal, preferring to focus on the improved efficiencies that could be achieved by restructuring the system and avoiding duplication and waste. Inherent within Ellis' comments was the acknowledgement that Australia's economy is much smaller than many of the nations it is competing against at the Olympic Games and that any increases in funding would necessarily be at the expense of other areas of public policy. As indicated earlier, the proportion of government spending allocated to sport remained static from 2005–06 to 2010–11. Even if funding to sport were to increase, it is unlikely that it would reach parity with countries such as China, the United States, Russia, Britain or Germany. The more likely scenario is that the Australian government will adopt a more targeted approach similar to Britain and Singapore in funding a smaller number of sports that have a greater chance at elite success.

The federal government will continue to work on developing policy aimed at reducing the use of performance enhancing and illicit drugs by Australian athletes competing internationally and within Australia's professional and elite domestic leagues. The investment required to do this will continue to grow as the science required for detection becomes increasingly costly and the reach of the testing regime requires greater resources.

The Australian sport policy will remain focused on using NSOs to deliver elite sport outcomes and to a lesser extent the targeted growth in participation rates. This dependence by the government on the nonprofit sector of sport will require them to maintain their interventionist policies of demanding and facilitating better governance and management from NSOs. The continued delivery of elite sport performances will require NSOs that manage the high performance programs to have the wherewithal to govern and manage such resources, and thus will be subject to continued performance assessments and interventions from the ASC.

Finally, sport's transfer to the 'health and ageing' department was foreshadowed in the Labor Party's 2007 election platform, in which sport and recreation were viewed as components of a broader health system that could improve the health and wellbeing of Australians. The 2008 discussion paper 'Australian sport: emerging challenges, new directions' appeared to establish a new agenda for Australian sport, and yet in 2010 it was unclear whether any significant changes had been achieved beyond moving sport to the Health and Ageing Portfolio. As previously noted, the Independent Sport Panel's report to the federal government created consternation among the sections of the sport industry that advocate for the importance of elite sport and continual government support of this area. The 'Australian sport: emerging challenges, new directions' discussion paper and the Independent Sport Panel report both appeared to indicate that the government funding imbalance towards elite sport might be about to redressed. However, as indicated by the figures in Table 4, the 2010/11 budget resulted in both an absolute and a proportional increase in funding to elite sport. In this context it remains to be seen how the federal government will meet the specific challenge of rising adult and child obesity levels, as well as the more fundamental challenge of making sport a more prominent feature of preventative health care in Australia.

References

Australian Bureau of Statistics (2006). *Government finance statistics 2004–2005 (Cat. 5512.0)*. Canberra: Australian Bureau of Statistics.

Australian Sports Anti-Doping Agency (2007). *Annual report 2006–2007*. Fyshwick: Australian Sports Anti-Doping Agency.

Australian Sports Commission (2004–2009). *Annual report 2003–2009*. Canberra: Australian Sports Commission.

Booth, D. (2001). *Australian beach cultures: the history of sun, sand and surf*. London: Frank Cass.

Bloomfield, J. (1973). *The role, scope and development of recreation in Australia* (The Bloomfield report). Canberra: Australian Government Printing Service.

Cashman, R. (1995). *Paradise of sport*. Melbourne: Oxford University Press.

Chapman, S., Byrne, F. & Carter, S. (2003). Australia is one of the darkest markets in the world: the global importance of Australian tobacco control. *Tobacco Control*, 12(4): iii1–iii3.

Coles, A. (1975). *Report of the Australian Sports Institute Study Group* (The Coles report). Canberra: Commonwealth Government Department of Tourism and Recreation.

Commercial Economic Advisory Service of Australia (2001). *Sponsorship of sport*. Sydney, Australia.

Commonwealth of Australia (2010). *Australian sport: the pathway to success*. Canberra: Commonwealth of Australia.

Commonwealth of Australia (2008). *Australian sport: emerging challenges, new directions*. Canberra: Australian Government Printing Service.

Commonwealth of Australia (2001a). *Backing Australia's sporting ability: a more active Australia*. Canberra: Australian Government Printing Service.

Commonwealth of Australia (2001b). *Commonwealth Grants Commission: review of operation of the Local Government (Financial Assistance) Act 1995*. Canberra: Australian Government Printing Service.

Commonwealth of Australia (1999). *Shaping up: a review of Commonwealth involvement in sport and recreation in Australia*. Canberra: Australian Government Printing Service.

Commonwealth of Australia (1985). *Australian Sports Commission Act 1985*. Canberra: Australian Government Printing Service.

Department for Victorian Communities (2007). *Annual report 2006–2007*. Melbourne: Department for Victorian Communities.

Green, M. (2007). Olympic glory or grass roots development? Sport policy priorities in Australia, Canada and the United Kingdom, 1960–2006. *International Journal of the History of Sport*, 24(7): 921–53.

Green, M. (2005). Integrating macro and meso-level approaches: a comparative analysis of elite sport development in Australia, Canada and the United Kingdom. *European Sport Management Quarterly*, 5(2): 143–66.

Green, M. & Houlihan, B. (2005). *Elite sport development: policy learning and political priorities*. London: Routledge.

Hess, R., Nicholson, M., Stewart, B. & de Moore, G. (2008). *A national game: the history of Australian Rules football*. Melbourne: Viking.

Hoye, R. (2005). Professional sport in Australia and New Zealand: an introduction to the special issue. *Sport Management Review*, 8: 89–94.

Hoye, R. & Nicholson, M. (2009). Australia. *International Journal of Sport Policy*, 1(2): 229–40.

Jaques, T. & Pavia, G. (1976). The Australian government and sport. In T. Jaques and G. Pavia, (Eds). *Sport in Australia* (pp. 148–57). Sydney: McGraw Hill.

Nicholson, M. (2007). *Sport and the media: managing the nexus*. London: Butterworth-Heinemann.

Parliament of the Commonwealth of Australia (2010). *Appropriation (Parliamentary Departments) Bill (No. 1) 2010–2011*.

Parliament of the Commonwealth of Australia (2009a). The 42nd Parliament Ministry List. [Online]. Available: www.aph.gov.au/library/parl/42/ministry/ministry9Jun09-14Dec09.htm [accessed 19 January 2011].

Parliament of the Commonwealth of Australia (2009b). *Appropriation (Parliamentary Departments) Bill (No. 1) 2009–2010*.

Parliament of the Commonwealth of Australia (2008b). *Parliamentary handbook of the Commonwealth of Australia*. [Online]. Available: www.aph.gov.au/library/handbook/historical/ministries/index.htm [accessed 19 January 2011].

Parliament of the Commonwealth of Australia (2003–08a). *Appropriation (Parliamentary Departments) Bill (No. 1) 2003–2009*.

Productivity Commission (1999). *Australia's gambling industries inquiry report No. 10*. Canberra: Productivity Commission.

Rowing Australia (2007). *Annual report 2006–2007*. Belconnen, ACT: Rowing Australia.

Rowing Victoria (2007). *Annual report 2006–2007*. Melbourne, Vic.: Rowing Victoria.

Sainsbury, M. (2005). Seven stitches tests rights and sets sights on footy. *The Australian*, 2 June, p. 32.

Shelton, J. (1999). 'Life. Be in it': from incrementalism to sharp policy reversals. Unpublished MA Thesis, The University of Melbourne.

State of New South Wales (2006). *Budget paper 3: budget estimates 2006–07*. Sydney, Australia: State of New South Wales.

State of Western Australia (2006). *Budget paper 3: budget statements 2006–07*. Perth, Australia: State of Western Australia.

Stewart, B., Nicholson, M., Smith, A. & Westerbeek, H. (2004). *Australian sport: better by design? The evolution of Australian sport policy*. London: Routledge.

Walter, B. (2005). NRL wants TV rights deal to start now, 20 May. [Online]. Available: www.smh.com.au/news/League/NRL-wants-TV-rights-deal-to-start-now/2005/05/19/1116361677981.html [accessed 15 February 2011].

Whitlam, G. (1972). It's time for leadership. [Online]. Available: whitlamdismissal.com/speeches/72-11-13_it's-time.shtml [accessed 15 February 2011].

4

Accessing youth sport in Australia: schools and clubs

Richard Light

Sport as we know it today originated from informal folk games rationalised into competitive games in the 19th-century schools of the rising English middle classes (Bourdieu 1978; Mangan 1981). Whether practised in stadiums before thousands of paying spectators as a form of entertainment, or informally among children in the backyard or on the beach, sport is essentially competitive. There is of course a range of non-competitive leisure activities such as bush or beach walking, cycling and body surfing available to Australian youth but this chapter is concerned with organised, competitive sport. The provision of sport for young people varies from country to country but is invariably accessed through schools or community-based and/or commercial sports clubs. Sport practised within educational institutions such as schools and universities is strongly influenced by conceptions of its having an educational role and forming part of the schooling experience. When youth participate in sport outside educational settings what they learn and what they experience are likely to be distinctly different. In many countries, such as the US, Japan and Singapore, most sport for young people is offered within educational institutions. In other countries such as Australia, New Zealand, Britain and Germany there is a very strong culture of making sport accessible outside schools through community-based and commercial clubs. The different institutional contexts within which children and young people participate in sport will exert very different influences on learning and the development of young people through participation in sport.

The organisation of sport through clubs is as old as sport itself is (Hargreaves 1986) and over the past decade or so there has been an expansion in the number of sport clubs and club membership in countries such as Australia and Britain where club sport is strong (Kirk & MacPhail 2003; Light 2008). Indeed, community-based club sport has come to form a prominent aspect of Australian cultural life (Light 2008). At the same time, competitive sport is offered in schools at intra and inter-school levels with sport and games still tending to form the bulk of physical education experiences for young people. There are thus two systems offering sport for youth that can be seen as running parallel to each other yet interlinked and offering quite different experiences. As Kirk (2010) suggests, children's experiences of sport may vary profoundly between its practice within the institutional settings of schools and outside them in the institution of sport. There is however, considerable overlap between the two systems with many children and young people playing sport in both systems. Children and young people who have a strong interest in sport typically play it during the week at school as well as playing for a club on the weekend in the same sport or in different sports. For example, in a study conducted on children aged nine to 12 years of age in an Australian swimming club they also participated in surf lifesaving (nippers), surfing, rugby and soccer with frequent clashes in their competition calendars (Light 2008). Sport is still immensely important in Australian culture but its place of importance in schools as school sport, and as taught in physical education, has diminished over the past few decades, particularly in government schools.

In addition to significant differences between experiences of sport in clubs and schools for Australian youth there can also be equally significant differences between government schools and the elite, independent schools where sport has had a history as a practice of distinction and a means of distancing such schools from what are perceived to be their social inferiors (Bourdieu 1986; Light & Kirk 2000). Performances in rugby and rowing in particular act as powerful markers of these school's worth where sport can be so consuming that students are often discouraged (or even forbidden) from participating in club sport outside the school and from sampling sports outside rugby, rowing, cricket or any sports valued in these schools. The place of such sports as rugby in theses schools of what Connell et al. (1982) call 'the ruling classes' is evident in the attendance at some GPS (Great Public Schools) rugby games in Sydney that can attract up to 15,000 spectators when Sydney premiership finals (for other sports) typically attract 5000. Since the 1950s when school sport was seen to feed into elite level international sport the place and role of sport in government schools has diminished due to changes in society and the role of education in it.

The following section provides some historical background and outlines the organisation and provision of sport for young Australians in the school and club systems. It is followed by an examination of swimming in NSW as an example to show differences between the two systems.

Sport in schools

Other than informal play in the playground, children are exposed to sport in contemporary Australian schools through physical education programs and school sport. The practice and cultural meaning of school sport is also quite different between government and non-government schools, and particularly in the elite independent schools. Sport has formed an important aspect of the schools of the social elite in Australia since the 1880s. The second half of the 18th century witnessed rapid development in the colonies culminating in Federation in 1901. This was an important period for the development of a sense of national identity and of an Australian culture profoundly shaped by sport. It also coincided with the diffusion of the English games ethic and the belief in the capacity of sport to develop morality and strength of character. For a colony anxious about the influence of its convict origins and the threat of the harsh natural environment, victories over touring English cricket teams from the later half of the century provided much needed confidence for the future of an emerging nation (Stoddart 1986). Cashman (1995) suggests that it was during this period that a uniquely Australian sporting culture emerged. Sport was of great importance in Australia during its development with the notion of sport as a central aspect of a middle class (for boys in particular) education imported from the mother country from the late 18th century. Sport was a little slower to be taken up in government schools but by the 1920s it was practised in many government schools and in the post-World War II period had become universal practice in government schools (Kirk et al. 1996).

Stimulated by the development of media technology and television in particular international sport expanded from the 1950s, which was a golden period in Australian sport. Within this context school sport was seen as providing a wide base from which sporting talent would be developed and channelled into the sports that Australia was successful in at international level (Kirk et al. 1996). Although this included swimming, tennis and athletics the emphasis was placed on team games such as cricket, rugby, netball, Rugby League and Australian Rules Football. Choices available in school sport were limited to major competitive sports and sport featured strongly in physical education curricula for several decades. The states that make up the Federation have traditionally enjoyed considerable power and autonomy with education being a state responsibility in Australia. There were thus considerable differences between the education systems of the various states that saw moves toward the development of a national curriculum in the late 1980s.

During the late 1980s increasing concern with the declining status of sport in schools lead to a Commonwealth government review of physical and sport education. The review suggested that there had been a significant decline in the content and quality of physical education and sport in schools linked to a reduction in the number of specialist physical education teachers, physical education being squeezed out of a crowded school curriculum, and the lack of clear aims and goals for the subject (Crowley 1992). It recommended that more physical education teachers needed to be recruited, the forging of better links between local, club-based sport and schools, and the development of a national curriculum. It also suggested reduction in the emphasis in schools on competition with significant implications for sport in schools. While there are still differences between states they have been considerably reduced as is evident in the ongoing development of a national curriculum. One of the more significant changes during this period was the development of curricula into a small number of Key Learning Areas (KLAs) that gave rise to the merging of health with physical education. This included a broadening of the physical education curriculum to move beyond sport in an attempt to provide students with more diverse experiences of physical activity. For example, in Victoria, health and physical education were merged into a new KLA, HPE (Health and Physical Education), in NSW health and physical education were merged with personal development to form the KLA, PDHPE (Personal Development, Health and Physical Education) and in Tasmania they were merged into the KLA, Health and Wellbeing.

Moves toward establishing a national curriculum in the 1990s led to the publication of a national statement and profile for health and physical education for Australian schools (Curriculum Corporation 1994a, 1994b) that established a common reference point for further development of state curricula (Penney 2010). The idea of a national curriculum is now further advanced in Australia with Penney suggesting that current developments represent, 'a significant shift toward far greater centralization' (2010, p. 5). Indeed, the development of a national curriculum has formed a prominent part of government education policy and has been taken forward by the National Curriculum Board and the Australian Curriculum, Assessment and Reporting Authority (ACARA) and is expected to be under way by 2013. This has led to significant changes in the conception of physical education's place and purpose in the school curriculum that have resulted in a considerable reduction in the importance and attention paid to sport. The emphasis in HPE and variations of this learning area name is now placed on providing education in learning how to lead healthy lifestyles with the professional body for HPE in Australia, ACHPER, suggesting that the role of HPE is to develop skills, knowledge and understandings that will counter lifestyle diseases (ACHPER 2009).

In the syllabi of the various states and territories sport now forms a smaller component of the physical activities offered than it did prior to the late 1980s. It is no longer seen as a means of providing a foundation for elite competitive sport nor of developing sporting talent. Instead, it is seen as one aspect of what Kirk (1999) calls physical culture that children and young people are exposed to with aims far removed from those of identifying and developing talent for elite level, professional, competitive sport. Public and government panic over rising childhood obesity has also strongly shaped ideas on the aims and purposes of physical education in schools leading to more emphasis on broadening participation and promoting healthy, active lifestyles. At the same time there is a growing concern with the negative aspects of competition and an over-emphasis on winning that excludes and marginalises the less skilled and less confident.

Sport in clubs

While sport has long been part of the school experience, it has a longer history as a form of community-based practice and is important for the development and maintenance of community identity in both urban and rural settings. It has long formed a central cultural practice for isolated rural communities in regional Australia. For example, commenting on a six-week Rugby League carnival held in 2007 in Dubbo (NSW) for years three and four primary school children from small towns in Western NSW, organiser, Russell Richardson said that, 'Sport is what keeps these communities together' (O'Brian 2007). Sports such as Rugby League and Australian Rules football in particular have a long history as practices that confirm and express community identity. The history of Rugby League in Sydney and Australian Rules football in Melbourne is intimately tied into the ways in which they have provided a powerful means of developing and expressing identity for local communities. It is strong enough to be often referred to as tribalism.

There is a large body of literature published on local identity with sports teams in Australia and particularly with Rugby League and Australian Rules football (for example see, Cottle & Keys 2007). Rugby League foundation clubs such as South Sydney Rabbitohs and Balmain Tigers in Rugby League in Sydney, and AFL clubs Collingwood and Melbourne have been very important in the development of suburban community identity. This is precisely why public opposition has been so intense when, as part of economic rationalisation strategies, governing bodies of sport decide to relocate teams, force mergers or remove them from the competition. In most cases passionate public protest is not enough to stop these activities, as in the cases of the relocation of AFL clubs Fitzroy and South Melbourne to Brisbane and Sydney to become the Brisbane Lions and the Sydney Swans respectively. However, sustained public opposition to removing South Sydney from the National Rugby League (NRL) competition did provide a 'win for the people'. The relocation of teams and the forced merging of others such as the unsuccessful merging of arch rivals Manly and North Sydney in Rugby League, and marketing that de-emphasises location operates to dilute long traditions of local identity with teams at the elite level. On the other hand, one of the key strategies that has helped the A League (football/soccer) succeed is the reduction in strong ethnic identity with teams by emphasising location in the names and promotion of the teams.

At the grassroots level club sport has long formed a prominent aspect of Australian culture and of youth experiences of growing up. In contemporary Australia it continues to do so with recent increases in children participating in organised sport. Of the 2,664,700 children aged between five and 14 in Australia in 2006, 63% (1,691,100) participated in sport outside schools in 2006 (ABS 2006). From 2000 to 2006 there was an increase in participation in organised sport from 59% to 63% with girls participation increasing by 6% to 58% and boys by 3% up to 69%. Of course this does not include participation in informal sport such as roller-blading, skateboarding or non-competitive surfing. The most popular (organised) sport for boys are soccer (22%) and swimming (16%) and for girls, netball (18%) and swimming (17%). The sport policy, *Backing Australia's Sporting Ability* (BASA), introduced by the Commonwealth government in 2001 was aimed at striking a balance between elite level, performance sport and community-based participation sport. While the two are not necessarily incompatible their aims, meaning and practices are very different. The BASA is aimed at fostering sport played at grassroots levels and particularly among school-aged children.

As Stewart et al. (2004) suggest, while youth sport development is essential for the future health of Australian sport it competes with many entertainment options for children that are sedentary in nature. Both government agencies such as the Australian Sports Commission (ASC) and independent sports organisations face the challenge of maintaining the attraction of organised sport for young Australians. The ASC is funded by the federal government and has a wide range of programs in place to promote sport from that practised at the most elite levels down to grassroots sport for young children, with policies in place aimed at increasing broad participation by children of all ages. It also distributes funding among the range of sport organisations in Australia to help them with promotion and development of their sports. Among these programs the model of modified sports for young people has proved to be successful in providing children and young people with satisfying and enjoyable sport experiences that would otherwise have been beyond them struggling to play adult games on adult fields using adult equipment. For example, the modified game of Kanga cricket with rules that are more forgiving, and the use of soft plastic and rubber equipment makes playing cricket more enjoyable and accessible for children. In addition to government developed sport programs aimed at increasing participation in general, individual sport organisations have developed their own programs.

The increasing commercialisation of sport in Australia has created a very competitive market for the hearts and bodies of youth that has led to the development of a range of versions of adult sports modified for children and young people. Most major sports such as Australian Rules football, football, Rugby Union, Rugby League, netball and cricket offer modified games for children as a means of attracting them to their particular sport.

Clubs in general have historically formed significant and distinctive aspects of Australian social life with many social clubs linked to sport. In most country towns and in many city suburbs social clubs function as meeting places for social interaction and the maintenance of a sense of identity with location. For example, most towns in NSW have a bowls (lawn bowls) club, a 'leagues club' (Rugby League) or an RSL (Returned Servicemen's League) club and form important social spaces for local communities. Most major social clubs also sponsor, or provide support in other ways for local sporting teams. Youth sport clubs are a feature of cultural life in Australia and play an important role in the social, physical and cultural development of children and young people. They also play an important role in maintaining social cohesion in many country towns and city suburbs (for example see, Daffey 2001; Tropp & Nauright 2007).

The significance of sport clubs on the Australian cultural landscape is reflected in Commonwealth government sport policy. The Commonwealth government's post-2000 Olympics sport policy, *Backing Australia's Sporting Ability*, explicitly recognises, and strives to enhance, the role of sport clubs in Australian society. BASA sees the sports club as a 'cornerstone of Australian society' (Stewart et al. 2004, p. 93) and important places for community activity and the development of a sense of local community. In a globalising world with its subsequent increases in social mobility and dislocation the enhancement of community-based sport clubs is seen as a means of countering the fracturing or weakening of local communities. In their book on Australian sport policy Stewart et al. (2004) outline how the BASA policy's aim of increasing participation in sport across Australia is divided into four strands that reflect recognition of the important social role that sport clubs play in Australia. The first strand aims to encourage young people, and particularly those in regional areas, to take up organised sport as a strategy for managing alienation, community fragmentation and social dislocation that increasing numbers of young people are experiencing. The next two strands aim at increasing membership in community-based sport clubs, fostering better links between schools and clubs and building better pathways from clubs to high performance sport. The final strand aims to educate the sporting community about the potential of community-based sport to perform an educative function in the development of morality and 'character', and as vehicles to address social problems such as racism and sexism. Without addressing the extent to which these objectives can be realistically achieved they do reflect the government's recognition of the place and importance of sport clubs in Australian society.

Youth sport in clubs and schools: swimming as an example

This section of the chapter provides an example of how the two structures of school and club sport function and how they are related to each other using the individual sport of swimming in NSW as an example. Australia has been a powerhouse in swimming from the turn of the 20th century when Australians held all the world swimming records and Fanny Durack broke every world women's record from February to March in 1912 (Light & Rockwell 2005). Australia remains one of the strongest swimming nations with swimming being the most popular sport in Australia for youth aged five to 14 (ABS 2006). The majority of Australians live close to the coastline making learning to swim a responsibility of schools for personal safety reasons and it enjoys a high profile as a sport across the country. At the 2009 ASA (Amateur Swimming Association) annual summit in Sheffield, England, a comparison of the number of Olympic (50-metre) pools between England and other countries highlighted the popularity of swimming in Australia by noting that, with a population of over 50 million, there are 18 Olympic size pools in England but there are 47 in the city of Sydney alone.

Australian children are exposed to swimming early in life through learn-to-swim classes after which many move into training squads aimed at developing competitive swimmers. Children and young people in swimming clubs typically begin learn-to-swim classes from one to three years of age and have their first experience of competitive swimming at the school swimming carnival at age eight (Light 2010). In Light's study, most of the talented 12-year-old swimmers followed a pattern of joining a commercial swimming school and club after positive experiences of the school swimming carnival making an early link between the school and club system that continued as they developed into talented swimmers.

Swimming as a school sport

In NSW swimming is organised within the Department of Education and Training (DET) School Sport Unit. Sport in primary schools is organised by the Primary Schools Sport Association (PSSA) with sport in secondary schools organised within the Combined High Schools Sports Association (CHSSA). Catholic and independent schools have their own sports organisations but compete at the state championships in an 'all schools' format at primary and secondary levels. This then leads into competition at the national championships conducted by School Sport Australia (SSA). This section of the chapter looks at the pathway provided for swimmers who attend government schools in NSW by the PSSA/CHSSA, which is separate to the Combined Independent School (CIS) and Catholic system until the state championships.

Most children begin competitive swimming by participating in the (primary) school swimming carnival from the age of eight. The school carnival typically aims at maximising participation, which is facilitated by having mostly 50-metre events. Primary schools will typically make the carnival a festive event and include some fun or novelty events if time allows. For most of the children at the swimming carnival it is the only competitive swim they have all year but for children who qualify by placing in the top two or three in an event they progress to the next level to represent the school in the 'Zone' Championships between local schools. Those who qualify by prevailing in the Zone Championships then represent their zone in the Area Championships contested by swimmers from all the zones in a larger 'area'. For example, children in schools on the lower North Shore region in Sydney compete in the North Shore Zone Championships and can then represent the North Shore Zone in the Sydney North Area Championships. In the NSW PSSA the state is divided into ten areas that join the Catholic and independent schools that have qualified through their own systems in the state championships.

Those who place in the NSW state championships progress to the SSA National Championships from 11 years of age. These championships are held in a different state each year with the primary school and high school championships run as separate events. Every fourth year swimmers have the opportunity of competing in the Pacific Schools Games (PSG) held in Australia. The PSG always include swimming and athletics with three other sports included in each game. In 2008 the PSG were held in Canberra with basketball, hockey and diving included along with swimming and athletics. Three thousand young athletes from 11 to 18 years competed in the event as members of teams from 23 countries and each state in Australia. Australia enters state representative teams but the other countries send selections rather than official national teams. While the teams from the Australian states are very large teams from some participating countries can be as small as a mere handful of participants.

The CHSSA is structured in a similar way. Government school swimmers progress through five stages before being able to compete against swimmers from Catholic and independent schools at the state championships. After that, they represent their state in an all schools' team at the SSA national championships. However, the high school carnival is typically a smaller event than its primary school equivalent. It is a competitive event whereas the primary school carnival is festive.

Swimming for a club

As illustrated, the school sport structure offers a series of levels through which swimmers must progress in order to compete at the national championships, and which vary from state to state. For example, in the primary school system the states of NSW, Victoria and Queensland have four levels up to and including the state championships but others can have as few as one level. Progression through the school systems depends upon earning a place at each level of competition and the age of the competitors is determined by the age of the student on their birthday that year. The structure of the club system is quite different. Like the school system, the club system is organised on a state basis with each state body sitting under the umbrella of the national body, Swimming Australia. Under the auspices of Swimming NSW swimmers in NSW clubs qualify for the state championships by making the minimum qualifying times set by Swimming NSW for each event in the relevant age group. Times must be achieved in carnivals recognised by Swimming NSW as qualifying meets but there is no need to earn a place in any meet. For example, swimmers in Sydney aiming to qualify for the state championships usually compete in the Metropolitan Championships and for those living outside Sydney, the NSW Country Championships. However they can still qualify for the NSW state championships without entering either the Metropolitan or Country Championships. They only need to meet the minimum qualifying times set for the state championships during the preceding year.

A wide range of carnivals is offered through the swimming season across the state as long course meets (contested in a 50-metre pool) over summer and short course meets (contested in 25-metre pools) over winter. Swimmers, their parents and coaches decide which events to enter over the season, typically training to make qualifying times for the metropolitan or country championships and state championships in particular events. Although those who qualify for the national championships tend to compete at state championships as a targeted meet this is not a prerequisite. While the school system offers the opportunity to compete at national level from 11, the club national championships begin from the under 13 years age group. However, the most significant difference between the two is the ways in which swimmers qualify for championships. Progression through the school system relies upon placings in the championships a level below, while qualification in the club system is dependent upon times being achieved. The school system provides a very clear marker of progress for swimmers but tends to stress the swimmer's achievement against others. It also gives no second chances by demanding success at each progressively difficult level whereas swimmers in the club system have all year to get a qualifying time.

Many swimmers competing in the club system had their first taste of competitive swimming at the school carnival. Swimmers and their parents are encouraged through this experience to develop any emerging talent by joining a swimming club. Apart from a few independent and Catholic schools, the school systems do not normally provide training. They merely provide a competitive structure and opportunities for developing talent but swimmers need to join a club to train. This means that the same 'serious' swimmers competing in the school carnivals compete in the club carnivals. Swimming is unusual here in that schools cannot normally provide the kind of training made available for team sports such as soccer, netball or touch rugby, or for individual sports like cross-country running or athletics. Even in schools that have a pool and provide coaching, the most competitive swimmers still train in their clubs with their club coaches. The exception is those schools which have established clubs registered with Swimming NSW, and which offer high quality coaches.

While there are two distinct structures within which young Australians can access sport there is a considerable overlap between them and swimmers participate with commitment in both school and club sports.

There are also differences in the identities developed by swimmers who progress to the state and national levels and this is most marked at the annual national championships. At the SSA national championships swimmers represent their state wearing the state uniform, and march under the state flag as a team. In the club system swimmers of the same age do not compete as a state team at the national championships but represent their club at national level. While there is intense competition between states at the national championships there is typically a stronger sense of identity with the state in the school system. There is, however, an annual inter-state meet in the club system contested in a state versus state format with swimmers wearing the state kit much like the schools SSA national championships.

Conclusion

As Kirk (2010) suggests, youth participation in sport within schools and in community-based clubs outside schools is likely to produce very different experiences. Such different experiences are, in turn, likely to generate different learning – and not just learning how to play the game or perform sport skills. For physical education teachers it is important to be aware of the values and beliefs that students develop through playing sport outside schools and their attitudes toward sport developed in different settings to schools (MacPhail et al. 2003). What students learn and their experiences of being in community-based sports clubs exert a significant influence on the ways in which they interpret learning experiences in PE. This is not only from being a member of the community of practice of a sports club (e.g. Light & Curry 2009) but also from the discourses of competitive sport and the impact that professional sport, as sport for entertainment, can have on them.

Any consideration of learning through youth sport must include a broader, unstated learning process that is so easy to miss. The range and depth of less noticeable learning such as social learning (for example see, Light 2010), moral learning and the identity development that is shaped and facilitated through participation in sport, highlights the significance of young people's engagement in sport. No learning takes place in a vacuum. Research on pedagogy in sport and physical education over the past two decades has emphasised the role of context in learning. One has only to think of the role physical education plays in the reproduction of unequal gender relations to highlight the depth and importance of embodied, implicit learning and how it is shaped by context. Youth live in complex worlds and experience things in many ways and many contexts. School sport, physical education and club-based sport are not the only places within which they engage in physical activity but they are very significant contexts for consideration in any research on youth sport in Australia.

References

Australian Bureau of Statistics (ABS) (2009). Children's participation in cultural and leisure activities, Australia. Australian Bureau of Statistics. [Online]. Available: www.abs.gov.au/AUSSTATS/abs@.nsf/ProductsbyCatalogue/0B14D86E14A1215ECA2569D70080031C [accessed 16 February 2011].

Australian Bureau of Statistics (ABS) (2006). Children's participation in cultural and leisure activities, Australia. Australian Bureau of Statistics. [Online]. Available: www.abs.gov.au/AUSSTATS/abs@.nsf/Lookup/4901.0Main+Features1Apr%202006?OpenDocument [accessed 16 February 2011].

ACHPER (2009). *The ACHPER national statement on the curriculum future of health and physical education in Australia.* Adelaide: ACHPER.

Bourdieu, P. (1986). *Distinction: a social critique of the judgement of taste.* London: Routledge.

Bourdieu, P. (1978). Sport and social class. *Social Science Information, 12*(6): 819–40.

Cashman, R. (1995). *Paradise of sport.* Melbourne: Oxford University Press.

Connell, R. W., Ashenden, D. J., Kessler, S. & Dowsett, G. W. (1982). *Making the difference: schools, families and social division.* Sydney: Allen & Unwin.

Cottle, D. & Keys, A. (2007). The fibro years: Roy Masters and Wests Rugby League Football Club, 1978–81. *Sporting Traditions, 21*(1): 67–74.

Curriculum Corporation. (1994a). *A statement on health and physical education for Australian schools.* Carlton: Curriculum Corporation.

Curriculum Corporation. (1994b). *Health and physical education: a curriculum profile for Australian schools.* Carlton: Curriculum Corporation.

Crowley, R. (1992). *Physical and sport education: report of Senate Committee on Environment, Recreation and the Arts.* Canberra: Australian Government Publishing Service.

Daffey, P. (2001). *Local rites: a year in grass roots football in Victoria and beyond.* Flemington, Victoria: Black Duck Publications.

Hargreaves, J. (1986). *Sport, power and culture: a social and historical analysis of popular sports in Britain.* Cambridge: Polity Press.

Kirk, D. (2010). *Physical education futures.* London: Routledge.

Kirk, D. (1999). Physical culture, physical education and relational analysis. *Sport, Education and Society, 4*(1): 63–73.

Kirk, D. & MacPhail, A. (2003). Social positioning and the construction of a youth sports club. *International Review for the Sociology of Sport, 38*(1): 23–44.

Kirk, D., Nauright, J. Hanrahan, S., Macdonald, D. & Jobling, I. (1996). *The socio-cultural foundations of human movement.* Melbourne: Macmillan Press.

Light, R. (2010). Children's social and personal development through sport: a case study of an Australia swimming club. *Journal of Sport and Social Issues, 34*(4): 266–82.

Light, R. (2008). *Sport in the lives of young Australians.* Sydney: Sydney University Press.

Light, R. (2006). Situated learning in an Australian surf club. *Sport, Education and Society, 11*(2): 155–72.

Light, R. & Curry, C. (2009). Children's reasons for joining sport clubs and staying in them: a case study in a Sydney soccer club. *ACHPER Healthy Lifestyles Journal, 56*(1): 23–27.

Light, R. & Kirk D. (2000). High school rugby, the body and the reproduction of hegemonic masculinity. *Sport, Education and Society, 5*(2): 163–76.

Light, R. & Rockwell, T. (2005). The cultural origins of competitive swimming in Australia. *Sporting Traditions, 21*(2): 21–38.

MacPhail, A., Gorley, T. & Kirk, D. (2003). Young people's socialisation into sport: a case study of an athletics club. *Sport, Education & Society, 8*(2): 251–67.

Mangan, J. A. (1981). *Athleticism in the Victorian and Edwardian public school: the emergence and consolidation of an educational ideology.* Cambridge, UK: Cambridge University Press.

O'Brian, B. (2007). Here's mud in your eye. *Sydney Morning Herald*, June 27, p. 7.

Penney, D. (2010). Health and physical education in Australia: a defining time? *Asia pacific Journal of Health, Sport & Physical Education, 1*(1): 5–12.

Stewart, B., Nicholson, M., Smith, A. & Westerbeek, H. (2004). *Australian sport: better by design? The evolution of Australian sport policy.* London & New York: Routledge.

Stoddart, B. (1986). *Saturday afternoon fever: sport in Australian culture*. Sydney: Angus & Roberston.

Tropp, D. & Nauright, J. (2007). Rugby league, community and identity in the Lockeyer Valley, Queensland. *Sporting Traditions, 21*(1): 53–66.

5

Compulsory heterosexuality and the construction of femininity and masculinity: issues of performance versus presentation

Kate Russell

This chapter provides an overview of the ways in which sport helps to construct gender for youth and those women and men who participate. It starts from the premise that sport reflects the culture within which it operates and therefore the perceptions and behaviours of those who organise, regulate and support sport and recreation in Australia. Aitchison argues that while sport can provide a possibility of 'resistance, contestation and transgression of hegemonic gender and sexual power relations' it also acts as an 'ambiguous site of visible and marked embodied identities where the discourses of power that are dominant within wider society can often be exaggerated' (2007, p. 1). Girls and boys, like women and men, have different experiences of sport. It is the processes and structures through which these differences exist and persist that this chapter seeks to explore. The chapter begins with a brief discussion of the need to differentiate between sex and gender. This provides a starting point to explore the relative dimensions of gender and its social construction in the 21st century. I will highlight how it has been the physicality of women that has often disrupted acceptable notions of femininity and masculinity, and how this embodiment has been both embraced and resisted by sportsmen and women alike. The notion of compulsory heterosexuality is discussed to evaluate one mechanism through which women's and men's bodies are controlled and how sport facilitates that process. It also provides an entry point to explore some of the issues around the sexualisation of sport and how the primacy of a heterosexual image helps to shape the identity development of many athletes.

Sex and gender: it's the same thing, right?

Biologists would argue that there are but two sexes: male and female. Sex is a biological characteristic (phenotype) that is associated with a particular genetic (chromosomal) makeup or genotype. Simply put females are XX and males are XY. This simplifies things for us; men and women have different tick boxes on passport forms, women and men compete in different races at the Olympic Games. Gender is described by the World Health Organization (2010) as the 'socially constructed roles, behaviours, activities, and attributes that a given society considers appropriate for men and women': often labelled masculine or feminine. As I will discuss later, this is often linked to an individual's sexuality. In very simple terms, sex is biological and fixed, gender is more fluid and socially constructed.

What the sex binary denies, however, are those individuals who are born intersex, formerly known as hermaphroditism, in which a child's genitals or reproductive organs are ambiguous in some way. It also ignores those individuals who have sex chromosome combinations other than XX or XY, such as Turner's syndrome (XO) or Klinefelter's syndrome (XXY) (Fausto-Sterling 2000). Fausto-Sterling estimates that the frequency of children born with various categories of intersexuality to be around 1.7%. Taking this into consideration, this would mean a city the size of Sydney (roughly 4.5 million) would have around 76,500 individuals with varying degrees of intersexual development (2000). More recent research has challenged this frequency because of the definitions of intersexuality used but even the most conservative estimates refer to a level of 0.018–0.2% of the population (Sax 2002) roughly equating to between two and 20 out of every 10,000 live births. Our Sydney example would still reflect a minimum of 810 to 9000 individuals who had the most obvious form of intersexuality. Early sex assignment (usually shortly after birth) by surgeons often determines the 'sex' of a child, based on the physical appearance of the genitals rather than a 'gender' preference identified by that child (which would surely take place at a later age). Regardless of the difference of opinion regarding the prevalence of intersex births Fausto-Sterling's (2000) book details numerous cases of parents (and their children) being lied to openly about the status of their condition, the lack of any appropriate support groups and a decision-making process of whether or not to operate based on the surgeon's own ideas about what is and is not a 'normal' looking penis, testicle, vagina or clitoris. Kitzinger (2004) explains that biology has given us a wide range of body types which society initially constructs as two sexes and then goes on to gender, even if this requires mutilation. According to Crawford gender is a 'system of meaning that organises interactions and governs access to power and resources' (2001, p. 231) and as such gender exists not necessarily in people but through the interactions and transactions they have with other people and in different contexts. In this way the act of *gendering* a body is overt and often invasive.

We may ask what this has to do with sport and performance, and the response is: everything. We come to understand what sex and gender mean through participation in our own culture, with its rules on what sports boys and girls should play, what clothes they should wear, or its assumptions about what sexual preference a female rugby player or male dancer may have. Even, as Fausto-Sterling would suggest, culture dictates the ways in which we identify newborns solely as girls or boys. I will argue that the way in which we *read* an individual as masculine/feminine depends on the ways in which certain ideals are constructed as valuable. Sport, as one of many structural components of society, is as complicit in that process as choosing to paint your son's bedroom blue. As the recent case of Caster Semenya indicates, identifying an individual as purely male or female can be problematic when we use such narrowly prescribed categories. Semenya's gender was challenged following her winning the women's 800-metre race at the World Championships in Berlin in 2009 (Kessel 2010). Speculation over her 'true' gender abounded because of her muscular physique and low voice which led to demands for gender verification by the IAAF.

Following extensive tests, Semenya has been cleared to race against women. Regardless of the physical condition she may or may not have, the furore over whether a young woman should be able to compete against other women purely based on physical characteristics is a clear example of the gendered construction of sport.

Gender construction of physical activity and sport

Sport in the 20th and 21st centuries has remained a highly gendered construct, a legacy of the Victorian-era demarcation of physical activity (in particular recreational) as male and female. Many Victorian ideals of the time medicalised female bodies to the extent that a myth of frailty persisted (Cahn 1994; Hargreaves 1994; Theberge 1989). In particular women of a higher social standing found that their bodies were valued for their ability to reproduce the next generation of Empire builders (Vertinsky 1988). The reproductive sacrifice was required in order to maintain the natural order of the world: men as superior and powerful and women as subservient and weak. This process of medicalisation led to physical activity being associated with certain 'mannish' behaviours and deemed wholly inappropriate (Cahn 1994). Concerns were not only founded on fears of women displaying lesbian tendencies, but that they may also behave in an overtly heterosexual manner, as men of poor moral quality did. The implication was that this behaviour simply reflected personal standards associated with an inferior social class. Again fear rested on the notion that women who pursued a promiscuous lifestyle (associated with low morals) would not provide heirs to continue British interests abroad or legitimate children to claim family fortunes.

Sabo and Messner (1993) argue that the prevailing model of masculinity in modern times emphasises aggression, dominance and physical strength. Femininity, they argue, encompass ideals of passivity, dependence and physical frailty; all aspects that were mirrored in appropriate sporting choices. Metheney's (1965) classic work concerning the definition of sports deemed appropriate for women and men has been found to hold true 25 and 35 years later. Kane and Snyder (1989) and Koivula (2001) confirmed gender stereotyping of sports and more explicitly identified physicality as the central feature (although Koivula did find that men tended to this more than women). Sports such as gymnastics, swimming and tennis are acceptable forms of exercise for women because they permit the athlete to maintain a level of gracefulness. The aesthetic quality of their bodies is enhanced and body contact is not required in competition. In contrast, sports such as wrestling, boxing or weight lifting require a substantial amount of bodily force being used. Resisting or overcoming an opponent is essential and sports can contain movements that do not lend themselves to traditionally 'feminine' patterns.

Connell (1995) and Dunning (1994) regarded sport as a male preserve, where young boys can 'test' their masculinity and through which expectations of themselves and others (boys who do not play sport and girls generally), promote 'ways of being' male (Whitson 1990). Evans et al. (2004) and Kirk (2006) have also highlighted the ways in which schools become places for the gendering of boys and girls in particular sporting behaviour (Scraton 1992) – the persisting model of sport for boys and dance for girls is an example (Wellard 2009). The 'problem' of sport is that it primarily distinguishes between male and female performances, valuing the male and rendering all male performances as 'normal' (Connell 2002). Sport acts to produce a dominant but problematic form of masculinity (and by comparison, femininity) that acts to marginalise alternative masculinities (and femininities) and to subordinate females (and other males). Research into the development of masculinities of young boys in an inner-city Sydney school have also indicated that boys are particularly aware of the ways in which gendered language can be used to control and dominate girls and non-sporty boys. In one example the boy's teacher saw that boys felt the need to exert power over girls in order to validate their masculinity. The teacher described the way in which the boys would enact violence in relation to the girls within the school. Boys mostly did this through language, aimed to shock the girls and get a reaction. The teacher describes how the boys used:

> female insults at girls ... Like calling someone a 'bitch' or something ... or worse. Because they feel that they can use language, or swearing as a form of power ... I think that language is power, a form of power or coercion over girls ... Sexualising language ... They put the 'c' word on a piece of paper and say 'You are one' to one of the girls or something like that.

Renold (2005) noted that boys tend to use highly sexual swearwords to unsettle and intimidate girls. The language used by boys in her study was also generally sexually abusive and aggressive, and was employed in an attempt to re-establish their masculinity and heterosexuality, as if girls in some way had challenged it. Likewise with non-sporty boys, I found, as did Renold (2003) that boys used the term 'gay' in a derogatory way. Some of the boys in a focus group recognised that dancing for boys was not usual: 'Some boys do dancing! What about Li Cunxin in *Mao's Last Dancer*? He was a guy!' and that this led to labelling 'Might call you a girlie girl or twinkle toes ... Gay'. Boys should play sport – and that is 'real' sport – and not to do so lent itself to assumptions of homosexuality. The boys' teacher also noted how dancing was viewed by the class, 'We had a boy that was the lead in a recent dance and other boys in Year 4 accused him of being gay! And that obviously is because that doesn't fit their idea of what a boy should do'. Whether or not the boys fully understood what the term implied, it was certainly used to derogate the boy who danced and in this sense the language used became performative (Butler 1990). It enacted preferred ways of being, in the same sense that 'throwing like a girl' is derogatory for boys and invalidates girls' experiences.

The sexualisation of female athletes: compulsory heterosexuality

One of the primary sites for the construction of notions of femininity and masculinity is the media, and in particular the ways in which it presents female and male sporting participants. Children and young people are exposed to these images and can internalise many of the subconscious messages around what is an acceptable sporting body to have and/or how to look generally. Duncan (1990) investigated the coverage of sprinter Florence Griffiths Joyner's 1988 Olympic performance and noted the focus of many journalists on the makeup, long nails and revealing running suits typical of 'Flo Jo' at that time. Such trivialisation and sexualisation of women's sport constitutes a denial of power for the sportswoman and only serves to promote the idea of female athleticism as less than male. More recent examinations (Markula 2009) found similar sexualisation practices being enacted upon women in the 2004 Olympic Games. Markula notes how media narratives shape an athletic feminine identity across the world, seeking marketable 'sex-appeal', whilst pursuing portrayals of the athletes' personal lives as mothers, sisters or daughters. This work continues Wright and Clarke's (1999) research focusing on the notion of compulsory heterosexuality for all female athletes. Through this dictate, Wright and Clarke argue that all other forms of sexuality are denied legitimacy resulting in a form of social and sexual control through the naturalising and normalising of (hetero)-sexual relations both within and outside of sport.

One explanation as to the root of this belief, I argue, is the link between a woman's physicality (her body shape and size, and her embodiment of that) and her perceived sexuality. We have seen earlier that there appears to be a connection between ideals of male and female sports, the level of physicality that is required to participate successfully in them and notions of homosexuality. Choi (2000) points to the threat of overdeveloped muscularity and the fear of appearing unfeminine amongst female bodybuilders. Here unfeminine equates with lesbianism. Research on other sports, including football (Kolnes 1995) and boxing (Halbert 1997), also indicate a similar perceptual relationship between women's physical expressions, the assumptions of unfeminine behaviour and the short leap to lesbian definitions. Elsewhere I note that female rugby players consistently fought this presumption of sexual preferences because of the more muscular build of their bodies (Russell 2004). For rugby women in general there tends to be a strong connection made between lesbianism and the open display of a muscular body. Whether or not the woman was a lesbian was irrelevant. The powerful display of her body was enough to brand her as one. Here we see a paradox for these women. On the one hand having a body that allowed them to perform their function on the pitch was perceived as valuable. This, however, became 'worthless' once in the social context because a muscular body did not fit the ideals of a feminine woman. This *transiency* of body satisfaction based on physical value demonstrates the changing positive-negative embodiment of female rugby players and many sportswomen. Many women have attempted to assuage such comments through feminising their sporting attire, for example wearing tassels on boxing shorts (Halbert 1997) or female body builders wearing makeup (Choi 2000). I also noted that many female netballers, for example, were also very mindful of the ways in which their bodies were developing and made a conscious effort to limit this physical change, for example, in the muscular development of biceps and calf muscles (Russell 2002). All this appears to go against the notion of pursuing the ultimate competitive body for your sport.

It is interesting to note that for women it is the demonstration and enacting of physicality and power that supports the labelling as lesbian. While it appears to be the absence of an open display of muscularity that categorises some male athletes as gay. Examples include dancers, ice skaters or divers who require more aesthetic qualities to perform.

While nearly 20 years have passed since Pat Griffin made the comment that 'women in sport must come to understand that it wouldn't matter if there were no lesbians in sport.

The lesbian label would still be used to intimidate and control women's athletics' (1992, p. 260) the questioning of both women's and men's sexuality in relation to sport choice is an enduring one. As Griffin goes onto explain and I would add in *some men*:

> the underlying fear is not that a female athlete or coach will appear too plain or out of style, the real fear is that she will look like a dyke or, even worse, is one. This intense blend of homophobic and sexist standards of feminine attractiveness remind women in sport that to be acceptable, we must monitor our behaviour and appearance at all times. (Griffin 1992, p. 254)

Identity development and sexualities: confirming masculinity and femininity

In order to understand the gender identity of sport participants (mainly female), researchers have tended to focus on the 'sex role' of those who do and do not participate in physical activity. Over the last 35 years or so the majority of research has demonstrated that female athletes tend to be more 'masculine' than female non-athletes (e.g. Hoferek & Hanick 1985; Matteo 1986, 1988; Wrisberg et al. 1988; Harrison & Lynch 2005). In general, more female athletes than non-athletes were classified as androgynous (somewhere in the mid-range between feminine and masculine), with many identified as having masculine traits, while more female non-athletes than athletes were categorised as feminine. No evidence was found that female athletes, regardless of sport, experienced a significant amount of role conflict between their role as an athlete and as a girl/woman. A recent paper for the internationally acclaimed journal *Sex Roles* (Knoppers & McDonald 2010) noted that studies in this area were usually based on the premise that 'women athletes were masculinised through their sport participation, especially in sports that were gender-typed as masculine, and that these athletes had to cope with role conflict' (p. 313). Krane et al. (2004) would go on to explore this notion as the tension between 'living the paradox' as female athlete and woman. Research in this area is highly problematic in the sense that the sport types studied were identified *a priori* as masculine or feminine and so it was no surprise to find that females participating in, for example, rugby would be identified as more masculine. If I were to ask a group of students for qualities that would be demonstrated by any athlete wanting to compete successfully (and I have), I would expect to receive the following descriptors: competitive, powerful, aggressive, determined, skilful, and a risk-taker. Asking again why female athletes are often categorised as masculine or androgynous, it becomes clear why they would be labelled as such. Competitiveness implies having those qualities. It is not a determinant of sex or gender – or at least should not be perceived as such. One way of viewing this material is as a helpful critique of the ways in which research helps to foster or, perhaps more accurately, reflect societal beliefs about gender, sex and identity development and would be therefore worthy of a deeper investigation.

There are many psychological and sociological theories that relate to identity development; one of the simplest being the self-categorisation theory (Turner et al. 1987). Turner argues that the way in which we see ourselves depends on the categories with which we define ourselves. This is ultimately determined by the social context of a given situation. For example, I see myself as a hockey player because I spend most of my time playing or training for that sport, my friends know I play hockey and ask me about it and so the context supports that identity. Goffman's (1963) notion of the hierarchy of body idioms provides an additional lens to provide a way to comprehend the ways in which individuals embrace and use their bodies to judge themselves and others. Both Shilling (1993) and Sparkes (1997) use this idea to help identify the dominant body stories of our time. These dominant stories are those which become valued and promoted over others, such as non-disabled bodies over disabled and thin over fat (Sparkes 1997). Shilling (1993) infers that the body, especially within the affluent West, has become a project. It is something that can be worked at and developed to produce an ideal identity. Sparkes (1997) argues that people are not free to choose just any kind of body project; individuals exist within systems of meaning and are thus directed by them. Western society provides an array of technical gadgets to aid transformation (in the guise of diet pills and cosmetic surgery), equalling the number of physical activities that can help one reach the goal of the subjectively interpreted perfect body. The body is viewed as a social product. The meanings and characteristics attributed to that body help distinguish different groups and mark the boundaries between what is acceptable and what is not. For Foucault (1977, 1979), the body is the ultimate site of political and ideological control, surveillance and regulation. Foucault would argue that various state apparatuses, such as medicine, education and the law, come to determine the limits or boundaries of acceptable behaviour. Bodies that transgress established boundaries are punished, creating bodies that are rendered docile but equally, politically and economically useful to the state. In this way what we as the society come to determine as useful and acceptable bodies, are directed not only by social processes but also the meanings given to certain bodies by the groups to which we belong. The physical body, and in particular the sporting body, becomes a site where the promotion of dominant bodily ideals takes precedence.

From a Foucauldian point of view, 'identity can be understood as constructed via experiences that are linked to the workings of discourse, power relations, disciplinary techniques and processes of active self-negotiation' (Markula & Pringle 2006, p. 99). The cultural practices, in short the context in which we live, provide the disciplining. Butler's (1990) account of gender performativity is helpful at this point to examine the ways in which identity is shaped and maintained. She argues that gender is a kind of 'enforced cultural performance, compelled by compulsory heterosexuality and as such is performative' (Jagger 2008, p. 20). Gender is understood, not as an expression of what one is, but as something one does. The performative 'enacts or produces what it names' and as such, there is no gendered self separate from, or prior to, its constitution as a series of bodily gestures, movements and styles (Butler 1993). Using this premise, Shogan (1999) applies the argument to a sporting context and further supports the notion of gendered performance when she notes 'disciplined athletic bodies are not "natural" or "normal", and there is nothing "natural" or "normal" about a body disciplined as feminine or masculine. Femininity and masculinity, like sport skills, are acts or performances that must be learned' (p. 51). She reiterates this point by indicating that the 'experiences of "female athletes" don't just happen. These experiences are the consequences of certain sets of discourses and technologies that make possible these experiences and not others' (p. 47). Shogan is arguing, as is Butler, that we have to recognise that athletes are not simply performing (or perhaps merely reflecting) their inherent femininity or masculinity. Bodies are shaped and disciplined by the practices in which they are bound. For example, the ways in which rules are enforced for gendered sporting attire (for example men's and women's beach volleyball), rules relating to the use of force or violence in different sports (and its relative value), the performance of male and female American football players (NFL and Lingerie League), or the way in which we value pain in our athletes and encourage individuals to 'get up' or 'stop playing like a girl'.

These disciplining practices begin at a young age and have an impact in the development of self-esteem and body image (as I will discuss in more detail in the chapter 'The media, body image and youth sport'). Garrett provides a specific Australian example of the ways in which young girls position their bodies in the shaping and maintaining of their identity. In particular, her work focuses on the role of physical activity in this development and the school as the site for managing that process. Garrett's work highlights that girls position their bodies in a number of ways, each serving a particular purpose. For example, there is the 'comfortable body': one that indicated acceptance and satisfaction with body shape and size. Physical activity influences this by providing a 'fit' body but one that has to be constrained – 'not too big'. The 'bad body' reflected those bodies perceived to be too big and were associated with negative body image. This body was also surveilled and internalised notions of 'fat' as 'bad'. This influenced the girls to the extent that it prevented them from active participation in physical activity and encouraged a pursuit of thinness (2004, pp. 145–50). Positively, Garrett also found some girls resisting the primacy of body shape and size on identity development with the 'different body' position. Here girls perceived themselves to operate outside existing discourses of 'body as everything' and focused on alternative aspects of their lives to provide them with positive lived experiences (Garrett 2004, pp. 150–53). Garrett's work provides a way in which to view the beginnings of concern over the body that is reflected at a later age (Russell 2002, 2004), demonstrating the role physicality and the gendering practices of sport has on identity. Drummond's (2001, 2003, 2008) work (see following chapter) provides support for this impact on young boys, an often-overlooked area of research. His work supports the link between boys' abilities at sport and perceptions of masculinity; the more sporty and able, the more masculine. Sporting practices facilitate the positioning of those boys who can against those who cannot. In so doing positive masculinity becomes and is a *sporting* masculinity and a body is 'successful'. For girls and women this is a difficult balancing act. Sport and physical activity does provide a significant level of body satisfaction (Russell 2004) but it has to be tempered. Too much of a good thing is not a good thing. Women and girls in particular are positioned as instigators of their own self-surveillance, monitoring and restraining any actions that might lend themselves to the development of alternative femininities or sexualities – anything that may challenge the compulsory heterosexuality of school and sporting systems.

Coming out in Australia

In the last section of this chapter I will focus on the experience of athletes who have been either labelled as gay or lesbian or who have chosen to 'come out' about their sexuality.

Very few ever do so while still active in their sports, and this in itself reflects the level of homophobia (perceived or otherwise) that these individuals have experienced. Russell (2007) identifies that the lesbian label itself is not always necessarily a negative one. Indeed many women in her study found that the assumption by others (in this case an assumed identification as lesbian that was true) allowed them to actively participate in their chosen sport without ever having to 'come out'. Likewise certain sports (such as rugby and cricket) that had connotations as a lesbian sport were actively joined in order to provide a 'safe haven' to find other women who were accepting of not just an alternative physicality (and therefore femininity) but also a 'gay-friendly' environment. Jefferson-Lenskyj (1994) found a similar philosophy in the development of the Notso Amazon softball league in Toronto. Both of these studies may reflect a greater acceptance of women rather than men coming out in competitive sport, as it is often the stories of professional sportsmen coming out that challenge our assumptions of ability and masculinity.

Ian Roberts was a highly successful Rugby League player in Australia during the 1980s and 1990s playing for the North Queensland Cowboys, Manly-Warringah Sea Eagles and South Sydney Rabbitohs. He was a New South Wales State of Origin player as well as an Australian international player. In 1995 he became the first football player in Australia to come out as a gay man. Doing this while still playing meant weathering the resulting backlash both on and off the field. In the 2005 documentary 'The lost boy' for the series *Australian Story*, Roberts described many aspects of his life that reflected the ways in which his sporting context allowed him to position himself as a 'straight' man in order to hide his true sexuality. This provided him with protection:

> With footballers, I would say there's a general perception in the public that's fighting, booze and women, they kind of all clump in. It wouldn't take much for me, for it to trigger for me to hit another player. It was living up to an image that you know, there's no way that a gay man would do this, so I'm going to do it.

He goes onto to discuss other mechanisms through which he presented himself as far away from a gay man as possible:

> I can honestly say that I've never, never been sexually attracted to a female as far back as I can remember. I can promise you, you know, I don't say this with any sense of shame or pride, I've had sex with loads of females. It was just, like peer group pressure, it was almost, you kind of go along living up to that stereotype and living up to that persona that I'd already placed upon myself, that, that I'd grown up to believe was what it was to be a sportsperson in that situation. But, I can honestly say, I never ever questioned that I was gay. To perpetuate that image, I would, I would always have a girl on my arm at any of the functions we had at Souths, any of the official do's Rugby League had, I was always out with the boys. After a while, I mean, living an untruthful life like that continuously, the truth is, I was never happy.

Ultimately, Roberts reflects on the ways in which many sports, and not just Rugby League, limit the possibilities for alternative masculinities – and in this case sexualities too:

> Like anyone else, many homosexuals love and thrive on sport. Not for the perv, for the sport. For actual love of the sport! But the footy subculture finds it hard to accept that. And it will continue to do so as long as the culture as a whole persists with its hideous reliance on separating and defining masculinity and femininity, as if each sex should display only one possible set of traits.

Here Roberts mirrors what many women who also played rugby found; that they had to justify their participation in some way. Often this meant having to 'spell it out' that participation was for the love of the sport and not because of a sexual preference:

> the only reason I play rugby is because ... I enjoy it, I like the game, I like getting dirty, I like the aggression ... I'm an aggressive person on the pitch but not off ... I like the girls, I like the people. I don't play rugby to make a statement about my life, don't play rugby to make a statement about the fact that I can play a man's sport so there! ... don't play rugby because I can say I'm not homophobic and I can get in the shower with a bunch of lesbians ... I don't do it for any other reasons than that I enjoy the game and I like the people who play (Sue: Rugby) (Russell 2002).

Regardless of someone's sexual or sporting preference it is important for individuals to feel that they 'can' play if they wish to. Young people are being encouraged to participate in physical activity to overcome concerns over being overweight or for the health benefits associated with lifelong physical activity (see for example Bailey et al. 2004). What we can do is to be mindful of the ways in which we set boundaries for acceptable behaviour at a young age, the ways in which we may talk about men and women who do not appear to have a 'normal' looking appearance and we can all certainly encourage a wider view of gender that takes us beyond the simplified notion of just female and male.

References

Aitchison, C. C. (2007). Gender, sport and identity: introducing discourses of masculinities, femininities and sexualities. In C. C. Aitchison (Ed.). *Sport and gender identities: Masculinities, femininities and sexualities* (pp. 1–4). London: Routledge.

The lost boy (2005). *Australian Story*, 26 September. [Online]. Available: www.abc.net.au/austory/content/2005/s1469590.htm [accessed 19 January 2011]

Bailey, R. P., Wellard, I. & Dismore, H. (2004). *Girls' participation in physical actiity and sports: benefits, patterns, influences and ways forward.* Technical report for the World Health Organization. Geneva: WHO.

Butler, J. (1993). *Bodies that matter: on the discursive limits of sex.* New York: Routledge.

Butler, J. (1990). *Gender trouble: feminism and the subversion of identity.* New York: Routledge

Cahn, S. (1994). *Coming on strong: gender and sexuality in twentieth century women's sport.* Cambridge, Massachusetts: Harvard University Press.

Choi, P. L. (2000). *Femininity and the physically active woman*. London: Routledge.

Connell, R. W. (2002). *Gender*. Cambridge: Polity Press.

Connell, R. W. (1995). *Masculinities*. Cambridge: Polity Press.

Crawford, M. (2001). Gender and language. In R. K. Unger (Ed.). *Handbook of psychology of women and gender* (pp. 228–44). New Jersey: John Wiley.

Drummond, M. J. N. (2008). Sport, aging men, and constructions of masculinities. *Generations, 32*(1): 32–35.

Drummond, M. J. N. (2003). The meaning of boys' bodies in physical education. *Journal of Men's Studies, 11*(2): 131–43.

Drummond, M. J. N. (2001). Boys' bodies in the context of sport and physical activity: implications for health. *Journal of Physical Education New Zealand, 34*(1): 53-64.

Duncan. M. S. (1990). Sports photographs and sexual difference: images of women and men in the 1984 and 1988 Olympic Games. *Sociology of Sport journal, 7*(1): 22-43.

Dunning, E. (1994). Sport as a male preserve: notes on the sources of masculine identity and its transformations. In S. Birrell & C. L. Cole (Eds). *Women, sport, and culture* (pp. 163–79). Champaign, IL: Human Kinetics.

Evans, J., Davies, B. & Wright, J. (Eds). (2004). *Body knowledge and control: studies in the sociology of physical education and health*. New York: Routledge.

Fausto-Sterling, A. (2000). *Sexing the body: gender politics and the construction of sexuality*. New York: Basic Books.

Foucault, M. (1979). *The history of sexuality*. Vol. 1. London: Penguin.

Foucault, M. (1977). *Discipline and punishment: the birth of the prison*. London: Penguin.

Garrett, R. (2004). Gendered bodies and physical identities. In J. Evans, B. Davies & J, Wright. (Eds). *Body knowledge and control: studies in the sociology of physical education and health* (pp. 140–56). New York: Routledge.

Goffman, E. (1963). *Behaviour in public places: notes on the social organisation of gatherings*. New York: The Free Press.

Griffin, P. (1992). Changing the game: homophobia, sexism, and lesbians in sport. *Quest, 44*: 251–65.

Halbert, C. (1997). Tough enough and woman enough: stereotypes, discrimination, and impression management among women professional boxers, *Journal of Sport and Social Issues, 21*(1): 7–36.

Hargreaves, J. (1994). *Sporting females: critical issues in the history and sociology of women's sports*. London: Routledge.

Harrison, L. & Lynch, A. (2005). Social role theory and the perceived gender role orientation of athletes. *Sex Roles, 52*: 227–36.

Hoferek, M. & Hanick, P. (1985). Woman and athlete: toward role consistency. *Sex Roles, 12*: 687–95.

Jagger, G. (2008). *Judith Butler: sexual politics, social change and the power of the performative*. N.Y: Routledge.

Jefferson Lenskyj, H. (1994). Sexuality and femininity in sport contexts: issues and alternatives. *Journal of Sport and Social Issues, 18*: 356–76.

Kane, M. J. & Snyder, E. (1989). Sport typing: the social containment of women in sport. *Arena Review, 13*(2): 77–96.

Kessel, A. (2010). Caster Semenya may return to track this month after IAAF clearance. *Guardian,* 6 July, [Online]. Available: www.guardian.co.uk/sport/2010/jul/06/caster-semenya-iaaf-clearance [accessed 19 January 2011].

Kirk, D. (2006). The obesity crisis and school physical education. *Sport, Education and Society, 11*(2): 121–34.

Kitzinger, C. (2004). Sexualities. In R. K. Unger (Ed.). *Handbook of psychology of women and gender,* New Jersey: John Wiley.

Knoppers, A. & McDonald, M. (2010). Scholarship on gender and sport in Sex Roles and beyond. *Sex Roles, 63*: 311–23.

Koivula, N. (2001). Perceived characteristics of sports categorized as gender-neutral, feminine and masculine. *Journal of Sport Behaviour, 24*: 377–93.

Kolnes, L. J. (1995). Heterosexuality as on ongoing principle in women's sport. *International Review for the Sociology of Sport, 30*(1): 61–75.

Krane, V., Choi, P. Y. L, Baird, S. M. & Aimar, C. M. (2004). Living the paradox: female athletes negotiate femininity and muscularity. *Sex Roles, 50*(5–6): 315–29.

Markula, P. (2009) (Ed.). *Olympic women and the media: international perspectives.* Basingstoke: Palgrave MacMillan.

Markula, P. & Pringle, R. (2006). *Foucault, sport and exercise: power, knowledge and transforming the self.* London: Routledge

Matteo, S. (1988). The effect of gender-schematic processing on decisions about sex-inappropriate sport behavior. *Sex Roles, 18*: 41–58.

Matteo, S. (1986). The effect of sex and gender-schematic processing on sport participation. *Sex Roles, 15*: 417–432.

Metheney, E. (1965). Symbolic forms of movement: the feminine image in sports. In E. Metheney, *Connotations of movement in sport and dance* (pp. 43–56). Dubuque, IA: Brown.

Renold, E. (2005). *Girls, boys and junior sexualities: exploring children's gender and sexual relations in the primary school.* New York: RoutledgeFalmer.

Renold, E. (2003). If you don't kiss me, you're dumped: boys, boyfriends and heterosexualised masculinities in the primary school. *Educational Review, 55*(2): 179–91.

Russell, K. M. (2007). Queers, even in netball?: positive and negative interpretations of the lesbian label among sportswomen. In C. C. Aitchison (Ed.) *Sport and gender identities: masculinities, femininities and sexualities* (pp. 106–21). London: Routledge.

Russell, K. M. (2004). On vs off the pitch: the transiency of body satisfaction among female rugby players, cricketers, and netballers. *Sex Roles, 51*: 561–74

Russell, K. M. (2002). Women's participation motivation in rugby, cricket and netball: body satisfaction and identity. Unpublished PhD thesis, Coventry University.

Sabo, D. & Messner, M. A. (1993). Whose body is this? Women's sports and sexual politics. In G. L. Cohen. (Ed.) *Women in sport: issues and controversies* (pp. 15–25). California: Sage.

Sax, L. (2002). How common is intersex? A response to Anne Fausto-Sterling. *Journal of Sex Research,* 39(3): 174–78.

Scraton, S. (1992). *Shaping up to womanhood: gender and girls' physical education.* Milton Keynes, England: Open University.

Shilling, C. (1993). *The body and social theory.* London: Sage.

Shogan, D. (1999). *The making of high performance athletes: discipline, diversity and ethics.* Toronto: University of Toronto Press.

Sparkes, A. C. (1997). Reflections on the socially constructed physical self. In K. R. Fox (Ed.). *The physical self: from motivation to well being* (pp. 83–110). Champaign, IL: Human Kinetics.

Theberge, N. (1989). Women's athletics and the myth of frailty. In J. Freeman (Ed.). *Women: a feminist perspective* (4th Ed) (pp. 507–22). Mountain View, CA: Mayfield.

Turner, J. C, Hogg, M. A., Oakes, P. J., Reicher, S. D. & Wetherell, M. S. (1987). *Rediscovering the social group: a self categorization theory.* Oxford and New York: Basil Blackwell

Vertinsky, P. (1988). Of no use without health: late nineteenth century medical prescriptions for female exercise through the life span. *Women and Health,* 14(1): 89–115.

Wellard, I. (2009). *Sport, masculinities and the body.* New York: Routledge.

Whitson, D. (1990). Sport in the social construction of masculinity. In M. A. Messner & D. F. Sabo (Eds). *Sport, men and the gender order* (pp. 19–30). Champaign, IL: Human Kinetics.

World Health Organization (2010). *Gender, women and health.* [Online]. Available: www.who.int/gender/whatisgender/en/index.html [accessed 25 October 2010].

Wright, L. & Clarke, G. (1999). Sport, the media and the construction of compulsory heterosexuality: a case study of women's rugby union. *International Review for the Sociology of Sport,* 34(3): 227–43

Wrisberg, C., Draper, M. V. & Everett, J. (1988). Sex role orientations of male and female collegiate athletes from selected individual and team sports. *Sex Roles, 19*: 81–90.

6

Sport, the body and boys' constructions of masculinity

Murray Drummond

Sport has long been regarded as a site for the construction of masculinised behaviours. In the 1960s the belief that sport built character in men was readily accepted throughout society (Messner & Sabo 1994). Sport has become one of the most important sites of masculinising practice and socialised boys into many of the values, attitudes and skills considered so important in the adult world of men. Even prior to the 1960s, history provided evidence of the importance, that politicians and military leaders placed upon sport, for instilling in boys and young men the courage and strength necessary to defend the nation (Messner 1992; Whitson 1990). It was also around this time that sports were intended to emphasise and teach 'manly' values and behaviours (Messner 1992). This type of ideology was commonplace in the post-World War II era of most Western cultural nations including Australia.

While various sports offered men the opportunity to display a form of masculinity, it was the organised, competitive sports that were perceived as being the primary sites in which boys were taught to be 'tough', thereby creating men who fit dominant forms of masculinity (Messner 1992; Drummond 1996). According to Messner (1992) these sports demonstrated that men's bodies could sustain physical punishment and engage in violence in ways that made them superior to feminised bodies. This superiority is underpinned by the notion of hegemonic masculinity.

Hegemonic masculinity

According to Connell (1995), hegemonic masculinity in Western society is equated to male dominance and the oppression of femininities, and subordinated and marginalised masculinities. Donaldson (1993) claimed that 'hegemonic masculinity' is a term that has been 'invented' with its main emphasis placed on the critique of masculinity. Sport has played a major part in the formation and perpetuation of masculine hegemonic ideology. Organised sports in particular have often been revered as a central site for the construction of masculinity (Messner & Sabo 1990). Further, it has been speculated that organised sport develops a sense of male solidarity, which encourages men to identify with one another thus providing a medium for the regular rehearsal of masculine identification (Whitson

1990). The playing arena at training or in competition, the locker room, or social settings beyond the sporting context, such as bars or night clubs, are all locations in which this masculine identification and solidarity is reinforced. Boys' sport has been identified as a testing ground for uncomplicated admission into manhood (Drummond 2003).

Sport is sometimes viewed as the last bastion of male power and privilege now that many of the traditional male social bases are perceived to be eroding as a consequence of social change and the advent of the feminist movement (Messner 1992; Drummond 1996). Further, Whitson (1990) argued that men regard the sporting domain as a stable environment in which masculinist ideals are upheld in the face of a culture perceived as becoming increasingly feminised.

The importance of sport as a masculinising institution

It could be claimed that sport plays an important role in the masculinisation of every male. Boys are introduced to sport at an early age. Without prior experience, it is the initial school year that acquaints them with the realm of sports. However, even before this period boys notice sport on television and pictures in newspapers, and quickly establish that the majority of people who play sport are men. Furthermore, it is generally their fathers, and other men, who take the most interest in sport whether it be watching or participating. Accordingly, Messner reported that the men involved in his research 'were introduced to organised sport by older brothers and fathers and, once involved, found themselves playing within an exclusively male world' (1992, p. 30). Additionally he suggested that as a consequence of sport being an exclusive male domain the men came to equate masculinity with competition, physical strength and skills while believing that girls did not, or could not, participate in such activities. Thus, sport establishes, and then highlights gender differences early in a man's life. As a boy he comes to view men and women as significantly different by the segregation of sexes in sport either as a participant in school sporting activities or as a spectator of adult sports.

The body becomes an important sociological tool where masculinity and sports are concerned. Through recognition of the sex-segregated, gendered activity of organised sport men perceive their bodies differently from women. A man's body has the capacity to confer masculinity upon him by using it in forceful and space occupying ways, and it is through sports that he can legitimately display such qualities. Rendering another man unconscious on the football field in applying a legitimate tackle is commonly seen as a signature of toughness and rugged masculinity yet, away from the playing arena it is a crime. Sport provides men with the opportunity to use their bodies as a display of masculine hierarchy. Not only is toughness a sign of masculinity but also being successful, regardless of body shape or size, is significant. Competition is important to men because it allows them to prove what their body is capable of achieving. Therefore heightened masculinity is achieved through winning and being successful.

The interrelationships that exist between masculinity and sports abound. Some men enjoy competition to demonstrate how well their body can perform; others see it as a legitimate arena in which they can prove their manhood by exhibiting strength and vigour. Whatever the reasons, men perceive sport as their territory. However, they are beginning to feel threatened and fear the intrusion of women in a similar manner to the way they intruded the masculine domain of the workplace. Thus it is arguable that men's sport is becoming more hegemonic in terms of masculinity in a bid to ward off feminist infiltration.

Boys, sport and masculinity

There is an underpinning notion that within contemporary Western culture a boy's social and cultural development is heavily influenced by the values attributed to sport (Connell 1983, 1990, 1995; Whitson 1990; Hayward & Mac an Ghaill 1996; Swain 2000). Booth provides an historical perspective to this argument claiming that New Zealand schools embraced rugby as a means by which 'the value of hard work, and determination, cooperation and teamwork, and character' (2000, p. 54) could be taught. Zavos concurs by claiming schoolboy rugby 'is one of those tribal experiences that has helped to create that unique and under-rated species, the New Zealand male' (1988, p. 118). Where boys are concerned, sport is often perceived as a rite of passage (Connell 1990; Messner 1992 and boys who do not engage in sport and physical activity are often marginalised, reinforcing the cultural perception that sport is a primary site for the social construction of masculinity (Whitson 1990; Davison 2000). Those boys who are good at sport are often popular among peers thereby enhancing self-esteem, self-image, and masculine identity due to the creation of dominant and subordinate groups (Wienke 1998; Swain 2000; Drummond 2003). Boys who are less skilled in the area of sport and school physical education, are often ridiculed thereby negatively impacting on their self-perception as 'worthy' males (Swain 2000). In addition such boys are often confronted with the possibility of total abstention from all forms of physical activity during childhood and adolescence through fear of failure and ridicule.

According to Baum (1998) it is the period of adolescence that is crucial in developing lifelong learning principles associated with long-term physical activity habits. It is also a crucial period in the development of self, body and masculine identity (Drummond 2003). Positive experiences in sport and physical activity have the capacity to enhance these domains. However, by disassociating themselves from sport and physical pursuits, these boys further limit skill development thereby reducing confidence to enter many forms of physical activity both now and later in life. The importance of physical activity for everyone where health and longevity are concerned is paramount. Not having the skills and ability to feel comfortable about pursuing physical activity throughout life may have detrimental effects on lifelong health (Drummond 2001). Apart from immediate social, emotional and psychological concerns for boys who abstain from physical activity, there are implications for their health as adult men later in life (Drummond 1996, 2008). Indeed, for these men, physical activity may be seen as a barrier and may not become an integral component of their lives. As the levels of obesity continue to rise for certain groups of men (Pritchard et al. 1997) physical activity becomes crucial to men's overall health and wellbeing.

There are certain societal expectations for boys to be accomplished at sport and physical activity. According to Gard and Meyenn (2000) those who do not live up to these ideals may feel unskilled and awkward. Additionally, abstaining from physical pursuits may become a meaningful alternative by eliminating the possibility of ridicule and humiliation. As a consequence their masculine identity is less likely to be challenged. It is within the masculinised arena of sports that one's masculinity is constantly being threatened and disputed. According to Curry (1991) challenges from peers are continually set down particularly in terms of appearance or size, performance, aggression, violence, as well as off-field behaviour. It is arguable, however, that competitive and skilful sporting performance is likely to override all of these masculine determinants (Drummond 1996). For the boys who do display high levels of skill and ability, and feel at ease participating in sports and physical activities, opportunities arise to continue engaging in a range of activities throughout their life as they develop sound motor skills and meaningful relationships with such activities. Due to the underpinning social and cultural importance that is placed on sport and physical activity for boys, the acquisition of such complex skills is likely to play a major role in enhancing one's masculine image and positive self-esteem.

Boys develop at various physiological and psychological rates (Pope et al. 2000). Those who mature early and display mesomorphic physiques have a distinct advantage over other boys, particularly in physical contact sports where size, musculature and strength are integral to success (Drummond 2003). Pope and colleagues (2000) argue that psychologically, boys who develop earlier have a distinct advantage at that time, where self-esteem and positive body identity is concerned. Regarding physical ability there is a greater likelihood that these boys will have the capacity to carry out strength tasks with relative ease over boys the same age. Such physical capacity is likely to promote positive self-esteem including masculine identity as a consequence of ongoing praise and recognition. As Pope et al. claim 'muscular bodies are strong, and they symbolize power, virility, and masculinity' (2000, p. 180).

While strong muscular boys may develop a positive masculine identity through their body, the same cannot be said for boys who are small and frail in size, and have developed a resultant poor body image and self-esteem. Similarly this cannot be assumed for boys who are overweight or obese. Davison (2000) who discussed some of these issues in his self-reflective paper on childhood physical education lessons claimed that changing clothes before and after physical education lessons was a significant deterrent for him and many boys. Embrey and Drummond (1997) concur in their research citing many of the boys interviewed identified showering, playing shirts on/shirts off competitions and scheduling swimming lessons with girls was problematic through being forced to display their bodies. It was claimed that having bodies that deviate significantly from the archetypal Western cultural male body, such as being overweight or underweight, was influential in determining one's positive or negative masculine identity.

The research underpinning this chapter will provide evidence on the way in which sport plays such a pivotal role in the construction of a boy's masculine identity. It will also highlight the issues boys face when they do not live up to certain archetypal sporting masculine ideals as well as the associated feelings of inadequacy where their bodies are concerned. In the following sections, the voices of boys will be presented to emphasise aspects linked to perceptions of bodies, sport and personal identity. Rich descriptive data emanating from boys who have been identified by their physical education teacher as being either highly skilled or less skilled in the area of sport and physical activity will be drawn upon. While it is important to understand the positive elements of sport and physical activity in the lives of boys, it is just as significant to understand the implications of not living up to certain social and cultural sporting ideals which suggest that boys must be proficient at sport and display high levels of skill and aptitude.

The research

This research is based on in-depth qualitative interviews with adolescent males ranging from 14 to 17 years of age. The primary reason for choosing boys in this age range is due to this period being one of immense physical and emotional change with respect to the body. As Davison has highlighted 'the high school "tweenage" years are particularly ripe for the exploration of gender identity negotiation and construction' (2000, p. 255). Additionally, it is possible to argue that boys are somewhat under-researched as a cohort when it comes to masculinities, sport and the body. Twenty-four males were interviewed within this research project with ten of the participants being identified as outstanding sporting achievers. The remaining 14 boys were identified by their physical education teachers as being non-achievers in sport and school physical activity. Similarly, these boys were also identified as those who abstain from physical education lessons and sporting involvement. The primary reason for utilising boys from opposite ends of the sporting spectrum, in terms of ability and participation, was to provide a basis upon which points of comparison could be made in order to understand the role of sport in the lives of boys.

In-depth interviews provide a rich source of data (Van Manen 1990; Osborne 1994) allowing for exploration of questions relating to meanings, perceptions, and expectations of male bodies within the context of masculinity. A guided questionnaire was used in conjunction with an unstructured interview method thereby enhancing information-rich descriptions of the boys and reflections of their body perceptions. Utilising open-ended questions and emphatic reflection 'helped to deepen the participants' self-exploration and explicate meanings and to limit the imposition of interviewer bias' (Webb & Daniluk 1999).

Most of the interviews with the boys were conducted within the school at which they attended. Despite being in the vicinity of a teacher at all times, they were not within 'ear shot' and therefore had the capacity to provide information without fear of retribution. Some of the older boys were interviewed at their homes, given their less structured timetables. In these cases a parent was at home at all times, but once again not in the vicinity where they could listen in. All of the boys' parents or caregivers provided written consent to be involved in the research as stipulated by the Institutional Human Research Ethics Committee guidelines. The interviews, which were recorded, took approximately one hour to complete with shorter follow-up interviews conducted where necessary to clarify issues. They were then transcribed verbatim and analysed using inductive thematic analysis to identify dominant themes.

Themes

There were a number of significant themes to emerge from the data. However, the dominant themes were essentially based around the implications of what the body looked like, particularly in terms of size, and what the body could do. Sport played in an integral part in these given that sport had the potential to vindicate certain body types with respect to the sports in which these bodies engaged or the body that was created through these sports. Indeed, questions were raised in terms of the meaning of masculinity if the boy did not live up to certain archetypal ideals around body shape and size as well as simply engaging in, or being skilled at masculinised sports. The following are some of the major themes to emerge.

Size, strength and masculinity

For the majority of the boys in this research, similar with much of the data that I have collected over the past 15 years, the size of one's body plays a significant role in the construction of masculine identity. There is a taken-for-granted assumption by the majority of the boys in this research that size and muscularity equates to strength, which in turn reflects one's masculinity. Accordingly the boys perceived the more masculine sports as those that require more strength and therefore muscularity by its participants. As one of the boys stated:

> I would like to be stronger, but then every guy would, so I can do more things. The more muscular you are the more things you can do better. I guess that goes for all aspects of life.

Another boy suggested that with a bigger body he would have the capacity to endure the rigours of masculinised sports far better. A bigger body was seen as integral to successful participation in masculinised sports.

> Yeah, I like my body. I guess I want to be a bit bigger to be able to take the hits a little better. I guess I am still young when it comes to playing league football. But it's a man's game and you have to be able to take it.

Contemporary Western culture places an inordinate amount of emphasis on the visual aspect of muscularity as being a key to the archetypal masculine male. Indeed, it is arguable that the majority of males who endorse such a notion are sportsmen whether consciously within paid advertisements that adorn billboards or sports and popular culture magazines, internet sites and television programs, or unknowingly as their images are displayed within the act of sporting participation throughout the same media. Regardless, the bodies of sportsmen provide young males with the opportunity to scrutinise and reflect upon the archetypal physique. Noteworthy, many of the physiques that are presented are those which are highly muscular or displaying acts of strength and immense physicality. It is the socially constructed endorsement of the archetypal male body through sports that places many boys in an invidious position. Some boys simply do not have the capacity to ever look like the men they see in such images while there are other boys who do not engage in masculinised sports for fear of retribution through their perceived lack of skill and physical ability. One of the boys articulated this notion well when he claimed:

> I would like to be stronger. I guess all my friends are stronger than me. So I would like to be able to beat them in arm wrestles and stuff and be more competitive. Looking stronger is always important for guys too.

Another boy reiterated this type of claim by stating:

> The thing is I am never happy with myself. I have always wanted to improve my body. I guess I find it's attractive to have a bigger body you know, because people think 'I don't want to start a fight with him because he's pretty big.'

It is clear from these comments that the body is central to the boys notion of contemporary masculinity. They view the body in terms of its physical size, its muscularity and its strength. The reasons for wanting to acquire a body that is strong, muscular and athletic is based upon 'looking' formidable as well as defeating opponents. These are key concepts within their constructions of masculinity. They view their bodies, as somewhat separate entities that can be shaped and manipulated at will. The following comment is representative of such a claim:

> I don't feel that good about my body and I don't like the way it looks. I would like to improve it. I would like to improve the fitness and I would like to have a big body, you know, muscly. Because I have always been into muscles and that sort of thing. I have always followed wrestling and I saw the wrestlers with big bodies. I look at them in awe.

It was not only in reference to their own bodies that these adolescent males discussed size, strength and masculinity. They also articulated their perceptions of other sportsmen in particular as men whom they admire. The reference to archetypal masculine figures was not only based on their strong, muscular aesthetic but also the controlling position they played on the ground and the dominant role that they played on the team. For example, one boy claimed his idols were the 'big men who play in controlling positions on the ground. They are the focal point of the team'. This boy was referring to both the centre half-forward and centre half-back within an Australian football team. These positions on the field, and the players who play in these positions are often seen as pivotal to the team. They are generally tall, strong and muscular. It is not uncommon for the sportsman in the centre half-forward, in particular, to be the captain of the team or at least recognised as a leader.

The body as a machine

Australian Rules football, in particular that which is played at the elite Australian Football League (AFL) level, was regularly identified as one of the sports that was highly masculinised. The players within the AFL were revered for their ability to engage in a highly skilled sport. They were revered more, however, for their capacity to engage in brutal body contact within the laws of the game. This was seen as being integral to the sport. While the boys were aware that they did not have the capability to replicate the intensity and physicality of the elite level footballers at this stage of their lives, they did have the opportunity to mimic certain types of behaviour in terms of using their bodies in a utilitarian manner to display acts of masculinity on the field. As one of the boys stated, 'I guess I see my body as a type of machine. It's there to do a job.' He further articulated this utilitarian ideology by suggesting that the some of the foods that he eats are not based on taste but rather providing 'fuel' for his body. He stated:

> I know I only eat some foods to give me fuel. I mean they don't taste great like chips or chocolate but stuff like pasta, and heaps of it, give you energy to perform.

This is certainly an interesting ideological perspective but is quite understandable, given the nature of sporting parlance within the media and now a broader contemporary culture that has been influenced by sports science terminology. Indeed it is arguable that school physical education, particularly at the higher year levels, condone and reinforces such notions as energy systems in which the body is seen as a machine where energy input must equal output to partake adequately in sporting contests. There is also a strong undertone within this ideological construct that the body is malleable and can be fixed when broken. It certainly does not take into consideration the associated psychosocial issues of pain, recuperation and possibly forced retirement that many participants must endure.

It is this notion of using the body as a machine that has the potential for immense implications for young males and the way in which they perceive themselves and their bodies. Early research into sport and masculinity by Messner (1992) identified this as the 'instrumental male' and Connell (1990) suggested that the body becomes the intense focus of the self.

As Messner (1992) identifies, the notion of regarding one's body as a machine or instrument is seen in a positive light within sports. Further he suggests that the 'instrumental male' is a somewhat alienated creature who can be goal oriented in work and personal relations while viewing others as objects that can be manipulated and defeated to achieve personal goals (Messner 1992). Therefore, in competitive sports where winning is a desirable outcome, perceiving one's body as a machine is seen as important element in gaining success. Indeed for the highly skilled young males involved in this research the greater the level of machine-like behaviour that is displayed the more success is perceived to eventuate. If the body is perceived as a machine and disassociated with emotion it provides the opportunity for the coaches of such masculinised sports to urge their players to 'attack' the ball and 'throw' themselves into packs, as the young males suggested, with the understanding that their bodies will heal if they happen to be injured. This ideology is often accepted and embraced as team ethos where, in turn, it is confirmed and reinforced.

Successful and unsuccessful bodies

The object of the original research was to investigate the meaning of masculinity and sports for boys who were identified by their physical education teacher as being skilled or less skilled at sports and physical activities. Therefore perceived success and failure were at the essence of many of the responses from the boys. It is noteworthy that the boys associated 'the body' with these elements of success or failure. It was evident amongst these boys that 'being good at sport', and having success, enhanced one's masculine identity, whether it be personal masculine identity or perceived masculine identity. Therefore for the boys in this research, success and sporting ability equated to positive masculinity. Some of the boys talked about winning and defeating opponents which, based on the socially constructed notion of success in sports, made them feel superior and dominant. As one of the boys stated:

> If I lose a game I go nuts, I can't stand it. I run around in circles, I climb the walls, I'm not a happy boy. I'm not approachable at that stage. But then again when I win again I'm quite happy. And after, you get a bit of a rush I suppose, a high feeling, a bit of euphoria or whatever.

Most of the boys, however, identified the exhilaration at simply engaging in sport and physical activity, and being able to use their body in a physical manner. Additionally there were many aspects of sport and physical activity beyond the element of winning that were appealing and provided them with a sense of wellbeing. For example, being a part of a team and developing camaraderie was important, as well as the involvement of parents, friends and peers. These were all critical in the significance of sport and physical activity in their lives. As one of the boys stated:

> The best thing I can remember about sport was when I was running in the final of the 400m event at state all schools championships. Hartley [secondary school] needed to win this final event to take out the championships. And this was against the private schools as well. I remember coming off the final bend knowing that I was in front. The crowd was going berserk and it carried me home. I did a PB [personal best] in that race and everyone just came up and swamped me and was cheering and stuff. It was the best. I had won for the school not just for myself.

The same boy described his sheer enjoyment at 'being able to run fast' and that in running fast 'you feel like your body is made to do it, just made to run fast. It's so hard to describe'. Another boy articulated the meaning of his positive relationship with sport and physical activity by emphasising the way in which he relished the opportunity to push his body 'to its limits'. In particular he enjoyed the euphoria that would wash over him after a hard training session knowing that 'you have achieved something'.

It is these types of comments that are critical to understanding the meaning and significance of sport and physical activity to some boys as well as the ease of physicality that some boys experience and the manner in which it impacts positively on their masculine identity. Conversely, the comments from boys who do not have similar positive experiences are stark and provide evidence of the significance that sport and physical activity play in the masculinisation process. It was the seemingly 'unsuccessful' bodies that emerged through the lack of skill and ability in sport and physical activity that impacted the way in which in these boys perceived themselves and their masculinity. One of the boys with a European background was vocal in his frustration at not being good at sports, which he regarded as integral to his European masculine heritage. He stated:

> European handball was one I hated and soccer. I guess it's because I can't really play them that well. I don't really have the experience and skills in games like that. I can't run and kick the ball at the same time. Like, you see the good soccer players on TV and they run

> and keep kicking the ball. I try to do that and it's impossible. I end up missing it or kicking badly and it goes in the wrong direction.

Another boy, like most of the others who were less skilled at sport and physical activity, claimed to be less popular than those boys who were more adept at sports and physical activity. This was evident in one of the boys' comments when he stated:

> No, I'm not very popular. I know because of the way some of the kids treat me. I guess me and my friends are a quiet group and the other kids think that's weird. I'm not really good at sport.

Such a comment provides evidence to suggest that sport plays a significant role in the socialisation and masculinisation process of young males in contemporary Australian society. In particular it highlights the way in which sport has come to be perceived as a normalised practice for boys. Such a notion carries ramifications for boys who do not enjoy sports or physical activities and therefore abstain from these activities.

One important distinction that emerged within this research was the recognition of these boys by themselves and others as being 'not good at sport' and yet most of the boys engaged in some kind of physical activity that was not traditionally sport-based such as the sports played and taught at school. While discussing the types of the sports in which they like to engage, many of these boys identified alternative activities such as BMX cycling or skateboarding or hiking. These are critical factors that need to be taken into consideration when discussing boys, sport and the process of masculinisation. Simply because they do not engage in stereotypical masculinised sports such as Australian Rules football or cricket and rugby, does not necessarily mean that these boys do not engage in physical activities. While there are many boys who do not engage, this notion provides the opportunity to explore ways of alternative pathways to physical activity participation. Indeed it may be the confines of the physical education environment at school that thwarts students' capacity to meaningfully engage in activities. One of the boys identified that while he played community-based basketball at a high level he did not participate in school due to, what he perceived as the draconian 'authoritarian' nature of the school sport and physical education system.

Conclusion

This chapter has attempted to identify the issues that young males face in contemporary Western culture surrounding sport, masculinity and the body. Navigating oneself through boyhood can be a difficult situation for boys who do not live up to archetypal expectations of what a male is 'supposed to be' in terms of sporting and physical activity participation. Being good at sport is seemingly a rite of passage for boys. As this chapter has identified, those boys who are good at sports and physical activity appear to enjoy the physicality of sport and using their bodies in what they would argue as a meaningful manner. Therefore they appear to have a stronger sense of masculine identity given the intrinsic benefits accrued through this physicality as well as the positive identification from others. The less skilled boys tended to have less positive self-perception, given the significance of their identity being inextricably linked to the socially constructed nature of boys supposedly being good at sports.

Understanding the meaning of sport and masculinity for boys has important implications for physical educators as well junior sports coaches and professional who engage with children and physical activity. We must be mindful that not all boys are going to be good at sports and physical activity. Indeed, not all boys will like sports and physical activity for a range of reasons beyond being less skilled. This certainly provides a dilemma for the ongoing physical activity participation for boys as they move into adolescence and on to adulthood where men's health issues, associated with lifestyle disease, is becoming a major concern. There is a need to establish alternative pathways into physical activity engagement for young males beyond the realm of sports. There is also a need to challenge the traditional masculinised sporting model in schools and champion other forms of sporting and physical activity endeavours as meaningful to the establishment of masculinity. Using contemporary approaches to engage boys in sports and physical activity other than the football, cricket, rugby, soccer model will enhance opportunities for engagement in heightening masculine identity. This means tapping into contemporary ideology around meaningful experiences for boys such as hip-hop dance, Capoiera and martial arts to name a few. While there are many boys who do like skateboarding, surfing, rock climbing and BMX cycling these are particularly litigious and costly activities within schools but must not be discounted as important masculinising activities. Contemporary physical education must adapt to engage with contemporary males otherwise an entire of generation of boys may be divided over, and therefore some lost to, sport and physical activity participation. This has immense implications for the masculinisation process of males as well as their health and the capacity to feel comfortable about engaging in sport and physical activity throughout their lives.

References

Baum, F. (1998). *The new public health: an Australian perspective.* South Melbourne: Oxford University Press.

Booth, D. (2000). Modern sport: emergence and experiences. In C. Collins (Ed.). *Sport in New Zealand society* (pp. 45–63). Palmerston North: Dunmore Press.

Connell, R. W. (1995). *Masculinities*. St Leonards, NSW: Allen & Unwin.

Connell, R. W. (1990). An iron man: the body and some contradictions of hegemonic masculinity. In M. Messner & D. Sabo (Eds). *Sport, men and the gender order: critical feminist perspectives* (pp. 83–95). Champaign, IL: Human Kinetics.

Connell, R. W. (1983). Men's bodies. *Australian Society, 2*(9): 33–39.

Curry, T. (1991). Fraternal bonding in the locker room: a profeminist analysis of talk about competition and women. *Sociology of Sport Journal, 8*: 119–35.

Davison, K. (2000). Boys' bodies in school: physical education. *The Journal of Men's Studies, 8*(2): 255–66.

Donaldson, M. (1993). What is hegemonic masculinity? *Theory and Society, 22*: 643–57.

Drummond, M. (2008). Sport, aging men, and constructions of masculinities. *Generations, 32*(1): 32–35.

Drummond, M. (2003). The meaning of boys' bodies in physical education. *Journal of Men's Studies, 11*(2): 131–43.

Drummond, M. (2001). Boys' bodies in the context of sport and physical activity: implications for health. *Journal of Physical Education New Zealand, 34*(1): 53–64.

Drummond, M. (1996). The social construction of masculinity as it relates to sport: an investigation into the lives of elite male athletes competing in individually oriented masculinised sports. Unpublished PhD thesis, Edith Cowan University, Perth, Australia.

Embrey, L. & Drummond, M. (1996). *Boys' and physical education project.* Report for Healthway. Western Australian Health Department.

Gard, M. & Meyenn, R. (2000). Boys, bodies, pleasure and pain: interrogating contact sports in schools. *Sport. Education and Society, 5*(1): 19–34.

Hayward, C. & Mac an Ghaill, M. (1996). Schooling masculinities. In: Mac an Ghaill (Ed.). *Understanding Masculinities* (pp. 55–60). Buckingham: Open University Press.

Messner, M. (1992). *Power at play.* Boston: Beacon Press.

Messner, M. & Sabo, D. (Eds) (1994). *Sex violence & power in sports: rethinking masculinity.* Freedom, CA: Crossing Press.

Messner, M. & Sabo, D. (Eds) (1990). *Sport, men and the gender order: critical feminist perspectives.* Champaign, IL: Human Kinetics.

Osborne, J. (1994). Some similarities and differences among phenomenological and other methods of pshychological qualitative research. *Canadian Psychology, 35:* 167–89.

Pope, H., Phillips, K. & Olivardia, R. (2000). *The Adonis complex: the secret crisis of male body obsession.* New York: The Free Press.

Pritchard, J., Nowson, C. & Wark, J. (1997). A worksite program for overweight middle-aged men achieves lesser weight loss with exercise than with dietary change. *Journal of the American Dietetic Association, 97*(1): 37–42.

Swain, J. (2000). The money's good, the fame's good, the girls are good: the role of playground football in the construction of young boys' masculinity in junior school. *British Journal of Sociology of Education, 21*(1): 97–106.

Van Manen, M. (1990). *Researching lived experience.* Ann Arbor, MI: Althouse.

Webb, R. & Daniluk, J. (1999). The end of the line: infertile men's experiences of being unable to produce a child. *Men and Masculinities, 2*(1): 6–25.

Whitson, D. (1990). Sport in the social construction of masculinity. In M. Messner & D. Sabo (Eds). *Sport, men and the gender order: critical feminist perspectives* (pp. 19–29). Champaign, IL: Human Kinetics.

Zavos, S. (1988). In praise of rugby. In M. King (Ed.). *One of the boys? Changing views of masculinity in New Zealand.* Auckland: Heinemann.

7

Can any*body* play? An introduction to the sociology of sport and disability

Nikki Wedgwood

Although most young people with impairments have the same preoccupations, interests and desires as their able-bodied peers – study, work, leisure, family, friends, sex and money – their experiences of growing up are often tainted by exclusion from everyday activities and ordinary relationships (Murray 2002, p. 13). Thus they experience much greater social isolation and loneliness than other disadvantaged groups, and suffer poorer health and wellbeing as a consequence (Shakespeare 2006, p. 170; Emerson et al. 2008). These negative outcomes are not purely the result of having an impairment but rather of the way in which ableist societies treat those of its members with visible differences. Indeed, despite the fact people with impairments in Australia have long been deinstitutionalised, thus are no longer physically segregated from the able-bodied majority, a form of 'social apartheid' continues today in more subtle, insidious forms (Goggin & Newell 2005). Therefore, in this chapter 'impairment' refers to a physiological condition, whereas 'disability' refers to the way society 'disables' people with impairments through attitudes, policies and built environments that exclude, oppress and/or make it difficult to participate in mainstream society.

These lower levels of social inclusion are apparent in every facet of life, including sport (ABS 2007). In developed countries the participation of people with impairments, who generally engage in less physical activity than their non-disabled counterparts (Sport England 2001; Murphy & Carbone 2008), is increasingly being promoted through government initiatives (EFDS 2004). In Australia this has been done through the Australian Sports Commission's Disability Sport Unit and federal programs like Project CONNECT and SportsAbility. This trend is partly due to greater financial imperatives for governments to encourage all of their citizens to be healthy and therefore less of an economic burden. It is also due to recent shifts towards more socially inclusive policies, coupled with the belief that sport for people with impairments promotes social inclusion. For instance, in one government report, sports participation with diverse others has been credited with the ability to 'overcome prejudice and discrimination (on the grounds of ethnicity, social background or disability, for example) and ... play a role in achieving an inclusive society' (Hannon 2005, p. 25).

Yet, people with impairments are not a homogenous group. Thus, although the health benefits of sports participation may be universal, other aspects of their sporting experiences will vary due to a wide range of factors. These include: type of impairment (physical, intellectual, sensory, congenital/acquired, visible/invisible and/or multiple); severity of impairment (mild, moderate or severe); and sporting context (disability-specific or able-bodied, elite or amateur, community-based or school-based, formal or informal and/or individual or team), along with social factors like class, race, sexuality, age and gender. Moreover, 'sport' is neither a monolithic institution nor a cure-all. Nor is it unusual for sports participation to heighten and underscore prejudice and discrimination, for instance on the grounds of ethnicity, class and/or gender (Foley 1990). This is because sport is not just a physical activity but is also a powerful social institution. That is to say sports do not develop in a social vacuum but rather they arise out of specific social and historical contexts, thus are often developed in accordance with the interests of dominant social groups and thereby reproduce broad social structures like gender, ethnicity, class and ableism (Messner 1990; Washington & Karen 2001; Anderson 2003). Indeed, sport ritually celebrates physical abilities as well as male superiority and thus is imbued with ableism. Yet, the sporting arena can also be the site of subversion, challenges or resistance to unequal power relations. It can sometimes be the site of both simultaneous reproduction and resistance (Hargreaves 1994). Thus, although sports do tend to reproduce dominant culture, they are deeply contradictory and also have the potential to transform culture (Hargreaves 1994, p. 289). Sport is neither a realm of absolute oppression nor an arena of absolute freedom and spontaneity, thus it must be examined within a theory that views human beings as active subjects who operate within historically constituted structural constraints (Gruneau 1983, p. 98).

The broad question then, for sports sociologists and sports providers alike, is: In what ways does sport reproduce and/or challenge ableism? With this question in mind, this chapter looks at the role of sport in the lives, not just of the minority of youth with impairments who play sport, but also the majority who do not. In the process it will briefly introduce some sociological concepts including: embodiment, governmentality, medical and social models of disability and hegemonic masculinity. The chapter is organised around several themes – social inclusion, gender and the body/empowerment – and concludes with a consideration of some of the implications for physical educators.

Sport and social inclusion

Along with improved general health and fitness from regular physical activity (WHO 2003), people with impairments also accrue the additional benefits of decreased rates of hospitalisation, co-morbidities and psychological sequelae associated with impairment (Rimmer 1999). Participation in sport, as opposed to physical activity alone, is said to have the added benefits of: enhancing feelings of wellbeing; reducing tension, anxiety and depression; improving self-concept, self-esteem and self-efficacy; and increasing the ability to perform daily activities (Hutzler & Bar-Eli 1993; Sherrill & Williams 1996). Sports participation may also help people with physical impairments to enhance pride in their bodies, redefine their physical capabilities and increase their confidence to pursue other physical activities (Blinde & McClung 1997; Guthrie 1999). It has also been associated with social integration (Blinde & Taub 1999). Indeed, from its earliest days disability sport has been credited with promoting the social inclusion of people with impairments into able-bodied society. Inspired by his patients' attempts to devise their own wheelchair sports and building on the competitive nature of his (mostly) young male patients, the neurosurgeon Sir Ludwig Guttman pioneered the use of sport in the physical, psychological and social rehabilitation of people with spinal cord injuries (Anderson 2003). He believed competition with able-bodied sportspeople would 'create a better understanding between the disabled and able-bodied and help the disabled in their social reintegration through the medium of sport' (Guttmann 1976, p. 13).

Like Guttman, some sociologists are keen to point out the social advantages of participating in sport for people with impairments. For instance, it is argued that playing sport can: enhance relations with peers (Taub & Greer 2000); expand social interactions, experiences and networks; and initiate other social activities (Blinde & McClung 1997). For children with impairments, playing sport is said to legitimate their social identity as 'typical' children and provide an opportunity to learn social skills like cooperation, sociability and forming alliances (Taub & Greer 2000). For physically impaired adults it is argued that sports participation can enhance perceptions of their effectiveness as social actors (Blinde & Taub 1999) and counter stigmatisation by giving able-bodied people the opportunity to see their athletic *abilities* (Taub et al. 1999). Yet, these positive experiences are far from universal. To begin with, of the few people with impairments who participate in sport, most do so in 'insular disability-specific clubs, organisations and competitions' (Hargreaves 2000, p. 202), which is unlikely to promote social inclusion into broader, able-bodied society. Even when they do participate in sport with their able-bodied peers, social integration is not necessarily always an outcome. Many young people with impairments who attend mainstream schools have negative experiences of physical education (Aitchison 2000, pp. 18–19; Finch et al. 2001). This is because social integration is not just a matter of adding people with impairments to able-bodied sport and stirring:

> Some [able-bodied] students do not develop an understanding for and tolerance of their classmates with disabilities. This problem becomes especially obvious during competitive activities in which winning is important to students. (Lienert et al. 2001, p. 10)

Thus a simple positive association between sport and the social inclusion of people with impairments belies a reality which is far more complex and contradictory.

Sport and gender

Experiences of social inclusion (or exclusion) are likely to vary widely according to sporting context, life phase, gender and so on. In the lives of male able-bodied adolescents, for instance, sport is one of the primary practices in which they construct their gender identities and their relationships with other males and thus is a source of kudos – those who excel at (not simply participate in) sport are often at the top of the peer hierarchy at school (Walker 1988; Foley 1990; Parker 1996; Wedgwood 2003). This is because men and boys in developed societies are not automatically considered 'masculine' merely on the basis that they are male. On the contrary, masculinity is conferred by one's male peers, thus cannot be assumed. For a boy to be called a 'sissy' or to be told that he runs or throws a ball 'like a girl' by his male peers is a dreadful insult; it means that other males as a group effectively deny him his claim to masculinity (Buchbinder 1994, p. 25). The particular importance of sport in masculinity construction is that '[w]hat it means to be masculine is, quite literally, to embody force, to embody competence' (Connell 1983, p. 27). Herein lies the rub for men and boys with physical impairments:

> Sport occupies a central place in the lives and in the social development of boys, promoting in them a sense of power, forcefulness, mastery, and skill. Today boys are still taught in a quite straightforward way that sport is a significant part of manliness. The achievement of basic skills of ball-throwing, kicking and batting, is a project to which boys are introduced at a young age. Female sport does not have similar significance for girls. Male sport, however, through its contribution to the construction of hegemonic masculinity actually reinforces traditional notions of femininity in which women are cast as passive, physically unskillful, and not forceful. Femininity is defined largely in the negative by male sport, as involving lack of skill and an inability to play valued games. A process of disparagement of that which is feminine is implicit in the celebration of masculinity. This is expressed in the abuse traditionally meted out by coaches and fans whom, when irritated by poor play, complain that their hero is 'playing like a girl'. (Bryson 1987, p. 155)

Men and boys with impairments therefore embody a lived contradiction between dominant or hegemonic forms of masculinity (embodied skill/power/agency) and impairment (reduced abilities/power/agency). In contemporary sociology the term 'hegemony' is used to describe a form of control or dominance which is persuasive, rather than coercive because it results from people's positive reactions to values and beliefs, which support established social relations and structures of power (Hargreaves 1994, p. 22). Hegemonic masculinity refers to particular kinds of behaviour and ways of being which are made culturally dominant and come to be seen as the pattern of masculinity in general (Kessler et al. 1982, p. 10).

Some sociologists have argued that participation in disability sports – particularly hyper-masculine sports – is a way for men with physical impairments to construct or recuperate a hegemonic masculinity (Berger 2008; Lindemann & Cherney 2008). For instance, in their study of men's quad rugby in the US, Lindemann and Cherney (2008) found that performing with athletic skill and embodying the hyper-masculine violence and aggression commonly seen in able-bodied sport enabled a form of gender and identity rehabilitation which helped players to go from self-loathing and stigma to acceptance and pride but, in doing so, they adopted sexist attitudes and ableist values to become more 'normal'. Yet, aside from evidence in the documentary *Murderball* (2005) of some elite quad rugby players developing sexual relationships with conventionally attractive young able-bodied women, there is little evidence to suggest that the male social power constructed and conferred within disability sports has much currency in broader able-bodied society, particularly at a non-elite level. A recent study by the author exploring whether playing sport is a form of cultural capital in the construction of a masculine identity and in gaining peer acceptance for young men with physical impairments suggests this may not necessarily be the case. Playing disability-specific sports was found to be beneficial in terms of meeting other young people with impairments. Yet social inclusion and social status among their able-bodied peers was associated more with doing well in able-bodied sports, from which they are mostly excluded (Wedgwood forthcoming [a]).

Whereas sport pervaded the life histories of the young men in the study and was a crucial part in many aspects their lives and identities, this was not the case for the only young woman in the study who, in contrast, stated 'I'm happy to be sailing but I'm sure I could do chess or something if I didn't do sailing' (Wedgwood forthcoming [b]). Given that sport is culturally defined as a masculine pursuit, this difference is very likely a gender difference. In particular, the young woman has participated in disability sailing for 13 years and competed at both a national and international level with the ultimate aim of competing in the Paralympics. Sailing is part of her identity as a 'person with abilities', yet it is not part of her gender identity and therefore does not have the same meaning for her as for the young men in the study: 'I'm not really a sporty person. Like I have a competitive edge once I'm on the water but getting me on the water is so hard'. Moreover, as Hargreaves has pointed out, disability sport has, in many respects, replicated the gender inequalities inherent in able-bodied sport – it is heavily male-dominated, with fewer female than male participants (2009, p. 193). Therefore, as with able-bodied sports, we should not assume that disability-specific sports are necessarily inclusive of all people with impairments, nor that social inclusion in sport has the same generic meaning for all people with impairments.

Sport, the body and empowerment

Our bodies – which we commonly think of as purely biological – are in fact also social entities. For centuries both in everyday life and in many academic disciplines we have thought about and treated our bodies as complex biological machines that are separate from (or at best conjoined to) our minds and ourselves. More recently, this way of viewing the body has been challenged, at least in the field of sociology where the body was 'brought back' over two decades ago (Frank 1990). Sociological insights into the body are based on the understanding that we are embodied, not in the sense that we have a body (as we have a car, a house, or other object) but in the sense that we are bodies – that is, we actively engage the everyday world through our body (Toombs 1995, pp. 10–11). Thus, we are who we are in and through our bodies, and we present ourselves to the world via our bodies. Disability then needs to be understood not just as a purely biological fact (though it is a physical reality as well) but also in terms of the relationship between body and society, which differs greatly from one society and historical period to another (Turner 2001, p. 259).

In contemporary Western societies people with physical impairments are faced with developing a sense of themselves within the context of an individualistic and hedonistic culture in which the body has become increasingly central to the modern person's sense of self-identity through diet, exercise, cosmetic surgery and cultural consumption (Turner 2001; Hughes 2002). With an emphasis on youth, youthfulness, health, physical fitness, productivity, sexuality and activity, ours is not a culture that celebrates physical difference, impairment or dependence (Toombs 1995, p. 18; Turner 2001, p. 259). Thus, ever-narrowing norms of the ideal body are problematic for people with impairments, particularly those with highly visible physical differences (Watson 1998, p. 147; Hughes 2002, p. 70).

> Embodiment has poignancy when applied to disabled people because they are looked upon, identified, judged and represented primarily through their bodies, which are perceived in popular consciousness to be imperfect, incomplete and inadequate. Because the lack of physical impairment is treated as the norm, the impaired body immediately and conspicuously signifies difference and abnormality. Thus the disabled body is tied to self and identity in a most intense and evocative way. (Hargreaves 2000, p. 185)

Consequently, people with impairments are generally perceived as different from ablebodied people – often thought of as 'that disabled person' rather than 'that student' or 'that person'. They attract unwanted pity and are also commonly seen as helpless, asexual or even socially invisible. For young people, having an impairment marks them out as different at a time when sameness is crucial and the emotional pain of social exclusion is heightened due to the intensive need to be 'normal' and accepted by peers.

In the field of sociology, the study of embodiment has proved particularly fruitful in researching how bodies not only shape, but are also extensively shaped by, social forces like gender. As feminists like Young (1998) have argued, some women literally *embody* their disempowered, inferior social status. By this she means that: 1) women typically use much less space than is available, keeping their limbs close to or closed around their bodies when sitting, standing, walking, even playing sport; 2) they tend to refrain from using their whole bodies in a task, usually concentrating motion in the part of the body most directly connected to the task, such as the arm while throwing, while the rest of the body remains relatively immobile (throwing like a girl); and 3) they often assume they are unable to accomplish easy tasks even before attempting them, in particular, those involving the use of force, such as carrying heavy objects, thus underusing and underestimating their potential physical power and skills and, in giving less than their full effort, fulfilling their own prophecy of incompetence. Of course, this is not the full story. Some women are strong, confident and/or masculinely embodied. Sport can also allow women to develop more powerful forms of embodiment by experiencing themselves as powerful, defensive, skillful, and assertive (Theberge 2003; Wedgwood 2004), thereby resisting at the embodied level the traditional ideal of women as fragile, defenseless and powerless sexual objects.

What we know about sport and gendered embodiment raises important questions about the embodiment of people with impairments. Namely, the extent to which people with impairments embody their marginal inferior status and the transformative potential of sports participation for people with impairments. We know, for instance, that the intrusion of body space for physical and medical care can prevent some people with impairments from developing ownership of their body (Kerr 1999, pp. 1–2). Yet because embodiment is an ongoing, dynamic process and because bodies have agency, they are also potentially significant sites of resistance and subversion. A good illustration is provided by the life history study of 'Ella', a young woman born with no limbs aside from a fraction of her leg with a partial foot and three toes with which she writes and operates her electronic wheelchair (Wedgwood forthcoming[b]). In contrast to some able-bodied women who assume they cannot do things because they are female (Young 1998), Ella never assumes she cannot do things because she has a severe physical impairment: 'I just usually do it if I want to do it. I'll work out some way' (Ella). Despite her inability to walk, get out of bed, toilet or eat unaided, Ella is a university student, an accomplished musician and an award-winning disability sportsperson. Given her sporting and other achievements it is unsurprising her impairment makes her feel, 'strong and confident'. Indeed, much of Ella's life – including her participation in a disability sport – can be viewed as lived and embodied resistance to ableist stereotypes of people with physical impairments as weak, pitiful, dependent and passive. Yet, despite her herculean efforts, Ella is seen first and foremost by most able-bodied people as a person with a severe physical impairment: 'Like, no-one knows [the name of my condition]. People just go, "Isn't that that girl that doesn't have any arms or legs?"' Though Ella may be confidently embodied and have the power to define and present herself to the world as 'a person with abilities', she has only limited influence over the way she is viewed by others and her subsequent levels of sexual and social inclusion (Wedgwood forthcoming[b]).

Just as important then as the lived embodied experience of participating in sport is the way in which that participation is viewed by the able-bodied majority. Indeed, disability activists, like Harlan Hahn, have critiqued the participation of people with impairments in any type of sport as inviting judgment by non-disabled standards and placing excessive emphasis on physicality in the assessment of human beings (Hahn 1984). With its roots in rehabilitation, disability sport has grown out of the 'medical model' of disability, which views disability simply as a personal misfortune requiring a medical, as opposed to a social, solution. Sport can thus be viewed, like rehabilitation, in Foucauldian terms as an ableist attempt to 'normalise' or 'discipline' the 'disabled body'. Yet people with impairments are not 'passive victims of a society that fails to include them' (Watson 1998, p. 150). They have the capacity as creative human agents to act in/on the world to either reproduce (or contest the reproduction of) social structures. An example is elite amputee athletes rejecting the 'normalising' aspects of cosmetic prosthetic limbs in favour of highly visible prosthetics:

> within the culture of Paralympians, most athletes do not bother to hide their amputation behind a cosmetic limb. In fact, most elite athletes are happy to wear either a technologically advanced leg ... or a more traditional prosthesis that is adorned with graphic art [which] ... makes the prosthesis highly visible ... and could be seen as the result of these athletes being more confident of the validity of their sporting achievements and about their bodies more generally. (Howe 2008, p. 130)

Though it is true that sports participation highlights the *inabilities* of people with impairments, it simultaneously highlights their *abilities,* providing an 'in ya face' challenge to ableist views of people with impairments as passive, pitiful charity cases.

Some feminists have argued that, over time, women's participation in sport has challenged sexist assumptions about gender and gendered embodiment:

> women's sports have the power to rearticulate gender ideals such that those very athletic women's bodies that, at one time, are considered outside the norm (too much, too masculine, even monstrous), can come, over time, to constitute a new ideal. (Butler 1998, p. 104)

Though it is difficult to measure and is very likely a slow, indiscernible process, disability sports may have a similar effect in challenging ableist assumptions about people with impairments – particularly high-profile, elite disability events like the Paralympics – but also at the everyday level, for instance in physical education.

Implications for physical educators

Due to enormous medical advances over the past 25 years, the survival rates of children with impairments have increased dramatically. By 2003 nearly 250,000 or just under 9% of Australians aged 12–24 years were living with a disability (AIHW 2007). At the same time, legislation and policies mandating social inclusion and equity of access are becoming more and more common in the developed world. One example is Article 30 of the Convention on the Rights of Persons with Disabilities, which states:

> With a view to enabling persons with disabilities to participate on an equal basis with others in recreational, leisure and sporting activities, States Parties shall take appropriate measures:
>
> 1) To encourage and promote the participation, to the fullest extent possible, of persons with disabilities in mainstream sporting activities at all levels ...
>
> 2) To ensure that children with disabilities have equal access with other children to participation in play, recreation and leisure and sporting activities, including those activities in the school system ... (United Nations 2006)

Subsequently, there is an increasing number of students with impairments, many of whom are attending mainstream schools. 'Inclusion', however, is not automatically achieved via legal mandates, government policies nor education curricula, as numerous studies of the impact of the UK government's inclusion policy goals articulated in the 2000 National Curriculum for Physical Education have shown (Barton 1993; Smith & Thomas 2006). Indeed, governments imposing 'social inclusion' from above can have unintended non-inclusive outcomes (Haycock & Smith 2010), and equal opportunity and social justice policies in education are frequently undermined by other policies like neoliberalisation (Barton 1993, p. 48; Evans & Lunt 2002, p. 12). Moreover social inclusion is achieved primarily through the everyday practices of schools, physical education (PE) teachers and students. Thus, ultimately, there is an increase in 'demand on teachers to plan for, teach and assess a wider range of individual needs' (Morley et al. 2005, p. 86).

A brief overview of research in the UK, US and Europe on the inclusion of students with impairments in mainstream PE from the point of view of both teachers and students indicates some broad patterns in everyday practice (Schmidt-Gotz et al. 1994; Blinde &

McCallister 1998; Goodwin & Watkinson 2000, Ninot et al. 2000; Lienert et al. 2001; Butler & Hodge 2004; Hodge et al. 2004; Smith 2004; ; Morley et al. 2005; Haycock & Smith 2010). To begin with, a wide range of approaches were evident, ranging from simply educating students with impairments alongside their able-bodied peers (integration), to changing existing mainstream PE classes to fully include students with impairments socially and educationally (inclusion). The research indicates that most practice falls somewhere in between integration and inclusion.

At one end of the integration/inclusion spectrum, it is not uncommon for some PE teachers simply to assign students with impairments to non-participatory roles in PE lessons (or parts of lessons), especially during complex skills training or team sports. These include spectating from the sidelines, pumping up balls, keeping score, marking boundaries or other marginal roles. In the words of one teacher:

> there are obviously some activities that they can't physically do, so we tend to maybe give them a different role. It could be officiating ... doing some sort of score keeping or analyzing a lesson ... getting them in that side of things. (Haycock & Smith 2010, p. 297)

This approach reflects a medical model view of disability – that the difficulties/inability to fully include students with impairments is due to the student's impairment rather than to teaching style, curriculum or lesson design. Some students who knew they could participate in physical activities (with some modifications to rules, equipment or attitudes) because they had done so in other contexts outside of PE, reported being excluded from those same activities in PE. Other commonly reported methods of integration (as opposed to inclusion) are teaching students with impairments separately to able-bodied students within the same class and/or removing them from the main PE lesson altogether to do different activities (like table tennis).

Most teachers in the studies reviewed were found to adapt or modify their lessons to one degree or another in order to better accommodate the needs of students with impairments. This included modifying rules, equipment, lesson plans, instructions, activities and/or teaching style. For instance, some teachers adapted games by introducing a five-count rule before a classmate is allowed to retrieve a ball hit by a student with an impairment or a five-foot radius wherein opponents cannot make contact with classmates with impairments (Hodge et al. 2004, p. 406). Even with such adaptations, students with impairments are still to a large extent expected to fit into the existing PE curricula, rather than the PE curricula being adapted to include students of all levels of ability. That is, PE programs which largely revolve around the provision of 'traditional', competitive, largely performance-oriented and team-based sports like football, basketball, netball, alongside individual activities like swimming, dancing and gymnastics (Barton 1993, p. 49; Haycock & Smith 2010, p. 299). In contrast, the social model of disability posits that, rather than adapting people with impairments to fit into the hegemonic sporting ideology, the dominant values of sport be questioned, challenged, adapted and changed in a way which makes PE more inclusive of people with impairments. There were no examples of this, more radical, approach to inclusion in the research reviewed – unsurprisingly given that PE teachers obviously have to work within the set curriculum of their school, region or country, rather than rewrite it.

Despite variations in education policies, PE curricula and schooling systems from one country or region to another, the factors which teachers sited as thwarting, limiting and/or adversely affecting their abilities and/or willingness to include students with impairments into their PE lessons, were remarkably consistent. Those being:

- concern about the safety of all the students when students with impairments are present in a class
- concern about individualised attention to students with impairments resulting in neglecting the needs of the rest of the class
- fears and assumptions about the abilities of students with impairments to enjoy active and meaningful participation in PE
- a lack of knowledge, experience and confidence in teaching and/or including students with impairments in mainstream PE classes leading to feelings of frustration, inadequacy and, in some cases, even guilt. This was primarily due to a lack of, or limited and inadequate, initial and/or continuing teacher training – particularly training on how to include students with impairments that meets the unique demands of the PE subject area which differs greatly in many ways from academic subjects taught primarily to students sitting behind desks in classrooms
- a lack of assistance from support staff – particularly compared to academic subjects – with any support received mostly being from staff untrained in PE
- ever-increasing class sizes, along with increasing numbers of students with impairments in mainstream educational settings making lesson planning, class management and teaching more and more complex and less conducive to being able to facilitate effective inclusion
- the challenges of including students with more complex, multiple, challenging and/or severe impairments
- inadequate facilities and/or levels of resourcing, staffing and support for the numbers or ratio of students with impairments.

Subsequently, teachers who were considered highly effective educators did not necessarily demonstrate effective inclusive practices and there was a wide variance in the effectiveness of teacher's adaptations to facilitate active and meaningful participation of all students, particularly those with a severe impairment (Hodge et al. 2004, pp. 414–15). Even PE teachers philosophically or theoretically supportive of inclusive PE and who believed or understood that adapting and modifying the learning environment is important, did not always do so or did so irregularly (Hodge et al. 2004, pp. 409, 414).

The research suggests that factors which facilitate effective inclusion of students with impairments in mainstream PE classes, include (but are by no means limited to):

- teacher creativity
- informed training
- preparedness
- availability of support
- a positive, open mind and high expectations of students with impairments
- positive attitudes towards disability and people with disability
- being sensitive to social interactions between able-bodied students and students with impairments, particularly put-downs, comparisons of ability and exclusion
- facilitating and fostering inclusive relationships between students with impairments and their able-bodied peer, for example via bi-directional, equal-status peer teaching
- taking advantage of a large selection of available resources (see below)
- listening to what students with disabilities have to say about their needs, desires and experiences and empowering them 'to be active in the learning process and initiators of strategies that will guide their own learning' (Goodwin & Watkinson 2000, p. 157).

The research reflecting the voices, experiences and perspectives of students with impairments in mainstream PE classes indicates that not all of the factors influencing effective inclusion are outside of the control of PE teachers. Teaching styles, teaching philosophies, attitudes towards disability and lesson plans all have a dramatic effect on the educational and social outcomes of all students in integrated PE classes.

Where students with impairments ended up being taught within the same PE class but separately from their able-bodied peers, they were not only receiving a physical education that was different, unequal to, and more limited and narrow to that of their able-bodied peers, they also remained socially isolated, missing out on important social interactions with able-bodied classmates (such as through high-status activities like team sports). This negatively impacted their self-esteem and social status. Both teachers and students with impairments 'perceived the status of the types of activities in which they were involved as inferior compared to those of others in the class' (Fitzgerald 2003 cited in Smith & Thomas 2006, p. 80). Though some students reported being embarrassed by not being able to perform the skills and movements required for success in an activity, the majority enjoyed participating in sport and games and did want to be fully included in PE, thus when they were excluded felt sad, angry, 'different,' hurt, upset and/or like unwanted outsiders (Blinde & McCallister 1998). This is important to understand because, although students with impairment may outwardly appear to accept a non-participant role in PE, this may be because the unequal power relationship between them and their teacher stops them from protesting or expressing their true feelings.

The experiences of students with impairments varied not only from one educational context to another but from one day to the next. In one study students described 'bad days' as those in which they were rejected, ignored, neglected, treated differently or made fun of by classmates and/or when active participation was inhibited by lack of support from teachers, classmates not including them in games (not passing to them) and/or constraints to participation were imposed by the instructional space for example, no wheelchair access (Goodwin & Watkinson 2000, pp. 151–54). 'Good days' were characterised by meaningful experiences in the regular program rather than in a segregated or 'special' program, which promoted a feeling of belonging and the opportunity to demonstrate skill proficiency to classmates (Goodwin & Watkinson 2000, p. 154). However, one study of a group of adolescents with mental impairments, found integrated PE significantly lowered their perceived athletic competence (Ninot et al. 2000).

The research showed mixed reports regarding the social benefits to students with impairments and their able-bodied peers of inclusive PE. Even where interactions between students with impairments and able-bodied students were primarily positive, they may be limited and infrequent (Butler & Hodge 2004). Where there were benefits like social acceptance, social inclusion and/or meaningful participation, it was unclear if these spilled over into other aspects of students' lives more generally. What was clear, however, was that positive and meaningful social interactions and inclusion are not an automatic byproduct of integration. Appropriate interactions between able-bodied students and students with impairments requires facilitation, endorsement, fostering and modeling by PE teachers. Though peer-teaching was reported by numerous teachers to be a useful teaching strategy (particularly given the lack of support many PE teachers reported), it mostly involved able-bodied students helping students with impairments, thus leading to uni-directional and unequal interactions. New approaches to peer teaching facilitate interactions which create a feeling of equal status between partners, which is more likely to produce desired attitude and behaviour changes (Sherrill et al. 1994, p. 28). Rather than one child being the tutor and the other being tutored, peer tutoring is carefully structured so that each child spends equal time in tutor and tutored roles, and contributes equally to the achievement of a common goal. In these bi-directional, equal-status relationships, both partners feel they are benefiting and find contact satisfying and self-actualising, thus are more beneficial to both students (Sherrill et al. 1994, pp. 28–30). Moreover, not only students with physical impairments but also those with learning disabilities, mild mental retardation, autism, and behaviour disorders can function effectively as peer tutors (Sherrill et al. 1994, p. 30).

Conclusions

In many ways a sociological understanding of sport is far more powerful in the hands (or minds) of sports providers than that of sociologists. It is with this in mind that I have provided a summary of the participation of people with impairments in sport – not simply as a form of physical exercise, competition or leisure – but as a social institution within which social structures and power relations are reproduced and sometimes challenged. In particular, I hope that thinking about sport from different (and perhaps personally challenging) perspectives will inform the practices of our future PE teachers, coaches and youth sport providers when it comes to the inclusion of people with impairments. To this end, this chapter has highlighted not only the way in which sporting practice in our society is heavily shaped and influenced by social structures like gender and ableism but also the fact that people who play sport or provide physical education are not completely constrained by these structures. After all, ableism is ultimately either reproduced or challenged by everyday practices, attitudes and behaviours:

> Sport may be a cultural sphere that is dominated by the values and relations of the dominant class, but it does not fully strip ... participants of the abilities to think critically and to reshape (at least in part) and redefine sport ... In essence, dominant classes place structural and ideological constraints around people's thoughts and actions, but these constraints do not fully determine the outcome – people retain the ability to act as historical agents, thinking critically and acting transformatively. (Messner 1990, p. 8)

While it is difficult for individual teachers to radically change the games-based curriculum overnight (even if they want to, which is unlikely), it is possible to make inclusive adaptations and modifications within the parameters of existing PE curricula. One example might be to provide a season of games which promote reverse integration, thus keeping the focus on games but reversing the onus of adaptation onto able-bodied students by getting both able-bodied students and students with impairments to participate in disability-specific sports like wheelchair basketball, goalball, visually impaired cricket or sitting volleyball.

References

Australian Bureau of Statistics (ABS) (2007). *Sports and physical recreation: a statistical overview*. Canberra: Australian Bureau of Statistics.

AIHW. (2007). *Young Australians: their health and wellbeing 2007*. Canberra: Australian Institute of Health and Wellbeing.

Aitchison, C. (2000). *Disability and social inclusion: leisure, sport and culture in the lives of young disabled people*. Cheltenham: Scope & Leisure and Sport Research Unit, Cheltenham & Gloucester College of Higher Education.

Anderson, J. (2003). Turned into taxpayers: paraplegia rehabilitation and sport at Stoke Mandeville, 1944–56. *Journal of Contemporary History, 38*(3): 461–75.

Barton, L. (1993). Disability, empowerment and physical education. In J. Evans (Ed.). *Equality, education and physical education* (pp. 43–54). London: Falmer Press.

Berger, R. (2008). Agency, structure, and the transition to disability: a case study with implications for life history research. *Sociological Quarterly, 49*: 309–33.

Blinde, E. & McCallister, S. (1998). Listening to the voices of students with physical disabilities. *Journal of Physical Education, Recreation & Dance, 69*(6): 64–68.

Blinde, E. & McClung, L. (1997). Enhancing the physical and social self through recreational activity: accounts of individuals with physical disabilities. *Adapted Physical Activity Quarterly, 14*(4): 327–44.

Blinde, E. & Taub, D. (1999). Personal empowerment through sport and physical fitness activity: perspectives from male college students with physical and sensory disabilities. *Journal of Sport Behaviour, 22*(2): 181–202.

Bryson, L. (1987). Sport and the maintenance of masculine hegemony. *Women's Studies International Forum, 10*(4): 349–60.

Buchbinder, D. (1994). *Masculinities and identities*. Melbourne: Melbourne University Press.

Butler, J. (1998). Athletic genders: hyperbolic instance and/or the overcoming of sexual binarism. *Stanford Humanities Review, 6*: 103–11.

Butler, R. & Hodge, S. (2004). Social inclusion of students with disabilities in middle school physical education classes. *Research in Middle Level Education Online, 27*(1): 1–10.

Connell, R. (1983). Men's bodies. In R. Connell (Ed.). *Which way is up? Essays on sex, class and culture* (pp. 17–32). Sydney: Allen & Unwin.

EFDS (2004). *Building a fairer sporting society, sport for disabled people in England: a four year development plan 2004–2008*. Loughborough: English Federation of Disability Sport.

Emerson, E., Honey, A. & Llewellyn, G. (2008). *The well-being and aspirations of Australian adolescents and young adults with a long-term health condition, disability or impairment*. Sydney: Faculty of Health Sciences, University of Sydney.

Evans, J. & Lunt, I. (2002). Inclusive education: are there limits? *European Journal of Special Needs Education, 17*(1): 1–14.

Finch, N., Lawton, D., Williams, J. & Sloper, P. (2001). *Disability survey 2000: young people with a disability & sport: headline findings*. London: Sport England.

Foley, D. (1990). The great American football ritual. In D. Foley (Ed.). *Learning capitalist culture: deep in the heart of Tejas* (pp. 28–62). Philadelphia: University of Pennsylvania Press.

Frank, A. W. (1990). Bringing bodies back in: a decade review. *Theory, Culture & Society, 7*: 131–62.

Goggin, G. & Newell, C. (2005). *Disability in Australia: exposing a social apartheid*. Sydney: UNSW Press.

Goodwin, D. & Watkinson, E. J. (2000). Inclusive physical education from the perspective of students with physical disabilities. *Adapted Physical Activity Quarterly, 17*(2): 144–60.

Gruneau, R. (1983). *Class, sports and social development*. Amherst: University of Massachusetts Press.

Guthrie, S. (1999). Managing imperfection in a perfectionist culture: physical activity and disability management among women with disabilities. *Quest, 51*: 369–81.

Guttmann, L. (1976). *Textbook of sport for the disabled*. Brisbane: University of Queensland Press.

Hahn, H. (1984). Sports and the political movement of disabled persons: examining nondisabled social values. *ARENA Review, 8*: 1–15.

Hannon, F. (2005). *Promoting the participation of people with disabilities in physical activity and sport in Ireland*. Dublin: National Disability Authority.

Hargreaves, J. (2000). *Heroines of sport: the politics of difference and identity*. London: Routledge.

Hargreaves, J. (1994). *Sporting females: critical issues in the history and sociology of women's sports*. London: Routledge.

Haycock, D. & Smith, A. (2010). Inclusive physical education? A study of the management of national curriculum physical education and unplanned outcomes in England. *British Journal of Sociology of Education, 31*(3): 291–305.

Hodge, S., Ammah, J., Casebolt, K., Lamaster, K. & O'Sullivan, M. (2004). High school general physical education teachers' behaviours and beliefs associated with inclusion. *Sport, Education and Society, 9*(3): 395–419.

Howe, P. D. (2008). *The cultural politics of the Paralympic movement: through an anthropological lens.* Abingdon: Routledge.

Hughes, B. (2002). Disability and the body. In C. Barnes, M. Oliver & L. Barton (Eds). *Disability studies today* (pp. 58–76). Cambridge: Polity.

Hutzler, Y. & Bar-Eli, M. (1993). Psychological benefits of sports for disabled people: a review. *Scandinavian Journal of Medicine & Science in Sports, 3*: 217–28.

Kerr, A. (1999). *Protecting disabled children and adults in sport and recreation: the guide.* Leeds: National Coaching Foundation.

Kessler, S., Ashenden, D., Connell, R. & Dowsett, G. (1982). *Ockers and disco-maniacs: sex, gender and secondary schooling.* Sydney: Inner City Education Centre.

Lienert, C., Sherrill, C. & Myers, B. (2001). Physical educators' concerns about integrating children with disabilties: a cross-cultural comparison. *Adapted Physical Activity Quarterly, 18*: 1–17.

Lindemann, K. & Cherney, J. (2008). Communicating in and through 'murderball': masculinity and disability in wheelchair rugby. *Western Journal of Communication, 72*(2): 107–25.

Messner, M. (Ed.). (1990). *Sport, men and the gender order: critical feminist perspectives.* Champaign, IL: Human Kinetics.

Morley, D., Bailey, R., Tan, J. & Cooke, B. (2005). Inclusive physical education: teachers' views of including pupils with special educational needs and/or disabilities in physical education. *European Physical Education Review, 11*(1): 84–107.

Murderball (2005). Rubin, H. A. & Shapiro, D. A. (Writers). J. Mandel & D. Shapiro (Producers). US: ThinkFilm.

Murphy, N. A. & Carbone, P. S. (2008). Promoting the participation of children with disabilities in sports, recreation, and physical activities. *Pediatrics, 121*(5): 1057–61.

Murray, P. (2002). *Hello! Are you listening? Disabled teenager's experience of access to inclusive leisure.* York: Joseph Rowntree Foundations.

Ninot, G., Bilard, J. & Delignières, D. (2000). Effects of integrated sport participation on perceived competence for adolescents with mental retardation. *Adapted Physical Activity Quarterly, 17*(2): 206–21.

Parker, A. (1996). The construction of masculinity within boys' physical education. *Gender and Education, 8*(2): 141–57.

Rimmer, J. (1999). Health promotion for people with disabilities: the emerging paradigm shift from disability prevention to prevention of secondary conditions. *Physical Therapy, 79*: 495–502.

Schmidt-Gotz, E., Doll-Tepper, G. & Lienert, C. (1994). Attitudes of university students and teachers towards integrating students with disabilities in regular physical education classes. *Physical Education Review, 17*(1): 45–57.

Shakespeare, T. (2006). *Disability rights and wrongs*. Abingdon, Oxon: Routledge.

Sherrill, C., Heikinaro-Johansson, P. & Slilinger, D. (1994). Equal-status relationships in the gym. *Journal of Physical Education, Recreation & Dance, 65*(1): 27–31.

Sherrill, C. & Williams, T. (1996). Disability and sport: psychosocial perspectives on inclusion, integration and participation. *Sport Science Review, 5*(1): 42–64.

Smith, A. (2004). The inclusion of pupils with special educational needs in secondary school physical education. *Physical Education and Sports Pedagogy. 9*(1): 37–54.

Smith, A. & Thomas, N. (2006). Including pupils with special educational needs and disabilities in National Curriculum Physical Education: a brief review. *European Journal of Special Needs Education, 21*(1): 69–83.

Sport England (2001). *Disability survey 2000: young people with a disability & sport* London: Sport England.

Taub, D., Blinde, E. & Greer, K. (1999). Stigma management through participation in sport and physical activity: experiences of male college students with physical disabilities. *Human Relations, 52*(11): 1469–84.

Taub, D. & Greer, K. (2000). Physical activity as a normalizing experience for school-age children with physical disabilities. *Journal of Sport & Social Issues, 24*(4): 395–414.

Theberge, N. (2003). No fear comes: adolescent girls, ice hockey, and the embodiment of gender. *Youth & Society, 34*(4): 497–516.

Thomas, N. & Green, K. (1994). Physical education teacher education and the 'special needs' of youngsters with disabilities: the need to confront PETE's attitude problem. *British Journal of Physical Education, 25*(4): 26–30.

Toombs, S. K. (1995). The lived experience of disability. *Human Studies, 18*(9): 9–23.

Turner, B. (2001). Disability and the sociology of the body. In G. Albrecht, K. Seelman & M. Bury, *Handbook of disability studies* (pp. 252–66). Thousand Oaks, CA: Sage.

United Nations (2006). Convention on the Rights of Persons with Disabilities, Article 30 C.F.R. [Online]. Available: www.un.org/disabilities/convention/conventionfull.shtml [accessed 16 February 2011].

Walker, J. (1988). *Louts and legends: male youth culture in an inner city school*. Sydney: Allen & Unwin.

Washington, R. & Karen, D. (2001). Sport and society. *Annual Review of Sociology, 27*: 187–212.

Watson, N. (1998). Enabling identity: disability, self and citizenship. In T. Shakespeare (Ed.). *The disability reader: social science perspectives* (pp. 147–62). London: Cassell.

Wedgwood, N. (forthcoming [a]). This sporting life: sport in the lives of young men with physical impairments. *Men and Masculinities, Special edition on Masculinity & Disability*.

Wedgwood, N. (forthcoming [b]). A person with abilities: the transition to adulthood of a young woman with a severe physical impairment. *Young – Nordic Journal of Youth Research*.

Wedgwood, N. (2004). Kicking like a boy: schoolgirl Australian Rules Football and bi-gendered female embodiment. *Sociology of Sport Journal, 21*(2): 140–62.

Wedgwood, N. (2003). Aussie rules! Schoolboy football and masculine embodiment. In S. Tomsen & M. Donaldson, *Male trouble: looking at Australian masculinities* (pp. 180–99). Melbourne: Pluto Press Australia.

WHO (2003). *Health and development through physical activity and sport*. Geneva: World Health Organization.

Young, I. M. (1998). Situated bodies: throwing like a girl. In D. Welton (Ed.). *Body and flesh: a philosophical reader* (pp. 259–73). Oxford: Blackwell.

8
A critical history of the Gay Games movement

Kellie Burns

The Gay Games are a quadrennial international sports and cultural festival. To date there have been eight games held in six different cities around the world. In the limited body of work written about the Gay Games or the event's parent organisation, the Federation of Gay Games (FGG), each event is described in terms of the organisational and financial struggles, the political triumphs and the celebratory sporting moments that shaped each event. This growing body of work analyses the games as a way of gaining insight into the experiences of participants and/or evaluating its political or cultural significance (Messner 1994; Cramer 1996; Krane & Waldron 2000; Pronger 2000; Krane et al. 2002; Lenskyj 2002; Symons 2002, 2004; Symons & Hemphill 2002; Rowe et al. 2006). This chapter, in keeping with more recent critical scholarship on the Gay Games (Probyn 2000; Miller 2001; Stevenson et al. 2005; Davidson 2008), focuses on analysing the event as a site of production, where normative meanings around sex, gender, citizenship and global living are constructed and contested.

Throughout the chapter the Gay Games are understood to be multiple assemblages that cannot be defined or described in simple or absolute terms. As such, the idea that one can trace a singular, linear history through the Gay Games movement is highly problematic and one that this chapter resists. French philosopher, Michel Foucault (2002) cautions against the use of linear approaches to history and disrupts the idea that events can be traced back to a beginning or an origin. He not only challenges the possibility of finding such beginnings, he also asks why it is that scholars desire linearity and crave rational models for thinking and/or modes for analysing questions around subjectivity. Sketching out some of the details of each of the games is thus not an effort to establish what the Gay Games movement *is* or *is not*, nor is it an attempt to link the individual games to one another in a neat and linear gay 'story' of progress. Instead, the overview offered in this chapter informs readers about the major dates, locations and issues that made each of the games 'newsworthy'. The aim is to provide the reader with some background information about the event and illustrate what details the 'history of the Gay Games' tends to draw upon. There are certain 'facts' within the story of the Gay Games that are deemed relevant to its storytellers whilst others remain peripheral or untold.

The Gay Games as we 'know' them

It was Olympic decathlete Tom Waddell who came up with the concept of an international gay and lesbian sporting competition, and it is Waddell who retains the title of 'founding father' of the Gay Games (Messner 1994; Waddell & Schaap 1996; Krane & Waldron 2000; Symons 2004; *Take the Flame!* 2006). Waddell founded San Francisco Arts and Athletics (SFAA) in 1981 and the group immediately began to organise for the first Gay *Olympic* Games. Waddell's intention was to create a space where gay men and lesbian women could enjoy the spirit of an international sporting competition like the Modern Olympic Games, only within a non-normative space, free of the homophobia inherent in mainstream sporting cultures. For Waddell and members of the SFAA, the games represented an opportunity to challenge dominant media representations of gays and lesbians. In Waddell's semi-autobiographical life story, the early objectives of the games are framed against Waddell's desire to improve the public image of the gay and lesbian community:

> Too often, Tom felt, the gay community was represented in public only by its most outrageous elements, by drag queens and leather boys, who were, in his view, only a small percentage of the community. The majority of the gay men, Tom knew, were, like himself, professionals, doctors, lawyers, advertising men, salesmen, men who went to the theatre and the cinema, voted and ate out, bowled and played softball and rooted for the 49ers. They were not flamboyantly lusting for attention. (Waddell & Schaap 1996, p. 145)

Closely linked to this aim was the SFAA's hope that the games would foster international goodwill and friendship amongst the various participants, encourage gays and lesbians to be fit and active, and to provide an international sporting space where being 'in the closet' was not a mandatory requirement. The Gay Games were intended to provide an alternative sporting experience where participation, team effort and the building of international community bridges were valued over national rivalries and competitiveness.

Despite the alternative ethos of the games, Tom Waddell and the SFAA went to great lengths to replicate both the format and the spirit of the mainstream modern Olympic Games. For instance, each of the Gay Games has begun with a formal ceremonial welcome and concluded with a similar closing celebration. Many of the games have formalised the opening ceremonies with the lighting of the Gay Olympic Flame. Likewise, in the four-year period between each of the games, the official Gay Games rainbow flag is debuted at a series of local gay and lesbian fun runs around the world as it makes its way from the previous games' host city to the next host city. This is intended to raise awareness about the event and to emulate the mainstream Olympic torch relay. The games have also adopted the tone, theatrics and production scale of the Olympics opening and closing ceremonies. Official speeches are blended with large-scale theatrics and athletes are ushered into the opening ceremonies stadium by country, dressed in matching team attire. The Gay Games also offer medals for achievement (gold, silver and bronze) and sporting performances are accredited with national and international sporting organisations.

Each of the seven games has been organised under the banner of the same motto: 'participation, inclusion and personal best'. As the succeeding subsections will demonstrate, each of the individual events follows a rather standardised format. Despite over two decades of political, social, economic and environmental change, organisers tend to hold on to the legacy and mandates of the first games, and the SFAA's original vision for the event. That said, despite only minor changes in the events' program structure and regardless of the fact that each host team has adopted very similar promotional strategies, a great deal has changed in terms of the events' conditions of production. One need only compare the footage of San Francisco 1982 and of Sydney 2002 or Cologne 2010 to acknowledge that being a participant today is a very different experience from what it was when the Gay Games movement was in its formative years. To begin with, at the first games there was barely a whisper around Human Immunodeficiency Virus (HIV) or Acquired Immunodeficiency Syndrome (AIDS); the world was yet to feel the impact of that epidemic. Furthermore, organisers depended upon 'snail mail' or word of mouth to promote the games as they did not have access to the new media technologies that organisers do today. The first games relied on local sponsorship to fund the event's modest budget whereas organisers of more recent games drummed up millions of dollars to stage their program and established government, media and corporate partnerships.

Again, this chapter sketches these changes, not to reinvent progress narratives but rather to consider how notions of 'progress' are used to frame the 'political' nature of the event and as a way of maintaining a normative public/media image.

Gay Games I: *Challenge '82*

The first games were called *Challenge '82* and were held in San Francisco. In the lead-up to these games, event organisers made national headline news when a lawsuit was begun against the SFAA. The United States Olympic Committee (USOC) wrote to the SFAA, citing copyright over the word 'Olympic' and requesting that it remove the word from all of its promotional items. At that time, the SFAA sought legal advice and was told to proceed as planned. After all, there were over a dozen American businesses and events that used the word Olympic in their titles: Olympic BBQ, The Xerox Olympics, The Crab Cooking Olympics, The Diaper Olympics, The Dog Olympics, The Special Olympics (Siegel 1994; Waddell & Schaap 1996; Miller 2001; *Take the Flame!* 2006). Why would the Gay Olympic Games be any different? The USOC then filed suit against the SFAA in the Federal District Court, where it was successful in getting a restraining order and preliminary injunction against the SFAA, both of which were upheld in the Circuit Court of Appeals.

The SFAA was ordered to ensure that the word 'Olympic', and any other word associated with the Olympic Games, was removed from the promotional items for the event, a process requiring a great deal of time and volunteer labour. The name Gay *Olympic* Games was simplified to the *Gay Games*, and has remained unchanged since. But again, the erasure of the word Olympic from the games materials in no way erased the spirit of Olympia, in fact, one could argue it made it stronger. The case of *USOC v. SFAA* continued until 24 March 1987, when the United States Supreme Court ruled that the USOC had exclusive proprietary rights over the word and a permanent injunction was issued preventing the use of the Olympic mark by the SFAA.

Gay Games I: *Challenge '82* attracted 1350 athletes from 11 nations, competing in 16 sporting events (Symons 2004). As mentioned above, one of the primary aims of *Challenge '82* was to shift the stereotypes of gays and lesbians within mainstream circles and demonstrate to the wider community that gays and lesbians were virtuous and upstanding members. The virtuous vision that organisers had in mind for these games was widely publicised throughout the event. At the opening ceremonies Waddell established the values and spirit that were central to *Challenge '82* in his welcoming address, which began with these words:

> Welcome to a dream that is now reality. Welcome to a celebration of freedom. These Gay Games, the first of their kind, are offered to gay and enlightened people from all over the world. They are a departure from other events of this scope and magnitude in that the underlying philosophy is one of self-fulfilment and a spirit of friendship. This is a first; it is our beginning, and as such, we expect these games to set a solid precedent for future games that are exemplary for wholesome and healthy athletics, devoid of the notion that beating someone is the criterion for winning. Participation makes us all winners. (Krane & Waldron 2000, p. 149)

His choice of words, 'celebration of freedom', 'gay and enlightened people', 'wholesome and healthy athletics', 'participation makes us all winners' again speak to the SFAA's efforts to challenge the stereotypes that have resulted in gays and lesbians being treated as second-class citizens. Sport is positioned as a space where the stereotypic image of the homosexual sissy and the queer social misfit could be contested. In a similar vein, in the *Challenge 1982 Official Programme*, SFAA members John Gildersleeve and Linda Wardlaw (1982) wrote:

> The Gay Games are one way to say, 'come and see how alike Gays and straights are. There are more similarities than differences'. The Games are open to everyone; that's a statement about love and acceptance. (p. 16)

While participants were encouraged to be 'out and proud', they were also given clear instructions around what did and did not constitute 'appropriate' Gay Games behaviour. Tom Waddell was especially committed to presenting a clean-cut image of games participants to mainstream media and sponsors, and he shamelessly worked to ensure that the community's 'undesirables' either conformed to this desired image or were excluded. Waddell visited members of San Francisco's drag and leather communities, urging them to alter their image if they wanted to be a part of the event. If they were unwilling, they were asked to sit the event out so as not to 'ruin' it for the rest of the community (Waddell & Schaap 1996). It is ironic then that Waddell espoused the importance of friendly competition, inclusiveness and goodwill, values that remain central to the Gay Games movement today. The first games had a modest budget of US$380,000 and finished with a surplus of US$15,000, assuring organisers that an international gay and lesbian sporting celebration was a financially viable option.

Gay Games II: *Triumph in '86* and Gay Games III: *Celebration '90*

It was not long before planning was underway for Gay Games II: *Triumph in '86*, hosted again in San Francisco. Organisers felt there was a need to 'refine [the Games] and work out the "bugs" before they [travelled] to other international sites' (Waddell 1984, p. 1). The aim of these games was to continue to challenge the idea that gays and lesbians were abnormal, sexually deviant and socially irresponsible. They welcomed 3500 sporting participants from 17 countries who were joined by thousands of spectators. These countries were: Australia, Brazil, Canada, England, France, Greece, Guam, Ireland, Israel, Italy, Japan, Mexico, The Netherlands, Nicaragua, New Zealand, Samoa, the US, the Virgin Islands and West Germany. The year 1986 was a precarious time to be staging an international gay and lesbian event and the SFAA was well aware of this. With the AIDS epidemic taking its toll on most of the Western world, border regulations in the US had tightened up, and people who were HIV positive (HIV+) and People With AIDS (PWA) were forced to identify themselves on immigration documents and most were denied entry visas. It should come as no surprise then that *Triumph in '86* was met with a great deal of disapproval and protest. According to Symons (2004), some of this resistance came from within the gay and lesbian community. Some community members felt that holding an event of this kind was inappropriate and a waste of community resources at a time when so many members of the San Francisco community were either sick and/or dying from AIDS. Despite the obstacles that visa granting posed, organisers felt that the games were an excellent opportunity to renew the community's spirit, to promote healthy and safe lifestyles, and to challenge the stereotypes around PWAs.

Apart from the 17 sporting events on the sports program, a 'Procession of Arts' that included conferences, exhibitions, concerts and plays was added to the program. Recognising the importance of the arts through the addition of this small cultural program was a significant change for the event. While Waddell himself was never entirely in support of the idea, many of the other organisers felt that it was important to provide a space for those who were less interested in sport to get involved in the spirit of the games. Symons (2002) points out that the cultural program was never a priority for Waddell, who saw sport and 'the arts' as two very different cultural spheres. For Waddell, the emphasis needed to be on changing the image of *athletes* in mainstream culture. He believed that individuals who participated in cultural sectors did not experience the same sets of discriminations or homophobia as athletes did. The outreach program that had got off to a slow start at *Challenge '82* became the portfolio of the SFAA's only African-American member, Lloyd Jenkins. The focus of the outreach program was to encourage gays and lesbians of colour, those living in 'disenfranchised American neighbourhoods' and delegates from 'Third World countries' to attend the event. Two other groups were targeted by the outreach program: women and gay and lesbian senior citizens in the community. The event had a budget of US$650,000 and finished with a small surplus. At the closing ceremony of *Triumph in '86* Waddell handed over the Gay Games flag to the Metropolitan Vancouver Arts and Athletics Association (MVAAA) and announced that the third celebration of the Gay Games would move across the 49th parallel from the United States to Canada.

Although the crowd at Kezar Stadium in San Francisco did not know it at the time, these would be Tom Waddell's last Gay Games. In the years between the second and third games, Waddell was diagnosed HIV positive and died in 1987 (at the age of 50) after a life of athletic and activist triumphs, including a sixth place finish in the decathlon at the 1968 Mexico City Olympic Games and several gold medal finishes at the first two Gay Games (Waddell & Schaap 1996). This was not the only significant change that took place between 1986 and 1990. The SFAA was reconfigured and renamed the Federation of the Gay Games (FGG), the international organisation that continues to oversee the games today.

Organising for Gay Games III: *Celebration '90* was not an easy task. The vast majority of participants at the first two games were from the US and this was the first time the event had left its host city. Vancouver was a much smaller city than San Francisco and the MVAAA had drafted an enormous budget of CAN$1.5 million. Failure to secure any significant sponsorship deals from large corporations, coupled with a lack of financial support from the British Columbia provincial government, meant that the MVAAA were working uphill from the start. The Canadian national government provided a substantial grant of CAN$45,000 to the event. Likewise, the city of Vancouver provided free transportation for participants. Symons (2004) criticises Canada's funding of the Vancouver Games, arguing that other major sporting events held in Canada at that time received much larger grants despite attracting significantly fewer athletes. While this is an excellent point, it is also important to point out that Canada was the first country to provide federal funding for a Gay Games festival. The symbolic gesture of a nation putting 'their money where their mouths are' is very important in unpacking the ways in which national governments strategically involve themselves in queer community activities. As organisers would come to learn, without a sizeable amount of the event's income generated in sponsorship, it would be hard to break even. There were 7250 athletes in attendance, registered in the 23 sports on the program. In addition, there were 750 participants taking part in the cultural festival (Forzley & Hughes 1990). Despite efforts to manage the budget, Vancouver was left with a CAN$100,000 deficit.

Gay Games IV: *Unity '94*

The 1994 Gay Games: *Unity '94* were held in New York City; the event also commemorated the 25th anniversary of the Stonewall Riots through a series of parallel conferences, protests and parties. The Stonewall Riots took place in June 1969 at a bar in Greenwich Village, New York City. When police aggressively raided this downtown community establishment, patrons fought back. Their efforts to resist the homophobic police brutality is memorialised as the first time gays and lesbians made a stand against their oppression in a public way and is said to have initiated a broader militancy within the community. The fourth games were certainly much more elaborate than the previous three games, and they were also far more controversial. Debates around HIV+ participants entering the US continued to be a major hurdle in event planning and this was mobilised as an issue for political action by *Unity '94* organisers. After a number of formal appeals, the US government temporarily lifted the immigration restriction to allow people living with HIV into the US in order to compete in the games. Over a million people attended *Unity '94*, with official sports participant numbers rising to 10,864 and the cultural festival participants numbering just over 4000. There were 40 countries represented at these games, 31 sporting events were on offer and the event budget had grown to US$7 million.

'Bigger and better' was the guiding principle of these games as organisers worked to put on the most elaborate Gay Games to date. They emphasised the positive impact the games would have on the city's local economy and used this as a selling point to secure a number of major sponsorship deals. It is estimated that US$316 million was injected into New York's economy over the eight-day sports and cultural festival. Max Harrold of Team New York, commenting on the role that sponsorship deals and global tourism played in the success of *Unity '94*, stated plainly 'Corporate America [had] finally discovered [the gay community]' (Harrold 1994, p. 98). Harrold's comment can be located within a broader move towards aligning queer community events with involvement from mainstream sponsors. This type of involvement has not only helped events grow in size and reach but it has also dictated the public image that organisers choose to portray to the rest of the (straight) world.

There are a few other significant factors that made the New York Games larger and more spectacular than its predecessors. The event opened and closed with headline performances by Cyndi Lauper and Patti LaBelle. Sporting and cultural events took place in renowned locations such as Madison Square Garden, Carnegie Hall, Yankee Stadium, Rutgers University, New York University and Central Park. As part of their outreach efforts, a small number of assistance scholarships were offered to athletes who would otherwise have been unable to attend the event. Other distinguishing moments for *Unity '94* included the 'The Rainbow Roll for the End of AIDS', an inline skating expedition that carried the Gay Games flag from San Francisco to New York and raised money for national HIV/AIDS research. The 'roll' covered 4500 miles and 18 US states. During the games another rainbow event took place, called 'Raise the rainbow'. On the 26th of June a mile-long and 30-feet wide rainbow flag snaked its way around the streets of Manhattan with more than a million people carrying it along. According to event organisers, this enormous flag, the largest flag ever made, was a symbol of the strength of queer unity both locally and globally, and was dedicated to the fight against AIDS.

The spirit of the 1969 Stonewall Riots was kept alive through a series of demonstrations. Most notable perhaps was the 'alternative' gay pride parade route where several hundred thousand marchers deviated from the scheduled *Unity '94/Stonewall 25* route. The scheduled march began at the United Nations building and culminated at Central Park; when marchers reached the original site of the Stonewall Riots a large group branched off and headed straight up Fifth Avenue until they reconnected with the original march. The deviation from the approved route was intended to send out the message to event organisers that not everyone was onboard the new mainstreaming agenda of the games. There was concern that important political issues were being overlooked because of the drive to please government officials and/or large corporate sponsors involved in the event. So while *Stonewall 25* was celebrated in conjunction with the 1994 Games, there were clearly struggles around what organisers of each event believed was the appropriate public image to put forth. Despite the increased interest of Corporate America in the Gay Games, *Unity '94* suffered a significant deficit (US$700,000) and eventually was declared bankrupt.

Gay Games V: *Friendship '98*

Amsterdam was the next city to host the Gay Games; these games were called *Friendship '98*. The 1998 host city was selected through a formal bid process. When Amsterdam won the bid, the games were truly committed to becoming a global event and only time would tell as to whether or not the event could be successful outside the North American context. With New York such a success in terms of generating corporate interest, there was debate around whether or not European sponsors would cash in on their piece of the pink guilder as eagerly as their American counterparts had the pink dollar in '94. The Netherlands national government and the European Parliament both endorsed Amsterdam's bid and pledged US$2 million upfront to support Team Amsterdam's early stages of planning. Team Stitching, the hosting team, was working with a budget of over NLG14 million (approx. US$7.68 million).

Despite this generous support, in the year leading up to the 1998 Games there was talk that Team Amsterdam was having dire financial problems and 'back-up cities' were organised in the event that the Amsterdam Games would fold. *Friendship '98* went ahead with a strong focus on human rights issues, international solidarity and understanding. Participant numbers totalled 16,026 and 68 different countries were represented in the opening ceremonies. Amsterdam offered athletes (all 14,716 of them!) 30 sports to participate in and worked to extend the cultural festival considerably. The outreach program was a central focus of these games and great efforts were made to provide financial assistance to athletes from former communist and developing countries so they could participate in the event. The government assisted this process by ensuring that appropriate visas were granted and, in some cases where coming to the games would have had political or personal repercussions for the athlete, the event's link to sexual politics was concealed. This program provided 238 athletes and cultural participants with travel, accommodation and local tour guides, waived registration fees and provided daily allowances to cover food and leisure activities. A social issues program was a significant addition to these games; this included a number of political, health-related and academic conferences. The number of women participants rose (42% of total participants) and there were various women-only events scheduled throughout the course of these games.

For the eight days of celebrations Amsterdam's small and intimate city centre came alive and the presence of the participants was certainly felt. Friendship Village was established in the city's main square and large numbers of participants gathered and socialised there between and after their sporting or cultural events for the day. Various venues were clustered in this area and entertainment was provided each evening. Over the course of the event an estimated US$79 million was injected into the local economy (Symons 2004). When all the medals were won and athletes returned home to tell tales of their fabulous time in Europe's queer hub, the host organisation was left with an enormous debt of NLG 3.5 million (approx. US$1.92 million).

Gay Games VI: *Under New Skies '02*

On 13 November 1997 the FGG announced that Sydney had put together the winning bid to host the 2002 Games. Sydney beat Dallas, Long Beach, Montréal and Toronto in the bid for the 2002 Games. Team Sydney had unsuccessfully bid for the 1994 Games and again for the 1998 Games. Securing the 2002 Gay Games was thus met with great relief by the Sydney Bid Committee, and by the local gay and lesbian community. The Sydney bid was strengthened by the international reputation of the annual Gay and Lesbian Mardi Gras Festival and the event infrastructure that would be in place by 2002, after the 2000 Sydney Olympic Games. The bid process was an expensive exercise, costing Sydney an estimated AU$75,000.

The Sydney 2002 Gay Games were called *Under New Skies '02* to mark the event's move to the Southern Hemisphere and also to signal a new face for the games to mark the second millennium (Sydney 2002 Gay Games Bid Ltd 1997). *The Sydney Morning Herald* stressed the financial benefits the Gay Games would have for the local community with a headline reading: 'We win – and it will be worth millions' (Bernoth 1997). It was estimated that *Under New Skies '02* would inject approximately AU$100 million into the local economy (Fitzsimons 1997). State government officials also emphasised the financial significance of the event, arguing that these games would give Sydney the economic boost needed following the tourism slump that was expected to follow the Sydney 2000 Olympics Games. The then Sports Minister Gabrielle Harrison commented that, 'I think when you're looking at tourism and jobs people will accept these games and support them' (Bernoth 1997). Harrison framed the government's decision to support the games in terms of the positive financial impact they would have on the local community. This is a familiar stance taken by mainstream sponsors and/or government bodies when describing their involvement in queer events; they adopt a 'business only' framework and make no mention of the social, cultural or political significance of the event (Sender 2004). Members of Team Sydney also emphasised the financial rewards rather than the cultural significance of hosting an event of this kind, particularly in the early stages of planning when they were eager to get large sponsors on board. Although a number of large corporations (Qantas Airlines, American Airlines) and widely subscribed-to media bodies (gay.com, Satellite Group Ltd) made early sponsorship arrangements with SGGB, a number of others were too overcommitted to the Sydney 2000 Olympics to make any financial promises for 2002 (Mills 2003a).

There were, of course, objections to the games taking place in Sydney. Most of these came from National Party and Christian Democratic Party members of the state Legislative Council, who dubbed these games the 'Sad Games' and objected to the government endorsing an event that 'promoted homosexual lifestyles'. Heading the campaign was Sydney's right-wing cleric-politician Reverend Fred Nile, who pushed for the government to make it mandatory for overseas athletes to be tested for HIV/AIDS before being admitted into Australia to compete (*The Canberra Times*, 15 November 1997, p. 5). News media accounts of Nile's objections quote him saying:

> The Carr Government is to be condemned that in the middle of a paedophile scare they actively promoted the Sydney bid and gave thousands of taxpayer dollars to help

finance the bid ... Sydney has enough social and moral problems without thousands of homosexuals descending on the city. (Bernoth 1997, p. 4)

Nile's comment makes reference to the paedophile 'witch hunts' that were taking place in Australia around the time of the bid. In 1994 the NSW Legislative Assembly called for a Royal Commission to be set up to crack down on adults having sex with underage children. Despite evidence that most children sexually abused in Australia are girls, a great deal of the Commission's efforts were focused on male, homosexual adults having sex with young boys. The campaign was supported in the media by Independent Upper House MP Franca Arena. The campaign escalated into a homophobic witch-hunt in the gay community with a number of prominent gay men implicated in the 'crack down' (see Riley 1997).

Despite conservative objections of this kind (which never went further than an in-house rant and a couple of news reports buried in the back pages of local newspapers), the then state premier, Bob Carr; the Governor of New South Wales, Professor Marie Bashir AC; Lord Mayor of Sydney, Frank Sartor AQ; Mayor of South Sydney, Tony Pooley; and Local MP Clover Moore issued formal messages of support for the games.

Organisers were working with a budget of approximately AU$10 million. The income for the games was mainly generated through participant registration costs, party ticket sales and sponsorship. The largest expenditures were administrative costs (for example personnel salaries and wages totalled over $1.7 million), the hiring of sporting venues ($598,000) and the opening and closing ceremonies ($1.1 million). As early as December 2000 there were suggestions that the Sydney 2002 Gay Games were in some financial trouble (*The Australian*, 23 December 2000, p. 7). Acting Chief Executive Officer (CEO) Garrie Gibson resigned when Premier Bob Carr rejected Sydney 2002's request for additional state funding. The Carr government had given Sydney Limited $75,000 for the bid and was providing office space and employment secondments to the value of $50,000. Geoffrey Williams subsequently replaced Gibson. Despite a change in leadership, complications continued to mount. The Satellite Group, one of the games' biggest media sponsors, and Australia's first public gay and lesbian company, went into receivership that year. Likewise, the American magazine HERO also folded soon after they had signed on as sponsors for Sydney 2002 (Mills 2003b). Although organisers had a few other sizeable sponsorship deals, most of these were providing value in kind, not dollars. As such, heading into the new millennium, concerns were being raised about the dearth of cash flow available to organisers. These concerns intensified when Mardi Gras was declared bankrupt and there was wide speculation about financial mismanagement by Mardi Gras board members.

By July 2001 local media raised doubts as to whether or not Gay Games organisers could keep the event afloat. The FGG – whom SGGB owed an AU$425,000 licensing fee – expressed concern that Sydney 2002 organisers needed to consider scaling the event down considerably. After the attacks on the World Trade Centre on 11 September 2001 global tourism took a dramatic dive and organisers had to account for the fact that many potential international competitors might elect to give these games a miss. In August 2002, Geoffrey Williams resigned and Karen Fletcher was appointed the acting CEO for Team Sydney.

However, the financial and public relations difficulties the games were experiencing did not drastically improve under yet another leadership arrangement. In late September, SBS broadcasters pulled the plug on their negotiations with Sydney 2002 to broadcast the opening ceremony and produce a nightly show about the games daily events (*The Adelaide Advertiser*, 27 September 2002, p. 15).

In addition to these difficulties, Australia's appeal as a safe holiday getaway was in question after the 12 October 2002 terrorist attacks in Bali nightclubs, which were predominantly filled with Australian tourists. The attack, led by members of Jemaah Islamiyah killed 202 people (88 of whom were Australians). There was a great deal of speculation around whether or not this attack was targeting Australia because of the government's backing of the US in the 'War on Terror'. While Sydney 2002 organisers assured overseas visitors the risk of terrorist activity in Australia had not risen and that the Gay Games were working closely with NSW Police to ensure there was no direct threat posed to participants, they also knew that these events would compound existing hesitations to partake in overseas travel.

In late October, only weeks away from the opening ceremony, news broke that the Sydney 2002 Ltd was in serious financial jeopardy. A large amount of revenue was tied up in ticket sales, processed by a local ticketing agency, Ticketek. In keeping with local legislation, Ticketek could not release the monies to Sydney 2002 Ltd in case the event fell through and ticket buyers were unable to get their money back. The Sydney 2002 executive worked to secure a bank loan of $2 million that would function as a guarantee to Ticketek that it was okay to release 50% of the money from ticket sales. Sydney 2002 approached South Sydney Council, asking them to support their loan application. The council refused and at the last minute a number of local gay and lesbian community members came together to personally back the bank loan. Community press publicised the generosity of these community 'elders' as a way of encouraging other members of the community to get out and buy tickets and thus do their part in making this community event happen.

Organisers and participants alike heaved a great sigh of relief when the three-and-a-half hour opening ceremony 'kicked off' at 7pm on 2 November 2002 in Aussie Stadium to a crowd of over 38,000. The sixth Gay Games, *Under New Skies '02* was held on 2–9 November 2002, with the event program organised into 'on-field' and 'off-field' sections. The on-field program included the 31 official sports events and the off-field program was made up of 97 cultural events, seven conferences and five event parties. A total of 12,099 participants were accredited at the games. There were 11,087 participants from 66 countries accredited in the sporting events, 704 conference participants and over 2500 artists, musicians and actors involved in the cultural events. The most popular sporting events were swimming (1387 participants) and the marathon, half-marathon and ten-kilometre road race (1297 participants) and the most widely acclaimed cultural events were *Blak, Queer 'n' Out There*, a showcase of Indigenous performers; the Poetry Slam finals and *Foreign Aids*, a one-man play written and performed by Pieter-Dirk Uys that addresses the political links between racism and government responses to HIV/AIDS in South Africa. The outreach and scholarship programs were expanded as organisers worked hard to include queer youth, women, Aboriginal Australians and participants from the Pacific region. Although 515 scholarships were offered, only 282 were taken up and although organisers aimed to have an equal number of female and male participants at the games, the final percentage of women in attendance was about 31% (Borrie, 2002).

Many of the sporting events took place at Sydney Olympic Park in Sydney's mid-western suburb, Homebush. In addition, the Botanic Gardens, Centennial Park, Sydney Town Hall, Darling Harbour Convention Centre, Fox Studios Showring and the Moore Park Golf Course were the main inner city spaces used to host the sporting events, with the remainder scattered across Sydney's inner suburbs and outer western suburbs. After eight days of sports and cultural celebrations, the games culminated with Tina Arena and Simon Burke performing at a fairly low-key closing ceremony at Fox Studios called Corroboree. A standing ovation was given to American Airlines hostess Alice Hogan, whose son Mark Bingham died during the 9/11 terrorist attacks. Bingham had intended to be at the games to play touch rugby and so his mother made the journey in his honour. Hogan addressed the crowd and helped present the Tom Waddell Award, an honour awarded at each of the games for outstanding dedication to the principles of the Gay Games – participation, inclusion and personal best. Lord Mayor Frank Sartor officially closed the games and handed the Gay Game flag over to a representative of Équipe/Team Montréal. Despite the financial turmoil that surrounded the planning of Sydney 2002, on 25 October 2001, the FGG had announced that Team Montréal had been chosen to host the 2006 Gay Games. There were five official bid city organisations bidding for the 2006 Gay Games: Montréal, Atlanta, Chicago and two teams from Los Angeles. One of the two LA teams was not shortlisted for the final presentations which took place at the AGM in Johannesburg, South Africa on October 25, 2001. Team Montréal used the celebrations at Sydney 2002 as an opportunity to promote the seventh Gay Games that were to be called *Rendez-Vous 2006*.

On Sunday, 10 November 2002 a headline in the late edition Sun Herald read, 'Thanks for having us Sydney, say gays'. In the news piece American Gay Games veteran Jim O'Donnell described his experience at Sydney 2002: 'Sydney was very welcoming, but on a more grand scale than, say, Amsterdam, which is a much more intimate place' (West 2002, p. 31). Both the mainstream, and gay and lesbian press proclaimed the Sydney 2002 Gay Games to be a success. Asked how effective he felt the games had been, Sydney 2002 Co-chair Peter Bailey stated: 'we have exceeded the expectations of our overseas visitors and Sydneysiders ... it's been incredibly rewarding to see this amazing event come together and to see the smiles of thousands of people who participated in the games in some way' (West 2002, p. 31). Kathleen Webster, FGG Co-president described the Sydney 2002 Gay Games as the 'best ever', offering that, 'Sydney 2002 has set a new height, it has brought the games to the next level, to another wonderful level' (Moran 2002). Despite what appeared to be general consensus around the games' success, the following month it was announced that Sydney 2002 Gay Games Ltd was insolvent, its final debt totalling AU$2.5 million, with some 150 creditors owed monies (Jacobsen 2002). Sydney 2002 Gay Games Ltd owed $516,000 to NSW government bodies, $425,000 to the FGG for licensing fees, $300,000 to the Australian Taxation Office, $211,000 to Qantas Airlines and the remainder to small businesses and venue operators. Eventually Sydney 2002 Gay Games Ltd went into voluntary administration and subsequently into liquidation (*The Hobart Mercury*, 5 December 2002, p. 4).

Co-chair Bev Lange maintained the Sydney games had been organised on 'sound business principles' (Jacobsen 2002, p. 4) and also stated that Sydney 2002 'set a benchmark for the delivery of the Gay Games in the future' (Mills 2003b). Although unintentional, Lange's words would foreshadow an immense amount of turmoil for the future of the Gay Games movement. The financial downfall of Sydney 2002 would have a significant impact on *Rendez-Vous 2006* and on the future of the Gay Games movement.

Gay Games VII and VIII

When the financial loss incurred by Sydney Gay Games Ltd was announced, the FGG felt strongly that it was time to carefully rethink the Gay Games financial model such that host cities were no longer left with the sort of hefty debts Amsterdam and Sydney had been. Montréal's original bid budget was CAN$20 million, and their estimated number of participants was over 20,000. During the bid, the FGG emphasised the necessity of scaling down these figures. By December 2002 the federation was putting pressure on Team Montréal to produce a more realistic budget, establish more realistic participant targets and focus on a more modest program of events so to safeguard against financial shortfalls. Team Montréal was yet to sign their event licensing agreement despite having traded under the Gay Games name (primarily securing sponsors and venues and appointing employees) for over a year. However, as both parties would soon discover, finalising the agreement would not be a simple task. Irreconcilable differences emerged. The FGG believed its role as the parent body who had witnessed the mistakes of former host cities was to 'break the cycle of financial deficits' (Federation of Gay Games 2003b, p. 11) by ensuring prudent financial plans were put in place for the 2006 Games. On the other hand, Team Montréal rejected the FGG's business plan and felt that the level of control exercised by the federation did not give host organisations the freedom to really make their event a success. For instance, the federation requires host teams to seek approval for all press releases, sponsorship agreements or employment contracts. Montréal wanted sole control over such matters and felt that having to get an 'okay' from the FGG on day-to-day operations prevented swift and professional business dealings. In addition, the FGG uses a formulaic business model that starts with modest projected numbers and builds upward. The FGG wanted Team Montréal to produce a draft budget for a projected 12,000 participants (10,000 sporting participants and 2000 cultural participants), but Team Montréal felt that they needed to plan for 16,000 participants in order to attract large sponsors and generate enough registration income to break even. The details of the negotiations around these budgetary details were extensive but it is important to point out that what Team Montréal saw as control, the FGG understood to be their consultative obligation, that is, to 'assess organisation readiness' (Federation of Gay Games 2003b, p. 8). After innumerable attempts to settle upon a licensing agreement, it became clear that the two groups' viewpoints of what the Gay Games event should look like could not be reconciled.

On 16 October 2003, in a media interview with Outsports.com, a gay and lesbian sports web portal, Team Montréal expressed freely and publicly many of their concerns about the negotiation process. The following day they circulated a worldwide press release that outlined, as they saw it, the tensions that were mounting between the two organisations. Then again on 3 November 2003 they sent an open letter to gay and lesbian organisations, media outlets and participants who had attended Sydney 2002 that clearly stated what they felt were the unreasonable 'demands' (Federation of Gay Games 2003b, p. 19) of the federation. Again the letter focused on differing views around participant numbers and budgetary figures. But this time Team Montréal stated that the FGG represents 'little more than itself, with only 21 of the 1000 teams around the world being FGG members' (Federation of Gay Games 2003b, p. 19). They also stated that FGG board members were 'out of touch' with the needs of today's LGBT (lesbian, gay, bisexual and transgender) communities. While the FGG wanted organisers to 'get back to basics' (Mills 2003a, p. 2), Montréal had in mind an enormous cultural event that would take place alongside the city's pride festival (Divers/Cité Pride) and that would be planned closely with the national and provincial tourism commissions. The FGG, which until this point had remained very quiet about the negotiations, released an extensive response to Montréal's claims, hoping to clear up what they saw as misinformation.

In their open letter, Team Montréal stated their intentions to end their affiliation with the FGG and host their own international gay and lesbian sport and cultural event, which would later be called the Montréal 2006 Outgames: *Rendez-Vous 2006*. Team Montréal established an independent sporting organisation called the Gay and Lesbian International Sporting Association (GLISA). Like the Federation of Gay Games, GLISA was to act as a parent body to support the running of a quadrennial sporting festival, with Montréal, of course, to be the first. The Montréal Outgames was scheduled to begin on 29 July 2006 and end on 5 August 2006.

The FGG, although more willing to express regret over the fallout with Montréal, maintained the professional stance that this small hiccup would not put an end to the games' 21-year legacy, stating that 'the Gay Games event does not belong to any one host city – it belongs to the world' (Federation of Gay Games 2003b, p. 6). Plans were quickly underway to ensure that Gay Games VII would find itself a new, and perhaps more agreeable host organisation. The FGG invited the four original bid finalists to re-pitch their plans for the 2006 Games, and both Chicago and Los Angeles came to the table. On 4 March 2004 Chicago was announced the winner of the bid and quickly began planning for Gay Games VII with only two years to get ready. These games were scheduled for 15–22 July 2006.

Despite efforts on behalf of Team Montréal and Team Chicago to downplay the rift that had occurred and to focus their energies on putting together successful events, the initial friction between the FGG and members of Team Montréal made a significant crack in the international gay and lesbian sporting community. At the local level debates raged as to whether one event should be supported over the other. Taking place back-to-back, both events were widely praised by those who attended and while both had a great deal of financial backing from government and sponsorship deals, the Chicago Games finished with a small surplus whereas Montréal incurred a deficit greater than CAN$5 million (Lysen 2006).

Critical reflections on the 'history' and future of the Gay Games

This chapter traced an historical narrative of the Gay Games movement and the inspirational slogans that dominated each event, focusing in particular on the Sydney 2002 Games. Both the Gay Games and the Outgames continue to host global sporting events around the world every four years. Since Montreal, regional Outgames have been hosted in North America, Europe and Australasia. In 2009 the second world Outgames were held in Copenhagen, Denmark and in 2013 the Outgames are scheduled to take place in Antwerp, Belgium. Likewise, the Federation of Gay Games continues to select host cities for its quadrennial event. In 2010 Gay Games VIII was held in Cologne Germany and in 2014 Cleveland, Ohio will host the ninth Gay Games.

These queer sporting events are markers of the increased visibility and acceptance gay, lesbian, bisexual, transgender and intersex people are experiencing across a number of domains, including sport. However, one must ask: At what cost? Are there more effective and less expensive ways to challenge those aspects of mainstream sport that are exclusive, sexist and/or homophobic? Furthermore, as these games continue to grow in size they become more and more reliant on large mega-event sponsorship and are therefore forced to promote a face of wholesome athleticism. Does this imperative create its own lines of inclusion and exclusion? Whose lives are intelligible at these Gay Games and whose are all but excluded?

References

Bernoth, A. (1997). We win–and it will be worth millions. *The Sydney Morning Herald*, 15 November, p. 4.

Borrie, S. (2002). *Sports programme post Games report*. Sydney: Sydney 2002 Gay Games Ltd.

Cramer, J. (1996). 'We're here, we're queer': breaking the silence with Gay Games IV. Unpublished doctoral dissertation, University of Michigan, Ann Arbor, Michigan.

Davidson, J. (2008). The necessity of queer shame for gay pride: the Gay Games and cultural events. In J. Caudwell (Ed.). *Sport, sexualities and queer/theory* (pp. 90–106). London: Routledge.

Federation of Gay Games. (2003). *Letter to Gay Games participants, friends and supporters*, 27 November, [Press release].

Fitzsimons, P. (1997). Sydney bids for 2002 Gay Games. *The Sydney Morning Herald*, 27 March, p. 8.

Forzley, R. & Hughes. D. (1990). The Gay Games: towards the next rainbow. In R. Forzley & D. Hughes (Eds). *The spirit captured: the official photojournal of Celebration '90 – Gay Games III & cultural festival* (pp. 12–13). Vancouver, Canada: For Eyes Press.

Foucault, M. (2002). *The archaeology of knowledge*. London: Routledge.

Gildersleeve, J. & Wardlaw, L. (1982). *Gay Games I: official programme for challenge 1982,* pp. 16–17.

Harrold, M. (1994). Corporate sponsors join the Games. In L. Labrecque (Ed.). *Unity: a celebration of Gay Games IV and Stonewall* (pp. 98–99). San Francisco: Labrecque Publishing.

Jacobsen, G. (2002). The game's up - now someone has to cough up. *The Sydney Morning Herald,* 5 December, p. 4.

Krane, V., Barber, H. & McClung, L. R. (2002). Social psychological benefits of Gay Games participation: a social identity theory exploration. *Journal of Applied Sport Psychology, 14*: 27–42.

Krane, V. & Waldron, J. (2000). The Gay Games: creating our own sports culture. In K. Schaffer & S. Smith (Eds). *The Olympics at the millennium: power politics and the Games* (pp. 147–66). Brunswick, NJ: Rutgers University Press.

Lenskyj, H. (2002). Gay Games or gay Olympics: implications for lesbian inclusion. *Canadian Woman Studies/Les Cahiers de la femme, 21*(3): 24-28.

Lysen, J. (2006). Outgames millions in debt, but planning more events: some doubt viability of two gay sporting competitions. *The New York Blade,* 29 December, p. 10.

Messner, M. (1994). Gay athletes and the Gay Games: an interview with Tom Waddell. In M. Messner & D. Sabo (Eds). *Sex, violence and power in sports* (pp. 113–19). Freedom, CA: The Crossing Press.

Miller, T. (2001). *Sportsex*. Philadelphia, PA: Temple University Press.

Mills, D. (2003a). Games loss affects Montreal. *Sydney Star Observer,* 20 March, pp. 1–3.

Mills, D. (2003b). Sydney 2002 administration continues. *Sydney Star Observer,* 30 October, p. 10.

Mills, D. (2002). The opening ceremony. *Sydney Star Observer,* 6 November, pp. 19–21.

Moran, J. (2002). Gay Games have 'renewed confidence in gay community'. *Australian Associated Press.*

Probyn, E. (2000). Sporting bodies: dynamics of shame and pride. *Body & Society, 6*(1): 13–28.

Pronger, B. (2000). Homosexuality and sport: who's winning? In J. McKay, M. A. Messner & D. Sabo (Eds). *Masculinities, gender relations and sport* (pp. 222–44). Thousand Oaks, CA: Sage Publications.

Riley, M. (1997). Arena hurt by blackmail letter targeting sons. *The Sydney Morning Herald,* 26 November, p. 13.

Rowe, D., Markwell, K. & Stevenson, D. (2006). Exploring participants' experiences of the Gay Games: intersections of sport, gender and sexuality. *International Journal of Media and Cultural Politics, 2*(2): 149–65.

Sender, K. (2004). *Business, not politics: the making of the gay market.* New York: Columbia University Press.

Siegel, P. (1994). On the owning of words: reflections on *San Francisco Arts and Athletics vs. United States Olympic Committee.* In R. J. Ringer (Ed.). *Queer words, queer images: communication and the construction of homosexuality* (pp. 30–44). New York: New York University Press.

Stevenson, D., Rowe, D. & Markwell, K. (2005). Explorations in 'event ecology': the case of the international Gay Games. *Social Identities, 11*(5): 447–65.

Sydney 2002 Gay Games Bid Ltd. (1997). *Sydney Gay Games VI: under new skies bid document.* Sydney, Australia: Sydney 2002 Gay Games Ltd.

Symons, C. (2004). The Gay Games: the play of sexuality, sport and community. Unpublished doctoral dissertation, Victoria University of Technology, Melbourne, Victoria, Australia.

Symons, C. (2002). The Gay Games and community. In D. A. Hemphill & C. Symons (Eds). *Gender, sexuality and sport: a dangerous mix* (pp. 101–14). Petersham, NSW, Australia: Walla Walla Press.

Symons, C. & Hemphill, D. (Eds). (2002). *Gender, sexuality and sport: a dangerous mix*. Sydney: Walla Walla Press.

Take the flame! Gay Games: grace, grit & glory (2006). Secter, D. (Producer/Writer). [Documentary]. Long Beach, CA: The Movie Secter.

Waddell, T. (1984, January). The promise of '86. *Triumph in '86, 1*: 1.

Waddell, T. & Schaap, D. (1996). *Gay Olympian: the life and death of Dr. Tom Waddell*. New York: Alfred A. Knopf.

West, A. (2002). Thanks for having us Sydney, say gays. *Sun Herald,* 10 November, p. 31.

9

Black and White in Australian sport

Colin Tatz

White Australia has always discerned Aborigines on a descending 'd' scale: as different, distinct, divergent, disordered, discordant and disparate. But essentially they have been seen as 'other' – not just different in quality but as *other as human*. They were treated as such for long periods from the beginning of white settlement in 1788. From the first anatomical classifications of human forms in the 19th century, from those (now) seemingly ridiculous divisions of 'races' into the woolly-, curly-, straight- or flaxen-haired, the broad- or convex-nosed, the white, red, yellow, brown and black peoples, the brachycephalic or dolichocephalic skull types, the 'Australoids' stood apart. (They still do, as we will see.) The wonder 'science' of craniology declared that the mean internal cubic capacity of the Aboriginal skull was significantly less than that of the consummate 'Caucasian' skull, thus predicating the biological destiny of Aborigines, their primitiveness, paganness and placing in the rankings of mankind.

The first officials and transported convicts Down Under did not need biology or anatomy lessons to arrive at dislike, disdain and, eventually, disregard for the humanity of the native peoples. This was despite edicts from the British Colonial Office to maintain friendly relations, not to disturb Aboriginal lands, to provide them with food, shelter, 'gratuitous medical assistance and relief' (Dunstan 1966, pp. 315–16). The newcomers, including Christian missionaries, saw them and described them variously as odious, 'scarcely human', 'hideous to look at', 'steeped in infamy', 'rotten in things sexual', 'sins against creation', 'wild animals', 'loathsome', 'vermin' and a 'nuisance' (Tatz 1999, p. 15). Disparateness was to become genocidal, mainly in the form of physical killing and the forcible transfer of their children into the mainstream society, part of a eugenicist fantasy to facilitate the disappearance of Aboriginality.

The respect factor

Nearly 40 years ago I compared race politics in Australia, New Zealand, Canada and South Africa. There was, and there is, I said, a direct correlation between the extent of indigenous rights and the degree to which the native peoples fought, or are fighting, against the dominant society (Tatz 1972, pp. 19–20). I called this 'the respect factor': the more respect the greater the rights. Respect does not have to mean a liking for; it can have the negative attribute of fear, even hatred. It means that the people concerned are 'people of account', to be taken into account and not relegated or consigned to the status of non-persons. Even in the worst of the apartheid years, black South Africans were regarded as a people of account by virtue of their numbers, military prowess, political and social organisation, animal husbandry and crop-growing. Maori as tribal warriors, modern soldiers, successful farmers and mighty players of religious rugby command respect. Less so the Indians and Inuit of Canada and – perhaps until the last two or three decades – so much less so the Aborigines, the people aptly described as the most *totally* conquered minority in Western history (Rowley 1970, pp. 2–9).

The hallmark of Aboriginal policy and administration, at least until the 1970s, was that they were treated as mute, malleable, movable, child-like and childish; since there was no (obvious) audible or visible resistance in the forms we recognise – like protest marches, strikes or violence – they appeared acquiescent in all that was done to, or for, them. For nearly a hundred years Aborigines were administered on the 'scientific' premises of men like Professor Baldwin Spencer, biologist and Australian Rules football administrator, who became Chief Protector of Aborigines in the Northern Territory: 'The aboriginal is, indeed, a very curious mixture: mentally, about the level of a child who has little control over his feelings and is liable to give way to violent fits of temper ... He has no sense of responsibility and, except in rare cases, no initiative' (Spencer 1913). Alas, he wrote, they did not even realise that they could make clothes out of kangaroo skins and, crucially, they did not cultivate crops or domesticate animals. The commodity of land, and the concomitant of labouring on it or profiting from it, was what the 18th-century philosopher John Locke considered the incarnation of civilisation: *ergo*, the Aboriginal hunter-gatherers were uncivilised and would remain so until they understood our concept of property.

What has changed since I wrote this in 1972 is that Aborigines have fought hard in three key arenas: in the politics of land rights and the acquisition of some very significant real estate across the continent, on several cultural stages both here and abroad and, especially, on the sports fields. They have become an ambiguous people, still excoriated and denigrated racially but often considered people of worth, virtue and value.

Ambiguity in race politics

Ambiguity is a major strategy in political science and public administration. It enables political candidates to express views on difficult topics without appearing to be on one side or the other: spin, elasticity, multiple meanings and a double-edged quality encourage listeners to hear what they want to hear. Ambiguity has more serious consequences in administration. It is a bureaucratic method of dealing with competing crises – a tactic of postponement or deflection or burial by way of diffusing responsibility, evading direct accountability, creating a sense of tentativeness, equivocation, enigma, perplexity and unclarity. Sir Humphrey Appleby, in that masterful *Yes, Minister* television series of the 1980s, was the apotheosis of ambiguity.

Aboriginal ambiguity has been stark. They were people but not people. They were *ferae naturae*, wild animals, and hence courts would come to deem the land *terra nullius*, an uninhabited land, when the settlers arrived. Later, they belonged as part of the nation, yet – in the phrase of genocide scholar Helen Fein – they were outside the nation's 'universe of obligation' and therefore disposable. For some legal purposes they were citizens, yet in a practical sense uncitizens for much of their daily lives. They were subject to the 'majesty' of the law, yet in practice were, and are, unprotected by its elementary rights and writs (as discussed later). Harsh and special laws applied only to them in a separate (and unchallengeable) legal system. They were removed from parents because 'no matter how frantic (a mother's) momentary grief might be at the time ... they soon forget their offspring' (Gale 1909, p. 9). They were British subjects, eventually protected by special laws and severe geographic isolation to save them from people who, in no particular order, wanted to kill them, remove their children, take their women and sell them opium. The protections soon became gross discriminations and violations of fundamental rights and freedoms. Elementary services – health, medical and dental care, schools, sanitation systems, clean water, garbage disposal, electricity, passable roads, adequate nutrition, basic housing, genuine artisan training, adequate wages, sport and leisure facilities – have been systematically absent, or denied, or provided half-heartedly, intermittently, inadequately, shoddily, maladroitly even as this is written. Friedrich Dürrenmatt, the renowned Swiss writer, wrote aptly enough (in an altogether different context): we 'do not do what we must do, obstinately never quite doing what must be done, but at best doing things only halfway, and even that grudgingly' (Dürrenmatt 1990, p. 33). The latest in a long line of governmental mantras and policy slogans is 'closing the gap', that is, reducing the difference between white male life expectancy, now said to be 77 to 79, and Aboriginal male life expectancy, ostensibly 57 to 59. The reality rather than the statistical probability is that in this land of 'the fair go' few Aboriginal men live beyond 50 – for a host of socioeconomic and politico-legal reasons, not because of a genetic predisposition to die, or want to die, early. A glance at any of the social indicators – life expectancy, infant mortality rates, morbidity rates, prevalence and incidence of communicable diseases, deaths from non-natural causes, school attainments, annual incomes and the like – show that Aborigines do not live the way of other Australians.

Abnormal society

A comment from Hassan Howa will long adorn the literature on racism in sport. When president of the South African Council on Sport and campaigning for sports boycotts in the most vicious years of apartheid, he said: 'there can be no normal sport in an abnormal society'. What would he have made of the levels of racism in the Aboriginal experience? In his *The nature of prejudice*, the Harvard psychologist Gordon Allport (1954) mistakenly linked several scales of prejudice in a causal syndrome: following scale one, antilocution (by which he meant 'bad-mouthing' and name-calling), he listed social exclusion, then geographic or regional exclusion, then physical attacks such as lynchings and, finally, extermination. Australian racism has been many of these things, not necessarily in any arithmetic sequence, but assuredly of an ingrained, patterned, institutionalised, systemic and pandemic nature. Aborigines have had to live with, and die from, an overt, physical racism that transcends all the offensiveness of verbal vilification.

Organised sport is most often concerned primarily with racist abuse of players by players and by fans in the stands. Most sports codes of conduct, especially in the four football genres, still treat 'sledging' (an Australian term for such abuse) as a form of 'illness' that requires *in camera* counselling, the offender meeting the offendee in private, conciliation, offers of apology and promises not to repeat the insult, and the 'victim-patient' hopefully healed. Codes of conduct have recently introduced game suspensions and hefty fines, but 'illness' remains the core diagnosis of these 'social' misdemeanours.

Maligning people is hardly on the same level as promiscuous and wholesale slaying. The organised massacres of the 19th century were essentially perpetrated by settlers, with the state authorities in the role of bystanders. (Rarely did the state prosecute white killers.) Later, state-run Native Police Forces became the instruments of killings. Settlers killed some 10,000 Aborigines in the colony of Queensland between 1824 and 1908. In 1883, the British High Commissioner in Queensland, Arthur Hamilton Gordon, wrote to his friend William Gladstone, then Prime Minister of England, that Aborigines were regarded 'as vermin to be cleared off the face of the earth': 'I have heard men of culture and refinement ... talk, not only of the *wholesale* butchery ... but of the *individual* murder of natives, exactly as they would talk of a day's sport, or having to kill some troublesome animal' (Evans et al. 1988, p. 78).

In 1896, the Queensland Colonial Secretary appointed Archibald Meston as Special Commissioner to investigate the Aboriginal condition. 'Men and women [were] hunted like wild beasts'; 'kidnapping of women and nameless outrages were reported'; in 25 years, one tribe of 3000 'was down to 100 survivors' as a result of 'the old style of "dispersal"'; 'boys and girls were frequently taken from their parents ... with no chance of returning'. All of which was 'a reproach to our common humanity' (Meston 1896, pp. 723–36). The 'only way to arrest their destruction', to 'save any part of the race from extinction', was to abolish the (homicidal) Native Police force, ban opium, and ensure the 'absolute isolation' from the whites who – 'coloured by prejudice, distorted by ignorance' – committed 'shameful deeds' (Meston 1896, pp. 733–34).

Can one play cricket and run track races amid genocidal killings? Yes. During the general carnage there was enough freedom to bat, bowl and run (Tatz 1995). In the 1890s, a number of Aborigines were playing cricket at Deebing Creek, near Ipswich, Queensland. Townspeople felt that 'every encouragement should be given to our ebony brethren'. People came to watch. They 'behaved like white gentlemen', said the *Queensland Times*. The Deebing Creek team won a major trophy in 1895 and then played the National Cricket Union in Brisbane. The Colonial Secretary, shortly before he received Meston's report, sent the Aborigines two cricket bats 'in appreciation of their excellent behaviour and smart turn-out'.

Across the land, cricket and massacres were widespread. Victoria was the first colony to enact safeguards, with the *Aborigines Protection Act 1869*. One year earlier, an Aboriginal cricket team toured England, a decade before a white team ventured abroad. The story is that an Edenhope grazier sent pictures of 'his' Aborigines to the owners of the Melbourne Cricket Ground refreshment tent, suggesting matches (Mulvaney & Harcourt 1988). In the

Lake Wallace district of Western Victoria, pastoralists had taught their servants the game because they and their sons had no one to play against. The names their 'owners' assigned to them illustrated their paternalistic attitudes: Jim Crow, Sundown, Redcap, Tarpot, King Cole, Mosquito, Tiger, Bullocky. Amid talk of commercial exploitation and associated skulduggery, and despite much illness among the players, hotelier Charles Lawrence agreed to coach the Aboriginal team for an English tour. The team landed in England in May 1868. Two players were ill enough to be sent home and King Cole died of tuberculosis on tour. They played 47 matches for 19 draws, 14 wins and 14 losses.

Historic, heroic, romantic, the subject of three books and innumerable photographic reproductions, the tour was also the beginning of sport exploitation, bad faith and ill treatment. The star of the tour, Johnny Mullagh (named after Mullagh Station, where he worked) was the only player to establish a cricket career on his return. Despite the general ethos of racial disdain, a memorial to this man was erected at rural Harrow and the local cricket oval bears his name. But later researchers have established that there was indignity, even cruelty, as the players went unpaid, were housed inadequately, and regarded as quaint circus-freak performers of various native sports rather than of cricket (Samson 2009). Had the Protection Board been in existence a year earlier, however, the famous tour would not have taken place.

In 1850, Reverend Matthew Blagden Hale's vision was to protect Aborigines from 'a vicious portion of the white population' (Tatz 1995, pp. 47–48). At Poonindie, 19 km from Port Lincoln in South Australia, he would 'train them in the habits of civilized life'. To overcome a 'native temperament' said to be distressed by 'continuous labour', illness and 'flagging spirits', he introduced cricket. The Aboriginal team won all but one of its local matches. In Adelaide, the Anglican Bishop attended a match between Poonindie and the upper-class Collegiate School of St Peter in 1872. Cricket, wrote Bishop Short in startling prose, proved 'incontestably that the Anglican aristocracy of England and the 'noble savage', who ran wild in the Australian woods, are linked together in one brotherhood of blood – moved by the same passions, desires, and affections'. Not so. Legal and physical separation of Aborigines were already under way. Increasing ill health, white complaints and pressure from neighbouring farmers to acquire Aboriginal land led to the end of the mission, and its cricket, in 1895.

Professional athletics, called pedestrianism, was a major gambling sport of the 19th century. Aborigines – seeking escape from isolated reserves and the incarceration of mission and government settlement life – were very good at it. Charlie Samuels, christened by his sheep property 'owner' as Sambo Combo, was the kingpin of the 1880s and 1890s. The leading sports paper, *The Referee*, wrote in 1894 that 'it might be a more pleasant reflection to Australians, perhaps, if a white man could be quoted as champion [of Australia] ... but a black aboriginal has to be accorded the laurel crown ... [He was] one of the best exponents of sprint running the world has ever seen' (Tatz 1995, p. 95). The most famous and richest of all the races, the Stawell Easter Gift in Victoria, was won by Aboriginal runners in 1883 (Bobby Kinnear), 1910 (Tom Dancey), 1929 (Lynch Cooper) and again in 2005 and 2006 (Joshua Ross).

Athletics officials created obstacles from the 1880s to the 1920s. So did the white athletes who wrote to the Governor of Queensland asking him to ban all Aborigines at Fraser Island – in effect because they always won. When Aborigines became prominent, separate initials began appearing after each runner's name in the official race programs, indicating that 'a' was Aboriginal, 'h.c.' a 'half-caste', and 'c.p.' a 'coloured person'. It was suggested that 'without these distinguishing marks ... the public are misled'. This practice lasted for some 40 years, but at least Aborigines were participants in the spiked-shoe business.

In 1976, Pastor Sir Douglas Nicholls became, briefly (due to illness), the Governor of South Australia. He remains the only Aboriginal Knight of the (Imperial) Realm. He hailed from Cummeragunja (Cummera), a mission on the Murray River between New South Wales (NSW) and Victoria, a small community that produced an assembly line of athletes, Australian Rules footballers, political figures and human rights activists. Doug tried out for Carlton Football Club but was told that because of his colour, he smelled. Fitzroy FC took him and his Australian Rules career was illustrious in the early 1930s. He had a stint in a travelling circus boxing tent and was a champion sprinter. In 1929, Nicholls won the 120-yards Warracknabeal Gift and with it a prize of 100 guineas (about AU$235 at face value). The money was a staggering sum, considering that the total annual income for Cummera's 140 farming people the previous year was a mere five times his winnings. Not surprisingly, Nicholls had a stronger motive to run than to reap.

Cummera began as a private mission in 1874. Daniel Matthews, an Echuca merchant, ran the original Maloga Mission on strictly religious principles. He was also prone to beating eloping girls. He resented their growing 'manifest ingratitude'. For him, cricket was 'an uncivilizing activity'. The Aborigines saw things differently. Matthews' biographer, Nancy Cato (1976, p. 128), wrote: 'They had discovered that their prowess in sport, particularly in cricket and running, gave them a passport to the white man's world, even to his respect and friendship'. He tried to prevent that passage. The Nicholls story is, of course, an extraordinary one but he did establish that sport was an escape from rigid isolation and an avenue to some social acceptance, even if transiently for the most part.

Monumental contradictions

At least 15 public monuments honour Aboriginal and Islander sports men and women. Victoria has an obelisk for sprinter Bobby Kinnear and a similar edifice for cricketer Johnny Mullagh; a Melbourne street plaque commemorates jockey Peter St Albans, winning jockey in the 1876 Melbourne Cup, while a suburban community centre is named after all-rounder Doug Nicholls. In NSW, a large roadside memorial celebrates middleweight boxer Dave Sands near Dungog, the scene of his fatal truck accident. Twice voted the most popular sportsman in Australia, his funeral drew one of the largest crowds ever seen in that state. There is an impressive Sands monument in Kempsey, NSW and a refurbished plaque at the juncture of two of Sydney's busiest inner city roads. The centre court at Homebush is named after tennis champion Evonne Goolagong. Two Queensland streets, in Cherbourg and in Dalby, commemorate boxer Jerry Jerome, the first Aborigine to win a national title (the middleweight championship in 1912). The entrance to Canberra Stadium has a life-size statue of Laurie Daley and the main stand bears the name of Mal Meninga, a South Sea Islander, and tributes to their Rugby League achievements. In Perth, the 'Polly' Farmer Room at Subiaco Oval honours the great Australian footballer; and in Darwin, the stadium restaurant is named after Tiwi Island footballer David Kantilla. A statue of fast bowler Eddie Gilbert, unveiled in November 2008, overlooks the headquarters of Queensland Cricket in Brisbane.

These monuments and arenas do not tell their stories. Rather, they hide or omit the realities of the lives they celebrate. Sport, wrote the late Ron Pickering (of the BBC), is based on an ethos of play, competition and opportunities being fair and equal for all. For Aborigines, Torres Strait Islanders and the South Sea Islanders, descendants of those 'blackbirded', that is, kidnapped, chained and brought here to work in sugar plantations between 1863 and 1904, there has been exclusion from competition, discrimination within it, and at times gross inequality of chances, choices and facilities – even in the early years of this new century. They have also had to overcome well-trained, experienced and talented opponents.

Sport is a litmus and a litany of ambiguity in the Aboriginal experience: there has been both denigration and adulation, contempt and respect, calumny and celebration, tolerance and bigotry, inclusion and exclusion.

The sport of inclusion

In the 1870s, the people at Coranderrk, near Healesville in Victoria, had proven themselves as farmers, musicians, cricketers, Christians and as peaceful and successful political demonstrators. Their success in crop-growing irritated white neighbours. Their cricket team won acceptance, and many games. Their Australian Rules football team, Badger Creek, was readily accepted and in 1906 contained an unimaginable man, Joseph Wandin, who became the first Aboriginal principal of a state primary school. The school was restored for centenary celebrations in 1994, but by then – and despite the earlier Aboriginal gains before royal commissions and parliamentary inquiries in the 1870s and 1880s – Coranderrk was no more, reduced to a quarter-acre plot with a memorial gravestone. The rest has become white suburbia, and a popular zoo.

Despite the views of Daniel Matthews, Imperial Britain used cricket as a civilising force in some colonies. But that a non-English-speaking Spanish monk should so view the game is quite startling. In 1879, Abbot Rosendo Salvado appointed a farmer, H. B. Lefroy, as coach of the New Norcia Mission team in Western Australia, situated some 120 km north of Perth, and began a series of matches in Perth. The team lost only once in 18 games. A Christian historian of the era remarked:

> The Australian native takes kindly to any form of sport he may set his mind upon. His inclination to labour is not at all so keen. But if labour could be placed before him in the form of a game of some kind, he would be an undoubted success in the world. (Tatz 1995, p. 57)

Neither Salvado nor cricket prevailed after 1905. Although an *Aborigines Protection Act* was introduced in 1886, it was the new law, the *Aborigines Act 1905*, that ended Aboriginal rights and freedoms. The Chief Protector became the legal guardian of every Aborigine under 16 and he could remove people to and from reserves at whim. Liquor was forbidden, as was any junior female presence 'within two miles of any creek or inlet used by pearlers between sunset and sunrise'. With the sexual ambiguities and fears about 'racial mixing', it was a given that inter-racial marriage was banned, unless by written permission of the Protector. Children were forcibly removed from their parents and placed in so-called assimilation homes – 'for their own good'.

Queensland in 1897 and Western Australia in 1905 set the tone for the rest of the country. Rigid law was now the instrument of social control and much of settler animus and prejudice were reflected in the statutes and draconian regulations. In the West, Aborigines could be punished for refusing to work, being cheeky, not emptying laundry tubs, leaving taps running, not parking the horse and dray and being untidy. In Queensland they could be imprisoned by officials and missionaries, for three weeks at a time on each 'charge', for refusing to work, committing adultery, playing cards, setting fire to the women's jail, and refusing to give a faeces sample to the visiting doctor. How did they play sport amidst all this? With difficulty.

South Australia was marginally, but only marginally, more humanitarian on Aboriginal matters. Koonibba, in the far west of the state, began as a Lutheran mission in 1897 and has had a successful Australian Rules football team since 1906, winning close on two dozen premierships. It is the oldest surviving Aboriginal team in Australia. In the 1950s, with too many Aborigines wanting to play, a sister team, Rovers, was admitted to the league, and within a year had won the 1958 premiership. We are constantly reminded of the gap between Aboriginal male and non-Aboriginal male life expectancy. Rovers presents a stark reality. Of the 18 men in that winning team, only one was alive in 1987: the other 17 men did not make it to the age of 50.

Port Lincoln, SA has the reputation of being a racist town. Nonetheless, the Mallee Park Football Club is based in a community centre, on 19 acres, in the town, complete with licence, function rooms and facilities. It is the football that has provided the necessary cohesion, especially as the team won the premiership 11 times between 1985 and 2001.

The Northern Territory (NT) is perhaps *the* measure of ambiguity. Settlement began as a tiny colonial outpost in Palmerston, now Darwin, with a few hundred pith-helmeted, boozy bearers of the Imperial message about civilisation and 'the white man's burden', men who saw themselves as 'practical bushmen', that is, men ever eager to give the natives 'lessons in gunpowder'. Kipling would have enjoyed a short visit. Horseracing was the great sport, from which blacks were excluded, except as grooms, stable hands and jockeys in the 'blackboys' races that were always a postscript to the today's outings.

Australian football came to the NT in 1916 and from then, to this day, it became the all-consuming sport. Astonishingly, two 'half-castes' were at the birth and became not only football champions, but winners of cricket, athletics matches, swimming, soccer and shooting competitions. Reuben Cooper and Willie Allen each had a white father and a tribal Aboriginal mother. Both broke through the colour bars because of the status (and protection) of their fathers, and both became leaders in several fields. Allen served in Egypt and Palestine during World War I even though Aborigines were exempt from military service (because they were deemed unreliable). Cooper challenged the racism so embedded and so endemic in that frontier society. He became a coach and a legend in eras when white teams refused to play under 'coloured' referees and when the football league banned all 'non-white' players between 1926 and 1929.

From the time of the 'emancipation' of 'half-castes' in 1957, NT sport has been powered and driven by Aboriginal performances – particularly in netball, basketball, softball, volleyball, field hockey, darts and, especially, Australian Rules football. The NT Hall of Champions is obviously 'over-represented' by Aborigines, while the Aboriginal and Islander Sports Hall of Fame has very strong NT representation.

A key story is that of the St Marys football team. In the 1940s and early 1950s, many young men from the Tiwi Islands (Bathurst and Melville) came to Darwin for three-month spells to work for the army and air force. Despite the uniforms, they were not allowed to be servicemen and worked essentially as domestic servants. The Bishop of Darwin felt that football might be 'a good thing' for the men. Despite objections from the town's administrators who did not want 'too many blackfellas around', the team was born in 1952, formed with the help of Ted Egan, then a patrol officer with the Department of Native Affairs. He initially coached and captained St Marys. In 1954–55 they won the first of many premierships, and a total of 26 Northern Territory Football League (NTFL) flags by the end of the 2007–08 season.

The politics of inclusion and exclusion has been long and painful. In the 2006–07 season, a team representing the Tiwi Islands Football League, the Tiwi Bombers, was admitted to the NTFL on a trial basis. The all-Aboriginal team played each of the seven NTFL teams in the first round of matches, winning six. The trial was a great success and proved most popular with the Darwin football public. The Bombers were finally admitted to the NTFL as its eighth team for the 2007–08 season.

Queensland remains the 'problem child' of Australian race relations. The *Protection Act* of 1897 saved at least half of the Aboriginal clans from massacre and the opium trade, but the legacies of racial hatred and contempt remained for a very long time. The legislation enabled full control of Aborigines and included, as most such laws did, a provision for exemption, the certificate of which basically indicated that the holder was, in effect, 'white folks'. Meston was the first Protector, and although a sports lover, he hated cricket. Walter Roth, his successor, disliked all sport and insisted on stopping it: the pedestrians ('peds') make 'plenty of money for a few years on behalf of the betting fraternity ... come back to us wrecks, as a rule, and a nuisance and a burden upon the rest' (Tatz 1995, p. 89). He banned all peds from earning their living by the strategy of prosecuting trainers for coaching them and race promoters for 'harbouring' them.

Jerry Jerome's manager gained him an exemption certificate, allowing him a long and popular career as a middleweight boxer. Roth loathed and hounded him, accusing 'this moneyed gentleman' of 'inciting Aborigines to refuse to work unless paid cash for it' at

Taroom settlement. The authorities got their man: when his boxing ended, they shipped him to Cherbourg settlement, took his earnings, and there he died, penniless. Ron Richards, possibly the best of all Australian boxers, hailed from Deebing Creek (Meston's first point of refuge for the victim peoples). In his career, exploited as most Aboriginal boxers were, he twice beat Gus Lesnevitch, considered one of the greatest light-heavyweight champions of the 20th century. He lost twice to the legendary Archie Moore. But if not for his exemption certificate, there would have been no place for him in history.

Jerome was the forerunner of Richards, and Richards led the way for what seemed like an avalanche of Aboriginal champions from Queensland: Elley Bennett, bantamweight champion of Australia, George Bracken, twice lightweight champion, Gary Cowburn, welterweight and junior welterweight champion, Jack Hassen, lightweight champion, Robert Peden, bantamweight champion. An all-time record was created at the Commonwealth Games in 1962: in Australia's amateur boxing team of eight, three men – Jeff Dynevor, Eddie Barney (Eddie Gilbert's son) and Adrian Blair – came from Cherbourg settlement with a population of just on a thousand. All three were 'controlled' Aborigines, needing dispensation to leave the reserve and fight in Perth. (Dynevor won the bantamweight gold.)

Given the tenor of race relations in Queensland, there were several unusual and unexpected stories. In 1893, Frank Ivory – 'a half-caste from Maryborough' – played Rugby Union for Queensland against NSW. Women's cricket began in 1929, basically as a 'silvertail' (upper-class) game, yet when an English team arrived on tour in 1934, two very poor-end-of-town black first cousins, Edna Crouch and Mabel Campbell, were picked for Queensland. Earlier, in 1925, Edna's brother Paddy was chosen for a Queensland Rugby League tour to New Zealand. Eddie Gilbert, who once famously bowled Don Bradman for a duck and who Bradman said was the fastest bowler he had ever faced, was a Cherbourg man who played for Queensland between 1930 and 1935. 'Controlled', he travelled to matches by train, while his team mates went together by car. Forever chaperoned lest he got too close to white ladies, he needed permission to play in each match. When his services were no longer needed, the Queensland Cricket Association did not send the notice to him but to his 'guardian', the settlement manager, with the request that the cricket clothing issued to Eddie be laundered and returned to headquarters in Brisbane. Nevertheless, he did play Sheffield Shield cricket for six years. (He died after 23 years in an overcrowded asylum, enduring much racial abuse.)

By the early 1970s, things were beginning to change across black Australia. Most states abolished their restrictive statutes, except Queensland, which followed suit in the mid-1980s. Rugby League was the major sport. Beginning with Lionel Morgan playing for Australia in 1962, an assembly line of stellar players emerged, especially in the ferocious State of Origin matches against NSW: Artie Beetson, a leviathan in the game then and since, Tony Currie, Colin Scott, Dale Shearer, Mal Meninga, Steve Renouf, Sam Backo, Gorden Tallis, Jonathon Thurston, Matt Bowen, Justin Hodges, Sam Thaiday and many others. Each is now a 'star', a hero, well-paid, carefully nurtured and managed, extravagantly paraded poster boy for all manner of commercial and public relations exercises intended to suggest level playing fields. More than any other sport, Queensland Rugby League illustrates the dialectical contradictions of denigration and adulation, vilification and adoration, omission and selection.

The sport of exclusion

Queensland passed its (genocide) *Protection Act* in 1897 and the other states soon followed that model. The restrictive laws prevented Aboriginal participation in virtually every economic activity, confining them to isolated mission stations and reserves for 'their own protection'. The Queensland Amateur Athletics Association tried to disbar all Aborigines on the spurious grounds that they either 'lacked moral character', 'had insufficient intelligence' or 'couldn't resist white vice'. These appalling excuses were rejected by the national athletics body, leading to the Queensland Association deeming them all professionals in 1903. In 1896, the Northern Territory settlers, small in numbers, ordained that 'no aborigines or other coloured races be allowed to compete in European events' – a response to the £10 Pine Creek Handicap victory in 1895 of an Aborigine named, unsurprisingly, Bismarck.

Exclusion does not have to be an overt racist act; omission is effective enough. The original Victorian Football League (VFL, renamed the AFL in 1990) began in 1897. Accused of being a colonial bastion with colonial attitudes, one can find only two Aboriginal names between the 1890s and the 1920s, and ten players from the start until the league's 75th anniversary in 1962. Aborigines certainly had the strength, speed or reaction skills needed for this game: their prowess in cricket, boxing and especially professional athletics had been well demonstrated in the century between the 1860s and the 1960s. This fast running, handling, kicking game on a large field seemed a 'natural' for sports-minded Aborigines, especially if *marn-grook* – the native game on which Australian football is said to be based – was the prevailing pastime of local tribesmen.

The trickle began in the 1950s but there were as few as 20 top players in the first 80 years of the competition. The (relative) flood of Aboriginal players began in the 1980s with six to seven times that earlier number emerging in the next 20 years. There is now an over-representation of Aboriginal players: Aborigines form 2.6% of the population (517,000 people) yet they now comprise between 13 and 14% of the senior players in AFL (and in Rugby League).

Exclusion led to bizarre situations. In the 1920s, Leo Appo, a champion axeman, could not get a place at the Royal Easter Show in Sydney. Encouraged to call himself a New Zealander, he gained entry and won several events before announcing his Aboriginality. To gain bouts, several mainline boxers became 'Greek'. Percy Hobson, chosen for the high jump at the 1962 Commonwealth Games, was told to 'play down' his Aboriginal origins. Frankie Reys, winner of the 1973 Melbourne Cup, said horseracing was so racist that he called himself a Filipino (which he was, in part), and in that identity he became president of the Victorian Jockeys' Association for ten years. Even in the 1960s and 1970s, several VFL players and Rugby League champions also 'suppressed', or were suppressed, but 'found' their Aboriginal origins on retirement.

Pre- and postwar Aboriginal teams in Australian Rules and in Rugby League have been refused admission or been expelled from various leagues. The Tweed Heads All-Blacks Rugby League team arose solely as a result of Aboriginal exclusion from white teams in 1930. Efforts 'to admit the dusky athletes to the white fold' in 1931 failed, 'the Noes having it by 17 votes to 15, with the result that the whites will have to struggle on as best they can' (Tatz 1995, p. 196). The famous Cherbourg teams of the 1920s and 1930s won many local league trophies in southern Queensland. Frank Fisher, grandfather of champion athlete Cathy Freeman, was a central figure in their successes. Invited to play professionally in England, the Aboriginal administration refused him permission to apply for a passport, claiming that one star from Cherbourg, Eddie Gilbert, was enough.

The importance of the Redfern All-Blacks Rugby League team in NSW does not lie in the pennants they have won. Rather, it was the focus of a strong sense of black identity in downtown Sydney, an urban society into which Aborigines, especially the rural 'half-castes', were meant to be assimilated to the point of their disappearance. The Foundation for Aboriginal Affairs was established near Redfern in 1963 as a way of assisting Aboriginal migration to the big city. Its founders were keenly aware of the struggle to survive discrimination, exploitation, poverty and, perhaps foremost, the pressure to surrender their identity. The All Blacks team defied the Liberal Coalition policy of the time which insisted that 'all Aborigines and part-Aborigines will attain the same manner of living as other Australians and live as members of a single community ... observing the same customs and influenced by the same beliefs, hopes and loyalties as other Australians' (Tatz 1964).

Narwan, in Armidale, NSW, was yet another team born out of discrimination. In the 1970s a number of players in white teams were forever sitting on the bench, not getting games and feeling unwanted. Amid loud cries of opposition from the town and the local university academics, they achieved an Aboriginal side in 1977. They won the Caltex Shield and in 1980 the Clayton Cup, country league's most prestigious event. They went on to win five premierships and four knockout competitions. Regrettably, as with so many teams, Narwan was expelled from Group 19 in country competition in 2005, ostensibly for unpaid debts. The Gimbisi Warriors were ejected from Group 2 for 'crowd behaviour' and Northern United were refused entry to Group 1.

The Moree Boomerangs have an outstanding record. Their team began in the 1940s, disappeared, then resurfaced in the 1970s. They won the prestigious Group 4 grand final in 1982 and again in 1992. Sadly, as the last century ended, the Boomerangs were excluded from the competition. Such exclusion has occurred in every state in the last three decades. Reasons vary from bad fan behaviour, to assaulting referees, unpaid dues and, in this land of excessive oaths and imprecations, excessive bad language.

The latest of many such sagas has been the attempt to create a 14-team competition called the Nations Aboriginal Rugby League in rural NSW. Why there is so much opposition, especially from Country Rugby League, is not clear: such bodies may well be part of the strong assimilationist thrusts still evident in Australian public life, or football administrators may not want to lose the many Aboriginal champions who now play for senior city teams.

The concept of 'All Blacks' is alive and well; Aborigines have shown, especially through the NSW Aboriginal Rugby League Knockout carnival, that they can run their own competitions, given a little breathing space and a ground to play on; and, significantly, the people of towns like Toomelah, Taree, Kempsey, Newcastle, Bourke, Walgett and Moree now see themselves as Aboriginal *nations*.

In the 2008 World Cup, the National Rugby League (NRL) presented a match as a curtain-raiser to the Australia *versus* New Zealand match: an 'Indigenous Dreamtime' team (34 points) won against a New Zealand Maori team (26). This led to an immediate clamour for both the Aboriginal and the Maori teams to be included officially in the next World Cup in 2013. Their playing styles attract fans, and pressure will mount for an Aboriginal team's inclusion – but that goal will depend on the willingness of the national team to forego their star Aboriginal players. It will also require a willingness to understand that Aboriginal culture is not solely about corroborees, body-painting and dancing, but is also very much about kinship, family and social ties that are enhanced by playing games together.

Appropriation, adulation and intervention

Evonne Goolagong-Cawley and Cathy Freeman are national treasures and both are adored internationally. The 'Evonne Goolagong Court' is the centrepiece at the new International Tennis Centre at Homebush, site of the 2000 Olympics. Cathy adorns covers of books, magazines and calendars, and is frequently seen on television news and sports program promotions and introductions. In 2009, French, Swedish and German journalists were still travelling to Australia to 'examine' Cathy's life after retirement, and she remains probably the most photographed sportsperson in Australia.

Cathy may be the forerunner of a generation of young women who can make it against the barriers of racism, sexism and stereotyping. Yet her breaking through makes her a convenient 'sample of one' – the attractive, sunny world champion whose very agreeable presence on centre stage 'proved' that Australians are not racist. She was always well aware of this tokenism and symbolism, the readiness of all to embrace her, to appropriate her as though she has single-handedly transformed the whole Aboriginal experience into the opposite of what it really is. There may well be neither malice nor ulterior motive in this taking over of Cathy, but her success is still portrayed, or sometimes interpreted, as proof of the (allegedly) vast improvements in Aboriginal life. Her belief 'that dreams really do come true' is, regrettably, not true for enough Aboriginal and Islander aspirants, most especially women. Evonne and Cathy are, in effect, aberrations – their careers and their chosen sports are not the norm for Aboriginal or Islander women.

In 2007, the Howard Coalition federal government launched an 'emergency intervention' in the Northern Territory, sending in civilian task forces (largely untrained in this work), and the military (even less qualified) 'to save the children' from reported child abuse, sexual molestation and neglect. Amid growing criticism, Kevin Rudd's Labor government has continued the program for at least another three years. The intervention involves the suspension (and therefore the protections) of the federal *Racial Discrimination Act* and the Northern Territory's anti-discrimination legislation; the suspension of the permit system which allows Aborigines to decide who can enter their domains; the search for sexual predators, but with not one charge or one arrest in over two year's of operation; the quarantining of all social welfare payments; the physical medical examination of children; the banning of alcohol and police raids on houses in search of yeast (lest they brew at home); and the extraction of rentals for Spinifex-grass 'humpies' and lean-to dwellings (to teach them the value of property). It affects some 82 communities and 47 town camps.

There is a Meston-like quality about this 'save-the-children' intervention. There are some positive outcomes to date, notably the reduction of alcohol-fuelled male pressures on women to hand over their food money, but it must be said that not very much has changed since Meston pushed for such protections 114 years ago: there is still a governmental philosophy of blanket ascription, that is, any instance of deviant behaviour by an individual, a group or a community is considered the behaviour of *all* Aborigines, and *all* must surrender to a national or state 'remedy'. Aborigines are back to where the *Aboriginals Ordinance 1911* began; only this time there are no exemption certificates.

In such contexts and environments, how do men and women go about the business of playing sport? Whether there is intervention of this military, and very old-fashioned, kind or whether communities attempt living under their own rules, the daily lives of those in remote and rural Australia are not normal in a first-world nation.

A matter of access

What are the norms for most Aborigines? Because of their place in the political, legal, economic and social system, Aborigines, Torres Strait and South Sea Islanders rarely get onto squash courts or championship golf courses or into ski lodges. They do not hang-glide, play polo, sail yachts, ride bikes for Yamaha (apart from the amazing Chad Reed, now in the United States) or drive cars for Ferrari. On remote or rural reserves, where most Aborigines have lived, there was and is no grass, no facilities, coaches, nutritionists, physiotherapists, personal trainers, motivators, let alone floodlights or change-rooms. Scholarship money is rare and even then transfer to sports institutes down south pose a problem for most Aboriginal sports apprentices: homesickness. Most dislike travel from home territory, let alone relocating to another state.

Sporting success has not ended their harsh experiences. Much remains unchanged: short lifespans, gross ill-health, lack of housing and sanitation, massive unemployment, less than adequate education, social breakdown in many communities, and a devastating youth suicide rate so indicative of the purposelessness of life. Yet sport is not a luxury or a leisure activity at the end of an arduous working week. For youth in many communities, it provides a sense of belonging and a feeling of coherence. Sport is more important to them than it is to any other segment of Australian society. It also lessens delinquency and, in an era in which suicide rates are grossly abnormal, it gives youth a sense of *belonging*. There is enough evidence to show that even if sport does not actually *prevent* suicide, it clearly defers that action, often allowing a time-out period to reconsider life's chances (Tatz 2007). It also offers a chance for a period of wellness. It is a powerful weapon in the fight against rampant diabetes; and many of today's illnesses, especially of the cardiac, renal and respiratory systems, are better controlled by physical regimens, including sporting competition. In many ways *sport is survival:* it provides purpose in life, an activity of real meaning, a sense of coherence, a reason for being, a sense of power and empowerment, and a feeling of autonomy, however brief.

References

Allport, G. (1954). *The nature of prejudice.* Cambridge, Massachusetts: Addison-Wesley.

Cato, N. (1976). *Mister Maloga.* St Lucia: University of Queensland Press.

Dunstan, D. (1966). Aboriginal land title and employment in South Australia. In I. G. Sharp & C. Tatz (Eds). *Aborigines in the economy: employment, wages and training* (pp. 314–26). Brisbane: Jacaranda Press.

Dürrenmatt, F. (1990). *The execution of justice*, London: Picador.

Evans, R., Saunders, K. & Cronin, K. (1988). *Race relations in colonial Queensland: a history of exclusion, exploitation and extermination.* St Lucia: University of Queensland Press.

Gale, C. F. (1909). *Report of the Chief Protector*, Western Australia Parliament, Votes and Proceedings, vol 2.

Meston, A. (1896). *Report on the Aboriginals of Queensland*, Queensland Parliament, Votes and Proceedings, IV (85).

Mulvaney, J. & Harcourt, R. (1988). *Cricket walkabout: the Australian Aborigines in England.* Melbourne: Macmillan.

Rowley, C. (1970). *The destruction of Aboriginal society: Aboriginal policy and practice*, (vol. 1). Canberra: Australian National University Press.

Samson, D. (2009). Culture, 'race' and discrimination in the 1868 Aboriginal cricket tour of England. *Australian Aboriginal Studies, 2*: 44–60.

Spencer, B. (1913). *Preliminary report on the Aboriginals of the Northern Territory*, Commonwealth of Australia, Parliamentary Papers, vol. III, 1913 – as part of the Report of the Administrator for the year 1912.

Tatz, C. (2007). *Aboriginal suicide is different: a portrait of life and self-destruction.* Canberra: Aboriginal Studies Press.

Tatz, C. (1999). *Genocide in Australia*, Research Discussion Paper no. 8, Australian Institute of Aboriginal and Torres Strait islander Studies, Canberra.

Tatz, C. (1995). *Obstacle race: Aborigines in sport.* Sydney: UNSW Press.

Tatz, C. (1972). Four kinds of dominion: comparative race politics in Australia, Canada, New Zealand and South Africa, inaugural public lecture, University of New England.

Tatz, C. (1964). Aboriginal administration in the Northern Territory of Australia, Unpublished PhD thesis, Australian National University, Canberra.

10

Beach sports

Douglas Booth[1]

> No matter what time you go to the beach you see [people exercising]. Breathing, stretching, yawning, yogaing, tai-chiing, wet sand jogging, punitively pounding along the promenade or slipping in soft sand, the whole beach is on the move. (Stewart 1984, p. 36)

Meg Stewart's comments above, made with specific reference to Bondi Beach, describe well the hive of physical activity observed on urban beaches across Australia. While the origins of that activity stretch back to the mid 19th century (Ford 2007), in this chapter I examine the physical cultures which developed around surf lifesaving and surfboard riding (or surfing) on Australia's urban beaches in the 20th century. Surf lifesavers and surfers comprise distinct cultures and occupy different spaces, but collectively they embody the most obvious forms of structured physicality on Australia's beaches.

This chapter contains two substantive sections. In the first I trace the origins and development of surf lifesaving and surfing as distinct sporting cultures in Australia. I argue that surf bathers formed surf lifesaving clubs in the early 20th century to legitimise their pastime during debates around the morality of bathing in public view, and that their sports, which were also a strategy of legitimisation, turned beaches into arenas. In the 1950s Californians introduced Australians to a new hedonistic beach culture based on (relatively) light and manoeuvrable surfboards. The so-called Malibu surfboard – named after the Californian beach where it became popular – redefined sand and surf in Australia. Ironically, just as surf bathers gained public acceptance by calling themselves surf lifesavers, so surfers achieved social credibility by labelling themselves sportspeople. Although surf lifesaving and surfing both attract the appellation 'sport', rather than acting as cultural glue, the term spawned philosophical and political division in both activities.

In the second section I examine surf lifesaving and surfing as fratriarchies, or brotherhoods, in which members bond through physical rites, intimidation, violence and denigrating women (Loy 1995). A key difference between the two fratriarchies is the way they demarcate their territory. Surf lifesavers exploit formal markers (e.g. clubhouses, uniforms, flags, insignia) reinforced by official signs (e.g. 'members only'); surfers use graffiti (e.g. 'locals only'), equipment (e.g. surfboards and towels) and sound (e.g. loud music, surfing argot).

---

1 I am grateful to Mark Falcous for his comments on a draft of this essay.

Sporting philosophies

Surf lifesaving and surfing emerged as physically grounded youth movements on Australian beaches in the early 20th century and after World War II respectively, and both initially struggled for social legitimacy. Here I look at the origins of these two sports and their associated sporting philosophies.

Surf lifesaving

In the late 19th and early 20th centuries, Australia's beaches were the site of social tension between surf bathers (many of whom entered the water naked) and moralists concerned by the former's lack of propriety. Surf bathers engaged rhetorics of health and wellbeing to justify their pastime. 'Sand, surf, sunshine and the free winds of heaven', championed Sydney's *Evening News* in 1907, 'make up the prescription which is confidently recommended as a sort of universal medicine. This, if not the elixir of life, must surely be part of it, and is certain to tone up the system and lengthen the life' (12 October). These claims failed to assuage concerns about indecent behaviour. Sydney's *Daily Telegraph* railed against beachgoers, calling them 'dirty ignorant louts ... dirty bodily and mentally', and condemned their 'unchecked ... horseplay' and nakedness (Brawley 1995, p. 11).

Disciplining beachgoers and providing a voluntary safety service underpinned the formation, in 1907, of the Surf Bathing Association of New South Wales (SBA), the predecessor of Surf Life Saving Australia (SLSA). The SBA advocated appropriate costumes for surf bathers and suggested rules for their proper conduct. In 1912 the SBA recommended to an official government inquiry into surf bathing that local councils appoint respectable members of surf bathing clubs as beach inspectors to police beachgoers (Surf Bathing Committee 1912, paras 148–49). One contemporary social commentator, Egbert Russell, reported club officials disciplining beachgoers. He observed one official 'sternly order[ing] a girl to cease diving from the shoulders of her male escort' and another ordering two youths to desist from dragging a third by his heels into the water. Thanks to these 'club men', Russell (1910, p. 265) wrote, 'it is rare ... that anybody hears of an incident which might not receive the hearty endorsement of the whole Council of Churches'.

Surf bathers also confronted sceptical residents and municipal councillors. They responded by structuring their clubs around beach patrols conducted by members experienced in the surf and knowledgeable about rescue techniques, first-aid and resuscitation. They introduced the bronze medallion as a basic qualification. Stressing physical fitness, strict discipline and mental alertness, the test for the bronze was, in the words of pioneer surf bather Arthur Lowe (1958, p. 93), 'one of the hardest examinations ... ever set'. But if patrols and a volunteer surf rescue service placated municipal councillors and local residents, they did not attract recruits. Social activities, camaraderie and clubhouses drew the majority of members to surf lifesaving with most joining as associate, rather than active (i.e. patrolling), members. Indeed, rules regarding patrol attendance, scrambles to fill patrol rosters and disciplinary proceedings against members who absented themselves from patrols, litter the histories of all surf lifesaving clubs. The initial rules of Bondi, for example, obliged active members to be 'on the beach at least twice each month'. Within two years of Bondi's formation the club had introduced the 'double duty penalty' for members who skipped patrols (Bondi Surf Bathers 1956, pp. 8–9).

The early surf bathing clubs quickly adopted sport – with its challenges, entertainment, diversions, competition and excitement – as a key tool of recruitment; sport also gave clubs broader social legitimacy. Surf bathing clubs employed competitions to test the fitness, efficiency and competency of members and they developed a new genre of sports based on rescuing patients. The core skills of surf lifesaving sports – swimming, running and teamwork – appealed to many leading athletes. Among the first members of early surf bathing /lifesaving clubs were the Olympians Andrew 'Boy' Charlton, Harold Hardwick, Cecil Healy and Bill Herald (all members of Manly), Reg 'Snowy' Baker (Maroubra), and Frank Beaurepaire (North Bondi). In addition to lifesaving sports, clubs sponsored rowing crews, and rugby and waterpolo teams. As well as highlighting the attraction of sport to potential recruits, clubs used it to discipline members: only those who completed patrols could represent club teams.

Sport, however, posed a dilemma for the SBA. On the one hand, it helped recruit members and give social legitimacy to the association. On the other, sport contradicted the SBA's claims to being a humanitarian organisation, a claim which was the basis of its autonomy on, and control over, the beach. Sport became more problematic after the SBA changed its name to the Surf Life Saving Association of Australia (subsequently Surf Life Saving Australia). Since the 1920s SLSA has released a stream of statements emphasising the subsidiary role of sport. In 1940, for example, SLSA described itself as 'a body formed primarily and principally with the humanitarian object of rendering safe the healthy and invigorating pastime of surf bathing'. In this role, competition introduces into the association 'a very definite sporting spirit which greatly benefits our ... work and our relations with the general public' (SLSA 1940). Clubs and members, however, generally privilege sport. While admitting that saving lives is 'a powerful ideal', Joe Henke, a founding member of the Victorian Centre, admitted that it was 'not enough to sustain either a club or our whole movement'. 'What appeals most to young people wanting to join, as well as to those who stay with the clubs', he believed, is 'physical fitness and competition' (Best 2002, p. 5).

Sport framed the culture and *esprit de corps* at scores of clubs. Most clubs channelled their resources into one or two sports. Earlier in its history Freshwater, for example, focused on developing boat crews and beach sprinters, and attached 'little or no importance' to swimming or rescue and resuscitation (Forbes 1958, p. 41). By contrast, the latter were traditional sports at Cottesloe and North Cottesloe with North also supporting surfboat rowing. Each surf lifesaving sport – swimming, rescue and resuscitation, beach sprinting, flags, boats – carries its own subculture and, prior to the acceptance of women as fully-qualified surf lifesavers in the 1980s (see below), its own distinct form of masculinity. Speaking in 1982 at a dinner to celebrate the 75th anniversary of SLSA, Peter Lacey, an all-time champion of the movement, humorously described the subcultures of the different sports. Having been a swimmer throughout my competitive career, Lacey began, I can happily nominate them as the 'most intelligent, bravest, toughest [and] strongest blokes'. They are 'fearless' and 'daring', venturing 'unprotected into the biggest of seas' and into 'the freezing conditions' of Victoria and Tasmania. Elite swimmers, Lacey continued, gravitate to the rescue and resuscitation. While this is 'a complex event that no one has ever owned up to inventing', the long costumes worn by competitors raise questions 'about their masculinity'. Beach sprinters are the 'prima donnas' of surf lifesaving, the ones 'who look great' but 'never even [get] their feet wet'.

Clarifying the origins of beach flags, a branch of sprinting, Lacey joked that it is not based on a patrol member reacting to a call to rescue; rather it derives from a member reacting to being caught in bed with the attractive wife of another member. 'The most dangerous of the competitive species' are the surf-ski racers: 'aggressive' and 'temperamental' they 'possess the cunning of a polar bear'. Converging at the buoy during races, they will 'hit each other with their paddles and hurl abuse ... and as they cross the finish line they smash their paddles and throw them to the sand and continue to hurl abuse – at officials'. (Galton 1984, pp. 229–30)

Lacey reserved most of his comments for the movement's infamous surfboat crews, boaties:

> They train like men possessed for nine months of the year – in gyms, rivers, lakes, and the surf. Then showing that brawn can outmanoeuvre brain, they begin a classic preparation for major races. Firstly, they protest about the depth of water in which they have to start, then they protest about the [positions of the buoys] and how they have been laid. Then they protest about the distance of the race. When they get through protesting ... they perform a barbaric and sometimes erotic ritual – they pull their costumes so tight as to expose the cheeks of their behinds to the public. At the starter's gun, they jump in, row like madmen backwards into crashing waves – this is so as not to anticipate the moment of impact as legs and arms are broken. (Galton 1984, p. 230)

The competition for status and prestige between sporting subcultures creates rivalries and tensions at many surf lifesaving clubs. Cottesloe's boaties achieved a long run of sporting success in the 1960s but they still felt like 'inferior citizens' in the club (Jaggard 1984, p. 145). Over time they turned these negative attitudes around by positioning themselves on different club committees and forcefully airing their views. Yet, even this strategy failed to win enduring respect.

SLSA progressively sanctioned and administered larger sporting events. For example, many of surf lifesaving's annual national championships involve more competitors than Commonwealth Games in corresponding years. By the 1990s only a handful of urban beaches supported the infrastructure to host national championships. Despite the centrality of sport, SLSA adopted an exceptionalist position in which it tries to distinguish itself from other sporting bodies. Far from resolving SLSA's philosophy of sport, exceptionalism left more than a few surf lifesaver sportsmen languishing on the sidelines during the association's struggles with amateurism and professionalism.

In the early 20th century an ideological chasm emerged between amateur and professional sport (Paddock 1994). Keen to recruit sportsmen irrespective of their status, the SBA/SLSA adopted a non-partisan position. The SBA did not affiliate to the Amateur Sports

Federation of New South Wales and it allowed organisers of surf lifesaving carnivals to award cash prizes. As amateurism gained ascendency in the 1930s, amateur swimming and athletics officials prohibited their members from competing in surf lifesaving carnivals against professional athletes and paid lifeguards, pool lessees and professional coaches. SLSA unsuccessfully tried to classify surf lifesaving as a service (alongside the army, navy and air force) but amateur zealotry prevailed and forced the association to effectively terminate the sporting careers of champions such as pool lessee Hayden Kenny (surf race) and swimming coach Rodney Hounslow (belt race) (Phillips 2006). In the 1980s the advocates of amateurism capitulated under commercial pressures; amateur bodies such as the International Olympic Committee, the International Amateur Athletic Federation and the Australian Swimming Union finally admitted professionals. Ironically, these same commercial pressures motivated a group of surf lifesavers to advocate for more professional sporting opportunities. Their actions divided the surf lifesaving movement in the 1990s. The catalyst for this rift was the ironman, a multi-discipline sport combining swimming, running, surf-skis and paddle-boards.

Introduced to Australia in 1965 by touring American lifeguards, the ironman is a test of stamina, strength and diverse skills. Exciting to watch, the ironman quickly emerged as the movement's glamour event and the embodiment of surf lifesaver masculinity. As Peter Lacey put it, the name ironman 'conjures up visions of John Wayne charging the beach at Iwo Jima' (Galton 1984, p. 230).

Corporations and the media immediately recognised the economic potential of the ironman and in the early 1980s commercial interests threatened to organise events independently of SLSA. The latter responded with a professional ironman in 1986, but this competition dissatisfied competitors. Demanding training regimes, high media profiles, lucrative sponsorships, and marketing and management consultants – none of which SLSA ever questioned – contributed to the ironmen's perception of themselves as professional athletes. The circuit raised their expectations as they were transformed from part-time semi-professional sportsmen into highly professional athletes. Ironmen competitors urged SLSA to redesign race circuits, build public awareness of the event, and increase prize monies. SLSA dismissed their demands; resorting to its exceptionalist position that surf lifesaving is first and foremost a humanitarian safety service. Led by Michael Porra and Grant Kenny, a small group of surf lifesavers formed a rebel competition, the Ironman Super Series, with its own sponsors. SLSA initially attempted to isolate the rebels and banned them from official competitions (e.g. branch, state and national titles). Of course, it did not extend the ban to lifesaving patrols! The rebels challenged the bans as a restraint of trade in the Federal Court before the two parties settled privately.

The Ironman Super Series folded in 2001 with the withdrawal of its key sponsor, Uncle Tobys. At the same time Kellogg, SLSA's longstanding backer, slashed its contribution to the official ironman circuit by more than 50%. SLSA restructured and downsized the elite ironman competition. Shortly after it replaced the ironman circuit with a national surf league which it claimed was a response to requests from ordinary lifesavers for a professional sporting competition based on a broader range of sports. The Surf League has not captured the public's imagination and has undergone numerous restructurings. Surf lifesaving is not unique in this respect; similar problems around philosophy, sponsorship and the design of appealing competitions also beset professional surfing.

Surfing

In Australia surfing developed under the auspices of SLSA with boardriders joining early surf bathing and lifesaving clubs. Men such as Claude West, Justin 'Snow' McAlister, Bert Chequer and Adrian Curlewis were well known for their surfing prowess within lifesaving circles. SLSA initially opposed the use of surfboards as rescue equipment but their buoyancy forced it to accept them as legitimate rescue craft. Logically, this meant adding board events to sporting programs. Clubs conducted board-paddling races at carnivals in the 1920s, and boards featured in official rescue competitions in the 1930s. The national titles in 1946 included board-paddling. However, many lifesavers also found pleasure in surfing as the complaints registered by Allan Kennedy, the superintendent of the Victorian Centre, in the 1940s attest. According to Kennedy, 'there are too many [surfers in] the club[s], who despite being fit and [energetic], avoid becoming active members ... and only use the club to house their boards' (Best 2002, p. 56).

In the summer of 1956–57, a team of American lifeguards, which included surfers Greg Noll, Tommy Zahn, Mike Bright and Bobby Moore, introduced Malibu boards to Australia. Invited by SLSA for a special international carnival coinciding with the Olympic Games in Melbourne, the lifeguards surfed before enthralled crowds at Torquay and Avalon. According to Zahn, Australian surfing at that stage was 'like nowhere. They were still going straight ... on 16 foot paddleboards' (Gault-Williams & Lynch 2000, p. 83) while Noll later recalled, 'we hit 'em like a comet. Took 'em from the horse and buggy straight to the Porsche' (Warshaw 2004, p. 413). The American lifeguards were part of an emerging Californian-based hedonistic beach and surfing culture that incorporated non-conformist and free-spirited beatnik philosophies. This culture produced its own language, humour, rituals, dress and hair styles and it rapidly diffused around the Pacific rim with travelling surfers, Hollywood beach movies (e.g. *Gidget* 1959), surfing films (e.g. *Slippery When Wet* 1958; *Cat on a Hot Foam Board* 1959; *Surf Fever* 1960) and surfing magazines (e.g. *The Surfer* 1960; *Surfing* 1964).

SLSA initially accommodated the new culture, co-sponsoring 'Miss Sydney Gidget' contests, sanctioning Malibu surfing events at the 1962–63 New South Wales championships, and introducing surfing to the Australian championships in 1965–66. Surfers, too, supported SLSA. *Surfing World*, the Australian-based surfing magazine, reported results from lifesaving carnivals as late as 1964. One aim of the Australian Surfriders Association (ASA), founded in August 1963, was to 'assist the SLSA in any way possible to help the public on the beaches' (Booth 2001, pp. 97–98). The press praised surfers for their initiative (e.g. *Manly Daily*, 15 May 1964).

Surfing won widespread acceptance because leading surfers defined themselves as sportspersons, which connoted structure and discipline. For example, editorials in surfing magazines implored surfers 'to preserve the images' of 'devoted and inconspicuous athletes' and of 'good, clean-living, average guys, out for a day's sport in the sun' (cited in Booth 2001, p. 98). Success in international competition added further credibility. Bernard 'Midget' Farrelly won the tenth International Surfing Championship at Makaha (Hawai'i) on New Year's Day 1963. Officials feted him upon his return and the following summer Farrelly began a regular column in the *Sun Herald*.

Public and official attitudes towards surfers deteriorated from the mid 1960s as boardriders abandoned surf lifesaving clubs in pursuit of waves. A war of words erupted with surfers criticising surf lifesavers' antiquated codes of masculinity and surf lifesaving clubs as 'rigid, old-fashioned and authoritarian'; surf lifesavers labelled surfers selfish and socially irresponsible (McGregor 1968, p. 285). Local councillors exacerbated cultural tensions between surfers and surf lifesavers when they ordered the latter to regulate the use of surfboards near bathing areas (on the valid grounds that boards threatened bathers). Attempts by surf lifesavers to police surfers led to several conflicts. In one incident, a furious argument erupted between the two groups at Palm Beach when surfboat crews tried to clear the water of surfers allegedly obstructing a bronze medallion test. One of the sweeps, John Windshuttle – a one-time boardrider – relished the task, boasting 'I creamed those surfers off wave after wave; I was like a road grader' (cited in Booth 2001, p. 110).

Technology helped ease tensions between surfers and surf lifesavers. In the mid 1970s surfers began attaching themselves to their boards with legropes which all but eliminated the problem of riderless boards washing through swimming areas. Around the same time the lifesaving movement adopted water-based, highly manoeuvrable motorised IRBs (inflatable rescue boats) as the principal means of patrol and rescue. IRBs reduced the visual presence of surf lifesavers on the beach. In short, these two technologies radically changed traditional spatial arrangements between surfers and surf lifesavers and increased the physical distances between them.

Surfers do not share a single conceptualisation of their pastime. Among those who view surfing as a 'dance' with a 'natural energy form' in which the dancer shares an intimate relationship with nature (Flynn 1987, p. 400), notions of sport and competition strike an uneasy accord. Bob Pike, a pioneer of big-wave riding captured this tension in the 1950s:

> I don't like to compete and I don't think any of the top board riders do. It takes too much of the pleasure out of the sport and creates too many jealousies. Competitions are all against the spirit of surfing which is supposed to be a communion with nature rather than a hectic chase for points (Australia's fifty 1992, p. 88).

Two decades later legendary Hawaiian surfer and contest winner Gerry Lopez repeated these sentiments when he said that 'trying to squash your opponents takes away from the experience of the dance' (Warshaw 2004, p. 345).

In the early 1970s, soul-surfing – riding waves for the benefit of one's soul – emerged with the counterculture as the defining motif of the pastime and stalled the development of competitive surfing, particularly in its professional form, until the formation of the International Professional Surfers (IPS) and the Association of Surfing Professionals (ASP) in the mid 1970s. Cultural tensions between Hawaiians and Australians plagued professional surfing in the mid 1970s and throughout the 1980s (Booth 2001; Tomson 2008), but the failure to attract a mass following, support from mainstream media, and a committed long-term umbrella sponsor, reveal the sport's structural limitations. Indeed, the unpredictable nature of the ocean and weather turn contest planning into a game of chance. The ocean is not a sports arena and contest directors cannot control the surf for live television broadcasts which require considerable on-location preparation. Potential sponsors thus face a major dilemma: do they support events on large urban beaches at fixed times in the hope of drawing large crowds who will (hopefully) overlook the (probably) poor waves and substandard performances? Or, do they stage contests at remote reef breaks which, while inaccessible to hordes of spectators, are more likely to produce quality surf for television?

Currently, major surf corporations (e.g. Rip Curl, Billabong, Quiksilver, Hurley) are the principal sponsors of events on the men's world championship tour, holding all eleven licenses (the ASP restructured the 2011 tour at the end of 2010). Events are a mixture of urban (e.g. Gold Coast), urban-periphery (e.g. Bells Beach) and remote (e.g. Teahupoo, Tahiti). License holders provide live coverage of events via the web and while the quality of webcasting has recently improved the format is inconsistent with respect to access and commentary. In the last decade two different parties, CSI (Communication Services International), a London-based distributor of sports programs, and ESPN, have proposed selling free-to-air television rights to the circuit and assorted fillers to the world pay-television market. Both proposals withered along with demands that the ASP restructure the tour and reduce the number of competitors (Booth 2001, p. 133; Baker 2009). Commenting on these moves, long time industry observer and surf journalist Nick Carroll (2009) observed that the realities of organising professional sports events, inevitably 'blow away' such proposals; sports events 'don't spring into being out of thin air' and other than air time the proposals contained no detail about 'all the boring yet critical infrastructure that makes multi-event global sports tours function with sanity and credibility'.

Lastly, surfing corporations face grassroots opposition from recreational and lifestyle surfers who oppose professional events at their breaks. In the words of David Shearer (2009, p. 81), an opponent of a proposed world tour event sponsored by Rip Curl at Lennox Head, communities wake up to find their beaches/headlands 'stuck all over with dinky structures selling trinkets, loudspeakers, sirens and flabby music ... the water filled with jetskis and cops clearing people out'. Citing a corporate insider who described the impact on local surfers of the annual Rip Curl-sponsored contest at Bells Beach as 'a nightmare' and 'a month of total mayhem and disruption', Shearer (2009, p. 83) poses the burning question: how do pro surfing contests benefit the mass of recreational surfers?

Fratriachal spaces

Different pasts and different foci mean that surf lifesavers and surfers occupy different spaces on the beach. In this section I outline the spatial aspects of surf lifesaving and surfing and the ways the two cultures demarcate their territories. Despite these spatial differences, surf lifesaving and surfing both developed as fratriarchies. Here I also examine the rituals, lores, and methods of intimidation and violence that surf lifesaving and surfing brotherhoods use to control their spaces.

Surf lifesaving

The hubs of surf lifesaving culture are (permanent) clubhouses and (temporary) triangles of sand between the patrol base and the flags at the water's edge. Surf lifesavers radiate from these hubs for training, rescues and sports. Traditionally, men excluded women from these spaces on the grounds that they were 'physically incapable of performing rescues'. Most clubs translated this lore into law and women entered these spaces only to 'make tea' or by invitation on clearly defined social occasions (Daly 2002, p. 63). SLSA admitted women as fully qualified members after 1980 from which time they began entering traditional male spaces.

Men dominated many institutions in the 20th century but the masculinity of surf lifesaving exhibited an 'extraordinary larrikinism' with surf lifesavers often displaying 'a cheerful contempt for authority' (Jaggard 1997, p. 183). Club histories are replete with examples. In 1949, 14 surf lifesavers from Palm Beach gate-crashed a function at the private residence of another member and proceeded to 'steal food and drink, damage the switch box while turning the lights on and off, and insult the hostess'; one gate-crasher 'knocked out the host' (Brawley 1996, p. 109). On another occasion, the Newport Arms Hotel banned the whole club 'after a member had a "misunderstanding" with a television set and threw a bottle through its screen' (Brawley 1996, p. 130). A local magistrate's court once convicted and fined six surf lifesavers from Collaroy for malicious damage. The intoxicated group fuelled a bonfire on the beach with council-owned signs and palings from the fence of a local hospital (Brawley 1995, pp. 187–89).

Larrikinism and vandalism serve social functions in male cultural groups, providing means by which members bond with each other and establish internal hierarchies (Loy 1995). Initiation rites serve the same roles and were practised across the movement. On the 'path to full membership', new members at Palm Beach, who were called freshers, had to 'jump through a few informal hoops' such as swallowing concoctions of tomato soup laced with gin. Over time, full members imposed greater demands on freshers:

> any full member could request a probationary member to perform some antic or menial task. Included in these tasks were jobs such as human cuckoo clocks, strutting into the lounge every fifteen minutes and squawking. Probationary members were physically accosted or deprived of the fresher's most prized possession – sleep. (Brawley 1996, p. 136)

Initiation rites at Collaroy in the late 1950s descended into humiliation. On Sunday afternoons surf lifesavers dug a hole, about six feet deep, in the sand and threw in as many young boys as they could catch. As the afternoon wore on and they became increasing intoxicated, the lifesavers amused themselves urinating and vomiting on their captives (Young 1998, p. 10).

In the summer of 1979–80, after a decade of heated internal debate which took place within a broader context of women's liberation and quality of life issues including the place of sport and recreation in the nation (Booth 2001, p. 143), SLSA officially approved women as active surf lifesavers (Brawley 2007, p. 256). But regardless of attitudinal shifts in the wider society, the first women to enter surf lifesaving clubs encountered fratriarchal cultures based on 'heavy drinking' and the denigration of women in 'sexual talk and blue movie stuff' (Coney 1985, p. 18). Some women faced overt verbal abuse. At Palm Beach male lifesavers invented a new moniker, 'pog', a combination of pig and dog; Kirsten Todd received 'pog' abuse every time she walked around a corner and was told she 'shouldn't be there' (Brawley 1996, pp. 209–13).

Initially, SLSA made no arrangements for women's sporting events. In the first two seasons after their admission women competed alongside men. Some, such as Carol Fox from Lorne, 'enjoyed the opportunity to race with the men' whom she described as 'really supportive' (Best 2002, p. 295). But at Portsea 'the blokes' gave Sue Dimmick 'hell':

> They were awful! They were all blokey blokes. [A] couple really gave me a hard time (these days you would sue for harassment or defamation of character, I'm sure). But because I was outspoken I could counter their really sexist comments with ones that were probably equally as sexist or demeaning. You definitely needed a sense of humour to survive. I would challenge the boys to a race and beat them and that confused them. (Best 2002, p. 295)

Women's events first appeared at the 1985 Australian championships but each new event precipitated controversy. Kim Tunnell of Manly opposed the introduction of the women's ski which she said was 'a step backwards': 'we'll lose our credibility. Women are just not as strong as men ... [and] if we go out there people will laugh at us'. A more positive Denby Stokes from Kawana Waters replied that even the men had to 'start somewhere', although she conceded that they never faced the 'close scrutiny of the public and the media' (Booth 2006, p. 104).

On the eve of surf lifesaving's centenary celebrations, women made up 35% of active members and 41% of total members (including active, active reserve, cadet, award, junior and other). Today, women hold official positions in club administration and serve as patrol captains.

Surfing

Surfers agree that unity with a wave is an orgasmic experience. Locked deep in the 'tube' – the cylinder created when the breaking crest pitches in front of the wall – boardriders discover a realm that 'tilts the otherwise ordinary planes of ... existence', where time has no meaning, where fear merges with joy in a rush of adrenalin, and the racing heart of danger and the ecstasy of dance become one (Tomson 2000, p. 15). Heavy and cumbersome boards meant that Australia's first surfers mostly stored their equipment at local surf lifesaving clubhouses and simply awaited the arrival of waves. Surges in private vehicle ownership and cheaper airfares after World War II gave surfers more mobility, and freedom, to seek waves (e.g. McTavish 2009). In surfing lexicon such searching was known as a surfari. In the mid 1960s Bruce Brown portrayed the ultimate surfari in *The endless summer* (1966) which followed the worldwide search for perfect waves by California duo Robert August and Mike Hynson. The surfari is not just a search for waves; it is also a release from mundanity. *Tracks* correspondent 'One-of-eight' (October 2005, p. 51) captures this in a reflection on a long-weekend surfari – 'I've never laughed so hard in all my life'. But comments on the relationship with his companions also reveal the fratriachal characteristics of the surfari: 'it was fantastic to sit there with a group of blokes talking shit and digging up forgotten misadventures from 20 years ago'. Newcastle surfer Noel Jackson's recipe for the perfect surfari confirms these dimensions: 'lots of surfing with grog, girls and jails' (Merewether Surfboard Club 1988, p. 14).

A few surfers extend the surfari into a lifestyle. 'I just turned 37 and I've never had a real job and I'm pretty proud of that, but I've had a lot of waves', says 'Camel', a West Australian surfer (Kennedy 2009, p. 46). Living on unemployment benefits, Camel's believes work would mean 'losing touch with the ocean ... the one thing I'm definitely in tune with' (Kennedy 2009, p. 46).

Yet, if the surfari is a defining characteristic of surfing culture, the peripatetic boardrider paradoxically exposes a dark side of the culture, localism. Some urban Australian beaches support as many as five local surfing spaces with crews holding 'onto whatever piece of sand or reef or point they can, like barnacles stubbornly clinging to a rock' (Evers 2010, p. 75). These spaces raise questions around the ownership of waves and surfing breaks, and individual and collective cultural identities. Unlike surf lifesaving spaces, which are fixed, formally defined and enforced by common property rights and local council by-laws, surfing spaces constantly shift in response to surfer movements. On the foreshore surfers paint 'locals only' across footpaths, rock walls and carparks and use noise (e.g. music, argot, offensive comments), movement (e.g. skateboarding), and boisterous behaviour (e.g. flicking towels, giving chase) to mark their territory and to warn off non-locals and newcomers who move too close (Evers 2010, p. 76). Newcastle surfer Brian Hoy recalls rising 'apprehension' whenever he ventured south of the stormwater pipe at Merewether: the local guys were 'not noted for their hospitality. Robbie Wood and Les Feighan always had a spare knuckle or two' (Merewether Surfboard Club 1988, p. 33).

At some breaks locals use intimidation and force to ensure they get priority on the waves. Non-locals who 'paddle out in at the wrong spot, or sit in the wrong place' may be told to 'fuck off'; 'at Burleigh Heads ... surfers are punched for trying to catch the same wave as a local, accidentally getting in the way, falling off or riding a longboard' (Evers 2010, p. 74). When experienced surfer Clif Evers entered an intense local line-up he obeyed all the rules – passing 'g'days' and smiles, waiting his turn – to no avail. Whenever he tried to catch a wave, one or another local would 'stroke to the inside, taking the right of way'. Finally, 'a bloke calls me off a wave I am in position for and I take off anyway. [A]t the end of the ride ... [a] local paddles past, staring into my eyes. I sit up on my board ... and prepare to fight' (Evers 2010, p. 71). The moment passed without violence and Evers finished the session with a few waves. But back at the carpark he found his windscreen smashed.

Surfing fratriarchies were no different from those in surf lifesaving with respect to their rivalries, use of initiation rites and attitudes to women. Rivalries loom large in Robbie Wood's early memories of surfing at Merewether: 'there were the surfies versus rocker battles, potshots at surfers at Leggy Point with .22 rifles, [and] great fights at the Town Hall dances and the Palais' (Merewether Surfboard Club 1988, p. 12). At Narrabeen older surfers initiated younger surfers by tying them to poles, locking them in the wire basket used by lifesavers to detain stray dogs, or burying them to the heads in the sand. On one occasion:

> they tied Robbo and Skiddy's arms behind their backs and buried them up to their necks about two metres apart, facing each other with only their heads sticking out of the sand. They had to have a spitting competition. They had to hack gollies at each other's heads. Robbo lost so they got his scum dog, Bandit, that used to hang around the carpark and shimmied Robbo's face with Bandit's arse. (Abraham 1999, p. 53)

Men and women initially shared waves in Australia until fratriarchies gained ascendancy and marginalised women. Gail Couper, winner of five Australian women's titles between 1966 and 1975, says women surfers were regularly 'harassed and put down' in the 1970s; she even claims to have been punched on one occasion (Booth 2001, p. 103). As a young teenager, Australian Pam Burridge, who went on to win a world championship in 1990, believed she was one of the surfer boys: 'if they were being derogatory towards women, it was other women not me. Then it slowly dawned on me that [I was not really part of their world]. It's like a family you're not allowed to belong to' (cited in Booth 2001, p. 103). Ironically, precisely as women began entering surf lifesaving clubs in the 1980s, the surfing media and contest directors began isolating female surfers (Stedman 1997; Booth 2001).

Since the mid 1990s women surfers have been more visible in the line up. Around this time surfing corporations began manufacturing and marketing products dedicated to women (Booth 2001, p. 177) and Surfing Australia, which succeeded the ASA, developed policies and strategies to promote women's surfing. While the latter is consistent with government policy, to which Surfing Australia conforms through its affiliation with the Australian Sports Commission, the organisation also has as its goal the development of surfing as 'a mainstream commercially sustainable sport' (Surfing Australia 2010). Surfing Australia boasts success here with 209 affiliated surf clubs (many of which had their origins in beach fratriarchies), 81 accredited learn-to-surf schools and nearly 23,000 members.

Conclusion

Surf lifesaving and surfing help define and shape our understanding of Australia's beaches. However, as I have demonstrated above, the meanings attached to surf lifesaving and surfing have always been fluid and contested. Nowhere is this more evident than when comparing contemporary official pronouncements (and images) with voices (and images) from the grassroots. It is doubtful whether core surfers share Surfing Australia CEO Andrew Stark's vision of surfing as a mainstream sport (e.g. Doherty 2010), or whether surf lifesaving's dedicated sportsmen and women understand SLSA's policies and rhetoric of humanitarianism and exceptionalism.

Paradoxically, the more people Surfing Australia and SLSA entice into their ranks, the greater the potential for divergent interpretations and, ultimately, the reconfiguring of cultural nuances and lores. Leanne Stedman (1997, p. 80) touched on this issue over a decade ago when she asked whether surfing could claim a collective culture identity under conditions where anyone can identify with it by simply wearing a branded T-shirt (see also Ishiwata 2002; Jarratt, 2010 pp. 210–12). The influx of women over the last two decades has weakened fratriarchal relationships in surf lifesaving, and SLSA's strategy of recruiting people from culturally and linguistically diverse backgrounds (SLSA 2007) promises more cultural shifts. The entry of women should similarly erode surfing's fratriachal structures. In May 2009 seven times women's world champion Layne Beachley joined Australia's most notorious surfing fratriarchy, the Bra Boys (see Evers 2010), at Ours, a Sydney break closely guarded by the gang. At the same time, we should not expect rapid change. One of Beachley's rides received a nomination for the Ride of the Year in the 2010 Billabong XXL Global Big Wave Awards and in true fratriarchal tradition not all commentators were complimentary. One called the ride 'lame', another observed that Beachley had been towed-in while the men were paddling-in (Billabong XXL, 2010).

The Australian beach seems certain to remain a site of sporting activity in the foreseeable future. As I have shown in this chapter, however, the precise forms of those activities, and the relationships they conjure, are not predetermined. Rather, they will shift in combination with technology, broader social trends, and cultural nuances including conceptualisations of space.

References

Abraham, P. (1999). Paradise or bust. *Deep*, Summer, pp. 42–57.

Australia's fifty most influential surfers (1992). *Australia's Surfing Life*, 50: 70–123.

Baker, T. (2009). Kelly Slater speaks about new tour. *Australia's Surfing Life*. [Online]. Available: www.surfinglife.com.au/news/asl-news/1278-kelly-slater-speaks-about-new tour [accessed 19 January 2011].

Best, A. (2002). *50 years and more: a history of surf life saving Victoria*. Melbourne: Surf Life Saving Victoria.

Billabong XXL Global Big Wave Awards (2010). Ride of the Year Entry, Layne Beachley at Ours. [Online]. Available at www.youtube.com/watch?v=AXSqiVqQPNA [accessed 19 January 2011].

Bondi Surf Bathers Life Saving Club (1956). *History of Bondi Surf Bathers' Life Saving Club, 1906–1956*. Sydney: Bondi Surf Bathers Life Saving Club.

Booth, D. (2006). Managing pleasure and discipline: Clubbies. In E. Jaggard (Ed.). *Between the flags: 100 summers of lifesaving* (pp. 75–105). Sydney: UNSW Press.

Booth, D. (2001). *Australian beach cultures: the history of sun, sand, and surf*. London: Frank Cass.

Brawley, S. (2007). *The Bondi lifesaver: a history of an Australian icon*. Sydney: ABC Books.

Brawley, S. (1996). *Beach beyond: a history of the Palm Beach Surf Club 1921–1996*. Sydney: UNSW Press.

Brawley, S. (1995). *Vigilant and victorious: a community history of the Collaroy Surf Life Saving Club 1911–1995*. Collaroy Beach, Sydney: Collaroy Surf Life Saving Club.

Carroll, N. (2009). Smoke and mirrors. *Australia's Surfing Life*. [Online]. Available: www.surfinglife.com.au/news/asl-news/1197-smoke-nd-mirrors [accessed 19 January 2011].

Coney, S. (1985). Amazons of the sea. *Broadsheet*, 14–19 April, pp. 14–19.

Daly, J. (2002). *Surf life saving in South Australia: a jubilee history*. Adelaide: Surf Life Saving South Australia.

Doherty, S. (2010). Andrew Stark. *Surfing World, 310*: 86.

Evers, C. (2010). *Notes for a young surfer*. Melbourne: Melbourne University Press.

Forbes, W. (1958). *The history of Freshwater Surf Life Saving Club, 1908–1958*. Sydney: Freshwater Surf Life Saving Club.

Ford, C. (2007). The first wave: the making of a beach culture in Sydney, 1810–1920. Unpublished PhD thesis, University of Sydney.

Flynn, P. J. (1987). Waves of semiosis: surfing's iconic progression. *The American Journal of Semiotics*, 5(3/4): 397–418.

Galton, B. (1984). *Gladiators of the surf*. Sydney: Reed.

Gault-Williams, M. & Lynch, G. (2000). Pulling seaward: Tommy Zahn. *The Surfer's Journal*, 9(2): 72–87.

Ishiwata, E. (2002). Local motions: surfing and the politics of wave sliding. *Cultural Values*, 6(3): 257–72.

Jaggard, E. (1997). Chamelons in the surf. *Journal of Australian Studies*, 53: 183–91.

Jaggard, E. (1984). *The premier club: Cottesloe Surf Life Saving Club's first seventy-five years*. Cottesloe, Western Australia: Cottesloe Surf Life Saving Club.

Jarratt, P. (2010). *Salts and suits*. Melbourne: Hardie Grant.

Kennedy, L. (2009). The magnificent seven. *Tracks*, November, pp. 34–47.

Lowe, A. (1958). *Surfing, surf-shooting and surf-lifesaving pioneering*. Sydney: Arthur Lowe.

Loy, J. (1995). The dark side of agon: fratriarchies, performative masculinities, sport involvement and the phenomenon of gang rape. In K. H. Bette and A. Rutten (Eds). *International sociology of sport contemporary issues: Festschrift in honor of Günther Luschen* (pp. 263–81). Stuttgart: Naglschmid.

Merewether Surfboard Club (1988). *The history of Merewether Surfboard Club*. Merewether: Merewether Surfboard Club.

McGregor, C. (1968). *Profile of Australia*. Chicago: Henry Regnery.

McTavish, B. (2009). *Stoked*. Huskisson, NSW: Hyams Publishing.

Paddock, R. (1994). Amateurism. In W. Vamplew et al. *The Oxford companion to Australian sport* (pp. 11–15). Melbourne: Oxford University Press.

Phillips, M. (2006). Dissension and challenges in surf lifesaving: amateurism and professionalism. In E. Jaggard (Ed.). *Between the flags: 100 summers of lifesaving* (pp. 165–87). Sydney: UNSW Press.

Russell, E. (1910). Australia's amphibians. *Lone Hand*, January, 252–65.

SLSA (2007). Inclusion strategy. [Online]. Available: www.slsa.com.au/site/_content/resource/00002226-docsource.pdf [accessed 20 January 2011]

SLSA (1940). *Thirty third annual report 1938–39*. Sydney: SLSA.

Shearer, D. (2009). David versus Rip Curl. *Kurungabaa*, *2*(2): 79–86.

Stedman, L. (1997). From Gidget to gonad man: surfers, feminists and postmodernisation. *ANZJS*, *33*(1): 75–90.

Stewart, M. (1984). Beachstruck on Bondi. In R. Drew et al. *Bondi* (pp. 28–53). Sydney: James Fraser.

Surf Bathing Committee (1912). Report Presented to the Legislative Council and the Legislative Assembly. New South Wales, Government Printer.

Surfing Australia (2010). [Online]. Available: www.surfingaustralia.com/ [accessed 19 January 2011].

Tomson, M. (2000). The horror: deconstructiong Teahupoo. *The Surfer's Journal*, *9*(3): 15.

Tomson, S. (2008). *Bustin' down the door: the surf revolution of '75*. New York: Abrams.

Warshaw, M. (2004). *The encyclopedia of surfing*. Melbourne: Viking.

Young, N. (1998). *Nat's Nat and that's that*. Angourie, New South Wales: Nymboida Press.

11

The role of physical education in promoting sport participation in school and beyond

Murray Drummond and Shane Pill

This chapter explores the role of physical education in promoting sport participation in school and beyond using a sociological perspective. A sociological lens encourages one to view through, behind and beyond the facades of social structures. Cliff et al. (2009) explain that a sociocultural perspective provides a means to critically 'read' and understand physical education content, shared ways of thinking and acting. We therefore aim to challenge what may have been 'taken for granted' or unproblematised assumptions about sport and physical education. We will consider the notion of participation and the place of physical education in stimulating, educating and encouraging involvement in sport. We will conclude with a consideration of a curriculum vision for sport in physical education that moves class participation beyond narrow technical and elite perspectives of sport participation to one which is more inclusive and understanding of broader sociological issues.

Sport in Australia

Australians are historically renowned for their *obsession* with sport. Whether the term 'obsession' is the most appropriate term is debatable given the contemporary societal influences on lifestyle choices and demands. Undoubtedly, early scholars of sport and society in Australia noted a cultural fixation around sport, which has sometimes been referred to as a 'passion' or 'religion', while its male sporting heroes have been perceived as gods (Land & Butner 1982). Dunstan stated that, 'it is important to examine the reasons why this sporting obsession came about' (1973 , p. 9). He argued that the primary reason for Australians' sporting desire was that the majority of the early settlers came from Britain, which, he claimed, was the most sport conscious nation on earth around the turn of the 19th century. Therefore sport became an expression of British 'Australianism' where organised games were thought to express social ideals that were fundamental to colonial society. A desire for cultural reproduction thereby formed one of the characteristics of Australian life (Land & Butner 1982). According to Veal and Lynch (1996), the new settlers to Australia brought with them the outdoor, physical and competitive sports of the 'mother country'. Moreover, the tough work involved in establishing a new colony necessitated opportunities for recreation and diversion from the hardship of early Australian white settlement. Veal and Lynch explained how Australia's predisposition towards sport endured from the initial 'cut from the British cloth' as the most durable and deeply embedded form of cultural identification with Anglo-European Australia. With the addition of notions of nationalism, a premise that sport built character and a sense of community, sport became arguably a dominant cultural artefact.

Land and Butner (1982) proposed the following as key determinants for the development of Australia's sporting obsession embedded in Australia's cultural heritage, physical environment and the values arising from a convict and pioneering beginning:

- The European Australians were mainly from Britain and Ireland – the home of most spectator sports.
- Australia inherited the British tradition of outdoor recreation and leisure.
- Australia generally has a mild climate encouraging outdoor recreation and leisure.
- Early settlers had vast amounts of open space for play.
- The settlement pattern with many neighbouring rural districts and towns encouraged local rivalry and competition.
- The large number of males in the early European population at a time when male dominance in sport was acceptable.
- The 'pioneering spirit' supposedly gave male Australians a unique sense of mateship, courage and manliness. In Australian literature and cultural education, these qualities were linked with sport.
- The lack of intellectual or wider cultural heritage was offset by more physically oriented pursuits suitable to the type of people attracted to a new settlement.
- The pioneering life was tough. Sport was seen as a means of release.
- European Australia's short history and convict origins resulted in a national inferiority complex. Sport was used as a form of nationalism to show superiority to other colonial nations, and especially Britain.

This historical backdrop surrounding sport involvement, and perception, is important considering the issues that face contemporary Australian culture and its relationship with sport. Contemporary Australia is multicultural, particularly within the metropolitan and urban areas. Regional, rural and remote areas of Australia have tended to maintain their traditional cultural demographics. Post-World War II governments have placed varying emphases on immigration from a range of continents including Europe, Asia and more recently Africa, thereby increasing population numbers and seeing the advent of multiculturalism. This multiculturalism has brought changes to traditional cultural ideologies.

Not only has the Australian demographic changed from largely white Anglo-Saxon to a milieu of races and ethnicities, but there are also significant globalisation issues that are impacting contemporary Australian life including global finances, technology and mass media to name a few. It therefore begs the question 'is sport in contemporary Australia as significant as it has been to previous generations?' This is an interesting question that we ask our pre-service physical and health education (PHE) teachers, which in turn creates a 'buzz' of excitement and multitude of responses. Among the first year PHE teachers it is not uncommon to hear the functionalist (Coakley et al. 2009) perspectives claiming that Australians as are 'obsessed with sport', that 'sport builds character' and that 'sport is healthy'. It is arguable that these functionalist perspectives have been successfully passed from one generation to the next, possibly through a lack of critical consideration, and assisted by perpetuation through the media and popular culture.

Sport does continue to play a significant role in contemporary Australia and its influence exists in three areas. The first and most visible is that of elite level sport, the second is community sport and the third is school sport and physical education. While few will make a living a from elite sports, many aspire to this level. This is because of its prominence in the media, which showcases high profile professional elite sports such as AFL football, cricket, netball, football as well as some Olympic-based sports. For many people it is this type of sport that provides them with a sense of identification and national identity. It is important to remember however, that this is not unique to Australian culture, which many pre-service PHE teachers tend to forget. We only need to reflect on the recent Football World Cup – it could be argued that Australians are less obsessed and gripped by sporting fervour than some of the South American countries.

Community-based sport is at the essence of Australian sporting culture. Weekend sport has remained a prominent part of the Australian sport experience for over a century but in particular since industrialisation and the advent of the 40-hour working week. In the era before the progressive deregulation of the working week, weekends were seen as the time for family leisure, recreation and sporting pursuits whereas for many individuals now, weekends and holidays are associated with work-related guilt and stress (Hilbrecht 2007). The erosion of the 'weekend' free of work and the rise of professional sport as lounge room entertainment mean that the 'weekend' model of sporting participation no longer suits many Australians' patterns of living. Nor does it provide a panacea for rising levels of sedentary behaviour, given the lack of motivation to participate and the relatively low numbers of adults engaging in sports at a level that would provide physiological health benefits (Koivula 1999). In contrast to the adult pattern, community sport participation among contemporary Australian youth is relatively high (ABS 2009). Participation in traditional sports such as Australian Rules football, cricket and netball are being challenged, however, by the popularity of sports with more 'edge', such as skateboarding, surfing, martial arts and BMX cycling.

The significance of multiculturalism cannot be underestimated either. The numbers of children engaging in football (soccer) as a primary sport is increasing rapidly. Indeed as Hay states, 'participation rates in the football codes, particularly among boys and girls up to the age of 15, show soccer leaving other football codes in its wake' (2006, p. 166). Will this be a 'phase', similar to basketball in the late 1980s to the mid 1990s, or does football represent a more substantial cultural shift in sport participation? It is important to recognise that during this period of increased basketball participation during the 1980s and 1990s the established sporting codes in Australia like netball, Australian Rules football and the two rugby codes (league and union) ultimately staved off this challenge, providing some evidence of the importance of having sport historically imbedded within a culture and its narrative.

Physical education

The significance of contemporary school physical education has never been more important to the debate around the relationship between school physical education, school sport and youth sport participation in Australia. Physical education has been justified within the curriculum by the claims of producing particular kinds of citizens (Wright & Burrows 2006). At a time when there is good deal of government and community discussion around the health of our children, lack of physical activity, rising obesity levels, possible lifestyle disease, and the encouragement of sedentariness by digital technologies, sport is seen to offer an alternative with potential health benefits. School sport participation in particular is expected to improve children's health.

School sport is often used as an interchangeable term for physical education in public discussions, while in fact sport is a content area of physical education. 'Sport' refers to a range of physical movement experiences or activities distinguished by accepted codifications of rules to enable participants to distinguish specific types of sporting activities. Indeed, sport has been variously suggested as integral to the meaning of physical education, a major orientating discourse (Tinning et al. 2001) providing a justification and a legitimating curriculum feature for physical education (Williams 1985 cited in Bailey & Kirk 2009, p. 3). Moreover, different sporting activities can contribute to the learning process, and enable participation in a broader spectrum of sport (Bailey 2005). This is significant for the development of the child and participation in physical activity through orientated learning beyond the school years. This learning process, however, is not an imbedded 'automatic' or a 'taken for granted' outcome that can be attributed to sporting experiences within physical education, or the school setting more broadly (such as lunchtime sports competitions and school sport programs). These learning outcomes through sport and from sport require specialised attention of the physical education teacher. They can then be translated into the lunchtime 'play' arena and beyond into the community context.

Contemporary PHE must challenge the notion that sport is intrinsically understood or that it is inherently valuable behaviour simply because one is Australian. There are many aspects of sport that need to be learned, nurtured and matured to assist an active and healthy life. The contribution of the social and educational aspects of sport within physical education cannot be underestimated – based on its functionalist positioning as part of the formation of physical competencies; its speculative benefits to personal character formation and broader sociological assumptions about sport's contribution to an understanding of Australian culture, gendered embodiment and sexuality. We need to acknowledge that tension also exists between curriculum theorists on the one hand, who advocate that physical education, and therefore sport in curriculum time, must justify its existence on its educative merit (Brooker & MacDonald 1993; Penney & Chandler 2000; Rossi 2006) and, on the other hand, those who seek to position physical education as a context of health benefits accumulation.

School physical education is often seen as the link between sport and health. Many people take a narrow ideological stance claiming that physical education should engage children in sporting activities, which in turn will make them fit and healthy. While this is problematic on a number of fronts – for example the limited amount of time allocated to physical education in the school curriculum – physical education is far more sophisticated than merely a site for physical activity accumulation. While school physical education may offer children an array of sporting experiences, that some might perceive as a 'suite of sports', it is the fundamental philosophies underpinning the sport experience within a program of instruction (curriculum), and the way it is enacted (pedagogy) that determines the student engagement with the sport experience. We argue that in Australia the student experience of sport comes from a narrow vision of sport. A technical paradigm foregrounding 'textbook technique' reproduction (Pigott 1982) within a multi-activity curriculum design (Alexander 2008) marginalises ways of knowing sport outside the skill acquisition/motor control paradigm. Within this paradigm, sport can become either 'too hard' for both teachers and students and become reduced to 'busy, happy, active time' (Placek 1983); or be reduced to an 'elite' talent identification filter to recognise students suitable for senior secondary physical education, school or community sport teams. Rather, all areas of study within the school curriculum should be justified in educational terms that articulate why they are worthwhile rather than terms of tradition (Peters 1966). Sport within physical education should assist physical education as an educational process, positioned within educational discourses and drawing upon educational argument (Brooker & MacDonald 1993) in order to promote, engage and facilitate sport participation within school and beyond.

Schools are a primary educational agency for young people. Schools provide a context within which they learn to live and contribute to their own cultural lives (Wadham et al. 2007). Through the agency of school and the experience of education young people are introduced to the values and attitudes, interests, skills and knowledge – in short the social and cultural way of life – current in groups of which the students are, or seek to become, members. Given that engagement in sport cannot be a taken-for-granted assumption, the role of physical education is central in the relationship between school and a multicultural contemporary Australian culture.

Physical education is an important component of education and schooling – certainly in its relationship to sport and active and healthy living, but also in broader aspects of life. But as previously identified, this can only occur through deliberate design and enactment. As Green (1998) highlighted, from a liberal analytical perspective physical education is relevant within the curriculum if it contains a distinctive body of knowledge requiring rational thought and inquiry as well as cultural significance. Physical education, however, has often been used in ways that are inconsistent with an education framing. For example, Tinning et al. cite the use of physical education in primary schools 'as either a cathartic or "kickstart" for the day's academic work, rather than as a worthwhile educational experience in itself' (1993, p. 9). Indeed a common perception for many people is that school physical education provides the capacity to 'blow away the cobwebs' to allow the 'real work' to begin.

This positioning of physical education does not sit comfortably with definitions of the subject. Wuest and Bucher (2006) define physical education as an interdisciplinary construct covering all areas relating to the transmission of knowledge, skills and understanding to an individual or a group, the application of these skills, and their results. Physical education provides a context for learning through physical, social, cognitive, moral and emotional learning through engagement in physical activity (Department of Education and Children's Services 2008). Physical activity is not physical education, but physical activity provides the medium through which learning is stimulated in physical education (Australian Council for Health, Physical Education and Recreation 1993). A key scholar, Arnold (1979) argued that physical education covers three 'types' of learning:

- Learning in movement – skill acquisition enabling an individual to be able to move efficiently and effectively
- Learning about movement – recognise that physical activity is structured in certain ways to bring about certain things
- Learning through movement – social, cognitive, moral and emotional learning available through engagement in physical activity.

Physical education, then, refers to an area of the school curriculum and by definition, should evidence a process of learning. Like all curriculum subjects, the purpose of this process is to develop specific knowledge, skills and understanding, to promote confidence and competence in school and beyond.

Challenging compensatory ideology

Gard and Wright (2005) have discussed the discourse surrounding the obesity epidemic that is said to exist in contemporary Australia. Increasingly schools are being targeted as the ideal site in which to address this 'epidemic' of inactivity and rising weight. As a consequence, the seemingly logical domain upon which this issue falls is the learning area of health and physical education. Hence, a compensatory ideology exists suggesting that sport can be panacea for other areas of society including the culturally endorsed 'obesity epidemic'. It is the notion that sport in physical education can help compensate for the poor/declining health of children by enhancing their interest, enjoyment in and motivation for involvement in physical activity and sport; and providing time and space for the accumulation of physical activity as a counter to the otherwise sedentary nature of the school day.

Contemporary physical education, while still heavily focused on sport skill reproduction, may be bestowed with the social and cultural responsibility of acting upon children and youth obesity. By default, physical education could also come to be seen as responsible for adult obesity, as an argument is mounted to suggest that skills and attitudes learnt in school around health and physical activity carry into adulthood. Physical education teachers could end up being accountable for students' fitness performance. There exists the possibility for immense accountability in a subject that is impacted by broader social and cultural issues. There is simply not enough time for physical education to be a compensatory site. Just considering the potential of physical education as an agent in the development of sporting competence, fundamental movement skill literature suggests it can take up to 600 minutes to learn one skill (Department of Education and Training 2005). The development of sport performance competence in a singular sport may take thousands of hours of directed practice (Ericsson 2003). Other research has also implied that the low percentage of class time allocated to physical activity and teaching fitness concepts problematises physical education as a context for fitness development and an understanding of concepts that may aid in the development of active and healthy living (Brown & Holland 2005).

A compensatory ideology may also move other valuable ways of knowing sport, such as cultural, historical and vocational, to peripheral considerations. Gard (2006) cautioned that the 'war on obesity' might even result in school physical education morphing into a resemblance of adult exercise classes unless physical education teachers critically assess the pressures and programs initiated in the fight against obesity. We argue that sport in physical education should result in 'a more able person' (Wright & Burrows 2006) capable of interaction with and in sport at school and beyond.

Sport in physical education can be an exclusive practice foregrounding and privileging those with movement skill competency and game knowledge largely acquired outside of the physical education 'classroom'. The dominant pedagogy and curriculum design privilege students who are talented. A multi-activity curriculum construction essentially provides a series of 'come and try' experiences. Those who can already do well and are identified on 'day one' as competent, and those who cannot are not exposed to the length or depth of experience necessary to learn anything of substance, improve movement skill competence or enhance self-confidence in sport activity settings.

Our experience as teachers, sport participants and sport educators lead us to a similar conclusion as Evans (2004), who claims that physical education largely ignores talk about sport and the nature of 'education' as the process of developing potential. The dominant discourse in physical education variously emphasises (unproblematically) assumptions about health-related behaviour and the role of sport teaching in facilitating 'fitness', 'health' *or* participation in school or community sport. It marginalises the potential of physical education as a site for learning the many capacities and participatory pathways that find expression in our sporting culture. For many students, sport experiences in physical education fail to make an impact on either the physical abilities or other cognitive, social or cultural abilities students develop in other areas of the curriculum or that they bring to school (Evans 2004). The persistence of sport teaching focusing on effort, compliance and the reproduction of very specific movement patterns may be a reason physical education continues to be situated at the margins of the academic goals of schooling (McDonald 1995; Harman & Marshall 2005). It also problematises any assertion that physical education contributes to sport participation in and beyond school. There is not sufficient time in each of the frequent short periods allowed within the multi-activity curriculum model to develop sport-specific competency in novice and inexperienced players. Further, the dominant pedagogical emphases on strict textbook instruction impact negatively on the experience of sport as a means of learning beyond sport-specific motor patterns.

A question of curriculum design and instructional strategy

The capacity of physical education to promote sport participation in school and beyond is a matter of curriculum design and pedagogy. A narrow mechanistic definition of sport teaching and learning delivered through a multi-activity program arguably leads to an embodied sense of incompetence rather than competency for many students. According to Hemphill (2008) this has created a scenario where sport has been devalued as a curriculum experience because it has been narrowed to little more than the demonstration of physical skill. Ennis (1999) for example, argued that no matter how well sport is taught using the multi-activity curriculum plan and traditional instructional emphasis, the majority of female students and less 'able' males will not be successful.

At some Australian universities, such as Flinders University, PHE pre-service teachers are encouraged to move beyond a bio-physical and mechanistic understanding of learning sport as part of a broad consideration of the social context of physical education. In this model, physical education and sport teaching are positioned within an educational discourse that considers school as one of the most important ways in which we learn to live within and contribute to our own cultural lives (Wadham et al. 2007). As an important part of the Australian cultural experience and arguably an artefact contributing to an understanding of what it means to be an Australian, sport is seen as a valid and highly regarded component of the school curriculum. This is only possible, however, when it is pedagogically constructed within a curriculum beyond the boundaries of normative textbook technique and physical activity discourses.

Remaining true to Arnold's (1979) definition of learning in physical education, sport teaching and learning is considered a context for:

- Learning in sport – sport skill acquisition enabling an individual to be able to move and make tactical decisions efficiently and effectively in game situations

- Learning about sport – recognising that sport is structured in certain ways to bring about certain things and

- Learning through sport – understanding the embodied experience of sport.

The vision for sport teaching and learning we promote is the functional use of sport knowledge for active and engaged citizenship (Pill 2009). Sporting intelligence is not narrowly considered as movement skill competency, knowledge of sport rules, and appreciation of intensity of effort as it is in the traditional technical and behaviourist paradigm. It includes appreciating the competitive play of sport, the structuring of sport contests, the cultural meaning and construction of sport, sport as a social instrument, and the business/vocation of sport. Known as sport literacy, four distinct understandings of knowledge are considered in the construction of sport within physical education:

- Sport is an applied, practised and situated set of skills
- Sport creates embodied meaning, and meaning that can be communicated, interpreted, understood, imaged and used creatively
- Sport creates a 'text', which can be read for understanding
- Understanding sport requires a learning process (Pill 2009).

Sport literacy presents sport as a physical, cultural, personal, social and cognitive experience for the demonstration of the acquisition and use of knowledge. It has two themes for the curriculum:

- Sport in physical education can enhance students access to practices and ideas that can enable them to make positive contributions to society
- Sport helps students to understand the self and the society in which they live.

Promoting sport participation in school and beyond

There are three examples of sport in physical education constructed to promote participation in and beyond school. The first two are examples of refinements to the sport education curriculum model (Siedentop 1994; Siedentop et al. 2004). Siedentop argued that sport is an important part of our culture and has considerable educative potential when the physical educator is repositioned from the technical specialist of traditional physical education to a facilitator of authentic learning experiences using a sporting context. With an emphasis on student accountability and responsibility, sport education promotes a more flexible approach to curriculum planning and a democratic student-centred style of teaching. This enables teachers to create an environment that can address many of the concerns raised about traditional physical education pedagogy and resultant student learning. Research identifies that students describe their experiences in sport education as preferable to other sport formats (Hastie 2003a). Girls and lower skilled students appear particularly receptive to sport education (Hastie 2003b). Penney et al. (2002) advocated that sport education could act as a 'connective specialism', capable of building a bridge between school sport and physical education experiences, on the one hand, and students' sustained and fulfilling engagement in sport beyond their school years on the other. Sport education offers a realistic curriculum structure to engage participation in physical education for the development of competencies that can be applied within school and beyond.

The above three examples represent intersecting roles of physical literacy, sport literacy and health literacy. Physical literacy is an emerging concept within physical education. In Canada it has been used to capture the curriculum importance of fundamental movement skill learning for an 'active start'. Many authors have written about the importance of fundamental movement skill learning in motivating and enabling engagement in physically active living (e.g. Sanders 2002; Okley & Booth 2004; Fisher et al. 2005). We have described in this chapter the use of sport literacy as a frame for active engagement in sport. This active engagement includes learning beyond the boundaries confined within narrow definitions of learning as textbook motor patterns and notions of fitness. It includes valued social, cultural and vocational understandings of sport as well as the cognitive ability to engage critically in sport perspectives. This 'critical' dimension to active engagement in sport encompasses notions of health literacy, where health literacy is defined as the capacity for sound health decisions. Sport literacy therefore provides a possible nexus through which to consider the work of health education and physical education as conceptually linked. This would stand in contrast to the more normative experience of health education and physical education as separate subjects within a co-joined learning area.

Conclusion

Throughout this chapter we have attempted to articulate the meaning of sport from a sociological perspective. Sport is certainly an important cultural construct for many Australians, providing active recreation, an avenue for elite performance for participants and passive leisure for spectators. The chapter has identified how sport is entwined in obesity discourses, which situates sport as a vehicle through which individuals can accumulate physical activity as part of a healthy 'lifestyle'. While we do not discount this ideological perspective, it is important to recognise that sport offers a range of learning opportunities beyond the stereotypical functionalist perspectives. Arguably, physical education remains the most appropriate site in which this learning can be achieved.

Physical education and school sport have a strongly related history. Experiences of sport in physical education, however, have largely been focused on 'skills and drills' (Pill 2007). The contribution of military physical training features in this pedagogical construction of direct and frequently command style teaching, which Metzler (2005) described as the physical education method, is still evident. The paradigm of contemporary physical education is shifting from methods and instructional strategies to instructional models. Instructional models provide a curriculum vision and theoretical basis for instruction (Metzler 2005; Buck et al. 2007). Within these models pedagogy includes the choice of instructional strategy or style to suit learner needs and task objectives. The *Spectrum of Teaching Approaches* (Mosston & Ashworth 2002) has been of particular benefit in this aspect of curriculum decision-making. Competing for physical education teachers' attention is a physical activity agenda where movement in physical education is simply an end in itself rather than a means through which to achieve a variety of outcomes (Metzler 2005). Irrespective of whether one chooses to adopt the stance promoted in the chapter around sport and physical education as a site for broader learning, physical education is simply not afforded the time within the school day to be a compensatory site through which to address children's health needs. The Australian Physical Activity Guidelines for Children and Youth recommend a minimum of 60 minutes and up to several hours of vigorous physical activity daily for health benefits (Australian Government Department of Health and Ageing 2010). There are broader multifaceted issues at play that have implications beyond the reach of physical education and sport. However, physical education can play its part in students establishing understanding of the meaning and significance of sport within a health-oriented physically active lifestyle at school, beyond the school, now and into the future.

Sport is a sound means through which contemporary physical education can achieve the hallmark vision of physical education as distinctive from physical training (Williams 1930; 1964). As a central component of the physical education curriculum, sport must be delivered through contemporary iterations of Sport Education, which bring social and cultural components, as well as the historically valued physical elements of sport. Although there are constant reminders to engage in sport as a valued form of community and health-enhancing physical activity, unfortunately, for many students sport in physical education is not a positive or affirming experience. Contemporary expressions of sport education and curriculum visions like sport literacy limit failure by broadening conceptions of ability and valued ways of knowing beyond competitive performance objectives. The role of physical education in promoting sport participation in school and beyond is linked with the development of skills and understandings enabling the functional use of sport knowledge within active and engaged citizenship. Assuming the potential of sport in schools to both galvanise and divide students into 'those who can and enjoy' sport and 'those who do not' creates a challenge for physical and sport educators to overcome. Curriculum and pedagogical decision-making are an integral part of efforts to move away from PE's branding as a 'marginal' concern of the curriculum (Hardman & Marshall 2005). Confronting the norms of the pedagogical status quo will play a pivotal role in educating through sport in areas of personal and social skill development, physical activity and participation, and health of individuals and communities.

References

Alexander, K. (2008). Is there a role for tactical and sport education models in school physical education? Keynote Address, 'Play to Educate' First Asia Pacific Sport in Education Conference, 21st January 2008. Sturt Campus, Flinders University School of Education, Adelaide. [Online]. Available: caef.flinders.edu.au/events/sie2008/presentations.php [accessed 20 January 2011].

Arnold, P. (1979). *Meaning in movement, sport and physical education*. London: Heinemann

Australian Bureau of Statistics (ABS) (2009). *Children's participation in cultural and leisure activities, Australia*, April 2009 (No. 4901.0). Canberra, Australian Capital Territory: Australian Bureau of Statistics.

Australian Council for Health, Physical Education and Recreation (1993). *Position statement: quality physical education in Australian schools*. Hindmarsh, South Australia.

Australian Government Department of Health and Ageing (2010). *Australia's physical activity recommendations for children and young people*. [Online]. Available: www.health.gov.au/internet/main/publishing.nsf/content/health-pubhlth-strateg-active-recommend.htm [accessed 20 January 2011].

Bailey, R. (2005). Evaluating the relationship between physical education, sport and social inclusion. *Educational Review, 57*(1): 71–90.

Bailey, R. & Kirk, D. (2009). Introduction. In R. Bailey & D. Kirk (Eds). *The Routledge physical education reader* (pp. 1–6). New York: Routledge.

Brooker, R. & Macdonald, D. (1993). Contextualising physical education and the national curriculum. *The ACHPER National Journal, 40*(1): 8–10.

Brown, T. & Holland, B. (2005). Student physical activity and lesson context during physical education. *ACHPER Healthy Lifestyles Journal, 52*(3/4): 17–23.

Buck, M., Lund, J., Harrison, J. & Blakemore Cook, C. (2007). *Instructional strategies for secondary physical education.* New York: McGraw-Hill.

Centre for Health Promotion: Children, Youth and Women's Health Service (2006). *Virtually healthy newsletter, 41*(3). [Online]. Available: healthpromotion.cywhs.sa.gov.au/library/vh43.pdf [accessed 19 January 2011].

Cliff, K., Wright, J. & Clarke, D. (2009). *What does a 'sociocultural perspective' mean in health and physical education?* University of Wollongong Faculty of Education Papers. [Online]. Available: ro.uow.edu.au/edupapers/96 [accessed 19 January 2011].

Coakley, J., Hallinan, C., Jackson, S. & Meweyy, P. (2009). *Sports in society: issues and controversies in Australia and New Zealand.* North Ryde, NSW: McGraw-Hill.

Department of Education and Children's Services (2008). *South Australian Curriculum Standards and Accountability Framework Online.* [Online]. Available: www.sacsa.sa.edu.au/ [accessed 19 January 2011].

Department of Education and Training (2005). *Get skilled get active.* NSW Department of Education and Training.

Dunstan, K. (1973). *Sports.* Melbourne: Cassell.

Ennis, C. (1999). Creating a cultural relevant curriculum for disengaged girls. *Sport, Education and Society, 4*(1): 31–50.

Ericsson, A. (2003). Development of elite performance and deliberate practice: an update from the perspective of the expert performance approach. In J. Starkes & A. Ericsson (Eds.), *Expert performance in sports: advances in research on sport expertise* (pp. 49–84). Champaign, IL: Human Kinetics.

Evans, J. (2004). Making a difference? Education and 'ability' in physical education. *European Physical Education Review, 10*(1): 95–108.

Fisher, A., Reilly, J., Kelly, L., Montgomery, C., Williamson, A., Paton, J. & Grant, S. (2005). Fundamental movement skills and habitual physical activity in young children. *Medicine and Science in Sports & Exercise, 37*(4): 684–88.

Gard, M. (2006). HPE and the 'obesity epidemic'. In R. Tinning, L. McCuaig & L. Hunter (Eds.), *Teaching health and physical education in Australian schools* (pp. 78–87). Frenchs Forest, NSW: Pearson Education Australia.

Gard, M. & Wright, J. (2005). *The obesity epidemic: science, morality and ideology.* USA: Routledge.

Green, K. (1998). Philosophies, ideologies and the practice of physical education. *Sport, Education and Society, 3*(2): 125–144.

Hardman, K. & Marshall, J. (2005). Update on the status of physical education worldwide. [Online].

Available: http://www.icsspe.org/documente/Status_PE_Hardman_and_Marshall.pdf [accessed 9 March 2011].

Hastie, P. (2003a). Teaching sport within physical education. In S. Silverman & C. Ennis (Eds.), *Student learning in physical education: applying research to enhance instruction* (pp. 109–28). Champaign, IL: Human Kinetics.

Hastie, P. (2003b). *Teaching for lifetime physical activity through quality high school physical education*. San Francisco: Benjamin Cummings.

Hay, R. (2006). 'Our wicked foreign game': why has Association Football (soccer) not become the main code of football in Australia? *Soccer and Society, 7*(2–3): 165–86.

Hemphill, D. (2008). Sport smart. *Education Review, 15*: 15.

Higgs, C., Balyi, I., Way, R., Cardinal., C., Norris, S. & Bluechardt, M. (n.d.). *Developing physical literacy: a guide for parents of children ages 0–12*. Canada: Canadian Sport Centres.

Hilbrecht, M. (2007). Changing perspectives on the work-leisure relationship. *Annals of Leisure Research, 10*(3–4): 368–90.

Koivula, N. (1999). Sport participation: differences in motivation and actual participation due to gender typing. *Journal of Sport Behaviour, 22*(3): 360–80.

Land, R. & Butner, G. (1982). *Time off: leisure, recreation and sport in Australia*. Sydney: CCH Australia.

Macdonald, D. (1995). The role of proletarianization in physical education teacher attrition. *Research Quarterly for Exercise and Sport, 66*(2): 129–41.

Metzler, M. (2005). *Instructional models for physical education*. Arizona: Holocomb Hathaway.

Moston, M. & Ashworth, S. (2002). *Teaching physical education*. San Francisco: Pearson Education.

Okely, A. & Booth, M. (2004). Mastery of fundamental movement skills among children in New South Wales: prevalence and socio-demographic distribution. *Journal of Science and Medicine in Sport, 7*(3): 358–72.

Penney, D. & Chandler, T. (2000). Physical education: what futures? *Sport, Education and Society, 5*(1): 71–88.

Penney, D., Clarke, G. & Kinchin, G. (2002). Developing physical education as a 'connective specialism': Is sport education he answer? *Sport, Education and Society, 7*(1): 55–64.

Peters, R. (1966). *Ethics and education*. London: Allen & Unwin.

Pigott, B. (1982). A pyschological basis for new trends in games teaching. *Bulletin of Physical Education, 18*(1): 17–22.

Pill, S. (2009). Sport teaching in physical education: considering sport literacy. Paper presented at the 26th ACHPER International Conference, 3–5 July, Brisbane.

Pill, S. (2007). *Play with purpose*. Hindmarsh, South Australia: Australian Council for Health, Physical Education and Recreation.

Placek, J. (1983). Conceptions of success in teaching: busy, happy, and good? In T. Templin and J. Olsen (Eds.). *Teaching in physical education* (pp. 45–56). Champaign, IL: Human Kinetics.

Rossi, T. (2006). An educational rationale for movement in education. In R. Tinning, L. McCuaig & L.

Hunter (Eds). *Teaching health and physical education in Australian schools* (pp. 9–16). Frenchs Forest: Pearson Education Australia.

Sanders, S. (2002). *The issues: the importance of developing fundamental motor skills: learning how to catch a ball.* [Online]. Available: www.pbs.org/teachers/earlychildhood/articles/motorskills.html [accessed 19 January 2011].

Siedentop, D. (1994). *Sport education: quality PE through positive sport experiences.* Champaign, IL: Human Kinetics.

Siedentop, D., Hastie, P. & van der Mars, H. (2004). *Complete guide to sport education.* Champaign, IL: Human Kinetics.

Tinning, R., Kirk, D. & Evans, J. (1993). *Learning to teach physical education.* Englewood Cliffs: Prentice Hall.

Tinning, R., MacDonald, D., Wright, J. & Hickey, C. (2001). *Becoming a physical education teacher: contemporary and enduring issues.* Frenchs Forest: Prentice Hall.

Veal, A. & Lynch, R. (1996). *Australian leisure.* Frenchs Forest, NSW: Hospitality Press.

Wadham, B., Pudsey, J. & Boyd, R. (2007). *Culture and education.* Frenchs Forest, NSW: Pearson Education Australia.

Williams, J. (1930). Education through the physical: a new view of physical education based on the biological unity of mind and body. *Journal of Higher Education, 5*(1): 279–82.

Williams, J. (1964). *The principles of physical education.* Saunders

Wright, J. & Burrows, L. (2006). Re-conceiving ability in physical education: a social analysis. *Sport, Education and Society, 11*(3): 275–91.

Wuest, D. & Bucher, C. (2006). *Foundations of physical education, exercise science and sport.* New York: McGraw Hill.

12

Are schools responsible for engaging youth in sport and physical activity?

Louisa Peralta

The promotion of physical activity is an essential public health and health promotion strategy to improve the health of individuals and populations (Brown & Summerbell 2009; WHO 2009). This has grown in importance over the last ten years, driven by issues related to accelerating overweight and obesity rates, and others related to the increasing burden of physical activity-related diseases, including some cancers, cardiovascular disease and Type II diabetes. For example, being inactive is estimated to cause 10% to 16% of cases each of breast cancer, colon and rectal cancers, as well as Type II diabetes, and 22% of coronary heart diseases (WHO 2009). In response to these issues, governments, along with health promotion advocates, educators and the general community, have looked at a number of ways to promote physical activity, particularly among children and adolescents. As a result, the school setting has often been postulated as an opportune environment. Hence, a myriad of school-based physical activity interventions worldwide have been implemented and reported in the literature. This paper will report on three of these interventions, which have been designed, implemented and evaluated in secondary school settings (both public and independent schools systems) in the United States (US) and Australia. The aim of reporting these three school-based physical activity interventions is to discuss and highlight the complexity of designing appropriate interventions and deciding whether schools are responsible for engaging youth in sport and physical activity.

Who is not engaged in youth sport and physical activity?

The literature has clearly noted that physical activity is important for young people's health (Biddle et al. 2004). Youth who participate in higher levels of physical activity are less likely to display risk factors for cardiovascular disease or Type II diabetes (Strong et al. 2005), and more able to regulate weight (Moore et al. 2003). Despite these health benefits, engagement in physical activity at a moderate-to-vigorous intensity, especially among particular population groups (such as children and adolescents), are lower than the Australian recommended guidelines of a minimum of 60 minutes per day (Commonwealth of Australia 2008). This is concerning, as those not adequately active during childhood and early adolescence are around five times less likely to be sufficiently active in adulthood (Telama et al. 2005).

There are a multitude of factors which may influence youths' engagement in sport and physical activity (Kohl & Hobbs 1998). These factors can be classified into four categories: physiological, psychological, sociocultural and ecological. Physiological determinants of sport and physical activity among youth include age, gender and ethnicity (Brodersen et al. 2007). In Australia, girls have been found to be less active than boys; older children and adolescents less active than younger children; and non-English speaking background youth less active than youth from English speaking backgrounds (Booth et al. 2002; 2006).

Psychological determinants include confidence in one's ability to engage in sport and physical activity (self-efficacy) (Dishman et al. 2004), perception of physical or sport competence (Sallis et al. 2000), having a positive attitude toward physical activity and sport (Trost et al. 1997), enjoyment of sport and physical activity (Dishman et al. 2005) and perceiving benefits from engaging in sport and physical activity (Zakarian et al. 1994). Conversely, perceived barriers to physical activity, such as lack of time or feeling tired, are negatively associated with physical activity among youth (Zakarian et al. 1994).

Sociocultural influences include support for and participation in physical activity from peers and siblings, parental level of physical activity, parental support and parental income. Two recent reviews showed differences in associations between physical activity and youth in regards to sociocultural influences (Sallis et al. 2000; van der Horst et al. 2007). For example in the review by Sallis et al. (2000), there were no positive associations between parents and youths' physical activity levels. In contrast, van der Horst and colleagues (2007) suggested that parental involvement in physical activities for boys and parental support for both genders were both positive influences on children's physical activity. Further, a number of cross-sectional studies have found that parental participation in physical activity and parental support of physical activity were positively related to children's physical activity levels (Sallis et al. 1988). In these studies, parents who actively participated in physical activity themselves and proactively supported physical activity were more likely to create an environment that promotes physical activity for their child, through providing transportation (Sallis et al. 1999) and positive role modelling (Bandura 1986). Currently, there is minimal evidence for siblings and peers' influence on youth physical activity and sport participation.

Ecological determinants of physical activity and sport include access to play spaces, facilities, availability of equipment and transportation to activities and programs. Population surveys of Australian children's participation in culture and leisure activities have been conducted in 2003, 2006 and 2009 (ABS 2009). Over this six-year period, data showed that the participation rate of youth (five–14 years) in organised sport remained stagnant (62% in 2003 to 63% in 2009). Participation rates for boys in at least one organised sport did not change. After showing an increase of three percentage points from 54% in 2003 to 57% in 2006, girl participation rates in at least one organised sport did not change in 2009 (56%) (ABS 2009).

An estimated 1.7 million (63%) Australian youth participated in at least one organised sport outside of school hours, in the 12 months to April 2009. Participation in organised sport was highest among nine- to 11-year-old children at 68% compared with 58% for five- to eight-year-olds and 65% for 12- to 14-year-olds. Participation rates were higher for boys across all age groups compared with girls, with the greatest difference being between 12- to 14-year-olds (boys 74% compared with 55% of girls). Further, an estimated 37% (1.0 million) of youth did not participate in any organised sport, 33% participated in one sport and 30% played two or more organised sports during the 12 month period (ABS 2009). These results are alarming, as they highlight that more than one-third of our youth (or two in every five) are not engaged in organised sport outside of school hours.

For those youth not involved in organised sport, the only opportunities for physical activity are in the school and home settings. The findings from two international physical activity reviews imply that participation in physical education and school sport are positively associated with youth physical activity and engagement in organised sport, but not for access to space, facilities and equipment in the home environment (Sallis et al. 2000; van der Horst et al. 2007). This suggests that physical education and school sport are important and positive influences on youth's physical activity levels (and particularly more so for those not participating in organised sport outside of school hours) and therefore play a key role in promoting physical activity and sport participation.

Are schools responsible?

The promotion of physical activity is an essential public health and health promotion strategy to improve the health of individuals and populations (Brown & Summerbell 2009; WHO 2009). A recent US nationwide survey found that 65% of parents and the wider public, cited schools (over and above health care providers, the government and parents themselves) as responsible for promoting physical activity and reducing childhood and adolescent obesity (Evans et al. 2005). The reason for this was that the school setting offered established links to other sectors – including federal, state and local governments, local communities and parents – and had access to most, if not all, youth. Therefore this setting had more opportunities to embed physical activity programs across the school, community and home settings.

For a number of years, research has also highlighted the school setting as having the greatest potential to make valuable contributions to the promotion of physical activity among youth. First, physical activity promotion aligns with the fundamental mission of Australian and NSW schools: educating young people to become healthy, productive citizens who can make meaningful contributions to society (NSWDET 2003). Second, schools offer continuous and intensive contact during the formative years (Doak et al. 2006; Flynn et al. 2006; Katz et al. 2008) and school programs have the potential to reach large numbers of youth through multiple avenues (Katz et al. 2008). School programs can be delivered at little or no cost to families and can reach low-income families who otherwise may not have access to programs, equipment and educated staff (Neumark-Sztainer et al. 2003). Third, the majority of youth enjoy school most of the time, find it a positive experience and can identify teachers whom they like and respect. The knowledge, rapport and support that the school teaching staff can bring to school programs may outweigh the support available in the home setting (Booth & Okely 2005). The combination of school linkages, infrastructure and the physical environment, which includes policies, classroom health education, physical education programs, co- and extracurricular programs, as well as qualified and skilled teaching staff, makes schools a viable forum for providing physical activity interventions in a cost-effective manner (Brown & Summerbell 2009; Dobbins et al. 2009).

While some have argued for the school as an opportune and dominant setting for promoting physical activity, others have questioned the ability of schools to make a difference (Kropski et al. 2008; Muller et al. 2005; Stice et al. 2006). The main grounds for these doubts include the focus and goals of education, the overcrowded curriculum and intensity of teacher workload, appropriateness of programs and the potential stigma that can be attached to students and programs.

Implementing school-based programs can be complex, with many realities possibly restricting effectiveness. For example, literacy and numeracy knowledge and skills rather than the broader development of students, are the primary focus for schools. This has become even more apparent in NSW and Australia in recent times, with the introduction of the National Assessment Program of Literacy and Numeracy (NAPLAN), school leader boards and the development of the Australian Curriculum (by the Australian Curriculum, Assessment and Reporting Authority [ACARA]). The first phase of the Australian curriculum was for English, Mathematics, Science and History and were closely linked to the current federal government's national literacy and numeracy goals, and the testing and distribution of these results on school leader boards. This is despite ACARA using the goals of the 2008 *Melbourne declaration of educational goals for young Australians*, which commits to supporting all young Australians to become successful learners, confident and creative individuals and active and informed citizens (MCEETYA 2008). It seems the goal of creating confident and creative individuals was considered in the second phase of the Australian curriculum with languages, geography and the arts being accepted in the next wave of development. This has left most researchers and educators in the Health and Physical Education (HPE) key learning area wondering about the placement of HPE, considering its main aim is to produce successful, active and informed citizens. With continued lobbying, this key learning area has been selected in the third phase. As a result, the message is clear: health promotion is a distant third, with educational goals focusing on literacy and numeracy prominent in Australian schools.

Additionally, schools typically have well-established cultures, which can be difficult and time consuming to change. Cultural change is usually needed for successful implementation of any new program within the school setting. This is primarily dependent on whether staff, students, parents and key stakeholders support the program, and the social and political environments are positive (Fullan 2001). The Active After-School Communities program (AASC) will be employed as it focuses on the availability of school property for recreational and sporting use outside school time, and the political and economic influences. Allowing community use of school property after school hours for the purpose of engaging youth, local sporting organisations and families in active sport and physical activity seems like a plausible option for improving the physical activity levels of youth (especially those not engaged in organised sport and/or coming from low socioeconomic status regions). Schools often have facilities (e.g. halls, gymnasiums, dance studios, grass fields and courts) that are appropriate for meeting the sporting and physical activity needs of their surrounding communities. The AASC program is a federal government funded program (introduced and funded by the previous federal government) that utilises this idea and provides primary-school-aged children with access to free, fun, safe, inclusive and structured physical activities, generally using the school's equipment and resources, in the after-school timeslot or window period (3–5pm). Running since 2005, this program has been designed to engage traditionally non-active children in structured physical activities that focus on fundamental movement skills and development. It also aims to build pathways with local community organisations in order to stimulate community involvement in delivering sport and physical activity programs and fostering school-community links. An interim report, released in 2008, reported that the program had met most of these goals, with over 150,000 students participating across 3250 schools, with 50% located in regional and remote areas (Australian Sports Commission 2008). Although the following physical activity results have to be viewed with caution, due to the physical activity measurement used (parent proxy report through web-based survey), youth doubled their structured physical activities per week, increasing their total physical activity levels by 1.4 hours (Australian Sports Commission 2008). Despite these positive results, the current federal government has slashed the funding and support allocated to the AASC program in 2010. The ramifications from the funding loss are yet to be seen, but schools which have embedded this program into their culture may be forced to fund these programs themselves and provide their own staff and personnel. In saying that, it is highly likely that most schools will not be able to sustain the program and will cut the program altogether.

Finally, there is potential for harmful social ramifications, such as labelling, coercion, stigma and discrimination associated with school-based physical activity programs. Such social ramifications were heightened in the 1970s and 1980s, when school-based programs targeted only overweight and obese students (Botvin et al. 1979; Brownell & Kaye 1982; Figueroa-Colon et al. 1996). Although, many of these interventions were effective in improving physical activity levels and achieving weight reductions, the psychosocial or adverse side effects potentially outweighed the benefits (Parcel et al. 1988; Gard & Wright 2005). However, recent school-based physical activity programs have taken the psychosocial aspects of their participants into consideration when designing and implementing their activities, which has been noted in van Wijnen and colleagues' review (2009). In fact, this review reports that school-based physical activity interventions had the potential to improve psychosocial aspects, especially interventions that were curriculum focused; embedded inclusiveness strategies and psychosocial skills; and universal (that is, did not target overweight and obese students only) (van Wijnen et al. 2009).

Although there are several realities of school-based interventions, it is likely that without a strong contribution from schools the levels of physical activity among youth will not improve. This has led to numerous researchers, departments, schools and teachers designing, implementing and evaluating a large number of school-based physical activity interventions all over the world.

What has been happening in schools?

Due to the large number of people designing, implementing and evaluating these school-based physical activity interventions, the aims, structure, length, components and activities of each of the programs can be quite different. Presently, the evidence gathered from school-based physical activity interventions to determine effectiveness is mixed. Hence, this section will describe three different school-based physical activity interventions, to emphasise the complexity in designing and implementing these programs, but also to show the potential for improving youth physical activity levels.

Given school-age youth spend a significant amount of their wakeful hours either in transit to or in the school setting, and that the majority of youth attend school until they reach adolescence, school-based physical activity interventions have potential to reduce population-wide chronic diseases. School-based interventions can target simultaneously, both youth at risk and not at risk for future chronic diseases, and can increase both knowledge and behaviour conducive to healthier lifestyles. School-based physical activity interventions usually focus on one of three aims:

- To increase the overall percentage of youth engaged in physical activity each day (either through curricular and/or non-curricular programs)
- To increase the duration of moderate to vigorous activity engaged in on a weekly basis
- To reduce the decline in physical activity that occurs as children reach adolescence (Dobbins et al. 2009).

Most of these school-based physical activity interventions plan to create a school environment that is more conducive to achieving higher rates of physical activity among youth, by promoting time spent in moderate to vigorous physical activity, and educating youth and encouraging healthier behaviours in the hope that these behaviours will track into adulthood. Generally this means changes to school curriculum and non-curriculum times during the school day.

The following three school-based physical activity interventions have been selected as case studies due to the quality of the research study, the selection of physical activity as a goal, their effectiveness (the ability to positively change physical activity behaviours) and curriculum focus. The interventions are: M-SPAN (Middle School Physical Activity and Nutrition program: Sallis et al. 2003); TAAG (Trial of Activity for Adolescent Girls: Webber et al. 2008) and The FILA Program (The Fitness Improvement, Lifestyle Awareness program: Peralta et al. 2009). The aim of presenting these case studies is to display school-based intervention programs that have similar aims regarding physical activity, but different structures, components, contexts and activities. By looking at each of these intervention programs and their findings, a number of clarities or queries may arise that may determine your response to the question: Are schools responsible for engaging youth in sport and physical activity?

Table 1 Descriptive characteristics of school-based intervention studies examining change in physical activity following an obesity prevention and/or physical activity intervention among older children and adolescents.

Author, year, country	Sample	Intervention groups	Length	Intervention and control content	PA change
M-SPAN Sallis et al. (2003) US	24 schools N = 1109±356, Years 6–8 (10–14yrs) 51% boys	1: Intervention (n = 12 schools) 2: Control (n = 12 schools)	2 school years	1: Increase PA in PE classes or on campus during leisure periods. Reduce total fat intake by provision of more low fat choices 2: Standard environment	Intervention increased boys' physical activity, but not girls
TAAG Webber et al. (2008) US	36 schools N = 3504, Years 6–8 (10–14yrs) 100% girls	1: Intervention (n = 18 schools) 2: Control (n = 18 schools)	3 school years	1: Create environmental and organisation changes supportive of PA and increase cues, messages and incentives to be more physically active 2: Standard environment	Intervention increased girls' physical activity after the third year of program
The FILA Program Peralta et al. (2009) Australia	1 school N = 33, 12.5±0.4 yrs, 100% boys.	1: Intervention (n = 16 boys) 2: Control (n = 17 boys)	6 months	1: Boys only PA Program 3 times per week. One theory session with behaviour modification skills, increase fruit and sweetened beverage and reduce small screen recreation activities. Two PA lunchtime sessions 2: Standard PE	Intervention increased boys' weekday MVPA, vigorous physical activity and total physical activity

Abbreviations: MVPA = moderate to vigorous physical activity; PA = physical activity; PE = Physical Education; N/n = number; yrs = years.

Of the three case studies presented, two were conducted in the US and the other in Australia. The two US studies were conducted in the middle-school setting (M-SPAN and TAAG), with the Australian study conducted in a secondary-school setting (The FILA Program). The average age of participants was 12.3 years, the average sample size was 1549, and the median intervention length was 22 months. These studies are summarised in Table 1.

Case Study 1: M-SPAN (Middle School Physical Activity and Nutrition) Intervention Program

The first case study (Sallis et al. 2003) describes a physical activity intervention that was implemented over a period of two years in 12 US middle schools. The intervention program was designed to increase physical activity in physical education (PE) classes and throughout the school day. This involved teachers and students engaging in policy change efforts and implementing a range of smaller programs within the school environment. PE was required daily in all years, and one intervention component was designed to increase physical activity in PE classes through changing lesson context, lesson structure, and teacher behaviour. Another intervention component was intended to increase physical activity throughout the school day during non-curricular periods when students could make choices (that is, before school, after lunch and after school). Consistent with these environmental changes, schools were to increase supervision, equipment and organised activities. Key school executive staff met with research staff to select and implement policy changes to create healthier school environments. Participants included administrators (principals, canteen personnel), faculty (PE teachers), staff (other keen teaching staff), parents, and students. The project requested three, 90-minute meetings per school across two years, and 80% of planned meetings were held. Parents were also included and updated on progress through existing school communication channels (e.g. newsletters, parent-teacher meetings).

The validated SOFIT (System for Observing Fitness Instruction Time) observation method (McKenzie et al. 2000) was used to evaluate student physical activity in a random sample of PE classes. The SOPLAY (System for Observing Play and Leisure Activity of Youth) observation method (McKenzie et al. 2000) was developed for the study to assess the number of students and their activity levels during non-curricular times. Intervention schools increased physical activity over time at a greater rate than control schools. In particular, the intervention was effective for increasing boys' physical activity ($p<0.001$), but not girls. Moreover, physical activity intervention was effective in increasing boys' physical activity levels only at school. There was no evidence that the school-based physical activity intervention improved physical activity behaviours outside school hours. The reasons for the lack of effect on girls' physical activity were not clear. Perhaps the activities were gender biased towards boys; or boys' participation in non-curricular activities limited girls' participation; or girls need a combination of opportunities, promotion and education.

Case Study 2: TAAG (Trial of Activity for Adolescent Girls) Intervention Program

The second case study (Webber et al. 2008) describes an all-girls physical activity intervention program. The primary aim of TAAG was to reduce by half the observed decline in moderate to vigorous physical activity (MVPA) experienced by adolescent girls. This was measured at the end of the research-staff-directed two-year intervention and again at the end of the schoolteacher-community-implemented third year of intervention. Intervention activities were targeted to create environmental and organisational changes, supportive of physical activity and cues; messages and incentives to be more physically active. Specifically, the intervention was designed to establish more opportunities; improve social support and norms; and increase self-efficacy, outcome expectations, and behavioural skills to foster greater MVPA among girls in Years 6, 7 and 8. Girls were the focus of the intervention, however both boys and girls received the PE components. An innovative feature of the intervention was linking school and community agencies to develop and promote physical activity programs for girls. These programs were delivered both on and off school property, in most cases either before or after school. Community partners included the YMCA or YWCA, local health clubs, and community recreation centres, providing programs such as lunchtime Dance Revolution, after-school step-aerobics classes, before-school open gym, basketball camp, touch football, and weekend canoe programs. Programs did not replace PE lessons. TAAG Physical Education lessons promoted MVPA for at least 50% of class time and encouraged teachers to promote physical activity outside of class. PE teachers were trained by TAAG research staff on classroom management strategies, skill-building activities, the importance of engaging girls in MVPA during class, and the provision of appropriate equipment and choices of physical activity.

Measurements were taken during spring 2003, 2005 and 2006. Physical activity was measured using Actigraph accelerometers (MTI model 7164). Each girl wore an accelerometer during waking hours for seven consecutive days. Data were collected and stored in 30-second intervals. Girls wore the accelerometer on their right hip, attached to a belt, except while bathing, swimming, or sleeping. Physical activity in PE lessons was measured by SOFIT. A minimum of four PE lessons were observed at each of the three visits to each intervention and control school during the three measurement semesters.

After the first two years of intervention, there was no difference in minutes of MVPA between Year 8 girls in schools assigned to intervention or control. The average daily minutes of MVPA declined from 146 (±81.8) in Year 6 girls (2003) to 136 (±74.3) in Year 8 girls (2005). However, after three years of intervention, Year 8 girls in the intervention schools had 10.9 more minutes of MVPA than Year 8 girls in the control schools ($p=0.03$). In PE lessons, the intervention schools had a 4% greater amount of time devoted to MVPA, compared with control schools. These findings show, in contrast to M-SPAN, that providing a school environment that encourages physical activity can make positive changes to adolescent girls' physical activity levels. Of particular interest, is the fact that TAAG was a single-sex intervention program and that the teacher-directed component of the physical activity intervention was the most effective. This suggests that interventions should be tailored specifically for gender differences and that the role of teachers in designing and implementing these programs is important.

Case Study 3: The FILA (Fitness Improvement, Lifestyle Awareness) Intervention Program

The primary aim of The FILA Program (Peralta et al. 2009) was to assess the feasibility, acceptability and potential efficacy of a six-month school-based obesity prevention program among adolescent boys with suboptimal cardiorespiratory fitness. It was hypothesised that boys in the intervention group, compared with those in the active comparison group, would show an increase in physical activity levels, as well as other outcomes.

Boys were recruited from the Year 7 student population of a single-sex (boys) secondary school in Sydney, Australia. The intervention program was implemented over a period of 16 weeks, with each week comprising one 60-minute curriculum session and two 20-minute lunchtime physical activity sessions. Each 60-minute curriculum session included practical and/or theoretical components. The theoretical components focused on promoting physical activity through increasing physical self-esteem and self-efficacy and the acquisition and practice of self-regulatory behaviours such as goal setting, time management, and identifying and overcoming barriers. Behaviour modification techniques (e.g. group goals converting time spent in physical activity to kilometres to reach a specific destination) were used throughout the program. The practical component of the intervention comprised modified games and activities, where boys had some choice. A combination of researcher, teacher and Year 11 peer role models implemented the intervention, although the researcher was the primary deliverer. Parents were also engaged throughout the intervention, through newsletters emailed or mailed regularly throughout the 16 weeks. Boys in the active comparison group were also involved in a physical activity program. This program comprised one 60-minute practical session per week and focused on improving boys cardiorespiratory fitness levels.

Measurements were taken at baseline and follow up. Physical activity was measured using Actigraph accelerometers (MTI model 7164). Each boy wore an accelerometer during waking hours for seven consecutive days. Data were collected and stored in 60-second intervals.

After the six-month intervention, the intervention boys' weekday vigorous physical activity (VPA), MVPA and total physical activity levels were greater (effect sizes of 0.86, 0.29 and 0.36, respectively), compared with the active comparison boys. However, the active comparison boys' weekend moderate physical activity (MPA), VPA, MVPA and total physical activity levels were greater (effect sizes of 0.72, 0.99, 0.72 and 0.44, respectively). This discrepancy in physical activity findings is hard to explain. It may be that regular contact between the teacher, researcher, Year 11 peer role models and intervention group participants reminded and motivated the boys to maintain high levels of physical activity during the week. Once they reached the weekend, however, they may have felt they could decrease physical activity levels to compensate for the higher levels during the week. Alternatively, participants may not have been motivated to be active on weekends or not confident that they could be active (that is, without the support of the researcher and teacher). The results also suggest the potential of single-sex interventions to positively change boys' physical activity levels, and the need to consider gender specific programs.

Conclusion

The three case studies were somewhat effective in making positive changes to physical activity levels. Each of the intervention programs had different aims, intervention approaches, structures, lengths and target participants. Despite their uniqueness and the trialing of a number of varied approaches, it would be appropriate to conclude that increasing youth physical activity levels is challenging and complex, with school-based physical activity reviews reporting ambiguity about which strategies might be effective in promoting physical activity. Van Sluijs et al. (2007) recommend that school-based physical activity intervention programs for youth must:

- Be multifaceted
- Utilise both curriculum and non curriculum elements
- Promote family or community involvement
- Be educational with policy and environmental changes.

Of interest, these recommendations have not included designing and implementing single-sex interventions or gender-tailored programs. However, it has been suggested that due to poor methodological quality (that is, study design and reporting) and lack of significant changes in outcomes, there is currently little evidence to suggest that single-sex interventions are more effective.

Are schools responsible for engaging youth in sport and physical activity?

As this chapter has shown, schools' responsibilities are numerous, with time being a valuable and scarce commodity. While many people in society, especially governments, health promotion advocates, researchers and parents, believe the promotion of youth physical activity and the fight to reduce youth overweight and obesity is a school priority and responsibility, the reality of taking on this responsibility is challenging and complex. More high quality research and evidence is needed to ensure schools are designing and implementing programs that are appropriate, cost savvy and effective.

Despite this, the case studies described above demonstrate that those schools, teachers and researchers who do decide to take on the responsibility, can make a difference. Each study shows the potential that schools and staff members have in promoting positive physical activity changes in youth. The decision to get involved is one that the school and its respective staff need to make as a collective. Without the total support of school staff (including the executive staff), it is unlikely that physical activity programs will be embraced and therefore succeed.

References

Australian Bureau of Statistics (ABS) (2009). *Children's participation in cultural and leisure activities, Australia*. Canberra: Australian Bureau of Statistics.

Australian Sports Commission (ASC) (2008). *Helping kids and communities get active: an interim report of the evaluation of the Active After-School Communities program 2005-2009*. Canberra: Australian Sports Commission.

Bandura, A. (1986). *Social foundations of thought and action*. Englewood Cliffs: Prentice-Hall.

Biddle, S. J., Gorely, T. & Stensel, D. J. (2004). Health-enhancing physical activity and sedentary behaviour in children and adolescents. *Journal of Sports Science, 22*: 679–701.

Booth, M. L. & Okely, A. D. (2005). Promoting physical activity among children and adolescents: The strengths and limitations of school-based approaches. *Health Promotion Journal of Australia, 16*:52–54.

Booth, M. L., Okely, A. D., Chey, T. & Bauman, A. (2002). The reliability and validity of the Adolescent Physical Activity Recall Questionnaire. *Medicine and Science in Sports and Exercise, 34*: 1986–1995.

Booth, M. L., Okely, A. D., Denney-Wilson, E., Hardy, L. L., Yang, B. & Dobbins, T. (2006). *NSW Schools Physical Activity and Nutrition Survey (SPANS) 2004: full report*. Sydney: New South Wales Department of Health.

Botvin, G. J., Cantlon, A., Carter, B. J. & Williams, C. L. (1979). Reducing adolescent obesity through a school health program. *Journal of Pediatrics, 95*: 1060–63.

Brodersen, N. H., Steptoe, A., Boniface, D. R. & Wardle, J. (2007). Trends in physical activity and sedentary behaviour in adolescence: ethnic and socio-economic differences. *British Journal of Sports Medicine, 41*: 140–144.

Brown, T. & Summerbell, C. (2009). Systematic review of school-based interventions that focus on changing dietary intake and physical activity levels to prevent childhood obesity: an update to the obesity guidance produced by the National Institute for Health and Clinical Excellence (NICE). *Obesity Reviews, 10*: 110–41.

Brownell, K. D. & Kaye, F. S. (1982). A school-based behaviour modification, nutrition education and physical activity program for obese children. *American Journal of Clinical Nutrition, 35*: 277–83.

Commonwealth of Australia (2008). *2007 Australian National Children's Nutrition and Physical Activity Survey: main findings*. Canberra, Australian Capital Territory: Commonwealth of Australia.

Dishman, R. K., Motl, R. W., Saunders, R., Felton, G., Ward, D. S., Dowda, M., et al. (2005). Enjoyment mediates effects of a school-based physical activity intervention. *Medicine & Science in Sports & Exercise, 37*: 478–87.

Dishman, R. K., Motl, R. W., Saunders, R., Felton, G., Ward, D. S., Dowda, M., et al. (2004). Self efficacy partially mediates the effect of a school-based physical activity intervention among adolescent girls. *Preventative Medicine, 38*: 628–36.

Doak, C. M., Visscher, T. L. S., Renders, C. M. & Seidell, J. C. (2006). The prevention of overweight and obesity in children and adolescents: a review of interventions and programs. *Obesity Reviews, 7*: 11–136.

Dobbins, M., DeCorby, K., Robeson, P., Husson, H. & Tirilis, D. (2009). School-based physical activity programs for promoting physical activity and fitness in children and adolescents aged 6–18. *Cochrane Database of Systematic Reviews*, CD007651.

Evans, W. D., Finkelstein, E. A., Kamerow, D. B. & Renaud, J. M. (2005). Public perceptions of childhood obesity. *American Journal of Preventive Medicine, 28*: 26–32.

Figueroa-Colon, R., Franklin, F. A., Lee, J. Y., von Almen, T. K. & Suskind, R. M. (1996). Feasibility of a clinic-based hypocaloric dietary intervention implemented in a school setting for obese children. *Obesity Research, 4*: 419–29.

Flynn, M. A. T., McNeil, D. A., Maloff, B., Mutasingwa, D., Wu, M., Ford, C., et al. (2006). Reducing obesity and related chronic disease risk in children and youth: a synthesis of evidence with 'best practice' recommendations. *Obesity Reviews, 7*: 7–66.

Fullan, M. (2001). *Leading in a culture of change*. San Francisco, USA: Jossey-Bass.

Gard, M. & Wright, J. (2005). *The obesity epidemic: science, mortality and ideology*. New York: Taylor & Francis Inc.

Gordon-Larsen, P., Nelson, M. C. & Popkin, B. M. (2004). Longitudinal physical activity and sedentary behaviour trends: adolescence to adulthood. *American Journal of Preventive Medicine, 27*: 277–83.

Katz, D. L., O'Connell, M., Njike, V. Y., Yeh, M. C. & Nawaz, H. (2008). Strategies for the prevention and control of obesity in the school setting: systematic review and meta-analysis. *International Journal of Obesity, (32)*: 1780–89.

Kohl, H.W. & Hobbs, K.E. (1998). Development of physical activity behaviours among children and adolescents. *Pediatrics, 101*: 549–54.

Kropski, J.A., Keckley, P.H. & Jensen, G.L. (2008). School-based obesity prevention programs: an evidence-based review. *Obesity, 16*: 1009–18.

McKenzie, T. L., Marshall, S. J., Sallis, J. F. & Conway, T. L. (2000). Leisure-time physical activity in school environments: an observational study using SOPLAY. *Preventative Medicine, 30*: 70–77.

Ministerial Council on Education, Employment, Training and Youth Affairs (MCEETYA) (2008). *Melbourne declaration on educational goals for young Australians*. Melbourne, Australia: Ministerial Council on Education, Employment, Training and Youth Affairs.

Moore, L. L., Gao, D., Bradlee, M. L., Cupples, L. A., Sundarajan-Ramamurti, A., Proctor, M. H., et al. (2003). Does early physical activity predict body fat change throughout childhood? *Preventive Medicine, 37*: 10–17.

Muller, M. J., Danielzik, S. & Pust, S. (2005). School- and family-based interventions to prevent overweight in children. *Proceedings of the Nutrition Society, 64*: 249–54.

Neumark-Sztainer, D., Story, M., Hannan, P. J. & Rex, J. (2003). New Moves: a school-based obesity prevention program for adolescent girls. *Preventive Medicine, 37*: 41–51.

New South Wales Department of Education (NSWDET) (2003). *Home, school and community partnerships*. Sydney, NSW: New South Wales Department of Education.

Parcel, G. S., Green, L. W. & Bettes, B. A. (1988). School-based programs to prevent or reduce obesity. In N. A. Krasnegor, G. D. Grave & N. Kretchmer (Eds). *Childhood obesity: a biobehavioural perspective* (pp. 143–60). New York, USA: The Telford Press.

Peralta, L. R., Jones, R. A. & Okely, A. D. (2009). Promoting healthy lifestyles among adolescent boys: the Fitness Improvement and Lifestyle Awareness Program RCT. *Preventive Medicine, 48*: 537–42.

Sallis, J. F., Alcaraz, J. E., McKenzie, T. L. & Hovell, M. F. (1999). Predictors of change in children's physical activity over 20 months: variations by gender and level of adiposity. *American Journal of Preventive Medicine, 16*: 222–29.

Sallis, J.F., McKenzie, T., Conway, T.L., Elder, J.P., Prochaska, J.J., Brown, M., et al. (2003). Environmental interventions for eating and physical activity: a randomised controlled trial in middle schools. *American Journal of Preventive Medicine, 24*: 209–17.

Sallis, J. F., Patterson, T. L., McKenzie, T. L. & Nader, P. R. (1988). Family variables and physical activity in preschool children. *Journal of Developmental & Behavioural Pediatrics, 9*: 57–61.

Sallis, J. F., Prochaska, J. J. & Taylor, W. C. (2000). A review of correlates of physical activity of children and adolescents. *Medicine and Science in Sports and Exercise, 32*: 963–75.

Stice, E., Shaw, H. & Marti, N. C. (2006). A meta-analytic review of obesity prevention programs for children and adolescents: the skinny on interventions that work. *Psychological Bulletin, 132*: 667–91.

Strong, W. B., Malina, R. M., Blimkie, C. J. R., Daniels, S. R., Dishman, R. K., Gutin, B., et al. (2005). Evidence based physical activity for school-age youth. *The Journal of Pediatrics, 146*: 732–37.

Telama, R., Yang, X., Viikari, J., Valimaki, I., Wanne, O. & Raitakari, O. (2005). Physical activity from childhood to adulthood: a 21-year tracking study. *Am J Prev Med, 28*: 267–73.

Trost, S. G., Pate, R. R., Saunders, R., Ward, D. S., Dowda, M. & Felton, G. (1997). A prospective study of the determinants of physical activity in rural fifth-grade children. *Preventive Medicine, 26*: 257–63.

van der Horst, K., Chinapaw, M. J., Twisk, J. W. R. & Van Mechelen, W. (2007). A brief review of correlates of physical activity and sedentariness in youth. *Medicine and Science in Sports and Exercise, 39*: 1241–50.

van Sluijs, E. M. F., McMinn, A. M. & Griffin, S. J. (2007). Effectiveness of interventions to promote physical activity in children and adolescents: systematic review of randomised trials. *British Medical Journal, 335*: 703–16.

van Wijnen, L. G. C., Wendel-Vos, G. C. W., Wammes, B. M. & Bemelmans, W. J. E. (2009). The impact of school-based prevention of overweight on psychosocial well-being of children. *Obesity Reviews, 10*: 298–312.

Webber, L. S., Catellier, D. J., Lytle, L. A., Murray, D. M., Pratt, C. A., Young, D. R., et al. (2008). Promoting physical activity in middle school girls: Trial of Activity for Adolescent Girls (TAAG). *American Journal of Preventive Medicine, (34)*: 173–84.

World Health Organization (WHO) (2009). *Global health risks: mortality and burden of disease attributable to selected major risks*. Geneva, Switzerland: Author.

Zakarian, J. M., Hovell, M. F., Hofstetter, C. R., Sallis, J. F. & Keating, K. J. (1994). Correlates of vigorous exercise in a predominantly low SES and minority high school population. *Preventive Medicine, (23)*: 314–21.

13

Factors influencing talent identification and athlete development in youth sport

Donna O'Connor

Australia's performance in recent Olympic Games is evidence of a national commitment and investment into developing its athletes. On medal count alone, Australia ranked fourth in both the 2000 and 2004 games and sixth in Beijing (2008). According to Hogan and Norton (2000) an Olympic gold medal costs the Australian government approximately $37 million. In 2010 the federal government allocated a record $1.2 billion to sport over a four-year period. As part of this strategy the talent identification program will be doubled 'to support 10,000 aspiring Australian athletes and employ more talent scouts' (Sports Minister Kate Ellis cited in Lewis 2010).

This leads us to a contentious issue – talent identification and athlete development. Talent identification has been defined as 'the screening of children and using selected tests of physical, physiological, and skill attributes in order to identify those with potential for success in a designated sport' (Ziemainz & Gulbin 2002, p. 28). This is similar to talent detection which attempts to discover potential athletes who are not currently involved in that particular sport (Williams & Reilly 2000). Advocates of talent identification systems highlight the opportunities it provides to accelerate potential athletes to elite status in a sport they are suited to rather than spending time in a sport they may not excel in. Opponents to talent identification point out the large number of young athletes who need to be initially tested, the reliance on physiological and anthropometric tests with results often skewed in favour of the early maturing athletes and the relevance of the tests to actual sporting performance. Talent selection, on the other hand, is an ongoing process of identifying current athletes within a sport who display prerequisite standards of performance for inclusion in a particular team or squad that will receive additional coaching and competitive opportunities (Williams & Reilly 2000; Bullock et al. 2009). The difficulty with talent identification and talent selection processes is determining the factors that predispose athletes towards success in a particular sport. There is no consensus in the literature or among coaches about the relative value of physiological, anthropometrical, psychological, and technical skills in predicting sporting success (Williams & Reilly 2000). In addition, athletes who have been identified or selected will generally be encouraged by their coach and parents to specialise in that particular sport.

Sport specialisation is a controversial issue among parents, coaches, educators and sport scientists. On the one hand is the perception that early specialisation will increase an athlete's chance of success while on the other hand the high pressure, year-round focus on one sport can lead to injury, burn out and drop out. Well-known early specialisers such as Tiger Woods, Andre Agassi, and Serena and Venus Williams 'serve as models for parents who want their children to be highly successful in sport' (Gould 2009, p. 35). This chapter will examine some of the main issues surrounding athlete development. The first section will provide an overview of the sampling versus early specialisation debate, and the significance of talent identification and early specialisation in the development of sporting expertise. The second section will explore the influence of two phenomena – the relative age effect and birthplace – on talent identification and athlete development.

Early sampling

The developmental model of sports participation (DMSP) consists of three stages: the sampling years (6–12 years), the specialising years (13–15 years) and the investment years (16+ years) (Côté et al. 2003). According to this model sports participants decide after the sampling stage whether they want to take a performance route (specialising then investing) or participate at a recreational level. Advocates for early sampling highlight the benefits of children participating in deliberate play and a variety of sports (Côté et al. 2009) during the early phase of development (6–12 years). Deliberate play refers to informal games that are aimed at maximising player fun and enjoyment, and are intrinsically motivating (Côté & Fraser-Thomas 2008). Examples include backyard footy and street cricket where the players determine the rules. According to Côté and colleagues, during deliberate play the players will modify the rules of the sport to suit their competence level or environment (equipment, number of players, space). Deliberate play provides opportunities for players to experiment and be creative 'without being told the right way to execute a skill' (Côté & Fraser-Thomas 2008, p. 20). There are no coaches, officials or uniforms (Côté et al. 2009). The amount of time spent on deliberate play should exceed the time spend on deliberate practice. During the sampling stage there should also be an emphasis on the development of fundamental movement skills as these will form the foundation for later sports participation and performance. Deliberate play has also been reported to be an important component in the development of anticipation and decision-making in team sports (Ford et al. 2009).

Coaching implications

When coaching during the sampling years the coach aims to create a supportive environment where the emphasis is on encouragement, fun and enjoyment, learning fundamental movement skills and providing opportunities for deliberate play. Coaches should provide a mastery-oriented climate (Smith et al. 2009) and avoid 'over coaching' and punishing mistakes.

Early specialisation

Early specialisation generally refers to children between the ages of six and 12 who commit to one sport and are involved in high intensity training and compete on a year-round basis (Wiersma 2000; Baker et al. 2009; Kaleth & Mikesky 2010). This premise is built on the relationship between time spent practising and achievement (Baker et al. 2009). The deliberate practice theory (Ericsson et al. 1993) has been used as a framework for the development of expertise in a number of domains (sport, music, chess, medicine and academia). Deliberate practice refers to structured practice that requires full concentration and effort for the purpose of improvement rather than enjoyment (Ericsson et al. 1993; Côté & Fraser-Thomas 2008). As a rule of thumb it has been proposed that a minimum of ten years or 10,000 hours of deliberate practice is necessary to attain expertise status and early specialisation is recommended to accumulate the required volume of practice (see Simon & Chase 1973; Bloom 1985; Ericsson et al. 1993). This theory suggests it is difficult to achieve expertise through late specialisation and experience in other sports which are not required or favoured (Bullock et al. 2009).

Training volume has also been reported as a distinguishing feature between expert and novice performers. Ericsson et al. (1993) found that expert musicians participate in deliberate practice for approximately 25 hours per week compared to novice musicians who train considerably less; in addition, elite athletes in individual sports such as karate, figure skating and wrestling participate in similar quantities of training (25–28 hours a week of practice; Helsen et al. 2000a). An important aspect of athlete development is the training quality as well as training volume. As an athlete's skill level improves training needs to be continually modified so that it is always challenging and places the athlete just outside their comfort zone (Coyle 2009). Athletes need lots of opportunities for practice, to make mistakes, receive feedback and accelerate learning (Ericsson 1996; Coyle 2009). This continually modified deliberate practice prevents performance plateaus (Baker & Cobley 2008).

A number of studies have recently questioned the necessity of early specialisation and expressed concerns about too much deliberate practice (for a review see Baker et al. 2009; Gould 2009). Excessive training at an early age has been linked to a greater risk of sustaining an injury (Kaleth & Mikesky 2009) with one study reporting that just over 50% of the 453 youth athletes sustained 492 injuries between them over a two-year period (Baxter-Jones and colleagues cited in Baker et al. 2009). Since the Women's Tennis Association Tour introduced an age eligibility rule there has been a reduction in the amount of stress reported by players and an increase in playing career length (Otis et al. 2006 cited in Gould 2009). Other concerns expressed in the literature include burnout, sport dropout, psycho-social development and eating disorders (Wiersma 2000; Wall & Côté 2007; Baker et al. 2009;). However Strachan et al. found there was no difference in the level of enjoyment between 'samplers' and early specialisers although the early specialisers did rate higher on the exhaustion dimension indicating they are probably tired from the additional training (2009, p. 88). Interested readers can also refer to the chapter on child protection in the later section of this book.

Coaching implications

The coach will devise training sessions throughout the year that focus on deliberate practice opportunities. This will include large amounts of repetition, structured drills and activities.

The coach will continually monitor progress, providing feedback and correcting errors to improve performance. The emphasis is on continual skill learning, development and large amounts of practice.

Is early specialisation necessary for success?

Evidence for early specialisation

In sports where peak performance occurs before puberty (e.g. gymnastics, rhythmic gymnastics and figure skating) there is evidence that elite athletes specialised earlier than sub-elite athletes. It has been suggested this is predominantly due to such a small time frame for accumulating the required practice compared to sports where peak performance occurs at a later age (Côté & Fraser-Thomas 2008). It has been reported that by the age of seven there was a difference in the amount of sport specific training between elite and sub-elite female gymnasts and figure skaters.

It appears that there is limited evidence for early specialisation in team sports. Côté and Fraser-Thomas (2008) indicate training differences do occur between elite and sub-elite players but not until after the age of 12 years (soccer: 13 yrs, hockey: 15 yrs, wrestling: 18 yrs, and triathlon: 20 yrs). However there is a lack of consensus regarding the age of specialisation and the development of football (soccer) expertise. There are a few studies that support early specialisation. Ford et al. (2009) suggest that during the ages from six to 12 years, large amounts of play and practice specific to football contribute to the development of elite players. Ward et al. (2004) found that players who attained professional level trained twice as much as sub-elite players in each age category. However there was no difference between elite and sub-elite on the number of sports played, the number of hours spent in other sports and the age they specialised in football. Helsen et al. (2000a) demonstrated that the amount of time spent in team practice was the strongest discriminator among soccer playing levels. All players commenced playing soccer around the age of five and started practice at seven years old. After 18 years in the sport the amount of accumulated practice hours were:

- 9332 (professional players)
- 7449 (semi-professional players)
- 5079 (amateur players).

The culture surrounding football (soccer) is certainly one of early specialisation. In 2007 Australia-born, nine-year-old Rhian Davis was signed by Manchester United after his grandfather sent the club a DVD featuring his footballing skills (Kent 2007). Only time will tell whether he makes it as a senior professional player. In Europe there is an abundance of football academies. As reported by Sokolove (2010), the Dutch club Ajax begins recruiting players as young as seven years for their systematic training. Rather than looking for immediate results, however, the aim is for long-term development. Nevertheless each year the players are reassessed and some are asked 'not to come back next year'.

With the increasing globalisation of the sport, which has driven the best players to richer leagues in England, Germany, Italy and Spain, the club has become a different kind of enterprise – a talent factory. It manufactures players and sells them, often for immense fees, on the world market. (Sokolove 2010, p. 1)

It has been reported that the club received 80 million euros as a transfer fee for five of its world class graduating players (for more detail see Sokolove 2010).

Evidence for late specialisation

Previous research indicates that elite athletes try a number of sports during childhood and often do not specialise in their chosen sport until adolescence (Hill 1993; Côté 1999; Baker et al. 2003; Soberlak & Côté 2003). This is particularly evident in sports where peak performance generally occurs in athletes who are in their 20s (hockey, basketball, netball, rowing). Examining the training background of professional ice hockey players revealed that they participated in over 10,000 hours in their sport between the ages of six and 20 years (Soberlak & Côté 2003). However this exposure was not limited to deliberate practice or early specialisation. Instead they participated in a combination of deliberate play (3500 hrs), other sports (2300 hrs), deliberate practice (3000 hrs) and organised ice hockey games (2400 hrs). An emphasis on deliberate practice and specialisation did not occur until the players were 15 years old.

Table 1 also demonstrates the success a number of athletes achieved within a four-year period after participating in a number of sports and specialising in their main sport during late adolescence.

Table 1 Rate of development of Australian elite athletes (adapted from Oldenziel et al. 2004).

	< 4 years (n=72)	> 10 years (n = 78)
Team sport (v individual sport)	31%	56% **
Starting age for main sport	17.1 + 4.5	7.9 + 2.5 ***
Number of sports before main sport	3.3 + 1.6	0.9 + 1.3 ***
Number of sports since starting main sport	0.2 + 0.5	2.4 + 1.8 ***

**$p < 0.01$ *** $p < 0.001$.

The results of these studies suggest there is a benefit in experiencing a variety of sports at an early age and waiting until late adolescence to focus on one sport (see Côté et al. 2009 for a position stand). There appears to be a transfer of learning between sports and a cross-training effect (Baker 2003). At this age an athlete is more likely to 'have the psychological, social, emotional and physical maturity to meet the demands of competitive sport' (Côté et al. 2009, p. 14). Many countries have implemented talent identification systems that identify, recruit and develop potential elite athletes from the ages of eight to 12 years

(Vaeyens et al. 2009, p. 1368). However literature now suggests that a large number of athletes identified at the youth level do not progress to become successful elite athletes at the senior level (Bompa 1995; Martindale et al. 2007; Vaeyens et al. 2009; Brouwers et al. 2009 cited in Gould 2009).

Table 2 outlines the age that Olympians (Athens 2004) began training for their current sport. When the 4455 Olympians were combined the average starting age in their chosen sport was 11.5 ± 4.6 years (Gullich 2007 cited in Vaeyens et al. 2009). This data indicates that a number of athletes did not specialise in their sport at an early age and still achieved Olympic selection. Interestingly 56% of these athletes made their international debut as senior athletes (22 ± 3.1 years) compared to 44% that competed internationally at the junior level (16.8 ± 2.5 yrs).

Table 2 Age when Olympians commenced training for main sport (adapted from Gullich 2007 cited in Vaeyens et al 2009).

Sport	Participants	Mean + SD	Sport	Participants	Mean + SD
Swimming	226	8.1 + 3.1	Wrestling	248	11.2 + 3.3
Hockey	167	8.9 + 3.5	Volleyball	125	13.8 + 4.3
Baseball/softball	98	10.4 + 4.6	Athletics	387	14.0 + 4.0
Basketball	89	11.1 + 2.9	Shooting	250	15.3 + 5.3
Handball	102	11.1 + 3.2	Rowing	283	15.4 + 3.1

In their review of talent identification programs Vaeyens et al. suggest that specialising in one sport and being part of a systematic talent promotion program through adolescence is not necessarily related to greater success at the senior elite level. Furthermore being a successful junior athlete does not equate to becoming a successful senior elite athlete. In fact the researchers highlight that examination of the Russian and German systems suggests that 'most of the early recruited and supported children never became successful senior elite athletes' (2009, p. 1371). Of the German medallists at the 2004 and 2006 Olympics 56% were recruited after the age of 15 years.

Bompa (1999) reported that the Romanian rowing talent identification program that commenced in 1976 resulted in five medals at the 1980 Moscow Olympics, five gold medals at the Los Angeles Olympics in 1984 and nine medals at the 1988 Seoul Olympics. More recently UK Sport implemented the Sporting Giants program to identify tall participants between the ages of 16 and 25 as potential Olympians in rowing, handball and volleyball. A number of these identified players are now with the national squad. Talent transfer, like the Australian skeleton program, is another initiative that a number of countries are utilising to fast-track athletes from one sport to another sport (see Bullock et al. 2009). Alex Croak was a gymnast at the Sydney Olympics, a diver at the 2006 and 2010 Commonwealth Games winning silver and gold respectively, while former Australian gymnast Alisa Camplin started skiing at the age of 22 and won Olympic gold in aerial skiing four years later. The UK Pitch2Podium program is aimed at young football and rugby players (18–22 yrs) who have been unsuccessful in securing a professional contract to transfer to an Olympic sport (UK Sport 2010).

Relative age effect (RAE)

The majority of youth sport competitions are structured around the chronological age of the participant often with a cut-off date of 1 January. For example athletes born from January through to December in the same 12-month period compete against each other. This means that players born in January will be 11 months older than athletes born in December. Additionally twins born ten minutes apart – one on 31 December at 11.55pm and one born on 1 January at 12.05am – equates to a 12-month age difference in terms of most sports. This large age discrepancy can lead to a significant variation in physical, mental, emotional and cognitive maturity (Musch & Grondin 2001; Jimenez & Pain 2008; Delorme et al. 2009; Williams 2010). The advantage that participants have when born in the first months following the cut-off date is referred to as the 'relative age effect'.

Research indicates that a relative age effect has been reported in many sports including soccer (Helsen et al. 2005; Vincent & Glamser 2006; Jimenez & Pain 2008; Carling et al. 2009; Mujika et al. 2009; Campo et al. 2010; Williams 2010), basketball (Delorme & Raspaud 2009), baseball (Grondin & Koren 2000), handball (Schorer et al. 2009), ice hockey (Barnsley et al. 1988; Baker & Logan 2007; Sherar et al. 2007), cricket (Edwards 1994), tennis (Musch & Grondin 2001; Edgar & O'Donoghue 2005) and swimming (O'Neil-Shaw 2010). Thus these sports have an over-representation of participants born in the early months of the selection year and an under-representation of participants born in the final months of the year. This trend suggests that coaches favour the older participant who is likely to be physically advanced compared to their younger and later maturing peers. However, other sports such as gymnastics, American football and basketball do not appear to have an RAE (Stanaway & Hines 1995; Delamore et al. 2009; MacDonald et al. 2009a). This may be due to factors such as the specialised and diverse positions in these team sports; American football at the youth level uses weight divisions as a subcategory to age divisions, and late maturation is viewed as a benefit in gymnastics.

The RAE has received much attention in team sports over the past decade and has been reported to be more prevalent in a country's popular sports compared to sports with fewer participants (Delamore et al. 2009, p. 337). According to a review conducted by Musch and Grondin (2001) nearly 60% of professional soccer players had a birthday in the first half of the selection year. This increased to 70% at the elite male youth level. The authors attributed this to the importance placed on stature and physical maturation. Williams (2010) analysed the FIFA U17 world cup competitions from 1997 to 2007 to determine if a relative age effect was present. Amongst players selected to compete in a world cup 40% were born in January–March compared to only 16% born in October–December. Interestingly this was a worlwide trend except for the African countries where a reverse age effect was evident. The researcher was unsure of the reason for this but did highlight that a number of births are not registered in some of the African nations leading to possible errors in date of birth data. This study supports the earlier work of Helsen et al. (2005) who reported an RAE at the under-15- through to under-18-years national youth teams.

Helsen et al. (2000b) were also able to demonstrate that when the cut-off date was moved to a different time of the year (from August to January) the RAE was still present for those participants (10–16 years) born just after the selection date. It has thus been suggested that the maturational benefits between athletes are a key contributor to the RAE. Coaches assume that greater height and mass provide an advantage for relatively older athletes in 'physically' dominated sports (Helsen et al. 2000b; Schorer et al. 2009). There is also evidence that early maturers (above average physical characteristics), even if relatively 'young', have a greater chance of being selected on the representative team (Sherar et al. 2007). This supports the notion of a selection bias by some coaches where size or physical strength rather than skill carries more weight when teams are selected.

To determine if a relative age effect existed in Australian sport the birthdates of professional Rugby League players and national level female basketball players were examined. Figure 1 illustrates that there is a relative age effect at three levels of Rugby League – State of Origin (SoO, NSW and QLD), National Rugby League (NRL), and National Youth Competition (NYC Under 20s).

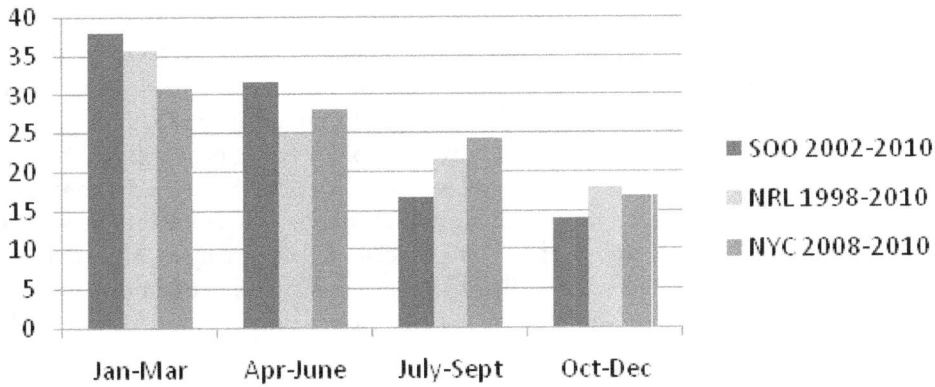

Fig 1 Quarterly birth rate distribution of professional Rugby League players.

Calculations were based on the following birthdate data:

- Players selected for each state of origin game (2002–1010) were counted separately (N=149)
- Any player that played at least one NRL game between 1998 and 2010 (N=1588)
- Players that competed in the NYC during 2008, 2009 and 2010 were added together (N=1520).

A more in-depth breakdown of NRL players is depicted in Table 3. Nearly twice as many players as expected were born in January and 35% of NRL players were born in the first quarter compared to an expected 25%. These trends are consistent with data from other team sports reported in the literature.

Table 3 Number of players from each month who played in the NRL during 1998–2010.

NRL players				
Month	Number of athletes	%	Quarter year of birth	%
Jan	248	15.6%	Q1: 565	35.6%
Feb	165	10.4%		
Mar	152	9.6%		
Apr	133	8.4%	Q2: 396	24.9%
May	148	9.3%		
June	115	7.2%		
July	128	8.1%	Q3: 342	21.5%
Aug	103	6.5%		
Sept	111	7.0%		
Oct	117	7.4%	Q4: 285	17.9%
Nov	77	4.8%		
Dec	91	5.7%		
Total	1588			

Q1 = Jan–March Q2 = April–June Q3 = July–Sept Q4 = Oct–Dec.

There was no relative age effect for players competing in the Women's National Basketball League (WNBL) during the 2010–11 season. But the RAE was present when the Australian national team that competed at the Beijing 2008 Olympics and 2010 World Cup were examined.

The presence of an RAE is not limited to team sports. Nearly 60% of elite junior (players with >120 pts on the ITF circuit) and elite senior tennis players (participated in a singles event at a grand slam during 2002–03) were born in the January–June period (Edgar & O'Donoghue 2005). This study also reported a similar RAE for female and male players. The authors point out that although players born late in the year are disadvantaged, December-born Aranxa Sanchez-Vicario and Richard Krajicek have both won grand slam singles events (2005, p. 1020). A strong relative age effect was also present in female swimmers (under 13 yrs, 14 yrs, and 15 yrs) who qualified for a final at the Australian Age Championships during 2001–10 (O'Neil-Shaw 2010).

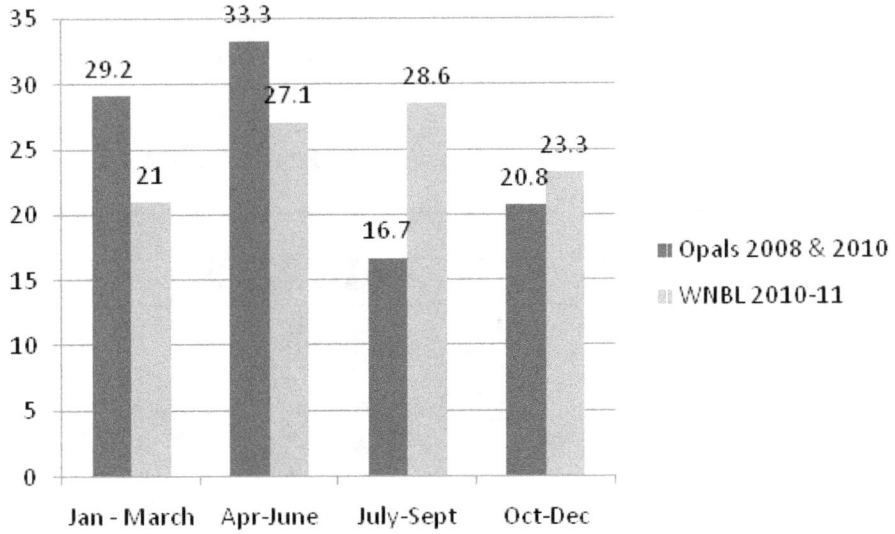

Figure 2 Quarterly birth rate distribution (%) for women's basketball players.

Analysis of birthdates of players in school sport teams also revealed a skewed distribution of birthdates (Wilson 1999; Cobley et al. 2008). Wilson (1999) found that boys born early in the year were twice as likely to make the school Rugby Union and soccer team and girls born during this time were three times more likely to be selected in the hockey and netball teams compared to students born later in the year. Although limited to a small sample there was also a trend that students born early in the year made the county representative teams as well. At this stage there have been no studies examining whether a relative age effect exists in Australian school teams.

These studies reveal that athletes born early in the selection year have an advantage over their peers. They are often bigger, stronger and faster and experience greater success during youth competitions based on their physical dominance. Often they have several months more experience in the sport which gives them an additional advantage (Ward & Williams 2003; Ward et al. 2004). These athletes are often perceived as 'talented' very early in their sporting careers. Consequently they are more likely to receive additional attention from the coach and are often given longer playing time. The relatively older and more mature athletes are also more likely to be selected for representative teams, providing them further opportunities for additional practice and better coaching at more advanced competitive levels (Mujika et al. 2009). They have a high perception of their competence levels which encourages them to continue to practise and improve. Participants are then recognised as 'rep' players and are often known by the selectors for the subsequent year (Vincent & Glasser 2006). Consequently the initial advantage of being born early leads to more opportunities for development which compounds over the years so eventually there is a large difference compared to their relatively younger peers. Therefore being born early in a selection year has an 'accumulative advantage' and you are more likely to play elite level sport.

For those born later in the year, however, it has been suggested that a lack of success, frustration and lack of motivation can increase perception of failure, and may lead to discontinued participation in sport (Baker & Logan 2007; Mujika et al. 2009). Take two boys playing under 15 football. Player 'A' is born in January, weighs 58 kg and is 169 cm; Player 'B' is born in November, weighs 52 kg and is 163 cm. Player A is selected in the representative team while Player B plays for his club team as he is considered 'too small' for the rep team. Fast forward six years and both players are now 177 cm and weigh 70 kg – Player A is a professional player while Player B has dropped out of sport due to limited opportunities and never realised his potential. Therefore coaches need to consider the impact of an RAE on participants born late in the year so they do not get disillusioned and drop out of sport at a young age (Musch & Grondin 2001; Helsen et al. 2005; Gil et al. 2007). It has been suggested that the level of withdrawal amongst relatively younger players increases the number of early-maturing players within a sport and has been suggested as a key contributing factor to the high occurrence of RAE in Olympic and professional teams.

Interestingly, there is now some evidence to suggest that the RAE may not be as advantageous as first thought. Although the relatively older players receive more game time and training opportunities during their adolescence they often base their performance solely on their physical attributes and spend less time improving their technical and tactical skill (Williams 2010). As they approach adulthood the physical advantage has often dissipated and they are unable to compete successfully at a senior level. Likewise at the elite or professional level the talent pool has diminished. At this level there is little variation in the physical attributes of players and more emphasis on skills and fitness as contributors to performance. The small talent pool may be due to the skilled, relatively younger and less mature players dropping out of sport through limited opportunities or the older more mature players not developing their technical skills.

The problem with sport based solely on chronological age is that it does not take biological age into account. Therefore this system provides an advantage to early maturers and participants born early in the selection year. Although intended to provide fair competition for participants and an equal chance of success this strategy does not seem to be sensitive enough to reduce the RAE in numerous sports (Helsen et al. 2005). Coaches, teachers and parents need to understand the maturation process and its consequences for athletes and youth sport generally. The aim should be to provide a positive sporting experience for the participant and ideally retain them in the sport. Coaches must consider the long-term development of their athletes rather than focus on winning now. They must be patient, ensure that all athletes receive equal opportunity for skills development, and be aware of any 'bias' in the selection process (Reilly 2010, p. 187). Coaches who give players equal game time and rotate positions at the youth level are more likely to minimise the RAE within their team. Coaches could also consider training or games where players can go 'up' or 'down' a level within a club. Coaches need to consider the skills of a player rather than rely soly on their current physical attributes. Who knows how much talent has been lost to sport because of current selection philosophies? Administrators may want to consider how they can reduce the RAE and the discrimination of athletes born late in the selection year. Strategies worth exploring include rotating the cut-off dates, reducing the age range (e.g. nine months), or grouping players based on skill level (low, medium and high-tier competitions) rather than solely on chronological age.

Birthplace effects

Some evidence exists to suggest that where a person is born can contribute to their likelihood of playing elite sport. When the birthplaces of Canadian and American elite ice hockey players (NHL and Olympians) were analysed, it was revealed that there was an under-representation of players born in large cities (Curtis & Birch 1987). This trend is supported by more recent studies in professional hockey, baseball, basketball, golf and American football (Côté et al. 2006; MacDonald et al. 2009a; MacDonald et al. 2009b). Table 4 illustrates that compared to population norms there was an over-representation of athletes born in small towns or cities (<500,000) and an under-representation of athletes born in large cities.

Table 4 Influence of birthplace size on US athletes in various sports (adapted from Côté et al. 2006; MacDonald et al. 2009a & b).

	US male/ female (%)	NHL (%)	NBA (%)	MLB (%)	PGA (%)	NFL (%)	LPGA (%)	WUSA %)
<50,000	26.4 /26.3	39.1	28.2	37.7	45.7	49.8	38.4	40.8
50,000–499,000	34.1 / 21.7	47.7	42.5	47.9	41.4	35.1	56.4	39.4
>500,000	39.4 / 51.9	13.2	29.4	14.6	13.1	15.1	15.2	19.7

Table 4 indicates that 48% of the female population are born in cities with a population of less than 500,000; yet this accounts for approximately 80% of professional female soccer players and 85% of the professional female golfers in the US. Although approximately 60% of males are born in relatively small cities (<500,000) there is an over-representation of professional players originating from here in American football (85%), golf (87%), baseball (85%) and ice hockey (87%). Baker and Logan (2007) also reported a birthplace effect for hockey draftees to the NHL during 2000–2005. They found, however, that most draftees came from city sizes of 100,000–999,999 inhabitants. The authors suggest the discrepancy in city size may be due to a different methodology in the studies (different years and subdivisions used for the census data) and may also highlight the need for further examination of birthplace effects in elite sport.

Abernethy and Farrow (2005) and O'Neil-Shaw (2010) demonstrated that the birthplace effect is also evident when the place of birth of Australian cricketers, NRL players and female swimmers is examined (Table 5).

Table 5 Influence of birthplace size on Australian athletes in various sports.

Size of city	Australian cricketers (2003–2004)		NRL players 2004		Female national age swimming finalists	
	Actual (%)	Expected (%)	Actual (%)	Expected (%)	Actual (%)	Expected (%)
>1 million	44	62	48	55	57.6	60.5
100,000–999,999					22.7	4.3
<100,000	44	25	37	26	19.7	35.2

The evidence suggests that small towns and cities have a positive influence on athlete development. The cause of this is likely to be multi-factorial but may be partly attributed to greater opportunities for practice (Abernethy & Farrow 2005). This may be due to the availability of more open playing spaces or perceived safer environment where parents allow their young children to play outside and experience greater amounts of deliberate play (MacDonald et al. 2009b). In Sydney, for example, a large number of junior sporting teams can only train once or twice a week and even then often have to share the playing field with other teams. Local community members in small cities may entice players to participate in more sports as teams may 'need the numbers' to be able to compete. It has also been suggested that athletes from smaller towns or cities are more likely to be introduced to playing against older (or adult) players at an earlier age either in organised sport or deliberate play (Côté et al. 2006). This also provides an opportunity for junior athletes to learn from older team-mates. Athletes from the larger cities are generally restricted to competing with and against athletes who are of the same age, developmental size and ability. As previously mentioned in this chapter, playing a variety of sports, participating in both deliberate play and deliberate practice under challenging conditions, plus competing against adults at an early age, are factors that have been linked to sporting expertise (Côté et al. 2003). Côté et al. also suggest that smaller cities may provide early opportunities for sporting success (big fish in little pond) 'which in turn would increase self-efficacy and the motivational drive to play and practise more' (2006, p. 1072).

Although children from larger cities often have access to more facilities and resources compared to their counterparts from smaller cities their court time may be reduced by the demand on the facility. As Curtis and Birch highlight, 'top players are more likely to come from communities large enough to build rinks, but not so large that the demand for ice time outweighs opportunities to skate' (1987, p. 239). If towns are too small (e.g. <1000 Côté et al. 2006) they may also disadvantage the development of athletes due to lack of resources, facilities, training partners and competitors. Finally, MacDonald et al. (2009a) propose that another reason for the successful development of athletes in smaller cities is that this environment reflects the eight features linked to positive youth development that were identified by NRCIM (2002 cited in MacDonald et al. 2009a):

- Physical and psychological safety
- Appropriate structures
- Opportunities for skill building
- Supportive relationships
- Opportunities to belong
- Positive social norms
- Support for efficacy
- Integration of family, school and community (MacDonald et al. 2009a, p. 87).

These factors could certainly facilitate better quality and quantity of play and practice in smaller cities (Côté et al. 2006).

Conclusion

Coaches have an influential role in determining whether the youth participant has a positive or negative sports experience (Gilbert et al. 2001; Hedstrom & Gould 2004). Coaches are encouraged to adopt an athlete-centred approach that focuses on the holistic development of the athlete, and incorporate a combination of deliberate play and deliberate practice. Although there is still debate regarding talent identification and athlete development, evidence exists that a coach's over-emphasis on winning and his/her influence on talent identification at an early age does not produce sporting success at the senior level. Perhaps we need to consciously plan for long-term athlete development, de-emphasise age group success and have flexible, ongoing development opportunities for all participants (Martindale et al. 2007). Coaches, teachers and sports administrators need to reconsider how we can recruit sport participants and encourage lifelong participation for all and specialisation for those striving to reach the top 'at the right time'.

References

Abernethy, B. & Farrow, D. (2005). Contextual factors influencing the development of expertise in Australian athletes. In *Proceedings of the ISSP 11th World Congress of Sport Psychology* (CD). Sydney: International Society of Sport Psychology.

Baker, J. (2003). Early specialisation in youth sport: a requirement for adult expertise? *High Ability Studies*, 14(1): 85–94.

Baker, J. & Cobley, S. (2008). Does practice make perfect: the role of training in developing the expert athlete. In D. Farrow, J. Baker & C. MacMahon (Eds). *Developing sports expertise: researchers and coaches put theory into practice* (pp. 29–40). London: Routledge.

Baker, J., Cobley, S. & Fraser-Thomas, J. (2009). What do we know about early sport specialisation? Not much! *High Ability Studies*, 20(1): 77–89.

Baker, J., Côté, J. & Abernethy, B. (2003). Sport specific practice and the development of expert decision-making in team ball sports. *Journal of Applied Sport Psychology*, *15*: 12–25.

Baker, J. & Logan, A. (2007). Developmental contexts and sporting success: birth date and birthplace effects in national hockey league draftees 2000–2005. *British Journal of Sports Medicine*, *41*: 515–17.

Barnsley, R., Thompson, A. & Barnsley, P. (1985). Hockey success and birthplace: the relative age effect. *Journal of the Canadian Association of Health, Physical Education and Recreation*, *51*: 23–28.

Baxter-Jones, A. (1995). Growth and development of young athletes: should competition levels be age related? *Sports Medicine*, *20*(2): 59–64.

Bloom, B. (1985). *Developing talent in young people*. New York; Ballantine.

Bompa, T. (1999). *Periodisation: theory and methodology of training* (4th ed.). Champaign, IL: Human Kinetics.

Bompa, T. (1995). *From childhood to champion athlete*. Toronto: Veritas.

Bullock, N., Gulbin, J., Martin, D., Ross, A., Holland, T. & Marino, F. (2009). Talent identification and deliberate programming in skeleton: ice novice to winter Olympian in 14 months. *Journal of Sports Sciences*, *27*(4): 397–404.

Campo, D., Vicedo, J., Villora, S. & Jordan, O. (2010). The relative age effect in youth soccer players from Spain. *Journal of Sports Science and Medicine*, *9*(2): 190–98.

Carling, C., Gall, F., Reilly, T. & Williams, A.M. (2009). Do anthropometric and fitness characteristics vary according to birth date distribution in elite youth academy soccer players? *Scandinavian Journal of Medicine and Science in Sports*, *19*: 3–9.

Cobley, S., Abraham, C. & Baker, J. (2008). Relative age effects on physical education attainment and school sport representation. *Physical Education and Sport Pedagogy*, *13*: 267–76.

Cobley, S., Baker, J., Wattie, N. & McKenna, J. (2009). Annual age-grouping and athlete development: a meta-analytical review of relative age effects in sport. *Sports Medicine*, *39*(3): 235–56.

Côté, J. (1999). The influence of the family in the development of talent in sports. *The Sport Psychologist*, *13*: 395–417.

Côté, J., Baker, J. & Abernethy, B. (2003). From play to practice: a developmental framework for the acquisition of expertise in team sports. In J. Starkes & K. Ericsson (Eds). *Recent advances in research on sport expertise* (pp. 89–110). Champaign, IL: Human Kinetics.

Côté, J. & Fraser-Thomas, J. (2008). Play, practice and athlete development. In D. Farrow, J. Baker & C. Macmahon (Eds). *Developing sport expertise* (pp. 17–28). London: Routledge.

Côté, J., Lidor, R. & Hackfort, D. (2009). ISSP position stand: to sample or to specialise? Seven postulates about youth sport activities that lead to continued participation and elite performance. *IJSEP*, *9*: 7–17.

Côté, J., Macdonald, D. J., Baker, J. & Abernethy, B. (2006). When 'where' is more important than 'when': birthplace and birthdate effects on the achievement of sporting expertise. *Journal of Sports Sciences*, *24*(10): 1065–73.

Coyle, D. (2009). *The talent code*. New York: Bantam.

Curtis, J. E. & Birch, J.S. (1987). Size of community of origin and recruitment to professional and Olympic hockey in North America. *Sociology of Sport Journal*, *4*: 229–44.

Delorme, N., Boiche, J. & Raspaud, M. (2009). The relative age effect in elite sport: the French case. *Research Quarterly for Exercise and Sport*, 80(20): 336–44.

Delorme, N. & Raspaud, M. (2009). The relative age effect in young French basketball players: a study on the whole population. *Scandinavian Journal of Medicine and Science in Sport*, 19(2): 235–42

Edgar, S. & O'Donoghue, P. (2005). Season of birth of elite tennis players. *Journal of Sports Sciences*, 23(10): 1013–20.

Edwards, S. (1994). Born too late to win? *Nature*, 370: 186.

Ericsson, K. A. (1996). The acquisition of expert performance: an introduction to some of the issues. In K.A. Ericsson (ed.), *The road to excellence: the acquisition of expert performance in the arts and sciences, sports and games* (pp. 1–50). Mahwah, NJ: Lawrence Erlbaum Associates.

Ericsson, K. A., Krampe, R. T. and Tesch-Römer, C. (1993) The role of deliberate practice in the acquisition of expert performance. *Psychological Review*, 100: 363–406.

Ford, P. R., Ward, P., Hodges, N. J. & Williams, A. M. (2009). The role of deliberate practice and play in career progression in sport: the early engagement hypothesis. *High Ability Studies*, 20(1): 65–75.

Gil, S., Ruiz, F., Irazusta, A., Gil, J. & Irazusta, J. (2007). Selection of young soccer players in terms of anthropometric and physiological factors. *Journal of Sports Medicine and Physical Fitness*, 47(1): 25–32.

Gilbert, W., Gilbert, J. & Trudel, P. (2001). Coaching strategies for youth sports. *JOPERD*, 72(4): 29–33.

Gould, D. (2009). Early sport specialisation: a psychological perspective. *JOPERD*, 81(8): 33–37.

Grondin, S. & Koren, S. (2000). The relative age effect in professional baseball: a look at the history of Major League Baseball and at current status in Japan. *Avante*, 6: 64–74.

Hedstrom, R. & Gould, D. (2004). *Research in youth sports: critical issues status*. [Online]. Available: www.educ.msu.edu/ysi/past_projects.htm. [accessed 20 January 2011].

Helsen, W. F., Hodges, N., van Wickel, J. & Starkes, J. (2000a). The roles of talent, physical precocity and practice in the development of soccer expertise. *Journal of Sports Sciences*, 18: 727–36.

Helsen, W. F., Starkes, J. L. & van Winckel, J. (2000b). Effect of change in selection year on success in male soccer players. *American Journal of Human Biology*, 12: 729–35.

Helsen, W. F., van Winckel, J. & Williams, A. M. (2005). The relative age effect in youth soccer across Europe. *Journal of Sports Sciences*, 23(6): 629–36.

Hensch, L. (2006). Specialisation or diversification in youth sport? *Strategies: A Journal for Physical and Sport educators*, 19(5): 21–27.

Hill, G. M. (1993). Youth sport participation of professional baseball players. *Sociology of Sport*, 10: 107–14.

Hill, G. (1990). The one sport athlete. *Strategies: A Journal for Physical and Sport educators*, 3(7): 5–7.

Hogan, K. & Norton, K. (2000). The 'price' of Olympic gold. *Journal of Science and Medicine in Sport*, 3(2): 203–18.

Jimenez, I. & Pain, M. (2008). Relative age effect in Spanish association football: its extent and implications for wasted potential. *Journal of Sports Sciences*, 26(10): 995–1003.

Kaleth, A. & Mikesky, A. (2009). Impact of early sport specialisation: a physiological perspective. *JOPHERD, 81*(8): 29–32.

Kent, P. (2007). Aussie wonder kid 'next Roo'. *Daily Telegraph*, August 3. [Online]. Available: www.news.com.au/aussie-wonder-kid-next-roo/story-e6frf4a3-1111114099205 [accessed 20 January 2011].

Lewis, D. (2010). $1.2bn to trim and support athletes. [Online]. Available: www.watoday.com.au/.../12bn-to-trim-and-support-athletes-20100511-uv2x.html [accessed 27 May 2010].

MacDonald, D., Cheung, M., Côté, J. & Abernethy, B. (2009a). Place but not date of birth influences the development and emergence of athletic talent in American Football. *Journal of Applied Sport Psychology, 21*(1): 80–90.

MacDonald, D., King, J., Côté, J. & Abernethy, B. (2009b). Birthplace effects on the development of female athletic talent. *Journal of Science and Medicine in Sport, 12*: 234–37.

Martindale, R., Collins, D. & Abraham, A. (2007). Effective talent development: the elite coach perspective in UK Sport. *Journal of Applied Sport Psychology, 19*: 187–206.

Mujika, I., Vaeyens, R., Matthys, S., Santisteban, J., Goiriena, J. & Philippaerts, R. (2009). The relative age effect in a professional football club setting. *Journal of Sports Sciences, 27*(11): 1153–58.

Musch, J. & Grondin, S. (2001). Unequal competition as an impediment to personal development: a review of the relative age effect in sport. *Developmental Review, 21*: 147–67.

Oldenziel, K., Gagne, F. & Gulbin, J. P. (2004). Factors affecting the rate of athlete development from novice to senior elite: how applicable is the 10-year-rule? Paper presented to the 2004 Pre-Olympic Congress – 'Sport Science Through the Ages', Thessaloniki, Greece. [Online]. Available: cev.org.br/biblioteca/factors-affecting-the-rate-of-athlete-development-from-novice-to-senior-elite-how-applicable-is-the-10-year-rule [accessed 24 February 2011].

O'Neil-Shaw, J. (2010). A statistical study of Australian age swimming (female): are performance outcomes influenced by where or when an athlete is born? Unpublished postgraduate dissertation, University of Sydney.

Reilly, T. (2010). *Ergonomics in sport and physical activity: enhancing performance and improving safety.* Champaign, IL: Human Kinetics.

Schorer, J., Baker, J., Busch, D., Wilhelm, A. & Pabst, J. (2009). Relative age, talent identification and youth skill development: do relatively younger athletes have superior technical skills? *Talent Development & Excellence, 1*(1): 45–56.

Sherar, L., Baxter-Jones, A., Faulkner, R. & Russell, K. (2007). Do physical maturity and birth date predict talent in male youth ice hockey players? *Journal of Sports Sciences, 25*: 879–86.

Simon, H. & Chase, W. (1973). Skill in chess. *American Scientist, 61*: 394–403.

Smith, R. E., Smoll, F.L. & Cumming, S. P. (2009). Motivational climate and changes in young athletes' achievement goal orientations. *Motivation and Emotion, 3*(2): 173–83.

Soberlak, P. & Côté, J. (2003). The developmental activities of elite ice hockey players. *Journal of Applied Sport Psychology, 15*: 41–49.

Sokolove, M. (2010). How a soccer star is made. *The New York Times*. 31 May. [Online]. Available: www.nytimes.com/2010/06/06/magazine/06Soccer-t.html [accessed 5 June 2010].

Stanaway, K. & Hines, T. (1995). Lack of a season birth effect among American athletes. *Perceptual and Motor Skills, 81*: 952–54.

Strachan, L., Côté, J. & Deakin, J. (2009). 'Specialisers' versus 'samplers' in youth sport: comparing experiences and outcomes. *The Sport Psychologist, 23*: 77–92.

UK Sport (2010) Pitch2podium. [Online]. Available: www.uksport.gov.uk/pages/pitch2podium/ [accessed 12 May 2010].

Vaeyens, R., Gullich, A. Warr, C. & Phillippaerts, R. (2009). Talent identification and promotion programmes of Olympic athletes. *Journal of Sports Sciences, 27*(13): 1367–80.

Vincent, J. & Glasser, F. (2006). Gender differences in the relative age effect among US Olympic development program youth soccer players. *Journal of Sports Sciences, 24*(4): 405–13.

Wall, M. & Côté, J. (2007). Developmental activities that lead to drop out and investment in sport. *Physical education and Sport Pedagogy, 12*: 77–87.

Ward, P., Hodges, N., Williams, M. & Starkes, J. (2004). Deliberate practice and expert performance: defining the path to excellence. In A. M. Williams & N. J. Hodges (Eds). *Skill acquisition in sport: research, theory and practice* (pp. 231–58). London: Routledge.

Ward, P. & Williams, A. M. (2003). Perceptual and cognitive skill development in soccer: the multidimensional nature of expert performance. *Journal of Sport and Exercise Psychology, 25*: 93–111.

Wattie, N., Cobley, S. & Baker, J. (2008). Towards a unified understanding of relative age effects. *Journal of Sport Sciences, 26*(13): 1403–09.

Wiersma, L.D. (2000). Risks and benefits of youth sport specialization: perspectives and recommendations. *Pediatric Exercise Science, 12*: 13–22.

Williams, J. (2010). Relative age effect in youth soccer: analysis of the FIFA U17 World Cup competition. *Scandinavian Journal of Medicine and Science in Sports, 20*: 502–08.

Williams, A. M. & Reilly, T. (2000). Talent identification and development in soccer. *Journal of Sports Sciences, 18*: 657–67.

Wilson, G. (1999). The birthdate effect in school sports teams. *European Journal of Physical Education, 4*: 139–45.

Ziemainz, H. & Gulbin, J. (2002). Talent selection: identification and development exemplified in the Australian talent search program. *New Studies in Athletics, 17*: 27–32.

14

Coaching and adherence issues in youth sport

Andrew Bennie

The United Nations (UN) describes sport as a universal language that endows people with a focus for their energy, worthwhile goals and that can teach the values of hard work, discipline and organisation. From the UN's perspective, sport also provides a forum for people to develop skills in leadership whilst assisting with the management of essential lessons in life such as victory and defeat (UN 2005, pp. 5–9). Few individuals escape contact with sport. It forms a significant part of our leisure, educational, economic and social experience, and contributes to a sense of national pride and unity (Moraes 1996; Lyle 2002). This could not be truer for the Australian context as stated by Faulkner and Free:

> Playing sport is an integral part of growing up in Australia. The majority of our young people are active participants in sport, whether it be in the schoolyard or backyard, the local park or in organised competitions. If children find their involvement enjoyable and fulfilling, they are more likely to continue it into their adult lives and the chance of lifelong participation is greatly increased. (1994, p. 1)

This poignant account by two former national government ministers identifies sport as a key aspect of Australian culture. Sport remains an integral part of the lives of young Australians, although recent changes in modern society has had implications for the nature and regularity of youth sport participation. The purpose of this chapter is to highlight two key themes. First, this chapter looks at an emerging field in the academic literature related to coaching in the youth sport context. The second theme describes reasons for youth sport participation including the motives for adherence to sport participation as well as the commonly identified reasons for sport withdrawal. Case-study examples are presented in the latter part of this section to explore key contextual instances for continued sport participation or withdrawal. Finally, the chapter outlines the implications of coaching within the youth sport setting in relation to continued participation into adulthood as well as for coach education.

The youth sport context

The role of physical educators in developing physically active and socially responsible youth has been closely scrutinised for centuries. Only recently has sport coaching become an important area for academic research on its influence on young people. Whether working with young children or professional athletes, coaches are significant figures, not just in the domain of sport, but also as role models, educators and leaders in society (Gilbert 2002). In the past ten years, there have been some interesting developments within sports coaching research about the definitions of coaching contexts. Lyle (2002) outlined two general coach contexts – participation and performance coaching. Trudel and Gilbert (2006) specified three developmental coaching contexts related to recreational sport, developmental sport, and elite sport.

Extending the recommendations of Lyle (2002), Trudel and Gilbert (2006) and Côté and Gilbert (2009) recently enunciated four coaching contexts:

- participation coaches for children
- participation coaches for adolescents and adults
- performance coaches for young adolescents
- performance coaches for older adolescents and adults.

In 2002, Lyle identified 'participation coaching' as teaching and sports leadership where participants are less intensively engaged and the performance or competition elements are not emphasised. The main purpose is to provide athletes with initial and positive experiences in sport. The alternate 'performance coaching' context requires intensive management of, and commitment to, competition goals and improving sport performance (Lyle 2002). This participation-performance perspective highlights the importance of applying a unique and individualised approach when delivering coaching programs to achieve context specific goals.

O'Connor and Bennie (2006) identified how coaching in a youth sport setting may be divided into three potential categories that distinguish between performance and participation coaches (see Table 1). According to O'Connor and Bennie (2006) youth sport coaches in the Australian context ranged from inexperienced parent-volunteers to highly skilled and paid coaches of elite youth programs. Their research highlights the different personnel that may be considered for various coaching positions in participation and performance contexts. Their assessment of the youth sport context, however, does not consider the various aims or objectives for coaches at this level.

On the basis of the participation-performance continuum from children to adults and an exhaustive review of the literature on sport coaching and athlete development, Côté and Gilbert (2009) outlined the objectives of coaching in different coaching contexts. This led to the development of various contextual features as summarised in Table 2.

When examining these coaching objectives across the participation-performance contexts, the participation framework focuses on inclusivity, personal improvement and fun as central to lifelong participation in sport. This is based on developing a sport environment that encourages athletes by promoting the physical and psycho-social benefits of sport involvement.

Table 1: Coaching categories and contexts (adapted from O'Connor & Bennie 2006).

		Coaching categories		
		Volunteer coaches	People who are paid to coach part time	People who are paid to coach full time
Coaching context	Participation context	Coach of a local youth sports club team	Junior school or early high school coach where the focus is on all round development and maximum participation for all athletes	Coaches who work in after school youth sport programs such as the Active After-school Communities Program developed by the Australian Sports Commission
Coaching context	Performance context	Coach of a representative youth sport team	School sport context where focus on winning becomes greater and potential for post-school sport participation becomes relevant	Institute of sport coach who works with potential future national representatives

Table 2: Coaching objectives for developing athlete outcomes in different contexts (adapted from Côté et al. 2003; Côté & Gilbert 2009, pp. 315–17)

Participation coach for children (6–12 years old)

1. Adopt an inclusive focus as opposed to an exclusive selection policy based on performance
2. Organise a mastery-oriented motivational climate (i.e. focus on personal improvement)
3. Set up safe opportunities for athletes to have fun and engage playfully in low-organisation games
4. Teach and assess the development of fundamental movements by focusing on the child first
5. Promote the social aspect of sport and sampling

Participation coach for adolescents and adults (13 years and older)

1. Provide opportunities for athletes to interact socially
2. Afford opportunities for athletes to have fun and playfully compete
3. Promote the development of fitness and health-related physical activities
4. Teach and assess sport-specific skills in a safe environment for long-term sport involvement
5. Teach personal and social assets through sport (citizenship)

Performance coach for young adolescents (13–15 years old)
1. Organise the sport experience to promote a focus on one sport
2. Teach 'rules of competition'
3. Offer opportunities for fun with increasingly greater demands for deliberate practice (i.e. repetitive sport specific practice)
4. Teach and assess physical, technical, perceptual, and mental skills in a safe environment
5. Present positive growth opportunities through sport (i.e. civic engagement, responsibility)
Performance coach for older adolescents and adults (16 years and older)
1. Set up training regime grounded in deliberate practice (i.e. repetitive sport specific practice)
2. Allow athletes appropriate mental and physical rest
3. Prepare athletes for consistent high-level competitive performance
4. Teach and assess physical, technical, perceptual, and mental skills in a safe environment
5. Provide opportunities for athletes to prepare for 'life after sport'

The performance climate centres on the development of technical, tactical and mental aspects of consistent sport performance. Interestingly, Côté and Gilbert (2009) also suggest that within this performance context, there is still a need to promote growth outside sport to develop positive citizenship during the young adolescent years (13–15-year-olds) that continues into older adolescence and adulthood (that is, life after sport). This means that in participation and performance contexts, coaches need to focus on the growth of the 'whole' person, who uses sport to develop positive behaviours within the sporting environment and as a general member of society. One recent study of expert coaches who work with young gymnasts suggested that reducing the coach's role to focusing only on increasing athletic performance misjudges the kinds of influence that coaches have on their athletes (Poczwardowski et al. 2006). Wayne Bennett, a Rugby League coach of professional athletes for more than 20 years in Australia, insisted that his players were there to learn and develop skills, knowledge and expertise not just in football, but also life (Bennett & Crawley 2002). It appears important for coaches to develop sport and life skills amongst their participant group as they progress through youth age groups to the adult context.

Côté and Gilbert (2009) recognised that the four contexts might overlap and vary between certain sports or cultures, yet they profess that these four contexts should form the foundation of coaching programs for the differing populations of athletes. This is an important acknowledgement given the difficulty of defining what age groups constitute the 'youth' context. The fact that Côté and Gilbert refer to the various contexts involving athletes aged from six to 16 (that is, potential age groupings for youth sport) as 'children', 'young adolescents', 'adolescents' and 'older adolescents', continues to raise questions about the boundaries of youth sport. This highlights an important avenue for future research with respect to validating the appropriateness of both the contextual descriptions and respective coaching objectives. For example, researchers could examine the proposed objectives of coaches, parents and administrators involved with participation and performance of the athletes aged six to 16 and compare their ideas with the reasons for participation amongst young athletes themselves. As well as evaluating Côté and Gilbert's (2009) propositions, this may enlighten coaches, parents, athletes and administrators about the value different stakeholders place on developing sport-specific and wider life skills within the youth sport environment.

Their suggestions open the debate about what coaches should focus on during the key developmental youth sport years and transition into adulthood. There are certain consistencies in terms of overall athlete development in the performance and participation context. It is clear, however, that coaches in youth sport must also carefully consider the specific context in which they work and the immediate and long-term interests of their athletes. Given that coaches are central to the positive and negative experiences within the youth sport setting, it is also imperative to understand which factors influence youth sport participation and withdrawal. The next section in this chapter explores the multifaceted nature of youth sport participation.

Sport participation: reasons for participation, adherence and withdrawal

The benefits of participation in sport have been acknowledged in the academic literature and amongst the general population. Past research indicates that participation in sport on a regular basis has positive effects on a person's physical and mental wellbeing (Koivula 1999). Sport aids the acquisition of motor skills, movement competence and body awareness whilst promoting general mental and physical growth and development (Gill 2000). Participation in sport also encourages self-discipline, organisation and time-management skills, dedication, and cooperation – all of which benefit the individual. Further, sport provides a medium that encourages people to socialise in and out of the competitive environment and contributes to the development of positive self-concepts, enhanced self-esteem and continued participation in sport (Gill 2000).

For many countries, a long-term goal of physical education curricula and sport policy is to promote lifelong physical activity (Telama et al. 2005). Governments also recognise the burgeoning fiscal and societal costs associated with physical inactivity. Sport organisations have a vested interest in maintaining sport participation to preserve historical traditions, encourage physical activity and maintain prominence within the community. They also aim to retain government funding to continue the production of highly successful athletes from a wide talent pool. For example, Netball Australia's (NA) 2007 strategic objectives aim to value netball traditions and culture, be embraced by commercial media and its audience and, maintain high performance excellence. Further objectives include being a community leader where coaches, umpires and players are household names and positive role models. Interestingly NA focuses on being relevant to new Australians in helping them engage with their local communities. Finally, NA aspires to encourage lifelong involvement in the sport by creating safe and supportive environments for enjoyable participation (NA 2006). NA clearly identifies key objectives that emphasise historical, community and commercial connections to promote long-term development of the organisation and the sport.

Despite the rising awareness of the costs and benefits associated with sport participation, the number of people and amount of time spent on participating in sports and physical recreation is declining (ABS 2009). The 2006 Time Use Survey (ABS) reports that Australians aged 15 years and over spent 4 hours 56 minutes (or 21%) of each day on free time. Over half (2 hours 20 minutes) of recreation and leisure time was spent on audio/visual media with only 19 minutes spent on sport and outdoor activity (down from 27 minutes in 1997). Perhaps more startling is the fact that approximately 5.5 million people (34% of the surveyed population) did not participate in any such physical activity (ABS 2009). It remains clear that participation in sport and physical activity is declining while the rate of overweight and obese Australians continues to rise. Parents, teachers, coaches and administrators must be sensitive to the reasons young athletes choose to participate in specific sports to perpetuate their interest, involvement and positive health outcomes over time.

Adults and children are motivated to participate in sports for similar reasons, although health concerns are more important for adults whilst skill development and competencies are more significant for children in exercise settings (Gill 2000). In addition, Koivula (1999) noted that competitive motives for participation were associated more with males whilst appearance-related motives featured more importantly for women. Further, Barber et al., identified that participant motivation differed by gender with boys being 'socialised to achieve/compete in sport, while girls are supposed to play' (1999, p. 178). It is beyond the scope of this chapter to fully explore such gender stereotypes. It is worth noting, however, that females may be equally motivated by competition, while the motivation to appear athletic resonates strongly with the modern male athlete.

Sport participation has been researched consistently over time in various contexts with most people defining several reasons for participation rather than just one fundamental motive (see Orlick 1974; Robinson & Carron 1982; Skard & Valgum 1989; Schmidt & Stein 1991; Gould 1993; Weigand & Broadhurst 1998; Gill 2000; Bennie & O'Connor 2004, 2006; Gaskin & Garland 2005; Fraser-Thomas et al. 2008). From their findings, the most notable reasons for participating in sport can be linked to the following key areas:

- enjoyment, excitement and having fun
- staying in shape and being physically fit
- playing as part of a team
- challenge associated with training and competition
- learning and improving skills
- wanting to go on to higher levels of competition.

At all levels of participation, the enjoyment derived from competing in organised sport has been central to participation (Scanlan et al. 1989; Bennie & O'Connor 2004, 2006). In fact, a recent report on Australian sport participation noted that enjoyment and health/fitness were the two main motives for participation (ABS 2007). Interestingly, 'winning' was not raised as a key motivator for participation. This is a critical point as sport coaches may at times overemphasise winning, give little positive reinforcement and provide athletes with non-contingent feedback (Gill 2000). Overall, most people define multiple reasons for participating in sport.

Motivation is a critical factor in long-term adherence to sport participation (Frederick & Morrison 1999). It initiates all thoughts, emotions and behaviours associated with any domain of activity. There is a common belief among researchers that intrinsically driven youth athletes who enjoy training and competing are more likely to continue with athletic endeavours (Weigand & Broadhurst 1998; Barber et al. 1999; Frederick & Morrison 1999; Gill 2000). Furthermore, the degree to which a person enjoys participating in turn relates to a person's commitment. Increasing rewards and satisfaction whilst minimising costs have been primarily associated with increased enjoyment and commitment (Barber et al. 1999). Other factors shown to maximise enjoyment within the youth sport setting include providing variety in training drills and routine, and imposing structural or rule changes that maximise skill development, promote safety and enhance fun (Strean 1995; Bennie & O'Connor 2004). For example, Bennie and O'Connor (2004) found that elite track and field athletes enjoyed training when coaches planned sessions at alternative venues to the track (e.g. sand hills at the beach). These athletes also suggested that coaches made training significantly more enjoyable by including warm-up games (e.g. games of touch football) as an occasional substitute for laps around the oval (Bennie & O'Connor 2004).

The motivation of sport participants to continue training and competing at any level wanes as a result of being physically and/or mentally 'burnt out'. Additional pressures of work and/or study and the culmination of a variety of new social experiences are other factors that negatively affect sport participation (Gould 1993; Horton & Mack 2000; Reimer et al. 2000; Tarbotton 2001; Bennie & O'Connor 2004). Motivation of youth sport participants was also negatively influenced by a belief that the ability to progress to the next level was beyond their capabilities (Weiss 1993; Gill 2000; Bennie & O'Connor 2004). Hedstrom and Gould (2004) noted that children who feel competent about their physical abilities were more likely to persist with physical activity while those that do not possess a sense of competence were more likely to discontinue. These final two points raise serious concerns about whether youth sport administrators, coaches, parents and athletes have an understanding of the broader social, mental and physical benefits of long-term sport participation.

Parents, teachers and coaches play an important role in the decision of youth sport participants to continue or discontinue with participation. Positive relations amongst peers have also been noted to encourage or limit participation (Douge 1987; Kenow & Williams, 1999; Horton & Mack 2000; Coakley 2001; Seabra et al. 2008). Douge (1987) for example, highlighted the importance of having a well-trained coach to assist in reducing the attrition of talented athletes from competitive sport. Further, Douge (1987) and Weib (2001) recommended that coaches must be knowledgeable in athlete preparation and program coordination, and aware of the participant's individual physical and mental wellbeing. In fact, Kenow and Williams (1999) established that if the sport participants' goals, personality, and beliefs were consistent with those of their coach, the interaction of the individuals was likely to be satisfactory, thereby producing a positive interpersonal atmosphere. Therefore, good athlete–coach relations are likely to increase enjoyment in training and competing. It is important for the coach to adapt his/her behaviour to suit the individual needs of each youth sport participant. This may enhance the interest of the young participants in continuing with the sport into future.

Parental pressure and lack of support from coaching staff served as additional forces that influenced the decision of youth sport participants to drop out from their respective programs (Morgan et al. 1988; Bianco et al. 1999; Kenow & Williams 1999; Butcher et al. 2002). Early research postulates that negative influences on youth sport participation includes lack of playing time, dislike of the coach/other athletes, boredom, and poor coaching (Robertson 1988; Ogilvie & Taylor 1993). According to Gill (2000), these behaviours may exacerbate competitive stress and lead to a decrease in self-esteem and motivation, which in turn could affect their commitment to sport participation. Other scholars also discovered that general poor peer relations, lack of enjoyment and dissatisfaction with the team seemed to lead individuals to lose interest and motivation in certain activities (Skard & Valgum 1989; Robinson & Carron 1982; Butcher et al. 2002). This, they suggest, influenced the dropout rate far more than competence, competitive anxiety and parental attitudes. Interestingly, while socialisation has been shown to be inhibiting for some, others have thrived on the affiliation established with their training group, citing that as a major reason for pushing on with sport participation (Gill 2000; Horton & Mack 2000; Coakley 2001).

The economic cost of sport often influences participation rates in junior and senior sport competitions, especially given that some families have multiple children who play sport all year round. For example, Coakley (2006) reported that parents of elite youth ice hockey players routinely spent between $5000 and $20,000 per year to support their sons' participation. Current evidence also highlights the immense pressure to sustain financial security or gain further education on completion of high school (Reimer et al. 2000) during a period in life where parents expect their children to become more independent and therefore responsible for financing more of life's costly facets. Hence, pressures to maintain independence post-high school often outweigh the financial incentive to continue. This often requires young athletes to decide between a career in sport or a career in the workforce (Hollings et al. 1997).

Another feature that can be tied into economic factors influencing sport participation at the youth level relates to socioeconomic status (SES) and geographic locality. Research has shown that youths from higher SES backgrounds represent a greater proportion of sport participants given their greater access to sport resources and programs. Those from lower SES backgrounds have less access, and receive less financial and emotional support to participate in youth sport programs (Dollman & Lewis 2010). Similarly, those from urban areas have greater access to sport program facilities, competitions and resources such as coaching. Those in regional and rural areas tend to experience limitations associated with facility provision, distance and cost, and a lack of competition due to fewer people competing (Australian Sports Commission 2005). Clearly local-, regional- and national-level sport organisations need to do more to supply funds, access and pathways for those from lower SES backgrounds and rural or remote areas.

Early specialisation is another contentious issue that has been shown to affect participation rates amongst our youth sport cohort. For example, Côté (2005) reported that elite gymnasts and hockey players who specialised in their sports before they reached 13 years of age experienced negative outcomes such as injury, low enjoyment and dropout. In contrast, children that sampled various sports in the early years of sport participation reported higher levels of enjoyment, fewer injuries and a continued engagement with youth sport (Côté 2005). Whether the aim is to perform at an elite or participation level into the future, Côté and his colleagues (2002, 2003, 2005) have recommended that youth sport participants experience a wide range of unstructured play and participation in a variety of sports before they choose to specialise in one sport. This developmental pathway for youth sport is more likely to enhance enjoyment, build various cognitive and physical skills and assist with long-term interest in sport participation.

Overall, previous research illustrates that there are a significant number of sport and non-sport variables that affect the decision of athletes whether to continue with sport participation. Although much of the research relating to sport adherence and withdrawal has been conducted with youth sport participants, few investigations have distinguished between the participation and performance context when carrying out their work. Future research should consider applying the parameters established by the recent cohort of coaching scholars to provide a more in-depth understanding of the appropriate context-specific coaching behaviours, training regimens and motives for long-term sport participation. This would allow administrators, coaches and parents to implement sport programs that are targeted more specifically to the needs and interests of young athletes.

The next section reviews two pertinent case studies of youth sport participation. These case studies provide recent examples of the reasons for continuation and discontinuation with sport participation in youth team (cricket) and individual (swimming) sport contexts. Although the research was carried out in New Zealand and Canada, the sports investigated represent sport activities with high participation rates among Australian youth. Ultimately, these case studies are important for demonstrating how the theoretical concepts of sport participation and withdrawal can be applied in real sport settings.

Case study 1: youth cricket in New Zealand

Gaskin and Garland (2005) examined participation motives within a youth team sport context in New Zealand. They surveyed 858 male and female 13–18-year-olds to explore motives for continuation/discontinuation, likelihood of playing into the future and the impact that various initiatives had on youths' inclination to continue playing. Of the survey sample, 718 were currently playing cricket while 140 had discontinued from playing cricket. Gaskin and Garland stated that the participants were chosen from school cricket teams yet it was not clear if the teams competed in a participation (e.g. sport held during school hours against other schools in a low intensity competition where no training is required) or performance-based context (e.g. compete in a highly structured and ratified weekend competition with mid-week training included). Regardless, their research aimed to investigate reasons for the downward trend in cricket participation from childhood through adolescence and adulthood (2005, p. 358), in order to improve retention rates, sport experience and programs.

New Zealand youth cricketers identified multiple motives for sport participation or withdrawal that were consistent with previous research. Fun was noted as the most important factor for playing cricket and this was strongly linked to enjoyment derived from being part of a team. Wanting to learn/develop skills and to be physically fit were also vital for continued participation. Although the main reason for cricketers stopping playing was linked to wanting to play another sport, a disturbing finding was that coaches played a major role in the decision to discontinue participation in cricket. For example, a lack of support and encouragement, dislike of coaches and inadequate playing time (which led to boredom) were actions that could have been positively or negatively influenced by the coach. Even with the narrow context in which the research was conducted, these findings highlight the impact that coaches have on the lives of young people.

Many of the participants currently involved in the game envisaged playing cricket again while few of those who had stopped playing cricket said that they would play again. Some of the projected initiatives related to playing in a more social competition with better and cheaper equipment. These ideas increased the likelihood of continued participation for those had dropped out. A unique finding from this study was that none of the proposed initiatives drastically influenced the views of the returning cricketers which may be due to their inherent satisfaction with the existing format for cricket. As such, the findings purport that it may not be plausible for a single product to cater for all the cricketer's needs. The researchers suggest the current forms of cricket are sufficient for most participants who plan to continue with playing cricket, while a second, socially oriented and less expensive form of the game may be more appealing to those who have discontinued with cricket. Furthermore, the findings indicate that these youth may not be lost to sport altogether; rather, they may have finished with cricket yet maintain participation in another sport.

The main research recommendations emphasised the need for administrators to consider various structural changes to suit the needs of New Zealand's youth cricket population – there were limited suggestions for coaches. Despite this, the implications are that cricket administrators, coaches and teachers need to emphasise personal improvement, affiliation with team mates and flexible playing arrangements to suit both social and more serious cricket participants. In fact, the researchers suggested that while current participants were happy, a modified version of the game could be played parallel to the current competition format. This would suit the needs of primary school children and maintain participation rates into the high school years and beyond.

Case study 2: youth swimming in Canada

The second case study examined continuation/discontinuation rates at a competitive youth swimming program in Canada (Fraser-Thomas et al. 2008). This research aimed to understand how training patterns and the roles of significant others' (coaches, parents, peers, and siblings) influenced adolescent swimmers' sport participation patterns during their developmental years (aged 13–18). Fraser-Thomas et al. specifically selected a group of 20 dropout (n=10) and engaged (n=10) swimmers who were involved in a competitive swimming program for at least four years and trained for a minimum ten hours per week. The male and female athletes in this study identified common factors that affected their willingness to continue with, or withdraw from, swimming in this performance-based context.

As with previous research on sport participation, coaches had a significant influence on their athletes' developmental experiences. Interestingly, both groups experienced supportive and unsupportive coaches who were caring, passionate and encouraging, or critical and intimidating. The dropouts and engaged athletes also encountered coaches who possessed excellent and poor communication skills. Excellent communicators listened, showed a genuine interest in individuals, were interactive and shared expertise clearly whereas poor communicators were autocratic, short tempered and could not relate to adolescents. A surprising finding was that throughout their early years, the nature of coach support did not have a major impact in terms of adherence and withdrawal despite the fact that negative coach behaviours have persistently been associated with negative youth sport outcomes (e.g. Barnett et al. 1992 cited in Fraser-Thomas et al. 2008, p. 658).

Coach favouritism was another factor perceived to influence athlete commitment to swimming. Engaged and dropout athletes acknowledged that favouritism was 'human nature' (Fraser-Thomas et al. 2008, p. 653) yet engaged athletes suggested that coaches favouritism was subtle and not just with the top swimmers – a feature contested by the dropouts who claimed that coaches blatantly ignored weaker swimmers and rarely offered one-on-one coaching. One noteworthy feature here is the notion of open communication between the coach and athlete. Engaged athletes suggested that coaches communicated openly with them when they contemplated withdrawal while dropout athletes did not recount any similar communications. Fraser-Thomas et al. suggest that this magnifies the importance of reciprocal coach–athlete relationships during the adolescent years where sport specialisation becomes more prevalent.

Both engaged and dropout athletes encountered aspects of 'play' (e.g. games, relays) and 'drill-based' training. These were described as positive and innate characteristics of competitive swimming. This suggests that appropriately balanced sessions which mix drills and play represent a suitable approach to training for adolescent athletes. One contentious issue within this youth sport context centred on the philosophical focus of training. For example, engaged athletes mentioned the 'developmental' philosophy at their club which delayed specialisation in swimming, included fewer practices and a focus on development of life skills such as organisation, time management, and leadership. The dropout cohort suggested that their training focused on specific investment and commitment to swimming as well as moving up to higher training squads before they were ready. As such, the philosophy toward training was an important factor with respect to commitment to swimming competitively, as engaged athletes found ways to be involved in activities besides swimming while dropout athletes suggested that the great time commitment required to be successful in swimming prevented them from being involved in other activities (Fraser-Thomas et al. 2008, p. 652).

The influence of parents, peers and siblings throughout the adolescent years has a significant impact on sport development. Both dropout and engaged athletes identified supportive parents as those who provided unstructured play opportunities (e.g. swimming in backyard pools or at beaches) or became involved in club events (e.g. fundraising, working a swim meets). Dropout athletes described, however, that their parents offered financial rewards for good performances, tips during practice/meets and pressured them to continue swimming. Clearly these are not the types of behaviour that one associates with support for long-term commitment to a sport. In contrast the parents of the engaged athletes did not interfere with their swimming yet always provided support, encouragement and flexibility – a balanced and indirect approach to supporting their child's interest in swimming.

Swimming peers positively influenced dropout and engaged athletes providing a supportive environment with a sense of family and common goals. School friends and competitive siblings negatively impacted on the continued participation of dropout athletes but had a positive influence on the engaged swimmers. These points demonstrate how peers can positively or negatively influence athlete participation either during developmental years.

In the concluding stages of this study, Fraser-Thomas et al. reported several clear implications for youth sport programs. They recommended that a broader psychosocial and physical developmental approach to athlete training instead of the early specialisation and elite focus of many current adolescent sport programs. To engage athletes in long-term participation they should be encouraged to participate in a diverse range of sporting (and other) activities. Given the critical influence of coaches, families and peers during adolescence, open communication and reciprocal, supporting relationships is as crucial as 'backing-off' (Fraser-Thomas et al. 2008, p. 660) in terms of influencing practice performance and long-term commitment to sport participation. Administrators and coaches need to provide parents and athletes with specific information regarding the philosophical approach of the club and the positive/negative consequences of youth sport participation.

This section analysed two case studies of youth sport participation. Cricketers identified that having fun, being part of a team, wanting to learn/develop skills and being physically fit were vital for continued participation. The cricketers who stopped playing either wanted to play another sport, experienced a lack of support and encouragement from coaches or disliked them for not giving the athletes adequate playing time. The swimming case study focused more specifically on the influence of significant others and training factors on engagement in their sport. Experiences with coaches (supportive and unsupportive), parent involvement and training session content during their adolescent years were similar regardless of whether athletes remained engaged or dropped out. The engaged athletes, however, outlined the importance of a developmental club philosophy, open communication with parents/coaches and the positive influence and support shown by peers and siblings. Dropouts reported that clubs focused on early specialisation in training and minimal one-on-one coaching. They also highlighted a lack of friendship amongst swimming peers, sibling rivalry and parental pressure during adolescence. Both studies reveal the importance of athlete relationships with family and friends, and clubs that tailor programs that encourage fun and provide developmental paths to maximise athlete engagement during adolescence. They also reveal the significant impact that coaches have on the lives of young people as they travel through their initial sporting experiences. These generic descriptors align with previously stated motives for participation or withdrawal (e.g. Weigand & Broadhurst 1998; Gill 2000; Horton & Mack 2000; Bennie & O'Connor 2004).

Implications for youth sport coaching

According to the *Junior Sport Guidelines* developed by the Australian Sports Commission, sport providers need to assure that coaches provide many opportunities for young people to learn, experience success and have fun. They recommend that young people need to feel like they are being treated fairly while participating in sport as shown by the following comment: 'It is important that sport be made to fit kids, and not the reverse. Modified rules, games and equipment assist in doing this, and help young people to experience success' (2003, p. 2). If coaches in youth participation sport settings focus on win/loss records with limited interest in the development of social relations with and between their athletes, there is likely to be minimal interest on the athletes' behalf in ongoing sport participation. Alternatively, if coaches are knowledgeable about the goals and interpersonal needs of athletes, they are more likely able to create training and competition scenarios that suit their athletes' interests. This may enhance the level of enjoyment and long-term commitment to sport participation.

Understanding the specific and unique contexts where sport takes place is crucial to ensuring long-term participation in sport programs. The recent and prudent differentiation between participation and performance contexts has provided a clear delineation of the various experiences and objectives of sport participants. This is particularly pertinent for youth sport where multiple changes in life take place. The deeper significance of appropriate coaching behaviours for targeted sport contexts has become apparent, with particular focus placed on how coaches can engage with their athletes before, during and after training and competition (see Côté et al. 2003, 2009).

Adequate training for coaches regarding the need to promote positive psychosocial outcomes through supportive, instructive and less punitive behaviours has been shown to enhance enjoyment, reduce anxiety and minimise withdrawal (see Smith et al. 1977, 1979, 2002; Smoll et al. 1993, 1995). Developing a deeper understanding of these youth (and adult) sport contexts may enable educators to deliver better programs that are more specific to needs of coaches and athletes. This might in turn lead to more positive sport and non-sport outcomes for young people with the ultimate objective to encourage long-term participation in sport. As Côté and Gilbert (2009) poignantly state, coaches require a different mix of professional, interpersonal, and intrapersonal knowledge to develop their athletes according to the different coaching contexts in which they work.

One Australian sports association that has attended to these needs through its coach development program is Football Federation Australia (FFA). Recently, the FFA reformatted its coach education pathway to provide more appropriate and contextually relevant information for 'community' (participation context) and 'advanced' (performance) coaches.

For example, the community coach education course focuses on developing grassroots and youth coaches who can deliver suitable game-centred practices with children aged 8–16. For those aspiring to coach at a higher level, advanced coaching licences are available. The C Licence, for example, is targeted towards coaches or prospective coaches of elite youth players who already possess experience and knowledge in working with participation-based teams. This stratification has enabled the FFA to deliver modern and applicable training programs that better cater for the coaches and athletes needs.

Conclusion

It is most important that youth sport administrators, teachers, coaches, parents and athletes are aware of the attributes that underlie continued athletic participation and the issues that contribute to sport withdrawal. This will assist in perpetuating sport participation beyond the youth sport context. The case studies illuminated current reasons for participation and withdrawal amongst youth team and individual sport. They examined both male and female perspectives using surveys and interviews to generate relevant data about the issues and challenges that sport organisers and participants face when planning, implementing and participating in youth sport. Their findings, in conjunction with previous research, highlight various key issues that influence the nature, rate of and motivations for participation. These studies emphasise that adequately preparing and supporting youth sport participants will encourage more athletes to continue to prosper in the years beyond their youth sporting experiences. Youth sport administrators, coaches and parents need to focus on creating environments in which athletes can enjoy themselves. This may be achieved by minimising the events that trigger sport withdrawal, coaching appropriately to the participation or performance context and relevant developmental age, whilst maximising opportunities for athletes to boost self-esteem and confidence in their ability to continue beyond the youth years. Overall, it is essential that coaches and administrators develop programs that meet the developmental and contextual needs of their athletes.

This chapter provided a brief introduction to issues associated with youth sport participation. The aim was to outline the importance of understanding the context when working in youth sport development. Generating and delivering context-appropriate sport programs are one of many features that are likely to influence positively long-term sport participation. This is crucial for Australian youth, given the critical role sport plays in Australian culture and in developing a healthy and happy population.

References

Australian Bureau of Statistics (ABS) (2009). *Sports and physical recreation: a statistical overview, Australia*. Australia: Australian Bureau of Statistics. [Online]. Available: www.abs.gov.au/ausstats/abs@.nsf/0/98B84CE4396FA84ECA2576570015DF5F?opendocument [accessed 19 January 2011].

Australian Bureau of Statistics (ABS) (2007). *Motivators and constraints to participation in sports and physical recreation*. Australia: Australian Bureau of Statistics. [Online]. Available: www.ausport.gov.

au/__data/assets/pdf_file/0011/142220/ABS_-_Motivators_and_Constraints_to_particpation_in_Sports_and_Physical_Recreation.pdf [accessed 19 January 2011].

Australian Sports Commission. (2003). *Guideline 1: long-term involvement.* [Online]. Available: www.ausport.gov.au/__data/assets/pdf_file/0017/144611/Long_Term_Involvement.pdf [accessed 12 October 2010]

Australian Sports Commission. (2005). *Guideline 2: getting young people involved.* [Online]. Available: www.ausport.gov.au/__data/assets/pdf_file/0018/144612/Getting_young_people_involved.pdf [accessed 12 October 2010]

Barber, H., Sukhi, H. & White, S. A. (1999). The influence of parent-coaches on participant motivation and competitive anxiety in youth sport participants. *Journal of Sport Behaviour,* 22(2): 162–80.

Bennett, W. & Crawley, S. (2002). *Don't die with the music in you.* Sydney: Australian Broadcasting Corporation.

Bennie, A. & O'Connor, D. (2006). Athletic transition: a qualitative investigation of elite track and field participation in the years following high school. *Change: Transformations in Education,* 9(1): 59–68.

Bennie, A. & O'Connor, D. (2004). Running into transition: a study of elite track and field athletes. *Modern Athlete and Coach,* 42(2): 19–24.

Bianco, T., Malo, S. & Orlick, T. (1999). Sport injury and illness: elite skiers describe their experiences. *Research Quarterly for Exercise and Sport,* 70(2): 157–69.

Butcher, J., Lindner, K. J. & Johns, D. P. (2002). Withdrawal from competitive youth sport: a retrospective ten-year study. *Journal of Sport Behaviour,* 25(2): 145–61.

Coakley, J. (2006). The good father: parental expectations and youth sports. *Leisure Studies,* 25(2): 153–16.

Coakley, J. (2001). *Sport in society: issues and controversies* (7th ed.). New York, NY: McGraw-Hill.

Côté, J. (2005). Building pathways towards youth sport performance and continued participation. *In 11th World Congress of Sport Psychology, 15–19 August, 2005,* Sydney, Australia.

Côté, J., Baker, J. & Abernethy, B. (2003). From play to practice: a developmental framework for the acquisition of expertise in team sport. In J. Starkes & K. A. Ericsson (Eds). *Recent advances in research on sport expertise* (pp. 89–114). Champaign, IL: Human Kinetics.

Côté, J. & Gilbert, W. (2009). An integrative definition of coaching effectiveness and expertise. *International Journal of Sports Science and Coaching,* 4(3): 307–23.

Côté, J. & Hay, J. (2002). Children's involvement in sport: a developmental perspective. In J. M. Silva & D. Stevens (Eds). *Psychological foundations of sport* (pp. 484–502). Boston: Merrill.

Dollman, J & Lewis N. (2010). The impact of socioeconomic position on sport participation among South Australian youth. *Journal of Science and Medicine in Sport,* 13: 178–81.

Douge, B. (1987). Coaching qualities of successful coaches: a checklist. *Sports Coach,* 10(4): 31–35.

Faulkner, J. & Free, R. (1994). *National junior sport policy: a framework for developing junior sport in Australia.* Canberra: Australian Sports Commission.

Fraser-Thomas, J., Côté, J. & Deakin, J. (2008). Understanding dropout and prolonged engagement in adolescent competitive sport. *Psychology of Sport and Exercise,* 9: 645–62.

Fraser-Thomas, J., Côté, J. & Deakin, J. (2005). Youth sport programs: an avenue to foster positive youth development. *Physical Education and Sport Pedagogy*, 10(1): 9–40.

Frederick, C. M. & Morrison, C. S. (1999). Collegiate coaches: an examination of motivational style and its relationship to decision making and personality. *Journal of Sport Behaviour*, 22(2): 221–33.

Gaskin, C., J. & Garland, R. (2005). Occupying the crease: an exploration of youth cricket in New Zealand. *European Sport Management Quarterly*, 5(4): 357–37.

Gilbert, W. D. (2002). *An annotated bibliography and analysis of coaching science*. Washington: American Alliance for Health, Physical Education, Recreation and Dance [Online]. Available: www.icsspe.org/documente/bibliography.pdf [accessed 20 January 2011].

Gill, D. L. (2000). *Psychological dynamics of sport and exercise* (2nd ed.). Champaign, IL: Human Kinetics.

Gould, D. (1993). Intensive sport participation and the prepubescent athletes: competitive stress and burnout. In B. R. Cahill & A. J. Pearl (Eds). *Intensive participation in children's sports* (pp. 19–38). Champaign, IL: Human Kinetics.

Hedstrom, R. & Gould, D. (2004). Research in youth sports: critical issues status. [Online]. Available: www.sportdevelopment.info/index.php?option=com_content&view=article&id=701:research-in-youth-sports-critical-issues-status&catid=55:researchsurveys&Itemid=82 [accessed 19 January 2011].

Hollings, S., Hume, P. & Trewin, C. (1997). *Successful athletes: the role of performance progression*. Auckland, New Zealand: Athletics New Zealand.

Horton, R. S. & Mack, D. E. (2000). Athletic identity in marathon runners: functional focus or dysfunctional commitment? *Journal of Sport Behaviour*, 23(2): 101–19.

Kenow, L. & Williams, J. M. (1999). Coach–athlete compatibility and athlete's perception of coaching behaviours. *Journal of Sport Behaviour*, 22(2): 251–59.

Koivula, N. (1999). Sport participation: differences in motivation and actual participation due to gender typing. *Journal of Sport Behaviour*, 22(3): 360–80.

Longhurst, K. & Spink, K. S. (1987). Participation motivation of Australian children involved in organised sport. *Canadian Journal of Sports Science*, 12(1): 24–30.

Lyle, J. (2002). *Sports coaching concepts: a framework for coaches' behaviour*. London: Routledge.

Moraes, L. (1996). Looking back and thinking ahead: reflections and recommendations. In J. H. Salmela (Ed.). *Great job coach! Getting the edge from proven winners* (pp. 207–26). Ottawa: Pontentium.

Morgan, W. R., O'Connor, P. J., Ellickson, K. A. & Bradley, P. W. (1988). Personality structure, mood states and performance in elite male distance runners. *International Journal of sports Psychology*, 19(4): 247–63.

Netball Australia (NA) (2007). *Strategic direction*. [Online]. Available: www.netball.asn.au/extra.asp?id=14&OrgID=1&menu=10690 [accessed 19 January 2011].

Netball Australia (NA) (2006). *Junior sport policy*. [Online]. Available: www.netball.asn.au/extra.asp?id=3040&OrgID=1&menu=10669 [accessed 19 January 2011].

O'Connor, D. & Bennie, A. (2006). The retention of youth sport coaches. *Change: Transformations in Education*, 9(1): 27–38.

Ogilvie, B. & Taylor, J. (1993). Career termination issues among elite athletes. In R. N. Singer, M. Murphey & L. K. Tennant (Eds). *Handbook of research on sport psychology* (pp. 760–75). New York, NY: Macmillan Publishing Company.

Orlick, T. (1974). The athletic dropout: a high price for inefficiency. *CAHPER Journal, 41*(2): 21–27.

Poczwardowski, A., Barott, J. E. & Jowett, S. (2006). Diversifying approaches to research on athlete coach relationship. *Psychology of Sport and Exercise, 7*: 125–42.

Reimer, B. A., Beal, B. & Schroeder, P. (2000). The influences of peer and university culture on female student athletes' perceptions of career termination, professionalization, and social isolation. *Journal of Sport Behaviour, 23*(4): 364–78.

Robertson, I. D. (1988). The coach and the dropout. *Sports Coach, 12*(3): 8–14.

Robinson, T. & Carron, A. (1982). Personal and situational factors associated with dropping out versus maintaining participation in competitive sport. *Journal of Sports Psychology, 4*(6): 364–78.

Scanlan, T. K., Stein, G. L. & Ravizza, K. (1989). An in-depth study of former elite figure skaters: II. Sources of enjoyment. *Journal of Sport and Exercise Psychology, 11*: 65–83.

Schmidt, G. W. & Stein, G. L. (1991). Sport commitment: a model integrating enjoyment, dropout and burnout. *Journal of Sport and Exercise Psychology, 13*(3): 254–65.

Seabra, A., Mendonça, D., Thomis, M., Peters, T. & Maia, J. (2008). Associations between sport participation, demographic and socio-cultural factors in Portuguese children and adolescents. *European Journal of Public Health, 18*(1): 25–30.

Skard, O. & Valgum, P. (1989). The influence of psychosocial and sports factors from boys' soccer: A prospective study. *Scandinavian Journal of Sports Sciences, 11*(2): 65–72.

Smith, R. E. & Smoll, F. L. (2002). *Way to go, coach! A scientifically-proven approach to coaching effectiveness* (2nd ed.). Portola Valley, CA: Warde.

Smith, R. E., Smoll, F. L. & Curtis, B. (1979). Coach effectiveness training: a cognitive-behavioural approach to enhancing relationship skills in youth sport coaches. *Journal of Sport Psychology, 1*: 59–75.

Smith, R. E., Smoll, F. L. & Hunt, E. (1977). A system for the behavioural assessment of athletic coaches. *Research Quarterly, 48*: 401–07.

Smoll, F. L., Smith, R. E. & Barnett, N. P. (1995). Reduction of children's sport performance anxiety through social support and stress-reduction training for coaches. *Journal of Applied Developmental Psychology, 16*: 125–42.

Smoll, F. L., Smith, R. E., Barnett, N. P. & Everett, J. J. (1993). Enhancement of children's self-esteem through social support training for youth sport coaches. *Journal of Applied Psychology, 78*: 602–10.

Smoll, F. L., Smith, R. E., Curtis, B. & Hunt, E. (1978). Toward and meditational model of coach-player relationships. *Research Quarterly, 49*: 528–41.

Strean, W. B. (1995). Youth sport contexts: coaches perceptions and implications for intervention. *Journal of Applied Sport Psychology, 7*(1): 23–37.

Tarbotton, D. (2001). Transition years. *The Journal of Athletics NSW, 9*(3): 1–9.

Telama R., Yang X., Viikari J., Välimäki I., Wanne O. & Raitakari O. (2005). Physical activity from childhood to adulthood: a 21-year tracking study. *American Journal of Preventative Medicine, 28*(3): 267–73.

Trudel, P. & Gilbert, W.D. (2006). Coaching and coach education. In D., Kirk, M., O'Sullivan & D., McDonald (Eds). *Handbook of physical education,* (pp. 516–39). Sage: London.

United Nations (2005). *International year of sport and physical education.* [Online]. Available: www.un.org/sport2005/resources/concept.pdf [accessed 5 December 2005].

Weib, S. (2001). More than just an athlete: the keys to achieving a lasting positive impact. *BC Coach's Perspective, 5*(3): 8–9.

Weigand, D. A. & Broadhurst, C. J. (1998). The relationship among perceived competence, intrinsic motivation and control perceptions in youth soccer. *International Journal of Sports Psychology, 29*(4): 324–38.

Weiss, M. R. (1993). Psychological effects of intensive sport participation on children and youth: self-esteem and motivation. In B. R. Cahill & A. J. Pearl (Eds). *Intensive participation in children's sports* (pp. 39–69). Champaign, IL: Human Kinetics.

15

Seen but not heard: child protection in sport

Kate Russell

> The Hickson case did a lot of damage to our profession. Now we have to establish the procedure that will make it easier for suspects to be dealt with. If anyone has any doubts about the conduct of one of our members they should come directly to me. (Mike Drew 1995, cited in Downes 2002)

Mike Drew, former Head of the Great Britain Swimming Coaches' Association spoke with disdain after hearing about the conviction of Paul Hickson, a former Great British Olympic swimming coach, who in 1995 was sentenced to 17 years in prison for rape and 15 other sexual offences against girls in his care. The case was not an isolated one and Drew's concern appears now, in hindsight at least, to be a perverse one. In 2001, Drew himself was convicted of sexually abusing children in his trust. The offences involved five boys, aged between 13 and 15, and ranged back over the previous 30 years. These incidents simply reflect one aspect of the varied child abuses and poor practices that can occur within the sporting/coaching environment. This chapter seeks to identify the key issues within the child protection field that pertain to both competitive and recreational sport and physical education. In particular, it seeks to provide a framework from which to build a critical understanding of the ways in which legislation, policy and professionalism have shaped not only how we view children as individuals but how we perceive the role of sport for our children.

The chapter begins with a brief historical investigation of the ways in which childhood has been perceived over the last 200 years or so and how legislation has shaped our understanding of young people as both in need of, and deserving of, care and protection. I will go on to highlight the incidence and prevalence of child abuse within the general and sporting population in an attempt to contextualise the current drives for child welfare. Using sources primarily from Australia and the UK, with reference to other European and North American research, I will present a number of factors that may indicate a child at 'risk' of abuse and the ways in which both government and sporting governing bodies have sought to address the issue.

The rise of child protection legislation

It was not until the 19th century that we start to see the role of the law in differentiating, and it could be argued, subsequently protecting children and young people in England.

Both the 1833 Factory Act and the 1834 Poor Law saw a dramatic shift in both the working conditions of children and the ways in which they were viewed by wider society – and not always to their benefit. The Factory Act of 1833 improved conditions for children working in factories in the following ways: no child workers under nine years of age; employers must have a medical or age certificate for child workers; children between the ages of nine and 13 to work no more than nine hours a day; children between 13 and 18 to work no more than 12 hours a day; children are not to work at night; and two hours schooling each day for children. Marshall and Bottomore (1992, cited in Brackenridge 2001) noted that while the Poor Law attempted to champion social rights it also placed the child as a potential delinquent. The law stated that if you required welfare you would have to substitute your rights as a citizen, thus often rendering you beyond the law (Brackenridge 2001). Other notable laws of the time raised the age of sexual consent to 13 for girls in 1875 (having been at 12 since 1285). In 1889 The Children's Charter was invoked. This was the first act of parliament for the prevention of cruelty to children. It enabled the state to intervene in relations between parents and children. Police could arrest anyone found ill-treating a child, and enter a home if a child was thought to be in danger. The act included guidelines on the employment of children and outlawed begging.

The law in the UK progressed steadily during the 20th century reflecting a change in the ways in which children were viewed – from a paternalistic viewpoint of requiring care towards a more autonomous view in which a child had individual rights. Acts such as the Children Act (1948), Children's Act (1989) The Protection of Children Act (1999) and more recently the 'Every Child Matters' Green Paper in 2003 which led to the development of the Children Act (2004) all served to create an environment where children were cared for but also recognised their individuality and need to represent themselves as citizens—ones with equal rights for protection and representation. Brackenridge (2001) provides a useful critique of the relative effectiveness of each act of parliament and an analysis of the ways in which the UK did and did not meet the ideal of the United Nations Children's Charter in 1989.

In contrast to the UK, Australia started from a very different place in regard to child protection. Fogarty (2008) and Tomison (2001) provide a useful history of policy development. Children were transported as convicts from the UK and as such were both treated and perceived quite differently from non-convict children. Abandoned and neglected children became an issue from the beginning of fleet arrivals and subsequently, during the gold rushes in the 1850s and 1860s. This led to the establishment of boarding houses and orphanages (Tomison 2001; Fogarty 2008). Australia matched the UK in the establishment of acts of parliament to protect children and also mirrored the development of the National Society for the Prevention of Cruelty to Children (NSPCC) established in 1883 in the UK with the Victorian Prevention of Cruelty to Children established in 1896. While many individuals believed wholeheartedly that they were 'rescuing' (Tomison 2001) these abandoned children, the development of institutions to house them was accompanied by interventions to prevent danger from occurring. This was unfortunately the case for many Indigenous children who were caught up in this process, reflecting the ways in which the White Australia policy institutionalised the removal of children from their families.

The current child protection system in Australia is very fragmented, with the responsibility for addressing cases of abuse and neglect subject to individual state and territorial governments (Goddard 1996). As a result, there are many variations in how issues of abuse and neglect are determined and addressed. Goddard (1996) argues, however, that despite these differences all states support the children in their care. According to Tomison (2001), many western nations (including the UK, US and Australia) have been working towards the professionalisation of child protection services and practices; the development of tools and policies to help determine if abuse is taking place (e.g. risk assessments) and ways to respond. Likewise, Bromfield and Holzer (2008) found that despite the many differences in policies (each state has its own child protection act) they are guided by common principles: the 'best interest' of the child; early intervention; involvement of children and young people in decision making; out of home care; culturally specific responses; after-care support; and permanency planning and stability of care. As an example, in New South Wales (NSW), the government has also implemented legislation in 2010 through the 'Keep Them Safe' program which provides explicit instructions on reporting and provides support for any individual dealing with a child protection incident. This legislation is particularly relevant to teachers who serve as one of the mandatory reporters.

Modern conceptions of childhood often reflect the ways in which government agencies choose to represent them. The law requires a boundary to be drawn between who is a child and who is an adult which can often appear to be arbitrary. For example, many cultures have established institutional ages of majority, which specify in a legal context the age at which adulthood begins. In the UK, criminal liability is set at age ten and yet sexual consent for both hetero- and homosexual relations does not occur until ages 16 (for girls) and 18 (for boys) with enfranchisement occurring at 18 for both groups. In Australia, criminal liability is at the age of ten across all the states and territories with the age of sexual consent 16 in NSW, Australian Capital Territory, Northern Territory, Victoria and Western Australia, and 17 in South Australia and Tasmania. Queensland has the only differentiated age of consent: 16 and 18 for heterosexual relations for boys and girls respectively, and 18 for male-to-male relations and 16 for female-to-female relations. Enfranchisement occurs for all at 18 years of age (Lamont 2010). The UN charter states that a child is someone under the age of 18 unless the age of majority in a country is less than that (see UNICEF 2010). So the situation is not clear and subsequently sport can often have an alternative set of measures to determine access to competition and training/performance expectations. It is often these differing perceptions of ability and capability within sport that creates tension between child welfare and sport participation.

Child protection development in sport

Celia Brackenridge is arguably the leading international academic in the field of harassment and abuse within sport. Her work over the last 25 years or so has influenced views of researchers and government bodies on the role and responsibilities of coaching and sport education in regard to child welfare (e.g. Brackenridge 1986, 1994, 1996, 1997, 2001, 2008, 2009; Brackenridge & Kirby 1997; Fasting et al. 2004; Fasting et al. 2008; Fasting & Brackenridge 2009; Fasting et al. 2010). Her early work on the development of a code of ethics and conduct for sport coaches (Brackenridge 1986), along with strong governing body reactions to cases of sexual abuse in sport through the media (e.g. Paul Hickson and Mike Drew) helped pave the way for the establishment of a National Child Protection in Sport Task Force by Sport England in October 1999 (Sport England 1999). As Brackenridge (2001, p. 172) argues, it 'represented a potential major breakthrough in the strategic efforts to deal with sexual and other forms of exploitation in sport'. Following this, in 2001 a permanent Child Protection in Sport Unit inside the NSPCC was established and represented a shift in the ways in which sporting governing bodies would be managed, from a laissez faire approach of the 1990s to a more coercive approach in the new millennium (Sport England 2000). Since then, all sporting organisations that receive funding from Sport England have to implement a Child Protection policy. Other independent large sporting organisation such as The Football Association in England, have also enlisted Brackenridge and colleagues (see Brackenridge et al. 2007) to provide developmental support and implementation strategies, as well as an evaluation of their child welfare campaign, 'The goal campaign'.

In Australia development in child protection law per se preceded the development of child protection legislation in sport. While each individual state or territory has specific child protection laws there are also some fundamental rights for all children. These include a right of every child to be safe from harm (*Children's Protection Act 1993*). In order to protect this right, every person has a legal duty of care to ensure all participants of an organisation's (including sporting) activities are given adequate protection from harm or injury. This duty of care is a common law responsibility that covers both action taken *and* inaction. This means that committee members, managers, coaches, staff members and volunteers have a legal responsibility to provide children with a safe environment in which to participate (see National Framework for Creating Child Safe Environments, 2005). The 'Play By The Rules' organisation is an excellent source of legal information on child welfare for all Australian states and territories in addition to providing training for coaches and administrators on how to manage and reduce risk. Play by the Rules is a unique partnership between the Australian Sports Commission, Human Rights and Equal Opportunity Commission, all state and territory sport and recreation and anti-discrimination agencies and the Queensland Commission for Children, Young People and Child Guardian (Play By The Rules 2010) and is essential viewing for all coaches.

These developments demonstrate the recognition of the unalienable rights of the child to be protected in any environment in which they interact. Paulo David (2005) provides an excellent account of the international development of the human rights of youth within sport including those outside of the Australian and UK context.

What do we know about abuse?

Neglect[1] refers to situations in which adults fail to: meet a child's basic needs (e.g. food or warm clothing); constantly leave children alone and unsupervised; or failing or refusing to

---

1 All definitions of the forms of abuse come from NSPCC 2010.

give their children love and affection. In sport, neglect would occur if children do not have proper supervision, clothing or are allowed or encouraged to play whilst injured. Physical abuse is used to describe situations in which adults: physically hurt or injure children (e.g. hitting, shaking, squeezing, burning, biting); give children alcohol, inappropriate drugs or poison; or attempt to suffocate or drown children. In sport, physical abuse occurs if intensity of training disregards a child's immature and growing body, or predisposes a child to injury because of fatigue. Drugs used to enhance performance or delay puberty can also have serious effects. Sexual abuse is used to describe incidents when: children are sexually abused by males and females who use them to meet their own sexual needs; have full sexual intercourse, masturbation, oral sex, anal intercourse and fondling with adults; when adults show children pornographic material; or if adults use sexually explicit language. In sport, sexual abuse can occur if photos are taken or adapted and placed on child pornography sites, where there is inappropriate touching or where an intimate relationship occurs. Emotional abuse can occur through: a persistent lack of love and affection; constant overprotection which denies children the opportunity to socialise; and verbal abuse (e.g. constantly being shouted at, taunted, or receiving racist, sexist or homophobic abuse). In sport, coaches or parents can be abusive if they constantly criticise, abuse their power or impose unrealistic pressure to perform at a high level. Initiation ceremonies can often result in emotional abuse as well. Bullying is a form of verbal, physical or emotional abuse. It is a deliberate act and might be inflicted by: a parent who pushes too hard; a coach or manager who has a 'win-at-all costs' philosophy or one child intimidating another. In sport, bullying occurs more often in places where adults are not around, such as the changing room.

The most recent data from the Australian Institute of Health and Welfare (AIHW) indicate that during 2008–2009 there were 339,454 reports of suspected child abuse and neglect made to Australian state and territory bodies. Of these, 54,621 were substantiated and 35,409 children placed under care orders (AIHW 2010). Aboriginal and Torres Strait Islander children were eight times more likely to have a substantiation or a care order than their non-Indigenous counterparts. In all states and territories in Australia, girls were much more likely than boys to have a substantiation of sexual abuse. In Western Australia, South Australia and Tasmania, three times as many girls were subject to a substantiation of sexual abuse than boys (AIHW 2010). These statistics reflects around 6–7% of the general child population as having experienced some form of abuse. Latest figures from the UK (NSPCC 2010) indicate that there were 31,919 children on child protection registers as of 31 March 2006 with the following national breakdowns: England 26,400, Northern Ireland 1639, Wales 2163 and Scotland 2288. In terms of prevalence, Cawson (2002) provides a close approximation to the level of abuse and neglect within the family, indicating that around 16% of children (one in six) experienced serious maltreatment by parents; one third experiencing more than one type.

Research into abuse in sport

Brackenridge (2001, pp. 46–48) provides a useful table, which identifies the number and types of work undertaken in the fields of harassment, bullying, abuse and coach-athlete relationships in sport covering 1985–2000. Not surprisingly, it is often difficult to pursue research in this field as many sporting organisations are unaware that they have a child protection 'problem' or the governing bodies are cautious about finding out material that may have a negative impact on future participation rates. Overall, Brackenridge (2000) notes that athletes generally are twice as likely as non-athletes to experience some form of sexual harassment from authority figures.

In Australia, Leahy et al. (2002) looked at regional and elite athletes and found that 31% of females and 21% of males reported sexual abuse at some point in their lives. Of this group 41% of females and 29% of males reported this happening in a sports setting. For the elite group 46.4% had reported being sexually abused by sports personnel. For the club group this was 25.6%. Kirby and Greaves (1996) investigated Canadian high performance and recently retired Olympic athletes. Their study found that 21.8% of 266 respondents replied that they had sexual intercourse with persons in authority in sport, 8.6% of persons reported forced sexual intercourse, or rape, with such persons. In Norway (Fasting et al. 2004) 28% of elite female athletes had experienced some form of sexual harassment in a sporting context. In the Czech Republic, Fasting et al. (2010) found that amongst a group of 595 elite, non-elite/competitive and general exercisers that the chances of being harassed by someone in sport increased with performance level; going from 29.7% among the exercisers to 55.2% among the elite performers. In UK, Gervis and Dunn (2004) noted that among elite child athletes, all had experienced some form of emotional abuse by their coaches during their time as elite performers. They summarise that the behaviour of some coaches is a threat to the psychological wellbeing and long-term development of these athletes. All of these studies indicate that abuse seems to occur at a higher level in the sport setting than the general population. The question is why?

Landmark cases in the sexual exploitation of sport

One of the first major cases to make headlines in the field of sexual abuse and sport was the case of Paul Hickson in 1993. As mentioned before, Hickson was a former British Olympic swimming coach, who was eventually sentenced to 17 years in prison in 1995 (after being on the run for two years) for rape and 15 other sexual offences against girls in his care. In 1997, Graham James, a renowned ice hockey coach in Canada was convicted of sexually abusing a male athlete in his care—Sheldon Kennedy, a respected National Hockey League player. Kennedy was a vulnerable child and from the age of 14 was abused over 350 times by James who only received three and a half years in jail and has gone on to coach other ice hockey teams. James was quoted at the time as saying that he felt 'surprised and betrayed by Kennedy's coming forward' (*Ottawa Citizen*, 1 August 1997). At the time of writing (December 2010) James has been named in another high profile case of suspected child abuse with another ice hockey player, former Calgary Flames captain Theoren Fleury. Mike Drew, the former Head of the Great Britain Swimming Coaches' Association was known as 'Dr Drew' by many of his victims who recalled incidences of hot baths and excessive massage in hotel rooms leading to abuse. Drew was finally sentenced to consecutive jail terms for his abuses in 2001 (Downes 2002). Brett Sutton was widely hailed as one of the most successful triathlon coaches of his time. In 1999, Sutton admitted five offences against a teenage girl in Australia, but never served a jail sentence. While he is banned from coaching in Australia for life, he now coaches professionally in Europe (Downes 2002). What all these cases have in common is access to athletes from a very early age and a position of trust that has been exploited. Many of the activities that preceded the abuse can be regarded as 'grooming' techniques or the 'normalisation of sporting practices' to the extent to which young people feel unable to question them. What follows is an attempt to understand the sporting context and the ways in which the potential for abuse may be generated.

Potential risk factors in sport

One of the potential risk factors for abuse happening within sport is the relatively young age at which children join many sporting organisations – in fact this is often regarded as 'best practice' in the sense that early introductions may lead to talent identification and enable directed training to occur. Brackenridge (2001) posits that young athletes are frequently away from parents or caregivers and are generally inexperienced in the sporting world compared to their coach; as such they often afford the coach a position of great power in relation to controlling their training and consequently, as performance levels increase, their life. She further suggests (Brackenridge 1997; Cense 1997; Cense & Brackenridge 2001) that in relation to many female athletes, low self-esteem is often a factor and targeted by the coach. Whilst also very talented, they were often on the edge of the highest performance level at the time they were first groomed; as one survivor described 'we were just ripe for the picking' (cited in Brackenridge 2001, p. 113). Brackenridge posits the theory that risk may be related to this 'stage of imminent achievement' with all of its anxieties over future success and direction in the balance (Brackenridge 2001; Brackenridge et al. 2009).

The sport itself may be a specific factor for increased risk of harm. Often sport is a paternalistic endeavour, in which easy access to athletes for those with less than honourable intentions is facilitated. This is particularly the case for recreational groups where checks and qualifications are often left unscrutinised. The type of sport may also influence the opportunities for abuse (Brackenridge 2001). For example, some sports such as swimming, gymnastics and figure skating often require minimal clothing and the use of 'spotting' or physical handling as methods for safety or correction. Whilst minimal clothing is often presented as an 'obvious' reason for increased risk of abuse, we have to be cautious about making such a firm distinction between such 'risky' and 'non-risky' sports. In particular, when we consider the extensive abuses that occurred within the sport of ice hockey and its extensive use of protective clothing, we can see that this assertion is not as straightforward as one would think (Fasting et al. 2000). Indeed, as Fasting et al. indicated after a later study, 'when it comes to female athletes' experiences of sexual harassment, sport type matters far less than sport participation per se' (2004, p. 373).

The coach him/herself is also a major factor in the development of potential for risk. Those individuals who derive self-esteem from placing themselves in a position of knowledge and power over the progress of athletes, who set very demanding technical or training goals, who push back interpersonal boundaries and who have access to isolated individuals (Brackenridge 2001, p. 196), are often more likely to be abusive. It is important at this point to recognise that we are focusing primarily on competitive and elite sport but the need to protect children in that intense environment as well as those in recreational sport is paramount. The 'win at all costs' mantra is a troubling one, especially when coaches are looking to find and develop the next national champion. The question surely remains, how do we achieve this without the athlete experiencing burn out, excessive punishment or even abuse? In his seminal work on elite gymnasts and figure skaters Ryan (1995) noted that often it was the coaches who believed that children were just as capable (as adults) of being ruthless and careless (with their own and each other's health) in order to win. Bela Karolyi, who trained both Romanian and American athletes, indicated: 'these girls are like little scorpions. You put them all in a bottle, and one scorpion will come out alive. That scorpion will be the champion' (Ryan 1995, p. 22).

In the best interests of the child?

David's (1995, cited in David 2005) work on human rights within youth sport provides some excellent examples of the ways in which sport normalises many practices that in any other context would be regarded as abusive and questions whether competitive sport is in the 'best interests of the child'. He notes that there are a number of factors within elite sport that can have a detrimental impact on young performers including (but not limited to): the age of competition and intensive training regimes.

The International Olympic Committee does not state a minimum age level for competition at the Olympic Games but refers to the different international sports federations to set those standards. Other organisations, such as the European Non-Governmental Sports Organisations made a recommendation that athletes under the age of 13 should only compete domestically and that an agreed age for international competition should be reached (David 1995, cited in David 2005), but this has yet to be attained. David also asserts that sports such as gymnastics often have children as young as 12 and 13 competing at the Olympic level, suggesting that the intensive training regimes that have to occur in order to reach that level would begin at around six years of age. It should be noted that gymnastics has made a number of shifts in regard to their minimum age standards for competition, which should be applauded. Gymnasts now have to be 16 years of age in the year of competition to be eligible to compete in major international events such as the Olympics and World Championships (Australian Institute of Sport 2010). With elite gymnasts often training 20–30 hours a week, we should also recognise that the opportunity for isolation and reliance on other adults other than parents/caregivers suggests that our drive for perfection could lead to harm.

Extensive training programs where children are asked to train for upwards of 50 hours a week (e.g. Donnelly 1993; Litsky 1998) indicate that children are being asked to do what adults often struggle with, at the same time as fulfilling their responsibilities as school students and to having some semblance of a social life. Often children sacrifice this aspect of their childhood, living up to many parental dreams for success (e.g. Quiner 1997; Baupere 2001). Countries such as Romania, the former Soviet Union and East Germany often exhibited many practices that were clearly abusive cases of corporeal punishment.

Willsher (1995, cited in David 2005, p. 70) interviewed team-mates of gymnast Adriana Giurca who was beaten to death by her Romanian coach at age 11 for not being able to complete an exercise. The athlete noted:

> we were regularly beaten when we did not perform perfectly during training as it was expected. Our trainer told us it was the best way to reach the height of performance. It was normal, but we didn't tell our parents or anyone else. We wanted to be gymnasts and we accepted it.

In the former East Germany, the use of performance enhancing drugs (including testosterone and anabolic steroids) was systematically and institutionally implemented throughout the 1960s, 1970s and 1980s (Yesalis et al. 2000; Noakes 2004). This has led many former athletes to develop depression and for some to even have gender reassignment surgery because of the damage caused by excessive testosterone injections. While many Western sport organisations refer to the practices of the old Eastern bloc countries as barbaric it belies the fact that many have taken on board the practices (and the coaches themselves) in order to achieve sporting success. Indeed, Bela Karolyri (famed gymnastic coach of Nadia Comanech, who defected from Romania) coached Mary Lou Retton to her Olympic Gold Medal in 1984. In more recent times, coaching from states such as China has generated cause for concern. In his exposé of gymnastic training practices in China for the BBC, Matthew Pinsent (himself a four time Olympic Gold medal winner for rowing) noted incidences of physical and emotional abuse (BBC 2005) against young children. While the IOC or Chinese officials have made no official response to this specific incident, China was recently stripped of an Olympic Bronze medal in gymnastics from the Sydney 2000 Games for fielding an underage athlete (Australian Olympic Committee 2010). These incidences raise general concerns about the expectations for our children, and the role coaches have in acting in the best interests of the child and protecting them from harm.

Conclusion

The question remains for scholars in the field of education, sport, sociology and child protection: what can we do to protect our children, whilst ensuring that our practices are reasonable and achievable by all those who have to deliver sport coaching and physical education teaching? The primary response is: education and training for coaches, teachers, parents *and* children. It is imperative that we understand the dynamics of the sporting and physical education field to reflect upon the unique environment and relationship that we develop with young children. We do not want to stop young children from playing sport or enjoying physical activity, or stop adults from volunteering their time, energy and expertise in guiding young people to achieve their physical aims; far from it. What we must endeavour to do is find ways in which to engage those stakeholders who have responsibility for working with our children to foster best practice. In this way we can pre-empt many situations that might have the potential to increase the risk of harm. Organisations such as Play By The Rules are essential in this process in Australia, as is the Safeguarding Children training run by the NSPCC in the UK.

We need to ask questions of the coaches who deliver our children's sessions; of the teachers who notice behaviour at school; of the parents who simply leave their children at 'the gate' or who display abusive behaviours at the 'pitch side' (Pitchford et al. 2004); and of the children who tell us that things are 'not quite right' or that someone told them to 'keep a secret'. In all these ways we become the guardians of our children and serve them well in our aim to protect.

Norman Brook, an experienced athletics coach and a child protection in sport educator notes the implicit trust we have for sport: 'Would you drive five miles to a place you don't know, knock on a door, hand over your child to whoever answers, and leave them for a couple of hours?' (Downes 2002).

References

Aries. P. (1962). *Centuries of childhood*. New York: Vintage Books.

Australian Institute of Health and Welfare (AIHW) (2010). *Child protection Australia 2008–09*. [Online]. Available: www.aihw.gov.au/publications/index.cfm/title/10859 [accessed 19 January 2011].

Australian Institute of Sport (2010). *Gymnastics*. [Online]. Available: www.ausport.gov.au/ais/nutrition/factsheets/sports/gymnastics [accessed 19 January 2011].

Australian Olympic Committee (2010). *China stripped of Sydney bronze*. [Online]. Available: corporate.olympics.com.au/news.cfm?ArticleID=10673 [accessed 19 January 2011].

Baupere, M. (2001). Jenny, fille de fer (Jenny, iron girl). *L'Equipe,* 28 January.

BBC (2005). Pinsent schocked by China training. 17 November [Online]. Available: news.bbc.co.uk/sport2/hi/other_sports/gymnastics/4445506.stm [accessed 20 January 2011].

Brackenridge, C. H. (2009). Olympic engagement in promoting athlete welfare. In XIII Olympic Congress Contributions, Copenhagen, 9 October 2009, pp. 65–66. Lausanne: International Olympic Committee.

Brackenridge, C.H. (2008). Coach swimmer interaction: traps, pitfalls and how to avoid them. *Journal of Sport Sciences,* 26(1): 3.

Brackenridge, C. H. (2001). *Spoilsports: understanding and preventing sexual exploitation in sport*. London: Routledge.

Brackenridge, C. H. (2000). Harassment, sexual abuse and safety of the female athlete. *Clinics in Sports Medicine,* 19(2): 187–98.

Brackenridge, C. H. (1997). Researching sexual abuse in sport. In G. Clarke and B. Humberstone (Eds), *Researching women in sport*, (pp. 126–41). London: Macmillan.

Brackenridge, C. H. (1994). Fair play or fair game: child sexual abuse in sport. *International Review for the Sociology of Sport,* 29(3): 287–99.

Brackenridge, C. H. (1986). Ethical problems in women's sport. *Coaching Focus*. Leeds: National Coaching Foundation.

Brackenridge, C. H. (Ed.) (1996). *Child protection in sport: policies, procedures and systems. Report of a Sports Council seminar for national governing bodies*. Cheltenham: The Countryside & Community Press.

Brackenridge, C. H. & Kirby, S. (1997). Playing safe: assessing the risk of sexual abuse to elite young athletes. *International Review for the Sociology of Sport*, *32*(4): 407–18

Brackenridge, C. H., Lindsey, I. & Telfer, H. (2009). *Sexual abuse risk in sport: testing the Stage of Imminent Achievement hypothesis*. London: Brunel University.

Brackenridge, C. H., Pitchford, A., Nutt, G. & Russell, K. (Eds) (2007). *Child welfare in football: an exploration of children's welfare in the modern game*. London: Routledge.

Bromfield, L. M. & Holzer, P. J. (2008). *A national approach for child protection: project report*. [Online]. Available: www.aifs.gov.au/nch/pubs/reports/cdsmac/cdsmac.pdf [accessed 19 January 2011].

Cawson, P. (2002). *Child maltreatment in the family: the experience of a national sample of young people*. London: National Society for Prevention of Cruelty to Children.

Cense, M. (1997). *Red card or carte blanche: risk factors for sexual harassment and sexual abuse in sport: summary, conclusions and recommendations*. Arnhem: Netherlands Olympic Committee, Netherlands Sports Federation.

Cense, M. & Brackenridge, C. H. (2001). Temporal and developmental risk factors for sexual harassment and abuse in sport. *European Physical Education Review, 7*(1): 61–79.

David, P. (2005). *Human rights in youth sport: a critical review of children's rights in competitive sports*. London: Routledge.

Donnelly, P. (1993). Problems associated with young involvement in high-performance sport. In B. R. Cahill and A. J. Pearl (Eds). *Intensive participation in children's sports* (pp. 95–126), American Orthopaedic Society for Sports Medicine, Champaign, IL: Human Kinetics.

Downes, S. (2002). Every parent's nightmare. *Observer Sport Monthly*, 7 April [Online]. Available: http://observer.guardian.co.uk/osm/story/0,,678189,00.html [accessed 20 January 2011].

Fasting, K. & Brackenridge, C. H. (2009). Coaches, sexual harassment and education. *Sport, Education and Society, 14*(1): 21–35.

Fasting, K., Brackenridge, C. H. & Knorre, N. (2010). Performance level and sexual harassment prevalence among female athletes in the Czech Republic. *Women in Sport and Physical Activity Journal, 19*(1): 26–32.

Fasting, K., Brackenridge, C. H., Miller, K. E. & Sabo, D. (2008). Participation in college sports and protection from sexual victimization. *International Journal of Sport and Exercise Psychology, Special Issue: Abuse and Harassment in Sport Implications for the Sport Psychology Profession* (Edited by T. Leahy), *16*(4): 427–41.

Fasting, K., Brackenridge, C. H. & Sundgot-Borgen, J. (2004). Prevalence of sexual harassment among Norwegian female elite athletes in relation to sport type. *International Review for the Sociology of Sport, 39*(4): 373–86.

Fasting, K., Brackenridge, C. H. & Sundgot-Borgen, J. (2000). *Sexual harassment in and outside sport*. Oslo: Norwegian Olympic Committee.

Fogarty, J. F. (2008). Some aspects of the early history of child protection in Australia. *Family Matters, 78*: 52–59.

Gervis, M. & Dunn, N. (2004). The emotional abuse of elite child athletes by their coaches. *Child Abuse Review, 13*(3): 215–33.

Goddard, C. R. (1996). *Child abuse and child protection: a guide for health, education and welfare workers.* South Melbourne: Churchill Livingstone.

Keep Them Safe (2010). [Online]. Available: www.keepthemsafe.nsw.gov.au/ [accessed 27 November 2010].

Kirby, S. & Greaves, L. (1996). Foul play: sexual abuse and harassment in sport, paper presented to the Pre-Olympic Scientific Congress, Dallas, TX, 11–14 July.

Lamont, A. (2010). Age of consent laws. [Online]. Available: www.aifs.gov.au/nch/pubs/sheets/rs16/rs16.html [accessed 19 January 2011].

Leahy, T., Pretty, G. & Tenenbaum, G. (2002). Prevalence of sexual abuse in sport in Australia. *Journal of Sexual Aggression, 8*(2): 16–36.

Litsky, F. (1998). She's only 16, but Sorgi is a rising talent in the diving world. *New York Times,* 18 July.

Community and Disability Services Ministers' Conference (2005). *Creating safe environments for children: organisations, employees and volunteers – national framework.* [Online]. Available http://www.ocsc.vic.gov.au/publications/childsafe_pubs.htm [accessed 21 February 2011].

Noakes, T. D. (2004). Tainted glory: doping and athletic performance. *New England Journal of Medicine, 351*: 847–49.

NSPCC (2010). *Prevalence and incidence of child abuse and neglect* [Online]. Available: www.nspcc.org.uk/Inform/research/statistics/prevalence_and_incidence_of_child_abuse_and_neglect_wda48740.html [accessed 19 January 2011].

Pitchford, A., Nutt, G., Brackenridge, C.H., Bringer, J.D., Cockburn, C., Pawlaczek, Z. & Russell, K. (2004). Children in football: seen but not heard. *Soccer and Society, 5*(1): 43–60.

Play By The Rules (2010). [Online]. Available: www.playbytherules.net.au/about-us [accessed 19 January 2011].

Quiner, K. (1997). *Dominique Monceanu: a gymnastic sensation.* New Jersey: The Bradford Book Company.

Ryan, J. (1995). *Little girls in pretty boxes,* New York: Doubleday.

Shahar, S. (1990). *Childhood and the Middle Ages.* London: Routledge.

Sport England (2000). Child protection in sport: action plan. London: Sport England.

Sport England (1999). Child protection: task force formed. Press release, London: Sport England.

Tomison, A. M. (2001). A history of child protection: back to the future? *Family Matters, 60*: 46–57.

UNICEF (2010). Rights under the Convention of the Rights of the Child: factsheet. [Online]. Available: www.unicef.org/crc/files/Rights_overview.pdf [accessed 19 January 2011].

Yesalis, C. E., Courson, S. P. & Wright, J. E. (2000). History of anabolic steroid use in sport and exercise. In C. E. Yesalis (Ed.). *Anabolic steroids in sport and exercise* (pp. 51–71). Champaign, IL: Human Kinetics.

16

The media, body image and youth sport

Kate Russell

The term 'body image' is widely used within the media, the classroom and even on the sporting field and yet it is a complex and multidimensional construct. There are both psychological and sociological definitions of the term, often situated within an historical, gendered, racial and class context. This can make it difficult to pin down and understand. Indeed, when this aspect was explored fully, Thompson et al. (1999) found that researchers and clinicians used 16 different definitions of body image in their work on unpacking the causes and treatment of body image disorders. For this chapter I have taken from Sarah Grogan who combined the multitude of definitions to simply determine that body image is 'a person's perceptions, thoughts, and feelings about his or her body' (Grogan 2008, p. 3). Likewise it is important for us to recognise that a person's body image can be both positive and negative, although often we only seem to reflect upon the level of dissatisfaction we have for ourselves. Factors such as the media feature strongly in any assessment of how and why we come to hold particular beliefs about our bodies and as I will argue later often become the focal point for retribution and blame. This chapter will examine the relative merits of such an absolute causal link and also reflect upon the ways in which both individual and social factors, such as gender, age and sport participation can mediate the process of body image development and maintenance. While the majority of research has been undertaken with adults (primarily female), more recent research has addressed men and children (Grogan 2008). The chapter begins with an examination of what we already know about body image; the forms of body image and the epidemiology of body image dissatisfaction. I will review the factors that can influence the perception of one's body as 'good', 'useful' and 'valuable'. I will then go onto evaluate the role of the media in the development of a body image and the potential impact of that process, whilst also providing possible alternative explanations for the ways in which we reinforce beliefs about our body shape and size through sport and physical activity.

What is body image?

From a psychological point of view, body image can reflect the perceptive, affective, cognitive or behavioural aspects of the relationship we have with our bodies. Perceptually this would reflect the picture we have in our mind about our body; how we see our bodies when we look in a mirror and how we imagine ourselves to look – thin or fat, short or tall, muscular or lean etc. Body dissatisfaction in this realm would indicate that there is a discrepancy between the perception of our body shape and size, and our ideal shape and size (and we view this negatively). Cognitive aspects of body image refer to how we think about or evaluate our body in terms of our appearance and function. We generate beliefs about attractiveness, strength and fitness of the body and its various parts. Dissatisfaction here would result from negative thoughts about that evaluation. The affective component of body image is strongly linked to the cognitive aspects and focuses on the feelings we associate with body appearance and function. We may have positive feelings of pride or comfort, while negative aspects could indicate shame, anxiety and disgust. The behavioural dimension of body image denotes the things we do that reflect our positive or negative perceptions, thoughts and feelings about our bodies. We may see, for example, the wearing of clothes to hide features of our body, the avoidance of behaviour such as exercising or swimming if we 'feel fat', or the restriction of eating.

Researchers in the area of body image also recognise that body image is subjective, how I may view my body may not be the way you view my body or how I would go onto interpret your body as attractive, useful etc. This subjectivity can be problematic for researchers who may wish to determine absolute reasons for dissatisfaction but we have come to understand that there are a number of individual and situational factors that can influence body image.

What do we know about body image?

What research tells us so far is that there are a number of individual factors that influence body image and in particular, levels of body dissatisfaction; that is the discrepancy between how an individual views their body and their ideal.

Gender and age

Most of the research concerning body image has focused primarily on women, although Grogan (2008) noted that the last 20 years or so had seen a marked increase in the interest and research into both men and boys. What we do know is that on the whole women are more dissatisfied with their bodies than men regardless of age or instruments used, in relation to weight and appearance (Silberstein et al. 1988; Davis & Cowles 1991; Cash & Henry 1995). Girls as young as five (Williamson & Delin 2001) and eight have been found to desire a thinner body (Gardner et al. 1997), while 77% of girls aged 14–16 (Grigg et al. 1996), 58% of women aged 20–34 (Webster, J. & Tiggemann, M. 2003) and 62% of women aged 65–74 (Allaz et al. 1998) all wanting to lose weight. When employing figural rating scales,[1] researchers in the US, Australia and UK have found that women have a tendency to pick a thinner ideal than their current figure (Cororve-Fingeret et al. 2004). Houn et al.'s (1990) Australian study found what many researchers have noted about women's perceptions of ideal body shape and size; that it is often how a woman perceives *other* women to see her body (rather than men) that influence perceptions of positive or negative

---

1 Figural rating scales are those that present a series of figures or silhouettes of body shapes ranging from very thin to very fat. Individuals are asked to identify their perceived body size and then their ideal. The discrepancy between the two provides an indication of the level of body dissatisfaction.

body image. It can also be the actual physical area of the body rather than the whole body that causes discomfort and this changes with age. Younger women are more critical of their hips, thighs and buttocks, whilst older women may be more concerned with the elasticity of their skin (Dionne et al. 1995) rather than weight for example.

In a recent review of the literature, Cohane and Pope found that 'although boys generally displayed less overall body concern than girls, many boys of all ages reported dissatisfaction with their bodies, often associated with reduced self-esteem' (2001, p. 373). The authors noted that girls typically wanted to be thinner, whereas boys wanted to be bigger. This appears to mirror earlier work with men who found that adding weight was not necessarily a problem as long as it related specifically to building up body mass and muscle (e.g. Mishkind et al. 1986). There appears to be a consensus with weight as an issue, but for girls and women it is about weight restriction, whereas for boys and men it is the nature of that weight which is important. More recent examinations of men's body image (see for example Pope et al. 2000; Cafri et al. 2005) have found that men are becoming increasingly concerned with perceived notions of a 'healthy' and 'sporty' body. The 'muscular ideal', often linked to low body fat and the visibility of stomach muscles, has become prominent in most Western societies (Cafri & Thompson 2004; McCabe & Ricciardelli 2004). For women, the ultra thin ideal pursued as vigorously as male counterparts, is clearly in opposition to the medical ideal of what constitutes a healthy body (Hesse-Biber 1996; Mutrie & Choi 2000; Murnen et al. 2003).

These beliefs appear to be deep seated and lend themselves to negative views of overweight/obese individuals, regardless of age. Both young girls and boys aged between seven and 11 years rate obese children as having fewer friends, being less liked by parents, doing less well at school, being lazier, less happy, and less attractive than average and thinner-sized children (Hill & Silver 1995; Tiggemann & Wilson-Barrett 1998). Shapiro et al. (1997) also found that in a population of children aged between seven and ten years, 45% of the girls and 38% of the boys in their study thought it was important for women to be thin, while 35% of the girls and 33% of the boys felt that it was also important for men to be thin. Other studies (e.g. Cramer & Steinwert 1998) have found that the mantra of 'thin is good, fat is bad' begins at a very young age. Their study found positive stereotypes of slenderness in American children as young as three to five. While it still remains clear that women are more dissatisfied with their bodies than men, this gap is closing.

Ethnicity and race

Overall research suggests that non-White women are less dissatisfied with their bodies than White women (Rucker & Cash 1992; Wildes et al. 2001). There appears to be less disparagement of obesity and greater body esteem among obese Black women compared to obese White women (Harris et al. 1991). In some instances we can also see the impact of country of residence having taken precedence over country of birth (and its associated belief systems). Kenyan Asians tended to perceive thin female shapes more negatively and fat shapes more positively than either British or British-Asian women (Furnham & Alibhai 1983). There also appears to be an interaction between class (social status) and body image suggesting that the body perception of African-American women of lower socioeconomic status (SES) was significantly different from African-American women of higher SES, and White women irrespective of SES (Allan et al. 1993; Abrams & Stormer 2002). Studies indicate that African-American women of lower SES were objectively heavier, viewed themselves as heavier and perceived an attractive body size to be larger. These women appear to find less stigma, if any, attached to obesity and subsequently perceived no pressure to engage in any weight-loss activities. One suggested reason was connected to traditional African-Caribbean cultures in which women with fuller figures are given a higher status. In comparison to White Americans, both adolescent and adult Black American women have been found to report lower levels of body dissatisfaction, less internalisation of the thin ideal, and less interest in pursuing the ideal feminine physique as portrayed in the media (Duke 2000). Samoans are another cultural group that values a larger body size (Pollock 1995) and perceive 'normal weight' to be a larger than that selected by Western groups (Brewis et al. 1998).

In an attempt to explore the body image of Indigenous Australians (a much under-represented group in research in this field), McCabe et al. (2005) found that while Indigenous Australian adolescent girls reported less body dissatisfaction than non-Indigenous girls, both Indigenous adolescent boys and girls engaged in more body change strategies to lose weight and increase muscles than did non-Indigenous adolescents. Ricciardelli et al. (2004) found that both Indigenous and non-Indigenous girls and boys perceived pressure to lose weight from the media and employed strategies to decrease weight. Interestingly, the Indigenous participants reported *more* perceived pressure from the media to lose weight than did the non-Indigenous adolescents. We might argue that one reason for this could be the increased vigilance of Indigenous bodies as 'at risk' of obesity and overweight.

Explanations of body image

Susan Bordo (1993, 2003) provided a useful explanation of the social meaning of the body. Her work examined the ways in which the ideal of 'slenderness' has permeated our belief systems and attached itself to notions of usefulness and acceptability. She noted how the idea of excess flesh somehow equated to a lack of will-power, low morality, and a sign of personal disorder. Slenderness on the other hand represents control; being 'firm' and toned equates to success. Muscles, often linked historically with notions of working-class status now operate as a sign of power and energy. Orbach (2009), while coming from a psychoanalytical perspective also provided many insights into the modern experience of body image disturbance. Orbach noted the marking of our bodies as culturally bound. She provided numerous incidences of the ways in which a person's body can be constructed and reconstructed through this process. She pointed to the ways in which, for instance, 50% of Korean girls had their eyelids Westernised and other women had their vaginas and labia reshaped after giving birth. Other examples include the revirginalising of female bodies, changing of skin colour, Chinese women inserting a 10cm rod in their upper thigh to become taller, and Scandinavian women having legs broken to shorten them (Orbach 2009, pp. 81–82). Orbach explored the modern phenomenon of cosmetic surgery noting how easy it had become to change our bodies; to become 'valuable'. Worldwide cosmetic surgery accounted for US$14 billion in 2007 (Mike Testa as cited by Orbach 2009, p. 85) equating to around 21 million operations. A third of the operations in the US are performed on individuals who have an income of $30,000 or less (2009, p. 87). In Argentina plastic surgery is so common that it is covered by health insurance (Orbach 2009, p. 85). Orbach made the argument that the success of shows such as *Extreme Makeover* in which individuals had their entire bodies reshaped provided an example of 'what you can achieve' and in this instance achievement meant physical reconstruction and personal success. The next question for us to consider is how did we get to this point and is it really just the media's fault?

The role of the media

I have discussed elsewhere (see the earlier chapter on compulsory heterosexuality and the construction of femininity and masculinity) that the way in which the media presents female athletes supports the drive for compulsory heterosexuality. There is a strong interaction between the perceived level of the acceptability of a female athlete's body (tied to issues of functionality and sexuality) and positive or negative interpretations of body image. Men and women are generally portrayed differently by the media, particularly in relation to body weight. Ferguson (1985) found that the media promoted a 'cult of femininity' through which notions of the thin ideal was prominent. More recently Strahan et al. reported that the cult was alive and well, noting, 'images of thin women are ubiquitous in the media' (2006, p. 211). According to Wykes and Gunter's critical work on the media and body image, regardless of the nature of the presentation (here either overt or covert) the media still engage in telling certain type of stories about femininity that are 'insidiously, repetitively and systematically engaged in a very particular construction of femininity that is deeply-body conscious and embedded within a particular gendered narrative' (2005, p. 95). This gendered narrative is endemic, even intruding on what I will go on to explore as the relative 'safety' of sporting activities in which many sports actually support the development of a positive body image. My own work with female rugby players, cricketers and netballers (Russell 2002) found that being body conscious was part of 'being girly'. This process was entirely naturalised within the context of being female and often contradicted their performance role. Rebecca, a rugby player described the inevitability and the 'naturalness' of the concern:

> my shoulders ... they're fairly broad and if you want to go out ... it's a complete girlie thing ... if you want to go out in a dress or whatever I am conscious of making sure that I've got the right shape dress on ... I damaged my shoulder seven years ago and ... my clavicle sticks up so again that's kind of, y'know off putting ... I do have very very broad shoulders that still ... don't tend to fit in with the rest of my body (laugh) ... I don't have sort of legs the size of tree trunks and I'm just like any other female I don't like the shape of my butt but ... what can you do about that (laugh). (Rebecca: Rugby)

Pope et al. (2000) investigated the development of men's body image and suggested that men in the late 20th and early 21st centuries have become as susceptible as women to concerns over body shape and size. Images of men with a V-shaped body, emphasising a lean, highly muscularised body (and in particular the abdominal muscles) have come to dominate magazines. Repeated exposure to such images has resulted in men, as it has for women, in poor body image and dissatisfaction with the self. The question is why does this happen?

Psychologists would argue that one of the strongest contributors to the development of body dissatisfaction is the internalisation of the thin ideal or in the case of men, the lean and muscular ideal. Individuals cognitively buy into socially defined ideals of attractiveness (in this case thin and lean) and this belief is then reflected in engagement in behaviours to achieve this ideal (e.g. dieting and exercising) and is socially reinforced by significant others. This internalisation was an additional predictor of body dissatisfaction in pre-teens (Cusumano & Thompson 2001) and increases in adolescent body dissatisfaction (Stice 2001). Botta (2003) incorporated the social comparison theory to illustrate the relationship between exposure to images and the development of poor body image. The theory postulates that we make sense of ourselves through comparison with others. Either we view media images and have an upward comparison (where we compare ourselves with others whom we idealise and in so doing develop poor body image) or a downward comparison (where we compare with others whom we would not want to be like and in so doing develop positive body image). Ideally we would have a scenario where we would critically view media images and as such they would have no effect; in so doing creating a happy and stable perception of ourselves.

Other research in this area compares the immediate (or direct) and prospective (long-term) effects of media exposure. Research on the direct impact of media exposure has suggested that there is generally a decrease in body satisfaction after viewing media. In particular, young females felt worse after exposure to images of thin women than to other types of images. Those women with a history of body dissatisfaction were more negatively affected than other women (Groetz et al. 2002), a point I will return to in a moment. Cattarin et al. (2000) found that when women were asked to focus on comparing themselves to the thin ideals in the media, body satisfaction dropped. Likewise, Bessenoff (2006) also found that those who were most likely to engage in social comparison were women who had the highest levels of body dissatisfaction. Similar trends have been noted for male populations, although the area has yet to be investigated as fully as for women (see for example Ogden & Mundray 1996). Not all studies, however, reflect what would appear to be the undeniable evidence for the causal link between exposure to the media and decreases in body image satisfaction. Stice et al. (2001) assigned a magazine prescription to teenage girls and found that there were no overall changes in body dissatisfaction or dieting, they noted, however, increases in body dissatisfaction among girls who were dissatisfied at the *outset* of project, who had a high perceived pressure to be thin and who perceived less social support. Stice et al. concluded that media exposure was not a sufficient condition for body dissatisfaction in itself, there had to be a notion of *vulnerability* and the relative importance of social support. This was, as Grogan (2008) concurred, an important distinction and one that was reflected in the few prospective studies undertaken. Tiggemann's (2006) Australian-based study 'demonstrated no causal role for media exposure in the body image of adolescent girls' (Tiggemann as cited in Grogan 2008, p. 112). Grogan highlighted that 'it is impossible to tell whether media exposure produced changes in satisfaction, or whether people who are less satisfied with their bodies gravitate towards particular kinds of media' (2008, p. 112). As Stice and others agreed, it may not have been the mere exposure to media that caused any concern, but the meanings attached to those images that were important, as well as the antecedents of any concerns with body image that interacted with an image.

The role of sport and exercise

Sport has been and still is one area in which self-esteem and positive body image can prosper. Fox (2000) indicated that while self-esteem was not directly related to increases in physical fitness, it was the perception of an improvement in fitness that was associated with positive self-esteem. He suggested that the results appeared stronger for aspects of the physical self and in particular aspects of body image. Fox argued, as I do, that the physical self may have the strongest impact on our overall self-esteem. Fox (1997) argued that having consistency in the self helped to develop unity, uniqueness, independence and control. This provides a framework for the self to organise and make sense of its interactions with life, a reification of the self. He further discussed the difficulty in hiding the physical self, as it is:

> subject to critical changes throughout the life span and therefore needs constant reappraisal. If the physical appearance or physical abilities are not consistent with the inner representations or aspirations of the self, then a sense of dissonance will emerge and act as a potential source of low self-esteem. (Fox 1997, p. 117)

Experimental results in this area show only limited effects of exercise on mood but this may be as a result of the people initially attracted to exercise studies. Such individuals may already be psychologically healthy and hence indicate little improvement in measures used to assess positive mood change (Mutrie & Biddle 1995). Although this may be the case, non-experimental research points to the positive effects of exercise on mood and self-esteem because individuals still perceive the benefits of exercise (Biddle & Mutrie 2001). The results of recent reviews (Ekeland et al. 2005: Spence et al. 2005) suggested that exercise could improve self-esteem, even if that was only moderate. This, according to Ekeland et al., confirmed what Gruger (1986) had suggested some 25 years ago: that directed play and/or physical education programs contributed to the development of self-esteem in elementary school-age children.

In relation to body image, the research is somewhat equivocal. Some researchers have found that female athletes have a more positive body image, healthier eating patterns, and are less likely to become pregnant accidentally than their non-athletic peers (Marten-DiBartolo & Shaffer 2002). Women who exercise have more positive perceptions of their own bodies and have an increased acceptance of their muscular shape (Richards et al. 1990; Furnham et al. 1994; Russell 2004). Yet, other researchers have found that the sport environment creates pressures that can lead to unhealthy practices such as disordered eating, excessive exercising and training through injuries (e.g. Striegel-Moore et al. 1986; Duquin 1994; Taub & Blinde 1994; Johns 1996; Krane et al. 1997; Petrie 1996). Leone et al. (2005) identified muscle dysmorphia as an emerging phenomenon in society. Pressure on males to appear more muscular and lean has prompted a concern in many areas of self-esteem and body image, as it is often likened to anorexia and bulimia nervosa. Athletes are particularly susceptible to developing body image disorders because of the pressures surrounding sport performance and societal trends promoting muscularity and leanness. Grogan et al. (2006) found that while men were less likely than women to take up sport or exercise for appearance reasons, many still wanted to use it as a way to change their looks – and this increased with age. Pope et al. (2000) and Thompson and Cafri (2007) have linked the increase in men's participation in gyms more closely with the drive for muscularity than the reduction of weight (often identified as the key motivator for women's exercise).

Furnham et al. (1994) and Russell (2004) found that that participants in less 'feminine' activities (such as body building or rugby respectively) appear to set less rigid definitions of what is acceptable and desirable in women. I have spoken elsewhere[2] about the ways in which women and men have been marginalised for taking part in activities some would regard as less feminine or masculine, but also about the positive nature of that undertaking (Russell 2007). In 2004 I examined the role of 'functionality' in sportswomen, finding that participants 'exalted the role of physical power and strength in their game [and] ... positively interpreted their bodies as tools for successful performance' (Russell 2004, p. 565). I argued that this functionality reflected what Furnham et al. (1994) had earlier called 'adhering to the norms of a given sport', in which having a large frame and muscular body allowed these women to perform their tasks on the pitch and be viewed as 'useful' and 'valuable' by their teammates and coaches. In this way body image was influenced positively. I also recognised strongly, however, that this functionality was transient. Once a valued sporting body was removed from the field, the body became subject to the restrictions and dictates of society, which interpreted female rugby players' bodies differently – negatively. While sport positively influenced levels of body satisfaction, the elasticity of body image meant that the context had a stronger influence on body image perceptions than mere participation (Russell 2002, 2004).

What we can ascertain from this research are three main points: firstly, sport does provide an avenue for the development of positive self-esteem and body image; secondly, the level of self-esteem and body satisfaction is most often tempered by the level of comparison with significant others in the sporting field; and finally the context in which you find your sporting body reflects notions of value and function.

Conclusions

This chapter has sought to provide an overview of the ways in which body image is developed and mediated by the media and sport. I have shown that body image impacts everyone in one way or another, either positively or negatively. The media as a whole is but one mechanism through which images of acceptable and non-acceptable bodies are

---

2 Interested readers should refer to the chapter on 'Compulsory heterosexuality and the construction of femininity and masculinity: issues of performance versus presentation' (this book) for further details on the ways in which female sportswomen have developed perceptions of acceptable body shape and size.

produced and reproduced. We must recognise that age, gender, ethnicity, sexuality, race and sporting choice can also influence the level of body satisfaction. In this way we come to appreciate the complex nature of body image development for all individuals and the need to be mindful of the ways in which we reproduce our own, often highly gendered ways of viewing sport participation. It is also important to be critical of the media images to which we expose our children and the way in which we view them. We need to understand that not one body is perfect and that not one way of participating in sport or physical activity is predetermined as suitable for young boys or girls. In this way we help to shape critical viewers and participants will be able to engage with a range of experiences with the knowledge that what we see is not always real and what we value may change over time.

References

Abrams, L. & Stormer, C. C. (2002). Sociocultural variations in the body image perceptions of urban adolescent females. *Journal of Youth and Adolescence, 3*: 443–50.

Allan, J., Mayo, K. & Michel, Y. (1993). Body size values of white and black women. *Journal of Consulting & Clinical Psychology, 16*: 323–33.

Allaz, A. F., Bernstein, M., Rouget, P., Archinard, M. & Morabia, A. (1998). Body weight preoccupation in middle-age and ageing women: a general population survey. *International Journal of Eating Disorders, 23*(3): 287–94.

Bessenoff, G. R. (2006). Can the media affect us? Social comparison, self-discrepancy and the thin ideal. *Psychology of Women Quarterly, 30*: 239–51.

Biddle, S. J. H. & Mutrie, N. (2001). *Psychology of physical activity*. London: Routledge.

Bordo, S. (2003). *Unbearable weight: feminism, Western culture and the body (10th anniversary edition)*. Berkeley, CA: University of California Press.

Bordo, S. (1993). *Unbearable weight: feminism, Western culture and the body*. Berkeley, CA: University of California Press.

Botta, R. A. (2003). For your health: the relationship between magazine reading and adolescents' body image and eating disturbances. *Sex Roles, 48*: 389–99.

Brewis, A. A., McGarvey, S. T., Jones, J. & Swinburn, B. A. (1998). Perceptions of body size in Pacific Islanders. *International Journal of Obesity and Related Metabolic Disorders, 22*(2): 185–89.

Cafri, G. & Thompson, J. K. (2004). Measuring male body image: a review of the current methodology. *Psychology of Men and Masculinity, 5*: 18–29.

Cafri, G., Thompson, J. K., Ricciardelli, L., McCabeb, M., Smolakc, L. & Yesalis, C. (2005). Pursuit of the muscular ideal: physical and psychological consequences and putative risk factors. *Clinical Psychology Review, 25*(2): 215–39.

Cash, T. & Henry, P. E. (1995). Women's body images: the results of a national survey in the USA. *Sex Roles, 33*(1–2): 19–28.

Cattarin, J. A., Thompson, J. K., Thomas, C. & Williams, R. (2000). Body image, mood, and televised images of attractiveness: the role of social comparison. *Journal of Social and Clinical Psychology, 19*: 220–39.

Cohane, G. H. & Pope, H. G. (2001). Body image in boys: a review of the literature. *International Journal of Eating Disorders, 29*(4): 373–79.

Cororve-Fingeret, M., Gleaves, D. H. & Pearson, C. C. (2004). On the methodology of body image assessment: the use of figural scales to evaluate body dissatisfaction and the ideal body standards of women. *Body Image: An International Journal of Research, 1*: 207–12.

Cramer, P. & Steinwert, T. (1998). Thin is good, fat is bad: how early does it begin? *Journal of Applied Developmental Psychology, 19*: 429–51.

Cusumano, D. L. & Thompson, J. K. (2001). Media influence and body image in 8–11 year old boys and girls: a preliminary report on the Multidimensional Media Influence Scale. *International Journal of Eating Disorders, 29*:37–44.

Davis, C. & Cowles, M. (1991). Body image and exercise: a study of the relationships and comparisons between physically active men and women. *Sex Roles, 25*: 33–44.

Dionne, M., Davis, C., Fox, J. & Gurevich, M. (1995). Feminist ideology as a predictor of body dissatisfaction in women. *Sex Roles, 33*(3–4): 277–88.

Duke, L. (2000). Black in a blonde world: race and girls' interpretations of the feminine ideal in teen magazines. *Journalism and Mass Communication Quarterly, 77*: 367–92.

Duquin, M. E. (1994). The body snatchers and Dr Frankenstein revisited: social construction and deconstruction of bodies and sport. *Journal of Sport and Social Issues, 18*: 268–81.

Ekeland, E., Heian, F. & Hagen, K. B. (2005). Can exercise improve self esteem in children and young people? A systematic review of randomised controlled trials. *British journal of Sports Medicine, 39*: 792–98.

Ferguson, M. (1985). *Forever feminine: women's magazines and the cult of femininity*. Aldershot, UK: Gower.

Fox, K. R. (1997). The physical self and processes in self-esteem development. In K. R. Fox (Ed.). *The physical self: from motivation to well being* (pp. 111–39). Champaign, IL: Human Kinetics.

Fox, K. R. (2000). The effects of exercise on self-perceptions and self-esteem. In S. J. H., Biddle, K. R. Fox & S. H. Boutcher (Eds). *Physical activity and psychological well-being* (pp. 88–117). London: Routledge.

Furnham, A. & Alibhai, N. (1983). Cross cultural differences in the perception of male and female body shapes. *Psychological Medicine, 13*: 829–37.

Furnham, A., Titman, P. & Sleeman, E. (1994). Perception of female body shapes as a function of exercise. *Journal of Social Behaviour and Personality, 9*(2): 332–52.

Gardner, R. M., Sorter, R. G. & Friedman, B. N. (1997). Developmental changes in children's body images. *Journal of Social Behavior and Personality, 12*: 1019–36.

Grigg, M., Bowman, J. & Redman, S. (1996). Disordered eating and unhealthy weight reduction practices among adolescent females. *Preventative Medicine, 25*: 748–56.

Groetz, L. M., Levine, M. P. & Murnen, S. K. (2002). The effect of experimental presentation of thin media images on body satisfaction: a meta-analytic review. *International Journal of Eating Disorders, 31*: 1–16.

Grogan, S. (2008). *Body image: understanding body dissatisfaction in men, women and children* (2nd ed.). London: Routledge.

Grogan, S., Shepherd, S., Evans, R., Wright, S. & Hunter, G. (2006). Experiences of anabolic steroid use: in-depth interviews with men and women body builders. *Journal of Health Psychology, 11*: 845–56.

Harris, M. B., Walters, L. C. & Waschull, S. (1991). Gender and ethnic differences in obesity-related behaviours and attitudes in a college sample. *Journal of Applied Social Psychology, 21*: 1545–66.

Hesse-Biber, S. J. (1996). *Am I thin enough yet? The cult of thinness and the commercialization of identity.* New York: Oxford University Press.

Hill, A. J. & Silver, E. K. (1995). Fat, friendless and unhealthy: 9-year-old children's perception of body shape and stereotypes. *International Journal of Obesity, 19*: 423–30.

Houn, G, Morris, S. & Brown, L. (1990). Differences between male and female preferences for female body size. *Australian Psychologist, 25*: 314–17.

Johns, D. (1996). Fasting and feasting: paradoxes of the sport ethic. *Sociology of Sport Journal, 15*: 41–63.

Krane, V., Greenleaf, C. & Snow, J. (1997). Reaching for gold and the price of glory: a motivational case study of a former elite gymnast. *The Sport Psychologist, 11*: 53–71.

Leone, J. E., Sedory, E. J. & Gray, K. A. (2005). Recognition and treatment of muscle dysmorphia and related body image disorders. *Journal of Athletic Training, 40*(4): 352–59.

Marten-DiBartolo, P. & Shaffer, C. (2002). A comparison of female college athletes and nonathletes: eating disorder symptomatology and psychological well-being. *Journal of Sport and Exercise Psychology, 24*: 33–41.

McCabe, M. P. & Ricciardelli, L. A. (2004). Weight and shape concerns of boys and men. In J. K. Thompson (Ed.). *Handbook of eating disorders and obesity* (pp. 606–36). Englewood Cliffs, NJ: Wiley.

McCabe, M. P., Ricciardelli, L. A., Mellor, D. & Ball, K. (2005). Media influences on body image and disordered eating among Indigenous adolescent Australians. *Adolescence, 40*(157): 115–27.

Mishkind, M. E., Rodin, J., Silberstein, L. R. & Striegel-Moore, R. H. (1986). The embodiment of masculinity. *American Behavioral Scientist, 29*: 545–62.

Murnen, S. L., Smolak, L., Mills, J. A. & Good, L. (2003). Thin, sexy women and strong, muscular men: grade-school children's responses to objectified images of women and men. *Sex Roles, 49*: 427–37.

Mutrie, N. & Biddle, S. J. H. (1995). The effects of exercise on mental health in nonclinical populations. In S. J. H. Biddle (Ed.). *European perspectives on exercise and sport psychology* (pp. 50–70). Champaign, IL: Human Kinetics.

Mutrie, N. & Choi, P. Y. L. (2000). Is 'fit' a feminist issue: dilemmas for exercise psychology. *Feminism and Psychology, 10*: 544–51.

Ogden, J. & Mundray, K. (1996). The effect of the media on body satisfaction: the role of gender and size. *European Eating Disorders Review, 4*: 171–82.

Orbach, S. (2009). *Bodies*. London: Profile Books.

Petrie, T. A. (1996). Differences between male and female college lean sport athletes, nonlean sport athletes, and nonathletes on behavioural and psychological indices of eating disorders. *Journal of Applied Sport Psychology, 8*(2): 218–30.

Pollock, N. (1995). Cultural elaborations of obesity-fattening practices in Pacific societies. *Asian Pacific Journal of Clinical Nutrition*, 4:357–60.

Pope, H. G., Phillips, K. A. & Olivardia, R. (2000). *The Adonis complex: the secret crisis of male body obsession*. New York: Free Press.

Ricciardelli, L. A., McCabe, M. P., Ball, K. & Mellor, D. (2004). Sociocultural influences on body image concerns and body change strategies among Indigenous and non-Indigenous Australian adolescent girls and boys. *Sex Roles, 51*(11–12): 731–41.

Richards, M., Peterson, A., Boxer, A. & Albrecht, S. (1990). Relation of weight to body image in pubertal girls and boys from two communities. *Developmental Psychology, 26*(2): 313–21.

Rucker, C. E. & Cash, T. F. (1992). Body images, body-size perceptions, and eating behaviors among African-American and White college women. *International Journal of Eating Disorders, 12*: 291–300.

Russell, K. M. (2002). Women's participation motivation in rugby, cricket and netball: body satisfaction and identity. Unpublished PhD thesis, Coventry University.

Russell, K. M. (2004). On vs off the pitch: the transiency of body satisfaction among female rugby players, cricketers, and netballers. *Sex Roles, 51*: 561–74.

Russell, K. M. (2007). Queers, even in netball? Positive and negative interpretations of the lesbian label among sportswomen. In C. C. Aitchison (Ed.) *Sport and gender identities: masculinities, femininities and sexualities*, (pp. 106–21). London: Routledge.

Shapiro, S., Newcomb, M. & Loeb, T. B. (1997). Fear of fat, disregulated-restrained eating, and bodyesteem: prevalence and gender differences among eight- to ten-year old children. *Journal of Clinical Child Psychology, 26*: 358–65.

Silberstein, L. R., Striegel-Moore, R. H., Timko, C. & Rodin, J. (1988). Behavioural and psychological implications of body dissatisfaction: do men and women differ? *Sex Roles, 19*: 219–32.

Spence, J. C. McGannon, K. R. & Poon, P. (2005). The effect of exercise on global self-esteem: a quantitative review. *Journal of Sport & Exercise Psychology, 27*: 311–34.

Stice, E., Spangler, D. & Agras, W. S. (2001). Exposure to media-portrayed thin-ideal images adversely affects vulnerable girls: a longitudinal experiment. *Journal of Social and Clinical Psychology, 20*(3): 270–88

Strahan, E. J., Wilson, A. E., Cressman, K. E. & Buote, V. M. (2006). Comparing to perfection: how cultural norms of appearance affect social comparison and self-image. *Body Image: An International Journal of Research, 3*: 211–28.

Striegel-Moore, R. H., Silberstein, L. R. & Rodin, J. (1986). Toward an understanding of risk factors for bulimia. *American Psychologist, 41*(3): 246–63.

Taub, D. E. & Blinde, E. M. (1994). Disordered eating and weight control among adolescent female athletes and performance squad members. *Journal of Adolescent Research, 9*(4): 483–97.

Thompson, J. K. & Cafri, G. (Eds) (2007). *The muscular ideal: psychological, social, and medical perspectives*. Washington DC: American Psychological Association.

Thompson, J. K., Heinberg, L., Altabe, M. & Tantleff-Dunn, S. (1999). *Exacting beauty: theory, assessment and treatment of body image disturbance*. Washington DC: American Psychological Association.

Tiggemann, M. & Wilson-Barrett, E. (1998). Children's figure ratings: relationship to self-esteem and negative stereotyping. *International Journal of Eating Disorders,* 23: 83–88.

Webster, J. & Tiggemann, M. (2003). The relationship between women's body satisfaction and self-image across the life span: the role of cognitive control. *The Journal of Genetic Psychology, 164*(2): 241–52.

Wildes, J. E., Emery, R. & Simons, A. D. (2001). The roles of ethnicity and culture in the development of eating disturbance and body dissatisfaction: a meta analytic review. *Clinical Psychology Review, 21*(4): 521–51.

Williamson, S. & Delin, C. (2001). Young children's figural selections: accuracy of reporting and body size dissatisfaction. *International Journal of Eating Disorders, 29*(1): 80–84.

Wykes, M. & Gunter, B. (2005). *The media and body image*. Los Angeles: Sage.

17

Celebrity, popular culture and sport

Bob Petersen

Celebrity is a species of fame. It has to do with time, with being famous and recognisable at the present moment. Julius Caesar and Alexander the Great have been famous for over 2000 years. They were celebrities in their day, and people went out to see them. It is unusual to speak of a dead celebrity; such people are said to be famous. If we want to see ancient celebrity, there is no better example than the victorious Olympic athlete, with his statue at Olympia itself and another in his hometown, with free meals for life and many other perks. We may doubt that many of today's celebrities will be famous 60 or 400 years from now, let alone 2000. But we have by now learned not to underestimate Madonna.

The ancient Greeks agreed that the bodies of professional athletes could not be beautiful, any more than could the bodies of tradesmen. Greek popular culture denied them beauty because they were not harmoniously developed. In his book Benjamin Lowe (1977) disagrees with this contention. The working class ploughed and hammered and shaped pots, while professional athletes ran or threw javelins or wrestled, so that in all cases one set of muscles was cultivated to the detriment of other muscles and the harmony of every part of the body in relation to all the other parts was lost. The Spartans refused to specialise and so regularly lost to professionals from other cities. The only Greeks considered beautiful were amateur sportsmen who had nothing better to do than to look harmonious. These were the Greeks who modelled the statues that are still called beautiful after thousands of years. Consequently they were the rich and privileged leisure class, living on slave labour. The people today closest to the ancient beautiful athletes are probably the bodybuilders who inhabit the gym, take their steroids, work on each muscle, and check out their 'pecs' and their 'lats' in the mirror – even if, all too often, the quest for mass leads bodybuilders to lose harmony and topple over into the grotesque. They do not use their bodies for anything. But modern bodybuilders are people too, with enough leisure and money to pursue their ambition.

All other modern athletes use their bodies to perform physical acts and therefore the modern Olympians resemble the ancient Olympians, wonderful achievers, champions, but physically no more harmoniously developed than a butcher or a waitress and so lacking beauty by classical standards. This can be studied on those naughty-sporty calendars issued around New Year, part of our popular culture. While *Les dieux du stade* is a well-known nude French calendar, according to David Coad (2008) the vogue began in Australia in

1993 with the 'men for all seasons' calendar of AFL players. But even earlier in 1989 in Adelaide, the South Australian Fire Brigades calendar featured husky firemen in various stages of undress. It was afterwards, with titles like Men of League and Nubile Netballers and Rugger-Buddies and even Gods of Sport, that the calendars went sporting and all nude; only a handy cricket bat retained, or some discreetly placed club colours. Professional photographers, with their posing and lighting perfected on models, create these calendars. These reveal, when used on athletes, a failure to reach the perfection of body that beauty requires. Those cyclists' legs, the thick necks, those swimmers' shoulders, the stringy thighs, will never cut it on the catwalk. To get photographed for a major fashion house, that famous soccer torso, efficient but not photogenic, will have to be covered up with tattoos. Later you can sell fridge magnets of it to gay men, as their maker proposes – or to tattoo freaks. But the idea of the beautiful body for athletes has to be given up, as the Greeks long ago decided. Anyway, everyone can have their own bare-chested calendar: New South Wales and Queensland have firefighter calendars, but with semi-clothed firies like Adelaide's; and these raise money for charity and for the biennial World Firefighters Games, held in Seoul in 2010 and in Sydney in 2012.

Generally we do not look in admiration towards athletes' physiques so much as to their sporting attainments. Almost no athlete becomes famous instantaneously without lead-up achievements, and most of those involve competition. One does not become a success because one looks the part or is seen on red carpets with the people who matter. It is possible, though very rare, to win international fame with a single act. Susan Boyle appeared unknown on *Britain's got talent* on 14 April 2009 and one can see celebrity being created on You-Tube. She had five million views in the first day. She was a world celebrity literally overnight. She had 50 million viewers in the first year. And it can happen to a sportsperson. When a young woman who had sailed alone around the world, east to west, put into Sydney Harbour she was welcomed by the Premier of New South Wales and the Prime Minister of Australia jointly. When she reached Brisbane, her home city, she enjoyed a civic reception with the Premier of Queensland. Once she had written and signed her autobiography called *True spirit* and put out with Sony's help a CD entitled 'Songs from the Pink Lady', comprising music played to herself while off Patagonia and in the Sargasso Sea but not sung by herself, Jessica Watson's future thereafter appeared uncertain, until she was appointed the Sailing Ambassador for tourist events in Queensland. As a sportsperson there was not much more she could do except sail round the world again west to east.

The first performers to be called stars were some pugilists of the 1820s. The term which started 200 years ago in boxing circles moved to stars of the stage by 1850 and is now most commonly used for famous movie actors, though there are other realms where the term is used, like pop star, literary star, and now, fashionably enough, back to sports star. In all cases however there is an idea of performance and achievement before an audience of some kind. There is a whole literature on film stars and the star system, most of it following Richard Dyer's lead (1998). There are a few books on sports stars.

'Star' is still used, of course, but the term 'celebrity' has become very common over the last 20 years, and there is a growing consensus that a lot of the celebrities do not do anything beyond 'being' themselves. They have no achievements. Boorstin (1992) said in 1961 that 'the celebrity is a person who is known for his well-knownness'. One website says it offers 'juicy' celebrity gossip, and that 'our site features thousands of the hottest male celebrities today'. (www.hunkymalestars.com). One must wonder how many male celebrities are merely known as hot; and how many female celebrities more or less hot there can possibly be. We seem to be heading for a surfeit of celebrities. On the web in June 2010 there were 1,500,000 sites dealing with 'Sports stars and legends' and 2,350,000 sites for 'Sports stars tomorrow'. Faced with huge populations in China, India, and South America now getting into sports, the Australian Sports Commission is mounting, we are told, a 'National Talent Identification Program' to unearth our next batch of celebrity athletes; and yet we beat them all at New Delhi.

All celebrity ends, all stars fade; but sports stars fade earlier than others because their achievements are premised on youth. Lawn bowls was perhaps the only sport where old people could star, but then youngsters of 35 and 40 moved in and cleaned up the prizes and now many bowling greens have been recycled for barefoot karma-bowling or are pushing up dandelions until the developers arrive. Other sports have no use for their players much after 35. Like fashion models they are retired early. Film stars may go on into their 90s making movies, but after a sports career you can only turn round to the management side, become a coach or referee, host a talk show, promote your own label of ugly underwear, or spruik goods on television until the day comes when people ask who that old guy in the project-home ads is supposed to be.

Sporting celebrities do not flourish for long, because athletes are almost all young people. But it is true generally of celebrities that they have a brief shelf-life. Woody Allen's *Celebrity*, filmed in 1998, was filled up with famous New York City residents who are now mostly off the scene; even Elaine's has turned into a tourist trap. The same with Ben Stiller's *Zoolander* from 2000, with all its fashion models. Rojak (2001) invented the term 'celetoid' for people who might last less than Andy Warhol's 15 minutes, people like the young women who fill the gossip columns from San Francisco to Shanghai to Barcelona – crazy lost young women like Lindsay Lowlife and Istanbul Hilton and Lady Agog who are talked about everywhere in the world these days. Their clothes, their men, their babies (some adopted in the Amazon), their breakdowns, their flirting with what we have learned to call 'a toxic mix of prescription drugs', their failed suicides – every day these provide the gossip of millions. Julie Wilson (2010) thinks these unfortunate celebrities are of interest primarily to other young women as exemplars of what they should not become.

It can be asked, just how influential gossip magazines are in shaping the behaviour of young women. The gossip may interest readers, but do the readers then go out and behave like the celebrity or contrary to the celebrity? Are celebrities models for ordinary people, or anti-models? There is some evidence, suggested by Jackie Stacey (1994) that female film stars influence the fashions of their fans, that the fans do their hair like their idol and buy clothes and perfumes that their idol recommends. But fans cannot follow the examples provided by a dozen stars all at once.

It is the same with young men, though the evidence is less compelling: they may copy a famous surfer, buying his sort of board shorts, close cropping their hair or sculpting it as he does. They can splash on some 'Intimately Beckham' brand of eau de toilette. 'Ideals of masculinity may include physical appearance', says Stacey:

> but this is typically only one amongst many options. Moreover it is not usually the most important one; success at work (be it technical, financial, intellectual, organisational or physical) and in leisure (be it sport, other hobbies, drinking or sex) tends to take priority. Ideals of femininity, on the other hand, conventionally include a central emphasis on physical appearance and sexual attractiveness to men. (1994, p. 216)

It is hard to say where Stacey places female CEOs and sportswomen. Stacey's contention is that 'femininity may thus be characterised as the constant reproduction of self as object for consumption for others, which is achieved through consumption of other objects' (1994, p. 225). We can see that the two decades since Stacey's work have brought some change to masculinity. This now involves some emphasis on physical appearance and sexual attractiveness to women – as witnessed by the toy-boys and the designer stubble and botox, though how long these will be fashionable is questionable. The firm of Sheridan, however, introduced Towel Man, with 'his brooding good looks' for anyone who looks at them, his precursor remembered as Sheridan's 1980s iconic Sheet Man who created a sensation on billboards 30 years ago. The 'Solo Man' was his contemporary, and he was also displayed on videos and sung about. And in effect, Kevin White (1993) described metrosexuals in 1920s America. The whole metrosexual phenomenon was hailed as bringing in a new era, but except in Tag Heuer land it has a weak hold on men.

In more general behavioural areas, outside of buying things like the celebrity has, nobody has definitely shown that a sporting celebrity's actions will be copied by those who read about him or her, or watch them play on television or live. It is so far down from the podium to the pavement. An athlete who signs their autograph books may be appreciated by the youngsters who surge around him, but it has not been shown that they become generous to charities or are nicer to their little sister because of the autograph. Nor has it been shown that some athlete's trashing of a hotel room has corrupted youngsters when or if ever they heard of it. The athletes who are featured on the sides of cereal boxes are more exposed to observers than any others. At countless breakfast tables their bodies and their cheery messages are viewed by countless youngsters – but who remembers them at lunchtime?

The managers of sports, that is the older people who have power over the younger sports people, like to say that their sport must be kept respectable, on and off the field, otherwise people will be corrupted. The temptation to use drugs, especially new or undetectable, is great. Parisotto (2006, p. 5) wrote of erythropoietin that 'performance-enhancing drugs like EPO were surely beneficial given the super media exposure and super money that surrounds super-human performances', meaning that a lot of people in the sporting world are far more interested in breaking records than in the longevity of the record-breakers. And the fans! Who would be satisfied if nobody could in future exceed the limits of human achievement? They could not be satisfied, it appears, merely by watching beautiful or technically perfect performances.

John Eales' compilation of 2006, *Learning from legends,* was prefaced by John Howard, Prime Minister of Australia and cricket celebrity, and is a monument to the traditional view. Howard says that:

> undoubtedly our elite sportsmen and women are leaders and role models. Their inspiration to young people is an important element of who they are and what they represent. They are living examples of the rewards that come from taking on personal responsibility, working together and having a go. (2006, p. 116)

Eales for his part agrees, saying 'in Australia a child is more likely to be influenced by Grant Hackett than the Prime Minister' (Eales 2006, p. 4). Each of the 41 athletes profiled in this book provides Eales with a dozen 'laws of leadership', which taken together constitute a gospel of impeccable advice. Sports people not only *do* act as moral examples, we are told, but *must* act as moral examples to the mass of the population, especially, of course, the young. We have the Stacey (1994) evidence of female film stars influencing young women, we do not have evidence about male film stars influencing young men; we do not have evidence about sports persons male and female influencing their fans of any gender persuasion. Chapter 10 on 'Sports fans and their heroes' in Wann (2001) reports that youngsters admire sportspeople, but reports little research on discernible practical outcomes. Parisotto (2006) asks: 'why do we scold an athlete who may have taken an upper legitimately yet often expect screen and stage performers to take them so that they can keep entertaining us? Ultimately what is the difference between the two?' Sometimes the necessity of being a moral exemplar is reinforced by saying piously that athletes have been given so much that they must give a lot in return. It is not entirely clear what this means.

The media ensures that the fans are fed gossip about their idols. Their images are easily found, performing their athletic feats, being crowned with wreaths, squirting magnums of champagne, waving from floats in back-home parades, but these images are always from a distance. Interviews on media are the crucial link between stars and their public. In the interview the stars tell the reporter or the talk-show host things that are consumed by their fans. It is a confession: 'yes I used to bite my nails as a little girl and I do not like avocadoes'; confessions which are added by the fans to their collection of information about the star. These are things one would only tell to one's friends. In fact one's friends would not be interested in such trivia, but here is the celebrity telling the whole world and amazingly the whole world is engrossed by such harmless information. This swimming celebrity was covering her mouth with her hand. Why? But why? It seems she had a cold sore. So now we know. This sportsman likes driving in the country, this one plays chess, this one has a lucky holey dollar, and so on. Such details humanise the star. Interviews create intimacy with each fan. A false intimacy, it is true, because it is all one way – the star does not learn a thing about the fan's preferences in salad.

Consider the barber shop. All men go to one unless they have dreadlocks or bought themselves clippers. The barber shop is a masculine space and has been for the past 200 years. Few women enter a barber shop. The barber shop has seen nothing like the invasion of women into hotel space, after a century of being confined to poky Ladies' Lounges: it may be the last entirely men's space. (Is there a drift by younger men to women's hairdressing salons?) The barber shop always had two or three calendars on the wall: advertising car batteries, advertising beer, and in the country advertising sheep-dip. Some calendars might show a curvaceous cutie but more likely a truck. It always had today's newspapers to read while waiting, more likely the tabloids than the papers of record, and men's magazines. *Gourmet Traveller* never graced those tables. The barber shop talk was about racing, gambling, other sports, politics, money. It went on between barber and customer, and between waiting customers, especially in a neighborhood barber shop. It was a site for gossip, the gossip of popular culture that gets swirled up to the heights of world gossip about avocadoes and cold sores.

But what is all this gossip? It is the culture of lost people looking for a culture, the culture of people who do not know even what they want to be. It is on the one hand that individuals are dreaming of being rescued from insignificance; on the other that here is somebody we can all talk about. Of course almost all these celetoids are American. But whatever else they may do they also provide the gossip of a universal culture, where all local traditions are breaking down and being forgotten, somebody in common for more than 500 million people actively logged-in to Facebook to discuss. In July 2010 the Twitter rumour mill went into overdrive on football player gossip. Experts warned that the internet was out of control after rumours about the alleged sexual life of a celebrity footballer circulated around the globe within a day. But 'sources close to the footballer' dismissed the rumours as fiction, again within hours. Boredom is impossible in this celebrity culture. Every year there is a Brownlow medallist, just as every year somebody wins the Stawell Gift. But which of these is remembered for more than a year or two, except by specialists? The line of Brownlow medallists stretches way off into the past, and all their celebrity is finished.

Folklore has vanished from the world. If you go on a cruise you will see local performers on the wharf below entertaining you with traditional dances and warrior exercises; it appears to be the case that such performances have died out on the islands and are nowadays for tourists. In fact we have to thank mass tourism with its scattered coins for preserving an idea of what culture used to be. What we have today is popular culture, created by the managers for the masses and only with difficulty and occasionally taken over and subverted by the masses to their own purposes. It spreads as inexorably as McDonalds, with movies released everywhere at once, with complete DVD sets of *I love Lucy* on sale in Buenos Aires, with consoles in Albania playing super-hero games. Who can resist, even protest? Authorities now erase graffiti overnight, so if the words of the prophets are written on the subway walls, as was once said, they can be read only for a few hours. The words of the profits are not erased. The internet has been hailed as the place where a genuine people's culture – interactive, organic, all the good terms – can flourish. But we know that the presidents of the United States now have the power to close the internet down.

Increasingly the matter of celebrity interests even academics, so that even the film-history journal *Velvet Light Trap* devoted its issue number 65 (spring 2010) to the subject, and to debates about what phenomena may properly be called celebrity. A lot of argument more or less vicious goes on about the difference between fame and celebrity. This would appear to be a false issue: nobody seems to know if there is a difference, though while famous people are found in all periods in history, all celebrities are still alive. But there are 'importance' and 'fame' and 'celebrity'. There are some people, like Bill Gates, who are not celebrities, though Gates has more money than Switzerland and his name is known worldwide. But do teenagers scream when he goes for a walk, even in Seattle? Do they mob his gorillas? And many very powerful people (bankers, for example) are neither celebrities nor famous, indeed they probably do their work best out of the light and unknown. At airports they frequent what are or were called VIP lounges, away from the mobs. To be a celebrity, you have to be recognised, recognisable. People have to know who you are when they see you in the street. This will involve cameras and the internet. Celebrity is unimaginable without the media.

International celebrity is what is best known. Everybody has heard of you or recognises you. Athletes who are international celebrities are few. World celebrity is not possible if you are a baseball player or a cricket player, and even for soccer players it is doubtful. American sports will not make you a celebrity outside of the US, just as international fame is enjoyed by no AFL player. The safest sports for world celebrity are golf, ice-skating, tennis, cycling, car racing and swimming; but it does help to be American, even in those. David Beckham has made the most notable effort as a non-American athlete to achieve international celebrity, even making the sacrifice of shifting to Los Angeles. Certainly he has appeared in two-metre posters on the wall of a *souk* in Marrakech; and in 2003 there was amazing excitement when he appeared in Hong Kong – though not in the flesh, rather in effigy at Madame Tussaud's. He advertises himself, and his wife advertises him. But has he made himself as universally well known as are the Americans Lance Armstrong and Tiger Woods? Coad (2002) is good on the links of athletes with advertising, and has sections on Ian Roberts, Pat Rafter, and Ian Thorpe. There are, around the world, athletes who are raising themselves by raising their sport. The World Ultimate Frisbee Championships were held in Florence and are held every four years like the Olympic and Commonwealth Games. Australia won the under-23 gold medal. Higher up are the World Frisbee Games, and the athletes hope eventually to have frisbee become an Olympic sport just as synchronised swimming did. But is frisbee a sport or a game? Is darts a sport? Is golf? Is ribbon-twirling?

For anyone who cannot make international celebrity, they can become famous in their own country. This has to be the case playing grid-iron in the United States or ice hockey in Canada. One can become famous across the nation like a talk-show host, but over the border nobody will want an autograph or no teenagers will start screaming. This was why *Field of dreams* (1989) failed. Even though it starred Kevin Costner, wildly popular at the time, most of the world watched it without sympathy because they did not know the baseball players nostalgically celebrated in the film. Babe Ruth we had heard of, but who were these guys? Apparently, and sadly, thousands of Americans every year still go to the place where *Field of dreams* was filmed. But technology can leap frontiers with a single bound! Major League Baseball is now being beamed down to pubs and clubs in Australia, and it may well be that the pitcher of the St Louis Cardinals will become a celebrity in Tasmania. How many Queenslanders can name the Brownlow medallists of the past three years?

Perhaps the nation's frontiers are not where you are headed but rather toward being famous among one group of people, reaching what is called 'sectional celebrity', among one characteristic segment of the population. Sectional celebrity is exemplified by success in the annual Caledonian or Highland games, where your success in tossing the caber will bring you notice from Scots at home and indeed around the world. Or your success in the Maccabean games will see you featured in the Jewish newspapers. For this kind of celebrity it is not in one place that you are famous, but among one sort of fans, religious or political or ethnic. Outside that distinct and scattered public you may well remain unknown. And some athletes stay quite content to be the best table-tennis player in Australia's Korean community until they are invited to the triennial games in Seoul – but still, perhaps, their celebrity would remain sectional.

The last kind of celebrity is topical, extending across one locality. The Gordon Junior Rugby Team in Sydney grows out of district clubs: Chatwood, Hornsby, Hunters Hill, Lane Cove, Lindfield, Roseville, St Ives, Wahroonga, and Killara/West Pymble, nine of them each fostering talent, each a venue. Many hotels find it pays to sponsor sports, either played in the hotel itself (like darts) or in the suburb round about, one perhaps as a district club. This is the most important level if our intention is to abolish couch potatoes by educating the grassroots to play sports.

In seaside towns around Australia in the ten years between World War II and the Melbourne Olympic Games with the introduction of television, the same young men were footballers in winter and lifesavers in summer. Everybody knew them by sight and to talk to. They continued their two sporting activities, season in and season out, until they married or moved away out of the circle. Cricket was not their game, and they would diversify their leisure only so far as to roar round town on Triumphs. Otherwise they had a beer at the pub where Catholics and Protestants mingled. Though in fact most were labourers or mechanics, their culture was that of a small elite group. It was hard to break into the circle because they had all grown up together and they all knew when the next joke was coming. Once or twice a week they could go to the pictures and meet girls, while once a month, it might be, there was a fifty-fifty dance at the local hall with a band playing the Pride of Erin and barn dances, and quick-steps and the occasional jazz waltz. People volunteered songs: 'Alice blue gown', 'Lover come back to me' in the style of Jack O'Hagan, and a grandiose 'Granada'. There might be a recitation: somebody would recite with elocutionist's art 'The green eye of the Little Yellow God'. The lifesavers-cum-footballers did not dance much; they hung out near the door where it was easier to smoke, and they were only ever cajoled into learning to waltz because of the town's weddings. Once a year, however, at the Christmas dance, they dressed up as women, big boofy women with bandanas and hints of Carmen Miranda, and performed a gross burlesque of their suppressed feminine side. These young men had a good life, everybody in town wished them well, they dreamed of rescuing their ideal girl, they feared only 'getting a girl into trouble' and the collapse of a sand bar. They were the town's heroes, and this is the lowest level on the ladder of celebrity, or maybe it is better to call it the fundamental level. We still do not pay our lifeguards, we do not pay our blood donors. If there is anything like folklore surviving, it will be found at this level.

A number of major libraries in Australia, however, battling with enormous banks of documents, have decided that the only sporting records they will store are those connected with prominent sportspeople and famous teams. This means that the record of Torrensville vigoro and the account books of the Brisbane Baptist Boys' Club will not be available for study, at least not in public collections; maybe in Halls of Fame (entrance fees). It appears that the libraries, obliged to choose, have chosen excellence: sport stars, celebrated teams. It seems that Aussie, Aussie, Aussie bronze does not matter, let alone Aussie lead. Only gold. Little battlers do not matter and their records will be lost.

Does anybody care?

References

Boorstin, D.J. (1992). *The image: a guide to pseudo-events in America.* New York: Vintage Books.

Coad, D. (2008). *The metrosexual: gender, sexuality, and sport.* Albany NY: State University of New York Press.

Coad, D. (2002). *Gender trouble Down Under: Australian masculinities.* Paris: Presses Universitaires de Valenciennes.

Dyer, R. & McDonald, P. (1998). *Stars.* London: BFI Publishing.

Eales, J. (2006). *Learning from legends.* Sydney: Fairfax Books.

Lowe, B. (1977). *The beauty of sport: a cross-disciplinary inquiry.* New Jersey: Prentice-Hall.

Luckett, M. (2010). Toxic: the implosion of Britney Spears's star image. *Velvet Light Trap, 65*(Spring 2010): 39–41.

Miller, T. (2001). *Sportsex.* Philadelphia: Temple University Press.

Parisotto, R. (2006). *Blood sports: the inside dope on drugs in sport.* Melbourne: Hardie Grant.

Rojek, C. (2001). *Celebrity.* London: Reaktion.

Stacey, J. (1994). *Star gazing: Hollywood cinema and female spectatorship.* London: Routledge.

Wann, D.L., et al. (2001). *Sport fans: the psychology and social impact of spectators.* New York: Routledge.

White, K. (1993). *The first sexual revolution: the emergence of male heterosexuality in modern America.* New York: New York University Press.

Wilson, J.A. (2010). Star testing: the emerging politics of celebrity gossip. *Velvet Light Trap, 65*(Spring 2010): 25–38.

18
Research methodology for youth sport

Rachel Wilson

Over the last two decades, there have been important insights into the nature of youth sport and the vital role it plays in promoting healthy development and personal wellbeing. Yet there has been little reflection on the part played by methodology in examining whether or not this area has been effectively researched. This is surprising since the nature of research methodology determines research validity and how quickly research progress can be made. Indeed, although there has been a rapid expansion of research in sport, there are few texts or journal articles which deal with research methodology in this area (Gratton & Jones 2004; Biddle et al. 2001). This chapter provides a brief introduction to the methodological possibilities in youth sport research. It also provides a critical perspective of different methodologies and how they have been applied in this field over the last three decades.

Much of this critique focuses on the lack of mixed methods approaches in youth sport. Youth sport research requires insight into both the physical and social aspects involved and there are clear benefits to mixing qualitative and quantitative approaches. The conventional methodology in physical research has been built upon positivist perspectives and quantitative measurement. This approach is exemplified in texts such as Thomas and Nelson (2005), and the dominance of quantitative studies is well established (Williams & Kendall 2007). In researching social aspects, however, qualitative and interpretivist approaches have much to contribute. Qualitative studies are less common and supported by specialist texts (Andrews et al. 2005; Hopper et al. 2008). Despite the convergence of physical and social worlds in youth sport studies, there are few studies combining both approaches.

The broad mixed methods approach to research is still in its adolescence (Leech 2009) and the field of sport studies which includes youth sport, provides a potential area for development. Rudd (2008) and Rauscher and Greenfield (2009) are among the first to recognise this potential and make well-reasoned arguments for a greater use of mixed methods. In a rare analysis of methodology in this field Rudd (2008) reports that in three prominent sport management journals only 2% of articles employed a mixed methods approach, while 55% were quantitative, 9% qualitative and the remaining 34% were conceptual.

It is now more than 20 years since social science methodology commentators highlighted the 'false dichotomy' of the quantitative and qualitative research divide (Lawrence 1993).

In many fields researchers have shifted from solely quantitative or qualitative studies. In recently published sports science methods texts, however, this divide is still presented as an acceptable, indeed logical, demarcation of how research is done. Texts typically devote substantial content to explaining the separateness and incompatibility of the two approaches despite arguments for strengthening validity and building diverse perspectives in research. In youth sport the importance of addressing both the physical and the social requires these diverse perspectives. Methodology scholars such as Tashakkori and Teddlie (2003) and Johnson and Onwuegbuzie (2004) argue that using a mixed method is superior to a single method research because it can answer research questions that cannot be answered by using the qualitative or the quantitative paradigm alone. The different perspectives provided in mixed method research by combining paradigms help to produce stronger research. Mixed studies can complement the strengths of an individual approach, while offsetting its weaknesses. Given this rationale, the adoption of mixed methods by youth-sport researchers will mean the production of more robust, valid findings. The adoption of mixed method approaches also has advantages in how research is interpreted by practitioners, policy makers and funding bodies. By providing evidence that comes from a range of data, methodological traditions and epistemologies, such studies have the potential to 'cover all bases' and engage wide audiences.

Tashakkori and Teddlie (2003) argue that those who teach research methodology now have a responsibility to prepare students for a professional world that is increasingly using mixed methods. Consequently, this chapter provides an introductory outline to research methodology for youth-sport studies which highlights the potential for mixed methods research.

Research paradigms

One might think that defining research is fairly straightforward until you attempt to do so in discussion with a range of students, researchers or professionals. A widely accepted view is that research is a systematic process of finding answers to specific questions concerning certain problems. But there are many varied perspectives and different views of what count as valid questions and how we can best get answers to these questions. These differences reflect different ways of seeing the world – ways of observing and understanding social reality. Different ways of seeing the world are often called research paradigms or epistemologies.

The four paradigms outlined here — positivist, interpretive, postmodernist and pragmatist — have practical consequences as to how a research project is developed. This distinction, commonly found in texts (e.g. Neuman 2003, pp. 70–91), is to a certain extent simplistic because many instances of social research cross-cut these boundaries and combine elements from two or more paradigms. Generally the positivist perspective is equated with quantitative research, while the interpretive and postmodern perspectives are associated with qualitative research. A mixed methods approach, in particular, advocates understanding and adopting combinations of research paradigms and methods in a single study, in order to tap into the strengths of each. This view has some strong validity, but has also been criticised (Freshwater 2007; Giddings & Grant 2007).

1. The positivist paradigm

This paradigm is often equated with the 'quantitative method' and it assumes that the phenomena being studied can be validly measured. Within this paradigm, research aims to uncover a social reality that exists independently of individual perceptions or beliefs. Objective social reality is assumed to be orderly and although individual perceptions are acknowledged and recognised, the broad social reality is viewed as stable, with patterns of varying complexity. Within this perspective youth-sport researchers describe and theorise on these patterns and the laws which govern them. Following a positivist paradigm means describing the problem or phenomena of interest in terms of how various variables are linked with each other.

An example of positivist research is a study of the relationships between weights status and child, parent and community characteristics in preschool children (Jones et al. 2009). In this study child characteristics like motor development, physical activity, even the child's own perceived physical and cognitive competence, are measured using objective scales. The analysis of the data draws on statistical traditions from science, and the overall interpretation of findings is framed within a perspective that assumes an independent, objective and measurable reality.

2. The interpretive paradigm

The interpretive paradigm is often associated with qualitative methods and regards social reality as something that is conceived of, or constructed, through social practices such as communication and negotiation of meanings. Consequently, social reality is not fixed but continuously constructed and varies from individual to individual. Interpretative research does not to claim that a single theory or reality is applicable to a population and it is not interested in claims of generalisability. Rather the aim is to explain the experiences and perspectives of a range of individuals.

This paradigm criticises positivism's lack of regard for people's capacity to construct personal meanings of their experiences. In youth-sport research, it is adopted to understand participants' personal experiences of sport. For example, in a study of adolescents with physical disabilities, Kristen et al. (2002) use a research strategy called phenomenography, to explore individual children's conceptions about their participation in sport. In this study the different conceptions or realities of individuals are explored.

3. Postmodern paradigms

Postmodern paradigms reject the modernist notion that there are standards of beauty, truth and morality, and share the interpretivist paradigm's view that individual realities are constructed by individuals within their own social worlds. But postmodernism also moves further to dismantle conventional views of social science. Polkinghorne (1992, pp.

146–65) gives a clear account (or as clear as is possible within a postmodernist perspective of subjective realities) outlining the critical characteristics of postmodern paradigms or epistemologies as:

- antifoundationalist: the foundations of knowledge are not secure
- neopragmatist: focus of local and applied knowledge; interest in historical and cultural perspectives
- fragmentary: there are many paths to knowledge and truth
- constructivist: the focus is on individual worlds and perspectives.

If truth has no objective and secure foundation, then claims of truth from science hold only the same value as claims of truth from any other source; including the arts or personal, everyday accounts of 'ordinary' people. Knowledge is seen as having numerous forms and knowledge coming from systematic empirical research is seen only as one form among many, with no special authority over other forms of knowledge.

Within postmodern paradigms, researchers then do not seek to be neutral or detached in reporting results of their studies, as if they are writing from an elevated place which enables them to see 'above' other people's perspectives. Rather, postmodern researchers write in a way that reveals their own identities and positions. Thus, the standard forms of academic reporting are rejected as the sole way of communicating research results; results of studies can be communicated in any form, including novels and art forms. This paradigm for research is rarely seen within youth sport, except when it is adopted by minority, standpoint researchers. Feminist sports research is one example, and you can see how this questions the foundations of conventional perspectives in Cole (1993). Research that explores the fragmentary and constructivist perspectives of how sport impacts upon identity is another example (Russell 2004).

4. Pragmatists and mixed method

Throughout the varied paradigms of research, the dichotomy of quantitative and qualitative research is often reinforced. Debates as to the superiority of one method over another continue: quantitative methods are said to be more objective and yield results that can be generalised, while qualitative methods are advocated as richer, more authentic, and do not reduce social phenomena to numbers. A fourth research paradigm exists that does not deny these debates but attempts to move beyond them in a pragmatic way by proposing the combining of methods, paradigms and epistemologies. For this reason proponents of this paradigm are sometimes referred to as methodological pragmatists.

When one contemplates how the paradigms or epistemologies outlined above might be merged in a single mixed methods study, the challenges are all too apparent. Can one adopt a quantitative, measurement approach to examine a group and still maintain interpretivist and postmodernist recognition of the complexity of individuals? How do the various paradigms influence the way both qualitative and quantitative data might be handled? These are complex issues, discussed in much greater detail by scholars in the field of mixed methods (Johnson et al. 2007; Leech & Onwuegbuzie 2007; Tashakkori & Teddlie 2004; Freshwater 2007; Giddings & Grant 2007)

There are currently very few examples of mixed methods research in youth sport. One of these is a study by Willenberg and colleagues who examine how school playground characteristics are associated with child activity levels (Willenberg et al. 2010). The study combines quantitative data (a structured observation of children's activity and playground equipment measures) with qualitative data from focus group discussions with the children, to develop a more interpretative understanding of how environmental characteristics impact on children's lunchtime activity and perceptions of play areas. By combining methods they were able to determine, not only the quantifiable relationships, but also individuals' perceptions. As such, it is clear that this study is built on both positivist and interpretivist foundations.

Having considered the epistemological foundation of research we can now move on to introduce the 'nuts and bolts'. What is provided here is an outline of what research methodology is. There are three primary elements of any research study:

- the research strategy and design
- data collection methods
- analysis.

There is not the scope here to cover these areas comprehensively, however references for further reading are provided, and a succinct approach is used so that the overall framework for research methodology can be understood. Once the structure of research methodology is clear, further reading and learning can be organised so that it is most useful – after all, research is all about being systematic and structuring our understanding.

Research strategies and designs

A research design outlines how your data collection method and analysis approach logically connects with the research objectives; it serves as a framework for the conduct of your study. General families or groups of research designs are referred to as research strategies. Common research strategies include: experiments, surveys and case studies. Developing a research question or hypothesis is an important step in determining what you want to research and how it might be done. There should be a strong alignment between the research question and the research strategy and design.

Of course, no study is developed in a vacuum and there is important work to be done prior to considering research design. A comprehensive review of literature in the field is necessary to develop a research project within the context of what is already known. A gap in the existing literature is an ideal starting place for developing a project. The literature review also informs the methodological issues that may be particular to the research topic and a good review not only considers what has been found, but how it was found. For a novice researcher, a methodological analysis of the existing literature will reveal potential research strategies and designs. A thorough guide to conducting and writing a literature review is provided by Hart (1998).

Four commonly used strategies include: surveys, experiments, case studies and ethnographies. In mixed method studies different strategies can be combined in a wide variety of ways, outlined by Leech and Onwuegbuzie (2009).

Within each research strategy, there are a number of specific designs that can be followed. For example, a survey looking at whether regular physical exercise affects mood might use questionnaires at a single, cross-sectional point in time, or it might apply a longitudinal design as Birkeland et al. (2009) do. All research designs can be classified as either cross-sectional or longitudinal. This distinction is related to how time is incorporated in the study. In general, cross-sectional research takes a snapshot of the phenomenon of interest, within a single (very short) time frame and no attempt is made to observe change over time. Longitudinal research specifically attempts to capture how things change and develop by collecting data over several time points. De Vaus (2001) outlines the advantages and disadvantages of longitudinal and cross-sectional research designs. Another universal dimension of design is whether a study is prospective (forward looking) or retrospective (backward looking).

Experiment

Experiments are the dominant research strategy within sports sciences research (Williams & Kendall 2007), but are less dominant within the field of youth sport where qualitative sociological perspectives are more established than in other areas of sport studies. Experiment is most suitable for determining whether one thing (e.g. exercising) causes another to happen (e.g. weight loss). The cause (exercise) is called the independent variable, and the effect (weight loss) is called the dependent variable. The logical structure of experiments means that the researchers are able to make claims about causal relationships in a way that no other strategy allows. Some examples of experiments include:

- drug trials, which examine whether a new drug has its intended effects
- comparison of two different ways of coaching/training
- evaluation of a self-esteem training/intervention.

The common design features of these experiments, and experimental logic, are outlined in Box 1.

Many variations on experimental design are available. Robson (1993) provides a good outline of this variety with a focus on applying experimental design to research outside the laboratory. This suits the requirements of sports research well, as this enables research in field settings (for instance, schools, communities, organisations). Some design types, with examples, are provided here.

> **Box 1 Experiments**
>
> *1. Manipulate (independent) variables.* This means that the researcher introduces something (an intervention, for example, a medical treatment) to some of the participants.
>
> *2. Compare at least two groups* of people who are placed under different experimental conditions. Usually, at least one group experiences the intervention (the independent variable) manipulated by the research, whereas the others (called control groups) don't.
>
> *3. Measure the effects of the manipulation.* This is to see if the intervention (independent variable) actually led to the intended effects (the dependent variables).
>
> *4. Control for other influential variables.* Experimental researchers need to control various confounding variables (other factors beside the independent variable) so that any observed effect can be said to occur because of the independent variable, and not because of any confounding variables.

In a simple two-group design participants are divided into two groups; one that receives the treatment/intervention (the experimental group), and one that doesn't (the control group). These two groups are formed by assigning participants randomly. After the treatment/intervention is completed, both groups complete a post-test (to measure the dependent or outcome variables). The post-test results of the experimental and control groups are compared. If the treatment/intervention does have an effect, then the post-test result in each group should be different.

An experimental approach would be helpful if you want to examine the effectiveness of 'Game Sense' pedagogy versus another pedagogical approach, in lifting students' participation in sport. In a simple two-group design, we need to randomly assign participants into two different groups. One group will receive the treatment (Game Sense), whereas the other will receive an alternative – the status quo pedagogy. After the pedagogy treatment is completed, participants from both groups will be tested using some measure of sports participation to see which produced the highest average levels.

Why do we need a control or comparison group? Let's imagine that you have only one group, and you measure this group's participation levels after they received the Game Sense program. Without a comparison, results of the post-test wouldn't be meaningful as we would expect all teaching to lift participation to some degree. In studying youth sport, it is always useful to consider not only whether an intervention is beneficial, but how it compares to other interventions and existing programs.

Why is it essential to form the two groups randomly? Imagine that you ask students to choose which group or condition they would like to join. In this situation, it would be likely that the two groups would differ in important ways (for example, those who choose to join the Game Sense group might be less enthusiastic sportspeople, who are not so confident of their abilities in drill and skill type classes). Therefore, even if you found in the post-test that the Game Sense group exhibited lower participation, this might be due to the characteristics of the participants in that group, rather than the qualities of the pedagogy intervention.

A variation on the simple two-group design, with the addition of a pre-test, is the before and after two-group design. The pre-test measures the level of the dependent, or outcome, variable prior to any intervention or treatment is given. The pre-test is useful as a double-check; to make sure that the two groups you are comparing have similar levels of the dependent variable (that is, participation in sport) before the intervention (Game Sense). Theoretically, the random assignment process already ensures that you have comparable groups, but including pre-tests is a way of making sure. This is particularly important if you have only a small number of participants in the experiment. In such situations, random assignment might not work so well. Imagine randomly assigning only eight participants into two groups; you might still end up with very different characteristics of participants in each group.

Another way to ensure that your experimental groups are comparable at the outset is to apply a matched-pair design. The unique feature of this design is that instead of randomly assigning participants to groups, you match them on certain factors which you think greatly influence the dependent variable. Continuing with the Game Sense example, if physical health is considered to have great influence on sport participation, you could measure this factor and match or pair participants with similar physical health and then randomly assign one of each pair to each of the two groups.

It is sensible to carry out matching if there are factors which exert great influence on the dependent variable; these should be evident in the literature review. There are often many things which might influence it – for instance sport participation is influenced by a variety of complex factors. The question then becomes: on what factor should we match? The matching procedure also becomes extremely complex if you want to match on many factors and there are many research contexts in which matching is ethically and/or logistically difficult. Indeed there are also many studies in which random assignment is also problematic; we can still apply the experimental approach here, but it is a modified or quasi approach.

Quasi-experiments are conducted when random assignment isn't possible. This is often the case in youth-sport research, where participants are in pre-existing groups – sporting clubs, schools, classes, teams, etc. To disrupt these naturally occurring groups by randomly splitting up teams and classes would be unethical – and it would also impact upon how the experimental research relates to the real world. By treating existing groups as experimental groups, quasi-experiments lose some of their power to determine causality. In doing so, however, they become more naturalistic representations of the phenomena studied.

A quasi-experimental study of Game Sense might involve identifying eight school classes and assigning four to the Game Sense pedagogy and leaving the remaining four with their current 'status quo' as the comparison pedagogy. Of course, these classes might be substantially different in their teachers and student profile. Thus, any differences you later observe (in the dependent variable) might have been caused by other differences that existed between the two groups, rather than by the pedagogy itself. In order to overcome this weakness, careful design is necessary to assess and account for any differences or 'non-equivalence' in groups. For example, a pre-test can be used to measure the level of dependent variable. With this information, the researcher will know how the two groups compare to each other before the pedagogy 'treatment' occurs. If we then observe in the post-test that the Game Sense group reports higher sport participation scores, is it safe to conclude that Game Sense encourages greater participation? Not yet. The researchers will need to look at the pattern of results, taking into account information from the pre-test. Statistical analyses that 'control' for the difference between the groups will need to be employed.

A final consideration in experimental design is whether you want to compare two different groups or whether it might be more appropriate to examine a single group as it experiences two, or more, different conditions. The later is known as a within-subjects or repeated-measures design and it is starkly different from the previous designs in that, instead of having two groups of participants, you have only one group which experiences both the treatment and control conditions. The advantage of this design is that, because you are comparing people with themselves, any differences between observations are likely due to the independent variable (and not caused by individual difference variables such as intelligence, health, gender, etc.).

In a within-subjects Game Sense design each participant experiences one term of Game Sense and one term of the alternative pedagogy, serving as his or her own comparison. Each individual's sports participation would be measured before the start of the study (pre-test) and after each condition. It is important to consider, however, order effects in this type of design. Perhaps the Game Sense classes would impact upon sport participation measured later after the alternative classes? Consequently within-subject designs usually require careful counter-balancing for order of treatments. Half the study sample should receive the Game Sense first and half should receive the alternative first.

In developing an experimental strategy, it is useful to compare designs – for example, classical and quasi-experimental; between subjects and within subjects. Robson (1993) provides a good discussion of three different quasi-experimental designs, and some comments on how quasi-experiments are different (and should be differentiated) from case studies and surveys.

Survey

A survey is simply research data collection across a set of cases. By comparison to experiments, surveys are straightforward as there is no intervention or manipulation in the study. The possible cases, or samples, studied in a survey are diverse; including people, texts, artefacts, flora, fauna, geographical regions. In social science research, the survey is the dominant research approach.

As in any other research strategies, data can be collected by asking, observing, looking things up, or by any combination of these, depending on the nature of the survey. For example, you can do a survey by asking a group of students about their sport participation, by observing sport classes, or by examining a collection of students' PDHPE (Personal Development, Health and Physical Education) reports.

One of the most common misconceptions in research is that a survey is a questionnaire. This has come about because of the ubiquity of the survey questionnaire. The two should not be equated, however, becauese in research methodology a survey is a strategy and a questionnaire is a data collection tool. It is important to remember this because surveys can be so much more than completed questionnaires. Surveys can collect both qualitative and quantitative data, they can employ multiple data collection techniques (interview, observation, and questionnaire) and are not constrained by the obvious limitations of questionnaires. Babbie (2004) provides a good overview of issues in conducting a survey and gives further clarification and examples related to the issues raised briefly here. In all cases surveys serve two purposes, see Box 2.

Box 2 Surveys
1. *Detail and describe the distributions* or variations of the characteristics of a population
2. *Explore the relationships* between different characteristics or variables.

Surveys research is sometimes referred to as correlational research. This is because surveys use the statistical analysis 'correlation' to examine the relationships between different variables. Correlational approaches take two variables – say, BMI and hours of TV watching – and examine how changes in one variable are accompanied by changes in the other; how they co-vary. A correlation coefficient is calculated that reflects the strength and direction of this relationship. It is important to remember, however, that this is a measure of association. It reflects how variables change, or operate, in similar ways. It does not reflect the causal direction of the relationship; in this case whether hours of TV watching impact on BMI or whether BMI impacts on hours of TV watching. Thus surveys are not able to make claims about what causes what. Carefully designed experiments are the only research studies which can determine causal relationships. Nevertheless, surveys do provide a straightforward and economical approach for examining relationships, and their first purpose – to describe the distribution and characteristics of a population – means they are a necessary foundation for research in all areas.

In youth-sport research surveys run second to experimental approaches in terms of popularity. The majority of survey studies rely on just one data collection approach – the questionnaire. Some researchers, however, employ diverse data collection techniques in order to access a wider range of data. For example, Kay and Bradbury (2009) surveyed youth-sport volunteers in the UK to examine social capital building processes. They used questionnaires on a larger sample (160) and interviewed 10 participants for more in-depth information. This sort of approach builds validity and authenticity into the research. Because of their summative and descriptive characteristics, surveys are also a common foundation in mixed methods studies. Willenberg and colleagues' study of how school playground characteristics are associated with child activity levels (Willenberg et al. 2010) is an example of this approach.

Case study

A case study is a systematic investigation of a contemporary case (or a collection of cases) within its real-life context using multiple sources of evidence (Robson 1993, p. 146). A case might consist of a range of entities, such as:

- individuals (e.g. an elite athlete)
- groups of people (e.g. a football team)
- organisations (e.g. a sporting club)
- geographical regions (e.g. a neighbourhood)
- events (e.g. the Special Olympics)
- cultural products (e.g. policies, films, magazines, etc.).

A case study is employed to provide an in-depth, context-bound, descriptive account of research phenomena. Not every study, however, which examines something in its real-life context is a case study. The defining characteristics of case study, according to Yin (1994, pp. 1–16) are outlined in Box 3.

Box 3 Case studies

1. Answer 'how' and 'why' questions. Case studies are able to provide detailed contextual information that can be used to develop theories as to how and why phenomena occur. For example, you might be interested in how and why a particular school became successful in improving minority students' sporting achievement.

2. Investigate contemporary phenomena over which the researcher has little or no control. The focus on contemporary phenomena distinguishes case study from history. Case studies use many of the techniques used in historical studies, with two additional sources of evidence: direct observation and systematic questioning (using either questionnaires or direct interviews). In addition, unlike quasi-experiments, case studies deal with phenomena that are beyond the researcher's control.

3. Rely on multiple sources of evidence. In case studies, usually there are more variables of interest than data points. Because of this, the researcher needs to rely on multiple sources of evidence. For example, to find out how a school managed to increase minority students' sporting achievements, you might need to survey minority and non-minority students, interview teachers and headmasters, review policy documents, observe how teachers run their classes, etc. Multiple data collection techniques are the hallmark of quality case studies.

Like experiments and surveys, there is a set of logical steps for designing case study research. Yin's (1994) text contains detail on the process of designing a good case study, from formulating the questions and propositions, determining the units of analysis, linking data to the propositions, and developing criteria for interpreting findings. There is also important information on the fact that a case study can have single or multiple units of analysis, as well as single or multiple cases.

Case studies are often valued by professionals and policy makers because they provide rich illustrations of real-life research contexts; showing how pedagogies or policies can be implemented in the most productive way (Wilson & Loble 2007).

The benefits of the case study approach are countered by some limitations. As you might imagine, much depends on the selection of the case. If a small number of cases are examined and the selection of these cannot determine whether they are representative of the larger population, then the claims made from the case study are limited. This ability to draw inferences from research participants to the greater population is known as generalisability. Case studies are usually seriously constrained by their generalisability. Although this is a limitation, it is not a heavy criticism, because generalisability is not one of the purposes of case studies and their strengths lie elsewhere.

The nature of case studies makes them complementary to many other research strategies. In mixed methods research, case studies can be embedded among other strategies. A large survey of sport participation, for example, would be enriched with the addition of several in-depth case studies of individuals who provide information on how and why they participate in sport. By employing this mixed method approach, the study would have the strengths of generalisability from the survey and rich description from the case study. Furthermore, if the survey is conducted first and the representativeness of the case studies can be established from the survey results, there is also the potential to make generalisable claims from the case study findings.

Ethnography

The key characteristic of an ethnographic study is that it explores culture. Ethnography originated in the practice of Western anthropologists studying the culture of people in pre-industrial societies. Although this kind of ethnography is still practised by some anthropologists, contemporary ethnography is also used to study subcultures (e.g. elite athletes, youth gangs, sports fans) and social institutions or organisations like clubs or schools within the researcher's own cultural context (Silverman 2006).

Whatever the object of study, traditional ethnography essentially involves 'extended participant observation'. Doing ethnography requires a commitment and engagement to be able to understand and participate in the culture being studied. This kind of cultural immersion takes much more time than other research strategies demand. It also requires considerable emotional energy to belong to the culture and yet create enough distance for critical observation. Consequently a new variant on ethnography – focused ethnography – has been developed, which enables researchers to access and immerse themselves in data, but which requires less time in the field and utilises recording technologies (Knoblauch 2005).

In addition to being a research strategy in its own right, ethnography includes principles of data collection (e.g. ethnographic-style interviews) that are now often incorporated into other research strategies. There is an important distinction between ethnographies and studies employing ethnographic 'flavour' in data collection; the ethnographic studies take an analytical approach to the cultural elements of the research context. Sanday (1979) discusses the historical development of ethnography and outlines how different theories of 'culture' shape an ethnographic analysis. Important concepts in ethnography quantitative data and statistics, can also include qualitative interviews (to provide stand-alone qualitative data, to develop high-quality questionnaire items or to triangulate the quantitative data). Furthermore, experimental studies – especially field experiments – might utilise observational data, sometimes referred to as 'process data' to record important qualitative information on the research process that can be used to inform interpretation of the findings.

An ethnographic study of 'sporting culture' in a school would most likely consider numerical data such as participation numbers and competition scores as well as behavioural observations. Similarly, an experiment comparing different pedagogical strategies to teach physical education might be supplemented with observational data from the classroom and interviews with teachers/students about their points of view regarding each of the pedagogical strategies. Therefore, whatever your research strategy is, you will benefit from having the skills to analyse both quantitative and qualitative data.

The data collection technique you choose should be largely driven by the research question. Using more than one data source is a recommended practice, as it can strengthen the conclusions you make in your analysis. A pilot study is another important consideration. A pilot is a small-scale trial of your study strategy, design and data collection; the benefits are listed in Box 5.

A pilot study can also be important in refining research analysis plans. One characteristic of high quality research is a focus, not on data, but on analysis. Analysis-driven research is preferable to data-driven research. Unfortunately, particularly with novice researchers, there is more attention paid to the active research process and the data collection phase than to analytical planning and analytical design. By focusing on the relationship between research questions, data and analysis methods, a researcher can produce a tighter fit between those research elements, which will ultimately mean that they more effectively answer the research questions. Data collection should be planned to produce data that is appropriate and of a suitable quality to answer the research questions. In order to do this effectively researchers need to have planned their analytical strategy before going out to collect data.

Box 5 Pilot studies

1. Evaluate the efficiency of your data collection process. Thus, you can calculate whether you have enough time and money to continue with your current plan.

2. Get an idea of the level of non-response. If too many respondents refuse or fail to participate in the study, you can find out the reason and try to address it (time required is prohibitive, questions might be worded in an offensive way). A random non-response pattern is acceptable but a systematic non-response pattern will bias your data and limit the claims you can make.

3. Estimate the variation of response and evaluate each question/observation in your instruments. For example, you can see if there are any questions which are answered only with 'agree' and 'strongly agree'. The wording of such questions might be leading (they give direction for most people to respond in the same way). In other words, such questions lack sensitivity to the variation of people's responses. In addition, you can also examine whether you have questions which are worded differently but could be perceived as meaning the same thing. Such questions lack specificity, and you can adjust their wording to discriminate them from other questions.

include reflexivity, intersubjectivity and the heuristic circle. The theoretical aspects may be completely absent in some studies which use the term errantly, or simply adopt the ethnographic data collection principles.

The leading youth-sport theorist David Kirk and his colleagues often employ ethnography to explore sporting cultures. O'Donovan and Kirk (2008), for example, conducted a ten-week ethnographic study of a coeducational Year 7 class. The study aimed to make sense of young girls' motivation and engagement in PE. Similar studies have explored youths' perspectives of sport in other contexts. In general, there remains a substantial potential for ethnographic studies to inform, and be informed by, other research approaches. To date there is no example of how they can be utilised in mixed methods studies in youth sport.

Data collection

While there are many strategies in social research, there are only three ways of collecting data: asking people, observing people or things, and looking things up; see Box 4.

Box 4 Data collection

1. Ask. Obviously, when we want to know how people view and experience things, we can simply ask them. This can be done through interviews, written questionnaires, and having a group of people discuss certain topics (a focus group). Although it may sound simple, there are quite a lot of things to prepare if you want to obtain high quality data by asking people.

2. Observe. In addition to asking, we can observe people's behaviour in the settings which are relevant for our research. This can be done in real time (in vivo), or it can be done with the help of recording devices. Again, conducting an observation might be more complicated than it sounds. Observation is necessarily selective (you can't observe everything), and to know the most important or relevant aspects, you will need focus and preparation.

3. Look things up. You might be interested to collect data from publicly available sources such as the mass media. Or you can access and analyse data collected by other people, such as census results or data from previous research (known as secondary data).

Many of the arguments dichotomising 'quant' and 'qual' methods have been refuted; Onwuegbuzie and Leech (2005) and Johnson and Onwuegbuzie (2004) provide convincing counter-arguments. One reason why the notion of 'quantitative v qualitative method' is misguided is because it conveys the false message that certain research methods/strategies only utilise quantitative data (numbers) and particular analysis techniques (using statistics); while others exclusively rely on qualitative data (words and visual images) and non-statistical analysis techniques.

The reality is, that although a research strategy may have preferences on the type of data and analysis technique, in principle both types of data and analysis techniques can be utilised within any research strategy. Thus, case studies can and often do use both numerical data (obtained from existing statistics or from questionnaires) and qualitative data (from unstructured interviews and observations). Survey studies, though frequently employing

Data analysis

As with data collection the focus here is on basic principles – often buried in more detailed texts. Quantitative data can be obtained by measuring (resulting in 'scores') and by counting (resulting in data about frequencies). Qualitative data is most commonly in the form of text, which comes from interview records, observational records or field notes, mass-media content, official documents and other sources. It stands to reason that the distinct qualities of quantitative and qualitative data require different analytical approaches.

In this section, we present the analysis of two different kinds of data: quantitative data, which is numerical; and qualitative data, which can be textual/verbal or visual. Although analysis of these differ in many respects, there are important common features outlined in Box 6 (see also Neuman 2003; Robson 1993). As with all analytical thinking it is helpful to take a critical or questioning stance with regard to your data and your techniques.

Box 6 Data analysis principles

1. Data analysis needs to be planned. It is wise to have an advance plan of how you will analyse your data. This is because your preferred analytic procedure might require certain types or amount of data and this in turn could influence practical decisions about data collection. For instance, certain statistical tests require a minimum number of cases (participants or data points) to be effective. Various methods of qualitative analysis might also require different approaches to data collection, for example, more or less detailed transcription of interviews. It is important to be familiar with the analytic approach you need to use, to answer your research questions before you begin collecting data.

2. Data analysis involves inference/interpretation. It is the researcher's job to tease out meaning from data. Doing analysis involves reducing, summarising, or simplifying the complexity of the 'raw' data, which is a process of abstraction, inference, and interpretation. Thus, no analysis can be completely objective; this applies equally to statistical analysis as to the analysis of qualitative data. In qualitative analysis, a corpus of textual or visual data are often summarised and abstracted through the identification of themes, concepts, or narratives. In quantitative analysis, data is often summarised by calculating certain properties such as central tendency and variability and presenting tables and graphs.

3. Data analysis needs to be rigorous and analytic procedures should be publicly reported. Because the goal of analysis is to draw inferences which are valid or trustworthy, analytical procedures need to be systematic and rigorous (although it is true that the interpretation of 'rigorous and systematic' varies slightly according to your analytic approach). As results of data analysis are dependent upon how the researcher approached the data, researchers are expected to describe in sufficient detail their analytic procedures, so that readers can make critical judgments or evaluations of the researchers' claims.

4. Immersion in data is necessary. Whether you are analysing a corpus of interview results or a quantitative dataset, you will need to immerse yourself in the dataset. This means exploring every part of it and becoming thoroughly familiar with its details.

Analysing quantitative data

There are abundant texts on statistical analysis but basic principles are rarely presented with the conciseness that is required in this chapter. The most skeletal principles are presented here according to the three phases of data analysis; this 'in a nutshell' approach may be useful as an overview.

1 Data preparation

1. *Data entry* into a spreadsheet or statistical software package. Interval/ratio level data (scores) can be entered directly. Categorical data (that is, counts/membership of categories) will need numerical codes assigned (assign '0' for male and '1' for female) Frequently researchers also want to analyse qualitative data, such as responses to open-ended questions; assigning codes here involves a large degree of interpretation.

2. Note and *identify missing cases* or unanswered items – give these clearly distinguished codes (e.g.–999) to differentiate them from valid responses.

3. *Data cleaning* involves checking the accuracy of the data entry, creating new variables (composite or calculated variables), ordering variables for ease of analysis, and any other preparation necessary. This also occurs naturally as part of data exploration.

2 Data familiarisation and exploration

Once your dataset is ready there is the potential to do exciting computations to answer the research question/s. Avoid jumping into your hypotheses and testing analysis, as it is always a good idea to explore your data first. *Exploratory Data Analysis (EDA)* is useful for:

- detecting any errors or anomalies in your data
- forming a tacit picture of the general patterns and important properties of data
- determining the kinds of statistical tests you can perform (because some have certain requirements or make assumptions about the data)
- obtaining new insights or unexpected patterns which are outside your original hypotheses but are interesting to explore further

Outline the data properties for each variable using descriptive statistics:

1. *Frequency counts*. Use these for categorical variables; including demographic variables (how many of your participants are male and female etc.). Represent frequency counts by using barcharts or piecharts.

2. *Shape of distribution*. This applies to continuous variables (or scores). Examine the shape of the distribution using a graph called a histogram. By looking at the shape you can gain important information; a skewed histogram (with many scores clustered at one end) suggests that there are some extreme scores in that variable. The shape of the distribution has consequences for later analyses; for a highly skewed distribution, you might choose the median value, and not the mean, to represent its central tendency.

3. *Central tendency*. There are three types of central tendency: the mode (the most frequently occurring value), median (the middle value), and mean (the average value). Beware – a measure of central tendency does not always accurately represent the dataset. For example, the average salary is not a good indicator of what most people earn, because there are several CEOs of big companies who receive millions of dollars each year.

4. *Variability*. Two datasets may have the same average score; students from two schools can have similar scores in a national exam ; say 70%. Does this mean that the students in the two schools have similar achievements? Not necessarily. We need to look at another property of the data – their variability. The test scores of School A might range from 40 to 100%, while in School B they range from 65 to 75%. Although they have the same average score, the two data sets differ in variability. Calculations of variability include variance and the standard deviations.

5. *Patterns of relationship*. Examine the pattern of relationship between variables. E.g. you might explore whether different demographic groups have different scores for certain variables. To graphically examine how two scores relate, you can draw scatter plots. Make cross-tabulations to see how two categorical variables relate. Many other techniques are also available.

Describe your sample characteristics using the above approaches. Include graphs and tables summarising the demographics (report in your methodology section on sampling) and their performance on the measures specific to your study (report in findings/results).

3 Answering research questions and making inferences

To *answer your research questions* a set of appropriate analyses needs to be planned. The choice depends on:

- The *type of question* you are asking: are you examining association or difference?

    Tests of association (including correlation and regression). Examine whether two or more variables systematically co-vary with each other, e.g. is an increase in praise associated with an increase in sport performance?

    Tests of difference (including t-test, z-test and analysis of variance ANOVA) are used to compare mean values of different groups of respondents by taking into account the variability around those means. For example, are boys different from girls in measures of body image?

- The *properties of your data*: how do they meet the requirements known as assumptions of different techniques?

- Your *technical abilities and enthusiasm*: statistics is a creative art.

If you are using a sample rather than whole population, you'll need to use inferential statistics to be able to generalise your findings to the broader population. Inferential statistics are used to derive whether any patterns of relationship occurred by chance (in your limited sample), or whether they are genuine relationships (applies to a wider population). Inferential testing is based on probability theory, with the logic that for each statistic (test result) you calculate there is a probability of it occurring due to chance or random factors. If this probability is low enough, we can say that the observed pattern or effect measured by that statistic is likely to be genuine. In social research, the cut-off is usually either 1% or 5%; if the probability of getting a result by chance is lower than this, then it can be considered to be genuine. To gain a deeper understanding of this logic see Rowntree (1991).

For further reading see Cohen and colleagues' (2007) chapter ('Quantitative Data Analysis') which provides a broad, albeit brief, discussion of various key concepts and statistical tests for social research. Field and Hole's (2003) chapter ('Descriptive statistics') is essential reading, especially if you're unfamiliar with quantitative analysis. It gives a thorough and accessible treatment of how to summarise, describe and visually present your data.

Analysing qualitative data

There are many different systematic approaches to analysing text and images. Examples include grounded theory methodology, narrative analysis, content analysis, phenomenography and ethnographic analysis. In this section, we will concentrate on general features of qualitative analysis rather than with specific analytic procedures.

At the outset: it is important to note that qualitative analysis is highly iterative; steps in the analysis are not linear; expect a lot of going back-and-forth in your analysis. Analysis often also takes place concurrently with the data collection, so that the emerging findings can inform further data collection.

For further reading on qualitative analysis see Ezzy's (2002) 'Coding data and interpreting texts: methods of analysis'. This chapter introduces several different approaches to coding qualitative data, including content analysis, grounded theory methodology and narrative analysis. Creswell (2003) also provides a useful discussion on how data analysis proceeds in the context of five different approaches (ethnography, case study, grounded theory, narrative analysis, and phenomenology). And finally Cohen and colleagues' (2007) chapter provides useful, rather detailed, examples from actual studies.

---

1 Data preparation

Transcription of talk/interview data can vary in the level of detail; ranging from verbatim uttered words alone through to full transcription of many subtle properties of speech such as pauses, overlaps, emphatics and unfinished words. Both the interviewer and the interviewee should be transcribed. Transcription also aids in data familiarisation.

Filing documents and field notes is also important as a way of organising and structuring data.

---

2 Data familiarisation and exploration

Data that have been prepared are *read and re-read* (viewed/reviewed) to search for patterns of meaning. During this process, the researchers write down thoughts or insights arising from their readings, often called memos. Their thinking is guided by the purpose of the study and by the theoretical framework(s) that underpin it.

Coding and structuring of data begins. This often begins with surface or superficial coding and proceeds to deeper, latent, or semiotic coding. Coding can be done inductively where codes and categories are developed directly from the data; or deductively where the data is classified into a set of pre-determined categories.

---

3 Answering research questions and developing theory

By *coding, classifying, structuring* researchers start to move away from the complex details of the data to try to tease out concepts, themes or narratives. This is a process of abstraction and conceptualisation as the researchers try to develop theories to explain the patterns in the data and answer their research questions. This is often described as a process of dismantling and reconstructing the data so that the underlying structure of relationships is understood. The structure of relationships, described through abstraction, is theory. The form of conceptualisation and abstraction varies with the theoretical and methodological framework used; for example, using grounded theory procedures, Ezzy (2002) constructed a theory to 'account for the different ways in which people with HIV/AIDS respond to their diagnosis'. The central theme which emerged was 'temporality': people's experience of HIV/AIDS seemed to revolve around the concept of time.

Re-presenting, visualising. Researchers must find ways to re-present their proposed theoretical explanation coherently. This phase is intertwined with the writing process. The kind of representation constructed also varies. In some, the outcome is often shown as revolving around key themes or concepts, which can be depicted using visual diagrams. In narrative analysis, the outcome is represented as stories with plots, actors, dominant metaphors, critical incidents, etc.

Mixed methods studies require ways of combining qualitative and qualitative analysis. Many papers explore the techniques for combing methods and several typologies of mixed methods have been proposed (Leech & Onwuegbuzie 2007; Bryman 2006). According to Bryman (2006, p. 96) important considerations include:

- *Priority*. Which type of data and analysis are given primacy over the other in answering the research questions?
- *Function of integration*. What is the function of combining qualitative and quantitative data? For triangulation, explanation, or exploration?
- *Time*. Will qualitative and quantitative data be collected simultaneously or sequentially?

In most cases mixed methods data is analysed separately, in qualitative and quantitative forms. The primary challenge is then to integrate the findings so that the empirical and theoretical outcomes can be maximised. Ultimately this sort of work, as with all analysis, relies on the creative abilities of the researcher. Researchers conducting mixed methods studies, particularly in fields like youth sport, where they are currently scant, will be required to develop innovative techniques and reporting. Such bold creative thinking can invigorate youth sport research, which is currently characterised and polarised by a lack of methodological diversity.

Conclusion

Reading and understanding a wide range of research methodologies is important to any informed perspective on youth sport. A brief introduction has been provided here, however there is much that has not been covered in this chapter – the ethics of research, debates over rigour, newer and innovative methodologies. What has been highlighted is a need for greater interest in research methodology among scholars in this field. A shift towards mixed methods might result from such interest. It is possible that youth-sport research continue in its current trajectory of dichotomised and separated qualitative and quantitative studies. These studies can, after all, be read together as a whole body of literature. If methodological approaches, however, are combined together within one study, with one set of participants and one research context this requires fresh epistemological perspectives and has added benefits. It is up to the next generation of researchers to see what insights this can bring.

References

Andrews, D., Mason, D & Silk, M. (2005). *Qualitative methods in sport studies*. Oxford: Berg.

Babbie, E. R. (2004). *The practice of social research*. (10th edition). Belmont, CA: Thomson/Wadsworth.

Biddle, S. J. H., Markland, D., Gilbourne, D., Chatzisarantis, N. L. D. and Sparkes, A. C. (2001). Research methods in sport and exercise psychology: quantitative and qualitative issues. *Journal of Sports Sciences*, *19*(1): 777–809.

Birkeland, M., Torsheim, T. & Wold, B. (2009) A longitudinal study of the relationship between leisure-time physical activity and depressed mood among adolescents. *Psychology of Sport and Exercise*, *10*(1): 25–34.

Bryman, A. (2006). Integrating quantitative and qualitative research: how is it done? *Qualitative Research*, *6*(1): 97–113.

Cohen, L., Manion, L &. Morrison, K. (2007). *Research methods in education*. (6th edition). New York: Routledge.

Cole, C (1993). Resisting the canon: feminist cultural studies, sport, and technologies of the body. *Journal of Sport and Social Issues, 17*(2): 77–97.

Cresswell, J. W. (2003). *Research design: qualitative, quantitative, and mixed methods approaches* (Chapter 1: Mixed-methods procedures). California: Sage Publications.

Ezzy, D. (2002). *Qualitative analysis: practice and innovation.* Crows Nest, NSW: Allen & Unwin.

Field, A. & Hole, G. (2003). *How to design and report experiments.* London: Sage Publications.

Freshwater, D. (2007). Reading mixed methods research: contexts for criticism. *Journal of Mixed Methods Research, 1*(2): 134–46.

Giddings, L. & Grant, B. (2007). A Trojan horse for positivism? A critique of mixed methods research. *Advanced Nursing Science, 30*(1): 52–60.

Gratton, C. & Jones, I. (2004). *Research methods for sport studies.* London: Routledge.

Hart, C. (1998). *Doing a literature review.* London: Sage.

Hopper, T., Madill, L., Bratseth, C., Cameron, K., Coble, J. & Nimmon, L. (2008). Multiple voices in health, sport, recreation, and physical education research: revealing unfamiliar spaces in a polyvocal review of qualitative research genres. *Quest, 60*(2): 214–35.

Johnson, R. B. & Onwuegbuzie, A. J. (2004). Mixed methods research: a research paradigm whose time has come. *Educational Researcher, 33*(7): 14–26.

Johnson, R. B., Onwuegbuzie A. & Turner, L. (2007). Toward a definition of mixed methods research. *Journal of Mixed Methods Research, 1*(2): 112–33.

Jones, R., Oakley, A., Gregory, P. & Cliff, D. (2009). Relationships between weights status and child, parent and community characteristics in preschool children. *International Journal of Pediatric Obesity, 4*(1): 54–60.

Kay, T. & Bradbury, S. (2009). Youth sport volunteering and the development of social capital? *Sport, Education and Society, 14*(1): 121–40.

Knoblauch, H. (2005). Focused ethnography. *Forum: Qualitative Social Research,* 6(3). [Online]. Available: www.qualitative-research.net/index.php/fqs/article/view/20/43 [accessed 28 February 2011].

Kristen, L., Patriksson, G. & Fridlund, B. (2002). Conceptions of children and adolescents with physical disabilities about their participation in a sports programme. *European Physical Education Review,* 8: 139–56.

Lawrence, D. (1993). Quantitative versus qualitative evaluation: a false dichotomy? *Environmental Impact Assessment Review, 13*(1): 3–11.

Leech, N. (2009). A typology of mixed methods research designs. *Quality and Quantity, 43*(2): 265–75.

Leech, N. & Onwuegbuzie, A. (2007). A typology of mixed methods research designs. *Quality Quantity, 43*(2): 265–75.

McFee, G., McNamee, M. J., Parry, J. & Reid, H. (2009). *Ethics, knowledge and truth in sports research: an epistemology of sport.* London: Routledge.

Neuman, W. L. (2003). *Social research methods: qualitative, and quantitative approaches.* Fifth edition. Boston: Allyn and Bacon.

O'Donovan, T. & Kirk, D. (2008). Reconceptualizing student motivation in physical education: an examination of what resources are valued by pre-adolescent girls in contemporary society. *European Physical Education Review, 14*(1): 71–91.

Onwuegbuzie, A. J. & Leech, N. L (2005). On becoming a pragmatic researcher: the importance of combining quantitative and qualitative research methodologies. *International Journal of Social Research Methodology*, 8(5): 375–87.

Polkinghorne, D. E. (1992). Postmodern epistemology of practice. In S. Kvale (ed.), *Psychology and postmodernism* (pp. 146–65). London: Sage.

Rauscher, L. & Greenfield, B. (2009). Advancements in contemporary physical therapy research: use of mixed methods designs. *Physical Therapy* 89: 91–100.

Robson, C. (1993). *Real world research*. Oxford: Blackwell.

Rowntree, D. (1991). *Statistics without tears : a primer for non-mathematicians*. Harmondsworth: Penguin.

Rudd, A. (2008). A call for more mixed methods in sport management research. *2008 North American Society for Sport Management Conference* (NASSM 2008). *Florida State University.* Saturday, 31 May 2008.

Russell, K. M. (2004). On vs off the pitch: the transiency of body satisfaction among female rugby players, cricketers, and netballers. *Sex Roles*, 51: 561–74.

Sanday, P. (1979). The ethnographic paradigm(s). *Administrative Science Quarterly*, 24: 527–38.

Silverman, D. (2006). *Interpreting qualitative data*. (3rd edition). Sage Publications: London.

Tashakkori, A. & Teddlie C. (2003). *Handbook of mixed methods in social & behavioral research*. Thousand Oaks, CA.

Thomas, J. & Nelson, J. (2005) *Research methods in physical activity*. Champaign, IL.: Human Kinetics Publishers.

Willenberg, L., Ashbolt, R., Holland, D., Gibbs, L., MacDougall, C., Garrard, J., Green, J. & Waters, E. (2010). Increasing school playground physical activity: a mixed methods study combining environmental measures and children's perspectives. *Journal of Science and Medicine in Sport, 13*(1): 210–16.

Williams, S. & Kendall, L.(2007). A profile of sports science research (1983–2003). *Journal of Science and Medicine in Sport, 10*(1): 193–200.

Wilson, R. & Loble, L. (2006). From evidence to policy: the policy maker's perspective. In Blackmore, J., Wright, J. & Harwood, V., *Counterpoints on the quality and impact of educational research* (pp. 159–74). Melbourne: AARE.

Yin, R. K. (1994). *Case study research: design and methods* (second ed.). Thousand Oaks: Sage Publications.

Index

A

ableism 97–98, 100, 103–04, 108
Aborigines 7–8, 52, 133–48
  Aborigines Act 1905 139
  Aborigines Protection Act 1869 136
  athletics 8, 10, 137–38, 140, 143, 145
  Australian Rules football 9, 138–41, 143–44
  body image 244
  boxing 8–9, 138, 142–43
  boys 8, 136, 244
  cricket 8, 136–40, 142–43
  culture 7–8, 145
  Gay Games 126
  girls 136, 138
  participation in sport 9
  Protection Act (1897) 141, 143
  Racial Discrimination Act 145
  Rugby League 9, 139, 142, 144–45
  Rugby Union 142
  schools and 135, 139
  soccer 140
  swimming 140
  tennis 8–9, 138, 145
abuse. *See also* child abuse; racism; sexist abuse; child sexual abuse; homophobia
  physical 233, 236–37
  psychological 100, 233–34, 237–38
ACHPER (Australian Council for Health, Physical Education and Recreation) 62
Active After-School Communities program (AASC) 182–83, 213
age of consent
  boys 231
  Britain 231
  girls 230–31
AIDS. *See* HIV/AIDS
Amateur Athletic Association of Great Public School (AAAGPS) 6, 29–30, 37
amateur sport 255
  athletics 153
  Australia 4–5, 8
  boxing 142
  disability 98
  Olympics 4, 153
  rowing 4
  Rugby Union 4
  soccer 196
  surf lifesaving 152–53
  swimming 153
  tennis 5
  Victorian Britain 4
Amateur Swimming Association (ASA) 65
anorexia. *See* eating disorders
ANZAC ix, 2
athleticism 3, 5, 7, 9, 27–28, 36, 39, 75, 77, 91, 129
  disability 99–100, 104, 108
athletics 4, 29, 53, 61, 66–67, 76, 118, 120, 153, 198, 216–17, 224, 238, 259
  Aborigines 8, 10, 137–38, 140, 143, 145
  amateur 153
  coaching 217
Australia
  amateur sport 4–5, 8
  child protection 229–35, 237
Australian Football League (AFL) 9, 11, 50, 61–62, 64, 91, 143, 167, 261. *See also* Australian Rules football
  Aborigines 9, 143
Australian Institute of Sport (AIS) 44–45, 47, 49–50, 53–54, 213

Australian Rules football 5, 7, 10, 27, 32, 50, 91, 94, 134, 136, 138, 167–68. *See also* Australian Football League (AFL)
   Aborigines 138–41, 143–44
   boys 94
   clubs 62
Australian sport: emerging challenges, new directions 46, 55
Australian Sports Anti-Doping Authority (ASADA) 49
Australian Sports Commission (ASC) 7, 45, 47, 49–55, 63, 160, 213, 223, 232, 257
   Disability Sport Unit 97
   sports promotion 63
Australian sport: the pathway to success 47

B

Backing Australia's sporting ability (BASA) 46–47, 63–64
baseball 13, 37, 198–99, 204, 261
basketball 29, 53, 66, 94, 105, 141, 167–68, 187, 197–202, 204
   national league 50
   wheelchair 109
bathing. *See* swimming
beaches 2–3, 35, 59, 149–61, 217, 222. *See also* surfing; surf lifesaving
body building 75, 248
body image 78, 88, 241–49. *See also* cosmetic surgery
   Aborigines 244
   boys 86–92, 242–43, 281
   girls 78, 242–44, 246, 281
   media's influence on 244–49
   men 241–43, 245–46, 248
   women 242–44, 247–48
boxing 73, 75, 256
   Aborigines 8–9, 138, 142–43
   amateur 142
boys 31–32, 38, 61, 71–72, 87, 89, 202–03
   Aboriginal 8, 136, 244
   age of consent 231
   Australian Rules football 94
   basketball 94
   body image 86–92, 242–43, 281
   cricket 94
   development 88
   disability 100
   masculinity 6, 73–74, 78, 85–94, 100
   obesity prevention 188
   participation in sport 63, 86, 88–90, 94, 180–81, 186, 216
   physical activity 87–88, 93–94, 180, 185–88, 249
   Rugby Union 6, 87, 202
   sexual offences against 229, 233
   soccer 63, 167, 202–03
   swimming 63
   violence 74
bulimia. *See* eating disorders
bullying 233

C

cadet scheme 36, 38–39
celebrity 255–63
child abuse 145, 229–33, 236–37
child protection 195, 229, 231, 234, 236–37
   Australia 229–35, 237
   Britain 229–34, 237
child protection policies 229, 231–32, 237
child sexual abuse 232–34
   Aborigines 145, 233
   boys 229, 233
   girls 124, 229, 233–34
Christianity 5, 123, 133, 139
citizenship 1, 52, 115, 168, 172, 175, 181–82, 213–14
class 4–5, 8, 36, 38, 59–61, 73, 98, 137, 142, 241, 243–44, 255
clubs 11–12, 50, 59–62, 64–65, 68, 203, 213, 221–22, 234, 256, 272, 275–76
   Australian Rules football 62
   cricket 13
   disability-specific 99
   golf 5, 8, 11
   health 187
   Jewish 11
   private 5, 8
   rowing 4
   Rugby League 62, 64
   Rugby Union 6, 262
   soccer 11, 13, 63, 196–97, 203
   surf lifesaving 3, 149–52, 154–55, 157–58, 160
   swimming 32, 34, 60, 65–68, 222

tennis 5, 8
coaching 5, 37, 50, 76, 92, 95, 100, 108, 137, 139, 141, 146, 193–94, 196, 199–200, 202–03, 206, 211–12, 214, 216–17, 219–20, 222–23, 229, 231–34, 236–38, 248, 270
  athletics 217
  participation 212–13
  performance 212, 214
  professional 38, 153
  swimming 67, 153
  volunteer 213
colonisation 1–4, 7–8, 27, 60, 133, 136, 139, 143, 165–66
Combined High Schools Sports Association (CHSSA) NSW 65–66
Combined Independent School (CIS) NSW 65
commercialisation 3, 12, 43, 49–50, 59, 64–65, 137, 142, 153, 215
Commonwealth Games 6, 9, 142–43, 152, 198, 261
community 3, 7, 11, 44, 62–63, 166, 168, 183, 187, 189, 205, 215, 223, 267, 270
  Aboriginal 7, 144, 146
  ethnic 11
  gay and lesbian 116, 118–21, 123–25, 128
community sport 44–47, 49–50, 52, 54, 59, 62–64, 68, 94, 98, 167, 169, 171, 175, 187. *See also* clubs
  development programs 49
compulsory heterosexuality 71–81, 245
cosmetic surgery 77, 101, 244–45. *See also* body image
Crawford Report 46
cricket 1–2, 5, 10, 13, 28–31, 36–37, 50, 60, 64, 79, 94–95, 136–37, 167, 194, 199, 204, 219, 222, 256, 259, 261–62
  Aborigines 8, 136–40, 142–43
  boys 94
  Britain 139
  clubs 13
  female players 245
  Kanga 63
  visually impaired 109
  World Series Cricket 5

culture
  Aboriginal 7–8, 145
  Australian 1–2, 59–60, 63, 166–69, 172, 211, 224
  beach 149, 154
  migrant 1–2, 10–11
  popular 90, 167, 255, 260, 275
  sporting 1, 9–12, 27, 31, 45, 59, 61–64, 71–72, 80, 89, 94, 109, 116, 149, 151–52, 165–68, 171, 196, 277–78
  surfing 149, 154–56, 159, 161
  surf lifesaving 149, 151, 155–58
curriculum 30–31, 39–40, 47, 62, 104–06, 109, 165, 168–75, 182–84, 188–89, 215
  Australian Curriculum, Assessment and Reporting Authority (ACARA) 62, 182
  national 40, 47, 61–62
  National Curriculum Board 62
  physical education (PE) 61, 105–06, 109, 215
  swimming (NSW) 34
  swimming (Victoria) 34
cycling 4, 9, 53, 59, 94–95, 167, 256, 261

D

Department of Education and Training (DET) NSW 65
developmental model of sports participation (DMSP) 194
disability 52, 77, 97–109
Disability Sport Unit: Australian Sports Commission (ASC) 97
discipline 30, 36, 38, 77–78, 103, 150–51, 154, 211, 215
discrimination 8, 10, 97–98, 119, 135, 139, 144–45, 183, 196, 203. *See also* homophobia; racism; sexism
Racial Discrimination Act 145
doping 45–46, 49, 54–55, 233, 237, 258
  Australian Sports Anti-Doping Authority (ASADA) 49
  Australian Sports Drug Agency (ASDA) 45
drilling 30–33, 36, 38, 174, 195, 217, 221, 271. *See also* cadet scheme
drugs 3, 233, 257. *See also* doping

E

eating disorders 195, 247–48. *See also* thin ideal; weight loss
elite schools. *See* private schools
ethnicity 3, 7, 10–11, 63, 97–98, 166, 180, 243, 249, 262

F

federal government (Australian) 43, 45–47, 51, 55, 63, 97, 150, 166, 181–83, 193. *See also* Australian Sports Commission (ASC); legislation; policy
Federation of Gay Games (FGG) 115, 120, 123–24, 126–28
femininity 6, 72–80, 85, 100, 248, 258
  construction of 245
  cult of 245
  media representations 244–45
feminism 6, 86–87, 102–03, 268
fitness 43–44, 48, 91, 98, 101, 116, 150–51, 154, 169, 171, 173, 188, 203, 213, 216, 220, 222–23, 242, 247
  National Coordinating Council for Physical Fitness 43
  National Fitness Act (1941) 43
Fitness Improvement, Lifestyle Awareness (FILA) program 184–85, 188
football. *See* soccer
Freeman, Cathy 9, 144–45

G

Gay Games 115–29
  Aborigines 126
gay men 74–75, 78–80, 115–29, 256. *See also* HIV/AIDS; homophobia
  age of consent 231
  magazines 124
gender 2–3, 6, 68, 76–78, 80, 86, 89, 98–103, 108, 115, 168, 180, 186–89, 216, 237, 241–42, 245, 249, 259, 273
  physical activity and 73–74, 76–78
  schools and 73
girls 6, 34, 36, 38, 71–74, 76, 78, 86, 100, 167, 173, 185, 187, 202, 216, 236. *See also* Trial of Activity for Adolescent Girls (TAAG)
  Aboriginal 136, 138
  age of consent 230–31
  body image 78, 242–44, 246, 281
  participation in sport 6, 63, 78, 86, 180–81, 186, 277
  physical activity 180, 185–87
  sexual offences against 124, 229, 233–34
  thinness 78, 242–43
golf 5, 8, 10–11, 146, 204, 261
  clubs 5, 8, 11
Goolagong-Cawley, Evonne 9, 138, 145
government schools 27–31, 33, 35–36, 38–40, 60–61, 179. *See also* Public Schools Amateur Athletic Association of New South Wales (PSAAA)
  physical education 60
  Victorian Associated Public Schools 28
GPS (Great Public Schools). *See* private schools
gymnastics 38, 73, 105, 196, 198, 214, 219, 235–37
gyms 29, 38, 152, 183, 187, 248, 255

H

Health and Physical Education (HPE) 61–62, 182
health and wellbeing 30–31, 46, 48, 55, 62, 80, 87, 95, 150–51, 179, 181, 184, 186, 215
  disability and 97–98
  Gay Games and 118–19
  National Coordinating Council for Physical Fitness 43
health promotion 62, 119, 179, 181–82, 189
hegemonic masculinity 71, 85, 87, 98, 100
high schools. *See* secondary schools
HIV/AIDS 117, 119, 121–23, 125, 282
hockey 53–54, 66, 76, 141, 196–98, 202, 204, 219
homophobia 76, 79–80, 116, 119–20, 123–24, 129, 233
homosexuality. *See also* gay men; lesbians
  age of consent 231

I

ice hockey 197, 199, 204, 218, 234–35, 261
impairments. *See* disability
independent schools. *See* private schools
Independent Sport Panel 46–47, 55
intersexuality 72–73, 129

interventions. *See* Middle School Physical Activity and Nutrition (M-SPAN) program; Trial of Activity for Adolescent Girls (TAAG)
ironman 153
  Ironman Super Series 153

K

key learning area (KLA) 61, 182

L

leanness 242, 246, 248
learn to swim (program) 34
legislation 8, 43, 45, 104, 125, 136, 139, 141, 143, 145–46, 229–32. *See also* policy
lesbians 73, 75, 78–80, 115–29. *See also* homophobia
  age of consent 231
lifeguards. *See* surf lifesaving
lifesaving 34, 43. *See also* surf lifesaving
  Royal Life Saving Society 35

M

magazines 145, 246, 275. *See also* media, the
  gay 124
  gossip 257
  men's 260
  popular culture 90
  sport 1
  surfing 154
masculinity 6, 71–74, 76, 77–80, 98, 100–02, 104, 151–53, 155, 157, 248, 258–59. *See also* compulsory heterosexuality; hegemonic masculinity
  boys 6, 73–74, 78, 85–94, 100
  construction of 245
media, the 1, 6, 11, 45, 47, 54, 61, 74–75, 117, 123–24, 128, 153, 156, 158, 167, 215–16, 232, 258–59, 261, 277, 279. *See also* magazines
  body image, and 241, 244–49
  homosexuality, representations of 116, 118
  masculinity, impact on 90, 92
  sport, impact on 12, 167
  surfing 160
Melbourne Cup 5, 138, 143
men 6, 8, 71, 73, 76, 78–80, 85–87, 90–91, 95, 99–101, 116, 124, 134–36, 138, 140–42, 146, 150, 152, 154, 156–58, 160–61
  body image 241–43, 245–46, 248
  media portrayals 245–59
Middle School Physical Activity and Nutrition (M-SPAN) program 184, 186
moderate to vigorous physical activity (MVPA) 185, 187–88
motivation 146, 167, 170, 173, 188, 194, 203, 205, 211, 213, 216–20, 223–24, 248, 277
multiculturalism 10–11, 52, 166–67, 169
muscularity 75, 88, 90–91, 246–48

N

National Coordinating Council for Physical Fitness 43
nationalism 2–3, 12, 54, 60, 166, 211
National Rugby League (NRL). *See* Rugby League
National Society for the Prevention of Cruelty to Children (NSPCC) 230, 232, 237
national sport organisations (NSOs) 50, 52–55, 116, 143, 218
netball 5–6, 61, 63–64, 67, 75, 105, 141, 167–68, 197, 202, 215, 245, 256
Netball Australia (NA) 215
New Zealand 50, 59, 87, 119, 133, 142–43, 145, 219–20
Nicholls, Pastor Sir Douglas 138
NSW Physical Education Primary School Syllabus 33

O

obesity 46, 54, 87–88, 170–71, 174, 179, 216, 243–44
  children, in 55, 62, 80, 168, 170, 183, 188–89, 243
Olympic Games 4, 6, 9, 29, 33, 35–36, 43–46, 51, 53–54, 64, 71, 74–75, 116–17, 120, 123, 151, 153–54, 167, 193, 198, 201, 203–04, 229, 234, 236–37, 255, 261–62

P

Paralympics 101, 103–04
parental pressure 218, 222, 233
pedagogy 68, 169, 171–75, 271–73, 275, 278
  Game Sense 271–72

Personal Development, Health and Physical Education (PDHPE) 61, 274
physical activity 6, 10, 30, 33, 36, 38–39, 43, 46–48, 61–62, 64, 68, 80, 87, 89, 149–51, 168–75, 179–89, 215, 217, 237, 241, 267, 270. See also Fitness Improvement, Lifestyle Awareness (FILA) program; moderate to vigorous physical activity (MVPA); Trial of Activity for Adolescent Girls (TAAG); vigorous physical activity (VPA)
   adult 43, 46, 48, 54, 149–61, 179–80, 216
   Australian Physical Activity Guidelines for Children and Youth 174
   boys 87–89, 92–94, 180, 185–88, 249
   club-based 64
   disability and 97–99, 105, 267
   gender and 73–80
   girls 180, 185–87
   National Coordinating Council for Physical Fitness 43
   promotion of 179–82, 184, 186–89, 212–13, 215, 229
physical and health education (PHE) 168
   teachers 167, 172
physical development 89, 91, 197, 199–200, 203, 215, 222. See also physical maturation
physical education (PE) 6, 28, 30–31, 33, 36, 38–39, 47, 59, 61, 68, 87–89, 92, 94–95, 104–06, 108, 165–75, 179–89, 211, 229, 237, 247, 278
   curriculum 61, 105–06, 109, 188, 215
   disability and 98–99, 104–09
   government schools 60
   promotion of 33
   teachers 33, 68, 89, 92, 104–05, 107–08, 186–87, 237
physical maturation 193, 197, 199–200, 202. See also physical development; relative age effect (RAE)
Play By The Rules 232, 237
policy 186, 189, 229, 266, 275. See also legislation
   Aboriginal 134–35
   anti-vilification 9
   Australian sport 33, 43–55, 63–64, 160, 182
   Backing Australia's Sporting Ability 63–64
   child protection 230–32
   education 62, 106
   multiculturalism 10
   National Sport and Active Recreation Policy Framework 47
   social inclusion 97, 104
   sport participation 213, 215
   White Australia Policy 8, 230
   women's surfing 160
pools. See swimming pools
popular culture 101
primary schools 27, 30, 32–33, 35–37, 62, 65–66, 139, 167, 169, 183, 186, 213, 220, 247. See also government schools
   NSW Physical Education Primary School Syllabus 33
   Primary Schools Sport Association (PSSA) NSW 65–66
private schools 27–30, 36–39, 60, 65–67, 93, 179
   Great Public Schools (GPS) 60
public schools. See government schools
Public Schools Amateur Athletic Association of New South Wales (PSAAA) 30–32, 34, 37, 39

Q

quad rugby 100

R

racism 7, 9, 64, 125, 135–36, 140–43, 145, 233
relative age effect (RAE) 194, 199–204. See also physical maturation
Rose, Lionel 9
rowing 2, 8, 28–29, 53–54, 60, 151, 197–98, 237
   amateur sport 4
   clubs 4
   Rowing Australia 50
Royal Life Saving Society 35
Rugby League 2, 5, 10–11, 13, 33, 50, 61, 63–64, 76, 79–80, 86, 90–91, 95, 136, 168, 200, 204, 214, 248, 256
   Aborigines 9, 139, 142, 144–45
   clubs 62, 64
   promotion of 33

Rugby Union 2, 4–5, 10, 13, 27–29, 33, 37, 50, 60–61, 64, 75, 79, 87, 94–95, 136, 151, 168, 199, 245, 248, 256
   Aborigines 142
   boys 6, 87, 202
   clubs 6, 262

S

sailing 2, 5, 8, 35, 53, 101, 146, 256
schools. *See also* government schools; secondary schools; primary schools; private schools
   Aboriginal people and 135, 139
   disability and 98–99, 104, 106
   gender and 73
   learn-to-surf 160
   physical education in 168–74, 181–83, 185
   promoting sport in 28, 30, 33–39, 165–75, 179, 181–83
School Sport Australia (SSA) 65–68
secondary schools 27, 32–33, 36–37, 65–66, 89, 92, 169, 179, 186, 213, 218, 220. *See also* government schools
self-esteem 78, 87–88, 98, 107, 188, 215, 218, 224, 235, 243, 247–48, 270
sexism 64, 145, 233
sexist abuse 74, 100, 158
soccer 10–11, 27, 29–30, 36–37, 50, 53, 60, 64, 75, 93, 95, 105, 136, 167, 196, 199, 203–04, 223, 232, 256, 260–61, 275
   Aborigines 140
   amateur 196
   boys 63, 167, 202–03
   clubs 11, 13, 63, 196–97, 203
   National Soccer League (NSL) 11
South Australian Primary Schools Amateur Sports Association 32
sport participation 1, 4–5, 33, 40, 45–47, 50–55, 59–60, 62–65, 67–68, 71–72, 75–76, 79–80, 86, 90, 180–81, 194, 203, 206, 211–13, 215, 215–23, 234–35, 241, 248–49, 267, 271–73, 276, 278
   Aborigines 9
   boys 63, 86, 88–90, 94, 180–81, 186, 216
   child welfare and 231
   developmental model of sports participation (DMSP) 194

   disabled people 97–109
   gay and lesbian 116, 118, 126
   girls 6, 63, 78, 86, 180–81, 186, 277
   policy 213, 215
   promotion of 165–75, 181
sports promotion 28, 63, 179–81, 212, 215, 265
   Australian Sports Commission (ASC) 63
   disability sport 97, 99
   in schools 28, 30, 33–39, 165–75, 182
   women's surfing 160
surfing 2–3, 9, 35, 60, 63, 95, 149–50, 154–56, 158–59, 161, 167, 257. *See also* beaches
   Association of Surfing Professionals (ASP) 155
   body surfing 59
   International Professional Surfers (IPS) 155
   magazines 154
   Surfing Australia 160
   violence 149, 157
   women's 160
surf lifesaving 3, 149–59, 161, 262
   amateur 152–53
   clubs 3, 149–52, 154–55, 157–58, 160
   nippers 60
   Surf Bathing Association of New South Wales (SBA) 150–52
   women 151, 157, 161
Surf Life Saving Australia (SLSA) 150–54, 157–58, 160
   Royal Life Saving Society 35
swimming 3, 6, 9, 31, 34–37, 53, 54, 60–61, 63, 65–68, 73, 88, 105, 125, 151–53, 155, 187, 198–99, 201, 204, 219–22, 229, 234–35, 242, 256, 259, 261
   Aborigines 140
   boys 63
   clubs 32, 34, 60, 65–68, 222
   curriculum (NSW) 34
   curriculum (Victoria) 34
   'learn to swim' program 34
   promotion of 34–35
swimming pools 3, 6, 35, 67, 222
   public 34–35, 65
   school 29, 36, 67

System for Observing Fitness Instruction Time (SOFIT) 186–87

T

talent development 62, 65, 67, 171
talent identification 169, 193–207, 235
   National Talent Identification Program 257
   programs 193, 198
talent pool 46, 61, 65, 203, 215
talent scouts 193
teachers
   physical and health education (PHE) 167
   physical education (PE) 33, 68, 89, 92, 104–05, 107–08, 186–87, 211, 237
tennis 5–6, 29, 31, 50, 61, 73, 138, 195, 199, 201, 261
   Aborigines 8–9, 138, 145
   amateur 5
   clubs 5, 8
thin ideal 242–46. *See also* eating disorders; weight loss
thinness 241, 243, 246
   girls and 78, 242–43
Trial of Activity for Adolescent Girls (TAAG) 184–87

V

Victorian Associated Public Schools 28
Victorian Institute of Sport 49
Victorian State Schools' Amateur Athletic Association (VSSAAA) 32
vigorous physical activity (VPA) 174, 179, 188
violence
   boys 74
   in sport 78, 85, 88, 100
   surfing 149, 157

W

weight loss 179, 183, 242–44, 248, 270
wellbeing. *See* health and wellbeing
women 6–7, 65, 71, 73–76, 78–80, 86–87, 100–04, 116, 119, 122, 126, 135–36, 138, 140, 142, 145–46, 149, 151, 157, 159, 161
   body image 242–44, 247–48
   media portrayals 245–46, 257, 259
Women's National Basketball League (WNBL) 201
Women's Tennis Association Tour 195
World War I 11, 27, 29, 33–34, 36, 141
World War II 10, 29, 34, 40, 43, 61, 85, 144, 150, 158, 166, 262

www.ingramcontent.com/pod-product-compliance
Lightning Source LLC
Chambersburg PA
CBHW080407230426
43662CB00016B/2345